JEFF

THE RISE AND FALL
OF A POLITICAL PHENOMENON

TONY PARKINSON

VIKING

For Sophie, Nicholas and Chloe

Viking
Penguin Books Australia Ltd
487 Maroondah Highway, PO Box 257
Ringwood, Victoria 3134, Australia
Penguin Books Ltd
Harmondsworth, Middlesex, England
Penguin Putnam Inc.
375 Hudson Street, New York, New York 10014, USA
Penguin Books Canada Limited
10 Alcorn Avenue, Toronto, Ontario, Canada M4V 3B2
Penguin Books (N.Z.) Ltd
Cnr Rosedale and Airborne Roads, Albany, Auckland, New Zealand
Penguin Books (South Africa) (Pty) Ltd
5 Watkins Street, Denver Ext 4, 2094, South Africa
Penguin Books India (P) Ltd
11, Community Centre, Panchsheel Park, New Delhi 110 017, India

First published by Penguin Books Australia Ltd 2000

10 9 8 7 6 5 4 3 2 1

Jacket and pages designed by Nikki Townsend, Penguin Design Studio
Typeset in Garamond 12.5/16.15 pt by Midland Typesetters, Maryborough, Victoria
Printed in Australia by Australian Print Group, Maryborough, Victoria

National Library of Australia
Cataloguing-in-Publication data

Parkinson, Tony, 1959– .
    Jeff: the rise and fall of a political phenomenon.

    Includes index.
    ISBN 0 670 88778 1.

    1. Kennett, Jeff. 2. Premiers – Victoria – Biography.
    3. Victoria – Politics and government – 1990– . I. Title.

994.5065092

www.penguin.com.au

CONTENTS

ACKNOWLEDGEMENTS

As followers of politics in the state of Victoria will be only too aware, this is not an authorised biography of Jeff Kennett, nor is it an official history of the seven years of the Kennett government. There have been no taxpayer funds involved in its research or publication. In essence, it has been a journalistic endeavour, possible only through the willingness of leading figures in public life over the past two decades – both friends and foes of the former premier – to contribute freely of their time and insights in this attempt to chronicle and explain an extraordinary period in the history of the state.

In striving to gain an understanding of the man and his methods, I sought and gained the assistance of informed observers from across the political spectrum. Many of the interviews were confidential, and some of the contributors did not wish to be identified. Others were happy to speak on the record, and I appreciate their candour. Of Jeff Kennett's former cabinet colleagues, I extend thanks to Rob Knowles, Alan Stockdale, Mark Birrell,

Roger Hallam and Louise Asher. Of those who served as senior advisers, I am grateful to Alister Drysdale, Anna Cronin and Steve Murphy from Kennett's private office and Ken Baxter, the Kennett government's first public service chief. Of Liberal MPs who were helpful in providing important detail on the Opposition years, I am especially appreciative of the contributions of Tom Austin, Geoff Connard, Reg Macey and Victor Perton. Likewise, I am grateful to David White and Ian Baker for their forthright assessments of the Kennett era from a Labor perspective. Several leading figures within the Victorian division of the Liberal Party have also been generous with their time: my thanks to Petro Georgiou, Peter Poggioli, Ted Baillieu, Tony Staley and Ron Walker. My gratitude also to Andrew Peacock, who interrupted his involvement in the momentous East Timor diplomacy of August 1999 to take an extended phone call in the early hours in Washington.

Given his well-known disdain for journalists, I was perhaps not entitled to expect much in the way of cooperation from Jeff Kennett himself. In fact, whatever his reservations about the outcome, the former premier allowed six hours of private interviews for this book, including a one-and-a-half-hour discussion in the aftermath of his election defeat. It need hardly be said that, without his involvement, any attempt to tell this story would be a hollow exercise. I would like to place on record my appreciation.

I also express gratitude to the *Age*, in particular for the support of editor Michael Gawenda – not least in allowing me leave to complete this project. I valued the advice and assistance of Ewin Hannan and Sandra McKay, who have trawled these waters many times. Tribute is also due to two decades of talented news photographers at the *Age*, and to Louise Graham and Sacha Kumbara for their help in assembling, and arranging permission to reprint, a collection of some of the more memorable images of the Kennett years. For support and suggestions along the way, I am also indebted to Bruce Davidson, Dallas Parkinson, Peter Ellingsen,

Michael Harvey, Karl Malakunas, Andrew Rule, Greg Scealy and Ian Smith.

This project was instigated by the publishing director of Penguin Australia, Robert Sessions. I thank Bob for his support, notwithstanding the punishing deadlines. I also express my appreciation to editors Katie Purvis and Laurie Critchley, and designer Nikki Townsend, for their professionalism and panache.

Finally, special thanks to Kirsty Simpson, for her superhuman display of patience, understanding and encouragement during a demanding and eventful year.

PROLOGUE

*'There is nothing more difficult to take in hand, more perilous to
conduct, or more uncertain in its success, than to take the lead in the
introduction of a new order of things, because the innovator has for
enemies all those who have done well under the old conditions, and
lukewarm defenders in those who may do well under the new.'*

MACHIAVELLI, *THE PRINCE*

On a hot autumn evening in late March 1999, Jeff Kennett
sat in his office at Treasury Place in Melbourne, sipping on
a whisky and sniffing the winds. Everything seemed to be falling
into place for the Victorian premier. The state's economy was
effervescing as seldom before. Unemployment was falling. Retail
spending was at record levels, and consumer confidence high. It
was the most benign economic climate in the state for 15 years.
The ideal setting, you would think, for an election campaign.

Only a week earlier, the premier had watched his political
opponents go through the ritual agonies of Opposition. Under the
pressure of poor opinion polls and an outbreak of poisonous
feuding within the Victorian branch of the Australian Labor Party,
John Brumby had been forced to resign as leader. He was replaced
by a political greenhorn, Steve Bracks, in a last despairing effort by
the ALP to haul itself back into contention.

In contrast, an AC Nielsen poll published in the *Age* newspaper
showed the premier's approval rating at a record 61 per cent.

Among 18 to 24-year-olds, he was rating an extraordinary 74 per cent. All the omens pointed to a government certain to sweep back into office for a third term. Kennett, though, was not convinced. Outwardly, he seemed calm and confident. Musing over the options with his two key advisers, Anna Cronin and Steve Murphy, he wandered across to his desk – the same desk behind which his feted Liberal predecessor, Sir Henry Bolte, had once sat – and put on a favourite Paul Robeson tape. Kennett hummed along for a few bars, jovially and pretty much in tune. But beneath his sunny disposition, he knew there was something missing in the atmospherics. He would always be at his best as a politician amid the blood and thunder of a genuine contest. 'I need some tension in the marketplace,' he would confide. Kennett sensed danger in the somnolent mood – a mysterious, malevolent shadow across the radar screen. Despite pressures to go to an early election in June, he held his nerve. And waited.

By mid-August, the premier had received news to gladden the heart of any political leader on the verge of an election campaign. The state Treasury had provided a confidential briefing on its revised budget forecasts. Revenue collections had surged beyond expectations. The state coffers were bulging with funds. The sustainable budget surplus had soared from the $68 million projected in May to $400 million, maybe more. The premier had a pot of gold at his disposal. He chose not to use it.

Kennett called a strategy meeting. Phil Gude, the education minister and Kennett's deputy leader, had lodged a submission requesting $45 million in extra spending in order to mount a campaign offensive in an area where the government was vulnerable. Kennett insisted this be trimmed back to $28 million. Gude was curious to know why. 'What's the surplus?' he asked.

Kennett briefed his colleagues on the budget update. Treasury was advising of a significant windfall that would push the surplus into some hundreds of millions of dollars beyond the original estimates. The government had money to burn. In virtually the next breath, however, the premier revealed a campaign strategy that left some of his colleagues perplexed. Despite having the funds to match or better any spending promises by the Opposition, Kennett had decided it would be best to resist the temptation to open a bidding war. He wanted to give his opponents no room for manoeuvre. The government would adhere to the modest spending proposals it had already drawn up. There would be no 'fistful of dollars' campaign. There would be no concession to the demands from country electorates for reinvestment in rural infrastructure. The government would stand on its record. It had developed its re-election strategy over many months of careful consideration, and it was leading comfortably in the polls. There was no need for panic or pork-barrelling. Strapped tightly into this self-imposed straitjacket of fiscal sobriety, Kennett called the election the following Wednesday 24 August.

Eight weeks later, Jeff Kennett was no longer premier. Rural electorates, weary of his constant exhortations to run harder and faster, had risen in revolt. Country voters faced with depressed rural industries had been demanding significant increases in government spending in their communities to counter the impact of deregulation and budget cuts on subsidised services. The mood of grievance was compounded by feelings of envy that Melbourne's revival as a metropolis had not been mirrored by a similar rejuvenation in smaller, outlying communities. The most conservative electorates in the state had decided to teach the premier the lesson of his life. He was a politician; he should behave like one. On election night, 18 September, eight non-metropolitan seats fell to Labor, a ninth to an independent. The Kennett era, as Victorians had come to know it, was over.

The unforeseen demise of the Kennett government reflects something of the enigma of its leader. As premier, Jeff Kennett always seemed to want to win arguments the hard way, as if temperamentally incapable of settling for a soft option. There were times when this dimension of his character confounded friends and enemies alike. Too often it seemed like bravado beyond the call of duty. The great irony of the election – apparent to his colleagues, if not to the man himself – was that he could so easily have launched a range of well-targeted spending initiatives across regional seats, without in any way compromising his government's financial management credentials. That Kennett refused was not really surprising: he was never one for the politics of appeasement.

Maybe, as his critics would suggest, Kennett had succumbed to the delusion of invincibility: planning strategies for his next term in office, believing that the 1999 election was as good as won. Doubtless, there was an element of arrogance and complacency guiding Kennett's calculations. But the answer to the riddle is just as likely to be found in the all-purpose one-liner used by Kennett aides on the regular occasions when they were asked to explain the inexplicable: 'It's just Jeffrey being Jeffrey.' It says something about the Kennett years in Victoria that this phrase requires almost no elaboration. It has its own ineffable logic.

No leader in postwar Australia succeeded so regularly in defying the predictable patterns of political behaviour. Jeff Kennett rejoiced in his image as a politician who dared to be different. He was a showman, a larrikin, a human headline. He said and did outrageous things. Often, it was enough to say no more than whatever he was thinking. Sometimes people laughed, sometimes they cringed, but he could never be ignored. His profile became such that it transcended the normal bounds of politics. When people spoke of the man, they spoke simply of 'Jeff'. He became one of the biggest brand names in the business.

Yet beneath the froth of celebrity status, there was always a jutting jawline, a steely professionalism, and a studied contempt for enemies and non-believers. In his policy agenda, Jeff Kennett was hard and unyielding. His government went after big licks of reform, imposing a difficult and gruelling reform program on the electorate. Aggressive and domineering, he trod unapologetically on the toes of any who stood in his path. It was a trademark style that was to become a model for the times, and a revolution of sorts: the Kennett revolution. Over his seven years as Victorian premier, Kennett became less a politician and more a phenomenon. This book is an attempt to explain that phenomenon, to chronicle an extraordinary life and career.

It took extraordinary circumstances for Kennett to be given an opportunity to lead the state. He arrived in the job largely by default. By 1992, his opponents had rendered themselves unelectable. Even so, critics assumed his style of government would last no time at all. Surely he would implode, self-destruct or taint himself with an outbreak of the silliness and excess for which he had been ridiculed in his early years as Opposition leader.

Instead, Jeff Kennett laid down a new model of leadership – aggressive, abrasive, swashbuckling. Australia seemed on the brink of a new era of conviction politics, in which governments would risk short-term popular support in pursuit of more ambitious policy outcomes. Kennett would lead the charge. Indeed, as his state was seen to regain purpose and momentum, there were repeated overtures for the Victorian premier to take his talents onto the national stage. Flattered by the attention, Kennett used his standing as a high-profile state leader to engage forcefully in many of the most important debates facing Australia at the end of the twentieth century: advocating new thinking in society's attitudes towards illegal drugs, coming out as an advocate of republicanism, opposing fiercely the anti-immigration sentiments of the One Nation movement, and prodding the Howard government to brace itself for the perilous challenge of instituting wide-ranging tax reform. Like few other state leaders, Kennett fought in the same weight division as prime ministers – and became a household name across the nation.

Part of Kennett's success can be put down to his irrepressible, indomitable enthusiasm. His single-minded refusal to be buffeted from the course he set for himself was a common cause of complaint from those who got in the way of his ambitions. But it proved an invaluable asset as Kennett sought to rekindle a city and a state's self-esteem. His determination to insinuate Melbourne into the international spotlight carried more than a tinge of parochialism and chauvinism. Yet, as a political strategy, it also had about it a touch of genius. Teamed with the marketing slogan 'On the Move' it created a sense of a community rediscovering its energy and vibrancy. Critically, it bought time for Kennett, while his government grappled with the imperative of financial reconstruction as well as the longer-term structural issues of how to generate a more competitive business ethos, stop the population drift to the northern sunbelt states, redress the decline of Victoria's industry and infrastructure, and counter the shift of money, power and influence to Sydney. Kennett was forever looking for frontiers where the state could establish an edge: high value-added food processing, advanced manufacturing, biotechnology and multimedia. Eager to understand the implications for government of the Internet, he launched himself into cyberspace, creating the first ministry for multimedia in Australia and becoming the first government leader to set up a workstation on his own office desk. In a memorable e-mail, Kennett also insisted each cabinet colleague follow his lead, adding, 'If you have not read this message and replied by 10 a.m. tomorrow, I will ring you to find out why.'

His blunt and demanding approach peeved some colleagues. Indeed, much has been said and written of Kennett's authoritarian streak, and not just within his own party. Through his years in power, he engaged in a running battle with fashionable opinion, rolling ruthlessly over the institutional speed humps preventing reform. His impetuosity, heavy-handedness and impatience with bureaucratic process were to see him clash heatedly with some of the most influential forces in the state: the legal profession, the *Age* newspaper, the unions, the churches, academia, the inner-city elites and, as often as not, his Liberal colleagues in the national capital. Kennett's was the politics of perpetual motion, and look out anyone who got in his way.

On the standard economic indicators – jobs, growth, budget outcomes – Jeff Kennett put runs on the board. In less than five years, his government succeeded in resurrecting the fortunes of a state that was considered an economic basket case. But at what cost to the old verities of government in the Westminster tradition, and with what changes – good or bad – to the social fabric of his community? As the steamroller rumbled through, what of those left behind in the trail of dust?

Perversely, though, Kennett turned community perceptions of his headstrong and maverick tendencies to his advantage. Although criticised constantly in sections of the media as bullying and bombastic, the flip side to this was a formidable public profile as a vigorous and daring leader. Thus in the 1990s Kennett came to be styled as a colossus of power politics: the Can-Do premier.

We in Victoria thought we knew him so well. As he pointed out famously during one of his weekly radio interviews with 3AW's Neil Mitchell, few politicians had been cross-examined as often or as comprehensively: 'You've been in me, up me, down me, vivisected me, dissected me – I don't know any part of my life that the public doesn't know about.' In fact, there were aspects to the Kennett character that remained forever hidden.

This was the premier, we were told, who governed only for the big end of town. Presumably, this is why nobody heard of him arriving unannounced at the annual Christmas drinks for Melbourne's taxi drivers. He liked to regard them as part of his team. They were the city's ambassadors: often the first impression visitors to the state received after they'd flown into Tullamarine airport or arrived at Spencer Street station. More than once, he went along to office parties to thank them for their contribution.

Jeff Kennett played his politics for keeps. He had enemies to whom he gave no quarter. This perhaps is why we never heard of the day when, as Opposition leader, he drove 150 kilometres west of Melbourne to be at the bedside of one of his old party-room antagonists, Harley Dickinson, who had been stricken by a heart attack. Dickinson was a rebel voice, a dissident who had resigned from the Liberal Party to contest the seat of South Barwon as an independent. Yet, according to colleagues, Kennett left his government car and driver behind – breaching protocol on their use – so that Dickinson's wife, who didn't drive, could visit her husband when he was transferred to a city hospital for intensive care. Kennett caught the train home.

As much as he thrived on the strongman image, it is odd that the public never learned of his regular visits to the hospital bed of a teenage worker who was wounded horribly when a poorly maintained boiler exploded during renovations at Treasury Place. For weeks the premier drove every morning to the burns unit at the Alfred Hospital to check on the welfare of the youngster and his three injured colleagues. When the Rolling Stones played the Melbourne Cricket Ground, Kennett arranged for the teenager, recovering but still desperately ill, to join him in a corporate superbox. He wheeled the youth into the stadium and sat by his side. One of the boy's few pleasures in life was to have a smoke. Kennett held a cigarette to his mouth as they watched the concert.

Jeff Kennett was highly protective of his freedom to do such things out of the public spotlight. Hence, we heard nothing of the Sunday afternoon when he drove 80 kilometres down the Princes Highway to console the players of the Geelong Football Club after their Grand Final loss to the West Coast Eagles – the first defeat of a Victorian side by an interstate club. This happened at the sharp end of the 1992 state election campaign, during Kennett's third attempt to become premier. He broke from his campaign schedule to make the trip. But there were no TV cameras present, no picture opportunities. Just a few quiet drinks in one of the local pubs, and a few words of sympathy. There was to be no feasting on the images, he insisted. It was a ritual of mourning, a private thing, nobody else's business.

Prominent Melbourne writer Les Carlyon once described Kennett as 'a biographer's dream'. Maybe so. But Jeff Kennett's is not a straightforward story to tell. How did a politician pilloried through his early years as a raw and undisciplined populist reinvent himself in the 1990s as one of the shrewdest and most effective politicians of his generation? What brought this man to the world of politics? What motivated him to step out of his advertising agency in Melbourne's eastern suburbs and decide he had the answers? How did he survive the furious helter-skelter of his early tempestuous months in office – the '100 days that shook Victoria'? Finally, and most intriguingly of all, how did he stumble to defeat in an election campaign he was universally expected to win, and win comfortably?

Tracing Jeff Kennett's life through his 23 years in public office, it is impossible not to be curious about, if not always admiring of, the individual and his idiosyncratic ways. Always with Kennett, it is in the many cross-currents and contradictions that the clues are to be found as to why things happened the way they did. There will always be an element of intrigue to the man.

Soon after Kennett's departure from office, former Liberal state president Michael Kroger, never an admirer of Jeff's style, said the great pity of the defeat was that it denied the Liberal Party an icon. In a speech delivered as part of the Menzies lecture series, Kroger said Australians only held up as heroes the champions who went out on top, undefeated, unbowed. In postwar Australia there had been only four politicians who could claim that mantle: Sir Robert Menzies himself, who had slipped gently from the scene like a stately steamship; Sir Charles Court, who had served until an advanced age as premier of Western Australia, apparently invincible; the long-serving Victorian premier Sir Henry Bolte, who had retired in 1972 sensing shrewdly that the mood of the day called for a different style of leadership than he – a man fixed in his ways – was ready or willing to offer; and, in more recent times, New South Wales premier 'Nifty' Neville Wran, who had succeeded in getting out with an element of grace before the voters or the plotters in his own caucus could catch up with him.

Jeff Kennett knew the sorry history of political leaders who out-stayed their welcome, and was intensely conscious of it in his latter years in office. After all, he had been taught to watch for the omens by one of the best in the business. In 1987 Kennett and Kroger had visited the old warhorse, Sir Henry Bolte, at his farm at Bamganie. The man who had ruled as premier for 17 years seemed troubled as he joined them in his loungeroom, the ubiquitous bottle of Scotch sitting alongside his armchair. He had been on the phone.

'What's the problem?' they asked.

'I have just been talking to Joh,' Bolte explained. Queensland's long-serving premier and one of the most powerful, if contro-versial, politicians of his day, Sir Joh Bjelke-Petersen, was on the skids. A royal commission into corruption in Queensland had destroyed his credibility, his National Party colleagues were des-perate for a fresh start, and the polls were at rock bottom. Joh had reached his use-by date.

'I told him he ought to retire,' said Bolte. 'I said, "Joh, for Christ's sake, you have to go. There comes a time for all of us." He said, "No, Henry, you don't understand. There's nobody else. I am the only one that can lead them."'

An exasperated Bolte looked at Kennett and Kroger sternly. 'Look, you young fellas, you have to know this. Leaders can't go on forever.'

CHAPTER ONE

BEGINNINGS

'A keen, pleasant though sometimes erratic boy.'
SCOTCH COLLEGE REPORT CARD, 1965

In 1964, Ken Kennett decided it was time for his first and only son to see the world. Ken was a successful airline marketing manager in Melbourne and had a standing invitation from one of his friends in business, Alitalia executive Renato Velli, to come and stay at his mansion on the Peak in Hong Kong. Ken decided to accept the offer and use it to give his 16-year-old son a taste of the excitement and exotica of Asia. The boy, though, had different ideas. Asserting his independence, Jeff told his father, 'You don't have to take me anywhere. I will go by myself.' And so he did. During his Fifth Form (Year 11) school vacation, the tall, lanky teenager flew out of Melbourne, bound for Hong Kong via Bangkok. He spoke no Asian languages. His life experience had been confined to the comfortable surrounds of middle-class Melbourne. He would be very much the innocent abroad. But this was to be his first great adventure, and he would go it alone.

Jeff Kennett was born into a tradition of risk-taking. On both sides of his family, driven individuals had pioneered family business ventures that had grown into major commercial enterprises. One of his forebears had crossed the oceans to Melbourne in search of business opportunities. There had been spectacular boom-and-bust cycles of significant wealth destroyed by the vicissitudes of war, depression and financial misadventure. Kennett's bloodlines contained three key traits: resourcefulness, a high-rolling instinct and a stout, even stubborn, resilience.

None of this was readily apparent in the modest affluence that characterised Jeff's childhood years. His parents, Ken and Wendy, both worked to put Kennett and his sisters, Judy and Sandra, through private-school education. The family lived at 61 Brandon Street, Burwood, in the middle-class suburbs to Melbourne's east. An elm-lined row of neat red-brick houses developed in the 1930s, the street offered uniform three-bedroom floor plans, enough land to establish a garden, and plenty of parkland nearby in which children could play. The neighbourhood was quiet, orderly and unpretentious – an ambience disturbed occasionally in the 1950s by the raucous sales pitch of a young and cheerful Jeff attempting to persuade passers-by to buy a cup of lemonade from a stall set up on the footpath outside the family home. In his teenage years, the Kennetts moved to the more salubrious suburb of Canterbury, with its impressive stone mansions and rambling gardens. Here, closer to the city, was the heart of old-moneyed Melbourne. For Jeff and his sisters, this might well have created a sense of upward mobility as their father made his mark in the airline business. For Ken and Wendy Kennett, however, it was merely a return to familiar territory. Only a generation earlier, both of their families had known great affluence and social status.

Wendy Kennett's great-grandfather, Hugo Wertheim, had made the long sea journey from Europe to Melbourne in 1875, intent on exploring new markets for his family's Frankfurt-based manufacturing business. He arrived in one of the most prosperous colonies in the British Empire. Underwritten by the gold rush of the 1850s, Victoria's living standards were enviable by any global measure. The brash and boastful British outpost was also blessed with some of the richest farming country in the world. The people of Melbourne were eager to demonstrate the conspicuous civility of their lifestyle. It was a city that prided itself on grand and ostentatious architecture and world-class public amenities, and was unabashed about flaunting its cultural and artistic pretensions. Hugo Wertheim had come with plans to sell sewing machines. But once in Victoria, he sensed there might be more lucrative markets to develop. He made plans to build the biggest piano factory in the world.

One of his sons, Herbert, was sent to the Boston Technological Institution to study piano-making. On his return, Herbert built a 4600-square-metre red-brick factory on 8 hectares in Bendigo Street, Richmond. Prime Minister Alfred Deakin laid the foundation stone in 1908. The Wertheim piano was to become one of the most successful brands in Australia. Using local timbers, it was proclaimed to be one of the 'instruments that stand highest on the honour roll of excellence.' Three hundred workers produced 2000 pianos a year. When at her home in Lilydale on Melbourne's outskirts, Dame Nellie Melba, Australia's first opera star of international renown, was said to have refused to sing with anything else.

The Wertheims soon became part of the city's wealthiest elite. They were the proud owners of Melbourne's twelfth private telephone line. Herbert Wertheim became one of the original investors in BHP. A non-practising Jew, he was admitted to the heart of the old establishment, the Melbourne Club, despite its notorious membership restrictions. The family lived in one of the most opulent mansions in Toorak, where Jeff Kennett's grandmother, Gladys, the youngest of six children, was educated by private tutors.

It is in her brother, Rupert 'Sos' Wertheim, however, that trace elements can perhaps be found of the gregarious characteristics that would later manifest themselves in Gladys' grandson. Sos was ranked among Australia's top six tennis players in the amateur era (playing Davis Cup against Czechoslovakia in 1922) and was something of a local celebrity. 'He had a lavish wardrobe, a taste for smart cars and was known as a wit and a society man. He also had a volatile temperament and was given to extravagant praise if his partner hit a winner, and searing looks if the partner served a double fault. He was a giant of a man, so tall that he once attracted the nickname of "the extension ladder".'

But Sos lived at the tail-end of what had been a glittering era for the Wertheims. World War One cruelled the circumstances of this prosperous and successful immigrant family. The Wertheims became targets for anti-German feeling, and were interned as 'hostile aliens' under the official policy of the day. This is doubtless an important episode in explaining Jeff Kennett's strong identification in later years with migrant communities, and his antipathy towards the xenophobic posturing of political movements such as One Nation. For the Wertheims, the impact of these wartime strictures on their business was drastic. The third generation proved less enthusiastic about rebuilding the enterprise, and their postwar attempts to rescue the piano-making operation were stymied by the impact of the wireless on more traditional forms of home entertainment. The family wealth began to dissipate. Then came the Great Depression. The Wertheim factory closed in 1935. Today, it is the home of the Melbourne studios of the Packer family's Nine Network.

Given the heavy-handed treatment of her family by the authorities during the war, it is perhaps surprising that Gladys married a military man. The 1924 wedding of the Wertheims' youngest daughter to Major William Fanning at Melbourne Grammar School's St Peter's Chapel featured in the pages of *The Home*, a glossy society magazine. Major Fanning, the son of a Sydney financier, had been exposed to the curse of chemical warfare that debilitated so many of the 'lucky ones' who survived the battlefields of the Great War. In another of life's ironies, he returned from Europe to rebuild his career as the general manager of Colonial Industrial Gases. Jeff Kennett remembers accompanying his grandfather to office Christmas parties at CIG, where Major Fanning would show off his musical talents on the banjo and ukelele. He was also a talented orator. Indeed, long after his retirement, the major was invited to address an annual dinner for the company in the 1970s. Tragically, he collapsed halfway through his speech and died.

Kennett speaks fondly of his grandmother, known affectionately as 'Gladdy Fanny'. She lived to the age of 88, and appears to have been an important formative influence in his early life. 'Her family lost their wealth but my grandmother never lost her strength, decency and politeness. She was just a wonderful woman.' Kennett tells the story of the day when, as a small boy at the beach at Frankston, he fell from a retaining wall and gashed his head. 'She said, "Jeff, don't cry, it's only a cut." There was blood everywhere, and I needed stitches and everything else. She wasn't – what's the word? – teutonic, or spartan. She was just very practical. No nonsense.'

Kennett's paternal grandfather, Charles E. Kennett, was also a successful businessman. He and his wife, Dagmar, had started out with very little. She had been a charwoman, riding her bicycle around South Melbourne to collect laundry, while her husband struggled to set up his own manufacturing company in City Road. In the interwar years, Kennett Ladders, like Wertheim Pianos, became a trademark business. The operations expanded interstate, with a branch office in Sydney run by Charles' younger brother, Lawrence. During these buoyant times the family moved to Kooyong, one of Melbourne's showpiece inner-eastern suburbs clustered around the Yarra River.

Born in June 1921, Kenneth Munro Gibb Kennett, Jeff's father, attended prestigious Scotch College, the oldest school in Melbourne. World War II came in his final school year and cut short his studies towards a career in accountancy. When a Japanese invasion of mainland Australia threatened, he answered the call to enlist and in 1941 joined the many thousands of young Australian volunteers for the army. He trained in an artillery regiment attached to the 4th Division of the Australian Infantry Forces and was sent into combat against the imperial Japanese army in Papua New Guinea and later Bougainville. As part of the grim defence of Australia's northern approaches, he did not come home until war's end in 1945.

Once back in Melbourne, Ken resumed work at the family business and met Wendy Anne Fanning, the only daughter of Major Fanning and Gladys Wertheim. Younger than the returned soldier by four years, she was studying arts at Melbourne University and working part-time in a chocolate shop. They married on 2 April 1947 at the Scotch College Chapel and moved into a house in upmarket Kew. On 2 March 1948 their first child, Jeffrey Gibb Kennett, was born at the Alfred Hospital.

After Jeff's birth, though, Ken and Wendy Kennett had to make a fresh start. The family business had run into trouble. When Lawrence Kennett died, a family dispute erupted over the ownership of the Sydney branch of the company's operations. In the early 1950s, Kennett's grandfather, Charles, lost much of what remained of his fortune when the stockmarket slumped.

'I was only six, but I remember the devastating impact it had on my grandfather,' recalls Kennett. 'He died soon after. This reduced my grandmother, Dagmar, from a position of great wealth to living in a one-room flat in Riversdale Road. She ended up, fundamentally, a pauper.'

The demise of the business meant that Ken Kennett had to start virtually from scratch in order to provide for his young family. He chose a career in marketing and accepted a job at the Heinz factory in Dandenong, on Melbourne's south-eastern outskirts. In 1953, in order to reduce his travel time to and from work, the family – by this time including Jeff and his sisters, Judy, two years younger, and baby Sandra, five years his junior – moved to the outlying bayside suburb of Mt Eliza. Jeff and Judy began their school life at the tiny Mt Eliza State School.

By 1960, Jeff's father had secured a job with TAA (later Australian Airlines), where he would ultimately become marketing director. The family moved to Burwood, in Melbourne's comfortable eastern suburbs. Nevertheless, the Kennetts kept their own henhouse to ensure a supply of fresh eggs and the occasional roast chicken dinner. 'It wasn't an affluent background at all,' Kennett insists. 'Although it might have started a bit more affluently, by the time I came along all that had gone. We lived in a small house. We never owned a new car. We were typically, I think, lower middle class. There was never any spare wealth but it didn't matter. My parents were wonderful people with a wide circle of friends, and it was a rich environment in which to grow up.'

His mother, Wendy, combined her home duties with a job as a librarian to pay for the children's private school fees. For his senior school years Jeff was enrolled at Scotch, his father's alma mater and one of the crucibles of the city's establishment. The school boasts an impressive alumni which includes many prominent figures in the affairs of the state and the nation: in law, in the churches and notably in public life. It has produced three federal cabinet ministers since the 1970s, all Liberals, including former federal Opposition leader and ambassador to Washington Andrew Peacock. In Victorian politics it can stake claim to two of the last four premiers, Jeff Kennett and John Cain, along with former attorney-general, Jim Kennan. The school's expectations of service and achievement are embodied in its motto, *Deo Patriae Litteris:* 'For God, for Country and for Learning'. Like most institutions of its ilk, Scotch sets high standards in scholarship and sport.

Kennett, however, did not excel academically. He also felt unable to live up to his father's reputation as an athlete. Ken Kennett had been a champion footballer in Scotch College's 1939 premiership team. In a centenary history of the school, he was named among the five 'great players' in the team that ended Melbourne Grammar's 10-year domination of the GPS competition. The title had been clinched with a tense two-point victory over Geelong Grammar in the final match of the season, and a report in the *Herald* had praised Kennett's starring role. This was the stuff of which schoolboy legends are made – and perhaps nowhere more so than at Scotch. The school's geography is dominated by a vast expanse of lush playing fields, extending from the red-brick Victorian schoolhouse buildings down past stands of native gum and across to the banks of the Yarra River. Scotch is a school that loves its sporting heroes, but Jeff was never able to emulate his father's prowess. He never made it higher than the fourth- or fifth-string football side. When he was mentioned in match reports, it was typically for his motivation of the team rather than his physical skills. But Jeff says this failure to measure up to the standards set by his father was never an issue with his parents – he was not pushed to achieve beyond his abilities, and was encouraged to develop broader interests such as model trains, photography and the school choir.

Even as a schoolboy, Jeff could never be ignored. He is remembered by fellow students as likeable and gregarious – a 'good all-round bloke'. Barrister Tony Kenna, who was a year ahead of Kennett, recalls: 'He was one of the popular kids. Well known, well liked. He had a presence. Jeff was never going to be a back-room boy. He was always going to be the type to attract attention.'

In his school records, Kennett garnered plaudits for his role as the ugly and misshapen hunchback, able seaman Dick Deadeye, in a school production of Gilbert and Sullivan's *HMS Pinafore*. The school newspaper, *Satura,* also praised him for the poise and conviction of his performance. 'Above all, his voice seemed ideally suited to the part,' the review noted. Indeed, Kennett's trademark foghorn baritone became the stuff of school legend, booming across the parade grounds and playing fields.

During his years at Scotch, Kennett mingled with the sons of Melbourne's well-to-do. And in the social interaction on the tram routes connecting the string of private schools in Hawthorn, Kew and Malvern, he also made it a habit to mingle with their daughters. 'Jeff was always a bit keen on jumping on and off trams,' says one colleague at school, remembering his eagerness to chat with the girls from Methodist Ladies' College, Genazzano and Ruyton. Fortuitously, his number 7 tram from Scotch back to Burwood also passed close by the Lauriston school for girls in Armadale. His sisters would board the tram here. So too would the Kellar sisters, Angela and Felicity, daughters of a prominent engineer. Felicity was three years younger than Kennett, but caught his eye. She, however, would remember Kennett as having a 'daggy' haircut and a military bearing. At the time, she was not impressed.

Jeff was distinguishing himself as a military cadet, but not as a student. His academic performance was lacklustre and caused some consternation within his family. During his Fourth Form (Year 10) studies in 1963, he even considered leaving. But his form master, 'Buster' Burt, persuaded the 15-year-old to persist in his studies, and he passed the year. In 1964, according to the head-master's progress report – the so-called 'blue card' – Kennett still lacked consistency of performance in the classroom: 'A confident and at times helpful student. Sometimes irritates. Sometimes works hard.' The report for his final year of 1965 added, perhaps wearily: 'He tries hard. He has taken an active part in school affairs and has been a splendid company sergeant major in the cadets. A keen, pleasant, though sometimes erratic boy.'

Self-evidently, Kennett was not deemed by his masters at Scotch to be destined for greatness. Even so, he believes the ethos of the school proved an important influence later in life: 'I look back at Scotch, and I ask myself was there a seminal advantage in going to Scotch as opposed to going through a secondary-level state school. I have to say I think if you are a bright student it doesn't really matter where you go. Unless the school community is terribly depressed, if you are a bright student, you will always do well in our system of education here in Victoria, or Australia. The education system is that good. But if you are very average academically, as I was, what is more important is the opportunity that private schools offer that state schools don't, like the clubs, the musical events, the debating clubs, the plays, the cadets and scouts, the rowing, the football and the cricket. I think the value of Scotch for a person like me was the ability to be exposed to all these things rather than just the straight raw discipline of academic achievement. Scotch was a very good instructor of values. It did broaden, I think, into the subject of public service. There was an expectation that some would go into the church, some would go into the military, some would go into politics.'

In his youth, Kennett had no thoughts of following in the footsteps of others from the school who had distinguished themselves in political life. 'My only association with politics was when I was out mowing the lawns, or helping Father in the garden, and watching the big, black car of Vern Wilcox [Bolte government minister and the Kennetts' local MLA] come up the road. He would often get out and speak to Father or talk to me, and that was my introduction to politics. I remember listening to political debate, and I have photos of Menzies coming to the school. But I didn't join the Young Liberals or any of that business.'

In the many profiles of Kennett written over the years, he is routinely described as an academic failure. In fact, he matriculated as an average student and won a scholarship with the insurance company Edward Lumley. 'They provided two scholarships a year. They started the process of selection in the first quarter of the year and then they whittled the list down. It was not just academically based, it was also judged on an aptitude scale. It was a wonderful thing because, well into my last year, I had no chance or desire to go to university. This gave me the opportunity to have specialised training and travel overseas.'

Overseas travel was a passion Ken and Wendy Kennett sought to instil in their children. Ken had taken Sandra on a trip to see friends in Canada, and Judy had accompanied him on a visit to Europe. Jeff's chance came in Fifth Form, when he set off alone on his voyage of discovery to Hong Kong. Although allowing his son the freedom to travel solo, Ken had issued strict instructions – especially when it came to how Jeff should behave in Bangkok. 'I got to my hotel and I didn't understand a word anyone was saying. My father had said to me, "When you arrive in Bangkok, just go to your room. Stay there. Don't go out."' Kennett went to his room and read a book. Then came a knock on the door. 'It was the first time I was propositioned,' Kennett recalls. 'During the night, three or four times, women came to the door, offering to come inside.'

Kennett insists he declined politely – which is why he found it even more galling to discover the following morning that he had been 'ripped off a huge amount of money' in his hotel bill. Strapped for cash and running late for his connecting flight to Hong Kong, he saw two limousines provided for Alitalia staff. 'Are you going out to the airport?' he asked cheekily. 'I would like a lift.' Told that the limousines could only be used by passengers in an emergency, the 16-year-old offered a garbled explanation of his plight, insisting, 'This *is* an emergency.' He talked his way into five-star service all the way through to Hong Kong.

Once there, Kennett checked into a flat at Repulse Bay for a few days before taking up the invitation of Renato Velli to stay as a guest at his house on the Peak. For the next fortnight, the youngster sampled life on the streets of Hong Kong. 'I just loved it. I loved the huge numbers of people, the intensity of it. Everyone was doing something. It was extraordinary.' Even as a raw and unsophisticated Australian teenager in 1966, Kennett had a sense of the dynamism of Asian societies, and of the likelihood that Australia's neighbours to the north were on the cusp of momentous change. 'There were very obvious differences between the authority and power of those who were associated with the non-Chinese as distinct from the Chinese themselves, who at that time were in this very subservient role.' Kennett would return regularly to Asia over subsequent years, and become a leading advocate of Australia engaging more closely in regional business and politics.

But, in 1967, Kennett's parents wanted him to have the necessary grounding before looking to distant horizons. When he left school, Kennett was anxious to begin work immediately with the insurance company. However, his father had applied on his son's behalf to enrol in the law faculty at the Australian National University in Canberra. 'I never applied for ANU, my father did. He thought one day much later I would come to regret that I didn't give university a try. I gave that some thought, and agreed he was probably right. So I threw in my Edward Lumley scholarship, which I felt very bad about, but I think Father's advice was right: whether you failed or succeeded at uni, you had to give it a go. So I packed my bags almost immediately, and went up there virtually that same day.

'By the time I enrolled, I had decided to do economics with a guy I met on the plane, which was fine except that I hadn't passed any maths subjects, or economic subjects, at school. In order to sit your final exams in economics, you had to pass a statistical subject. I passed all my economic subjects in the first term, but I got 13 per cent for statistics. I was not going to be able to sit the exams. In the second term, I got about 30 or 35 per cent. I passed all my economic subjects but still didn't qualify on stats. I realised I was in a bit of bother so I got some tutoring. I ended up getting 80 per cent for stats and failing all my economics subjects. The university said, "Well, it's obvious what's happened here. You have given too much focus to one discipline, so why not come back next year? You can start again, now you have qualified in your stats." I said, "No. I've had my chance and I've blown it. I will go back to the real world."'

Kennett concedes there is another equally convincing explanation for his substandard university results: an overinvestment in the extracurricular activities attached to university life. He was boisterous and companionable, enjoyed a drink and a lively argument, and was known to croon along to the songs of Edith Piaf. 'We had a good time. We lived in a university residence on Northbourne

Avenue and you had all these students and lecturers and professors
and everyone else. It was a good mix of people. We put in a fair bit
of work but we also played pretty hard, yes.' A favourite anecdote
involves Kennett's attempt, at the urging of fellow students, to
meet the visiting US president, Lyndon Baines Johnson, in 1966.
Kennett posed as an incapacitated Vietnam veteran. 'We were trying to work out how we were going to get LBJ to stop and talk to
us. So they bandaged me up, put me in a wheelchair, and took me
out into the crowd lining the street. The only problem was that
LBJ's security people had decided to switch the route. They didn't
come anywhere near us.' This triviality was about the extent of
Kennett's interest in politics. Although he acknowledges he spent
many hours on the local golf courses, he cannot remember from
his student days in Canberra a single visit to the seat of the federal
parliament.

Kennett returned to Melbourne eager to make a start in the
world of commerce and industry. He secured a job in the advertising department of the retail giant Myer. These were familiar
surroundings: he had worked there as a casual employee during
school holidays, sweeping floors and running messages. One of his
menial tasks had been to maintain the 'guide books' – collections
of advertisements Myer had placed in the city's newspapers. This
had given him an early eye for layout and design techniques in
advertising. He was employed as a cadet to help prepare the
company's full-page print advertisements, usually for homewares,
to be placed in the *Herald* and the *Age*.

Unlike many other major companies, who by the 1960s were
beginning to contract out their advertising and marketing roles to
industry specialists, Myer maintained its own large in-house advertising department of more than 200 staff. Although operating
under a conservative corporate ethos, the retailer's weight and influence in the Melbourne market provided its trainees with invaluable
connections to the city's commercial and media networks. Kennett
came under the watchful eye of Wally O'Donoghue, known as

'O.D.' and something of a guru of the advertising industry. Jeff
came to idolise him. 'He was a wonderful, creative retail advertising man. He was a red-headed Irish guy and he was a lot of fun. He
had big ideas. He had a wonderful relationship with the juniors he
trained. There are many people of my age around the traps who
owe a lot of their success in life to his formative training. We wore
suits, our hair was short, we were clean, we were punctual.'

After the disappointment of his failure to come to terms with
university life, Kennett appears to have thrived in the advertising
business. He enjoyed the discipline and the demands; according to
former colleagues, he also brought great enthusiasm and a sense of
fun to his work. He became popular with clients for his energetic
and 'in-your-face' approach. But Kennett's career in advertising was
cut short. In 1968, the twenty-year-old was conscripted as one of
the tens of thousands of young Australian soldiers being trained
for the battlefields of Asia. Despite mounting anger among his contemporaries over Australia's support of the United States' military
campaigns in Indochina, Kennett did not question being drafted for
military service. He headed off to the Puckapunyal training base in
central Victoria determined to make the best of it. The experience
was to change his attitudes and outlook forever.

CHAPTER TWO

OFFICER MATERIAL

'It was there, it was happening. Whether I liked it or not,
the government had committed Australia to it . . . that was
fine with me. Once we were there, bingo.'

JEFF KENNETT

It was 16 July 1969. Second Lieutenant Jeff Kennett, commander of the 1st platoon, A company, Royal Australian Regiment, led his men out of the jungles of East Malaysia. They had spent weeks trudging though the leech-infested rainforest. They were filthy and fatigued. Under Kennett's command, they crept stealthily onto a rubber plantation in their jungle greens. This was not a secret mission; nor, strictly speaking, had it been authorised by military command: Jeff Kennett's men had come to watch Neil Armstrong's first step on the moon.

As a junior officer with the Australian forces in South-East Asia, Kennett had been assiduously building up his local networks. He had befriended the French family who ran the plantation, and they had agreed to create a makeshift amphitheatre for the Australians in the gardens of their villa, setting up a television so Kennett and his mates could watch the historic telecast. As the soldiers emerged from the jungle, there to greet them were dozens of Indian rubber tappers, curious as to what all the fuss was about.

'You had this incredible dichotomy,' Kennett recalls. 'Young men watching the history of man walking on the moon, with Indian plantation workers watching TV for the first time and wondering what the hell was going on.'

The day was a highlight of Kennett's tour of duty in Malaysia and Singapore. In a stint that stretched for just over a year, he did not once engage in hostilities. But there is little doubt that his time in the military set him apart from many of his contemporaries. While tens of thousands of his generation marched the streets in protest at the Australian government's involvement in the Indochinese wars, Jeff Kennett was making his way into the junior officer ranks of the army. After an impressive performance at the notorious Scheyville army training camp west of Sydney, the 21-year-old university drop-out had been deemed officer material. He was promptly dispatched to Malacca in 1969 as a spear-carrier for the so-called 'domino theory' of forward defence – Australia's deployment of expeditionary forces into mainland South-East Asia aimed at stopping the spread of revolutionary communism. His was the last garrison based on the Malay Peninsula.

The Gorton government in Canberra, facing mounting domestic criticism, was beginning the process of phased withdrawal from the region. Kennett and his troops, many of whom were Vietnam veterans resting and retraining before a return to war, were ordered back to Singapore within a year and based at Changi. Forward defence was now a discredited theory. Hundreds of young Australians had become casualties of a war that it was clear the US and its Australian allies could never win. Ho Chi Minh's revolutionary movement, though Marxist in ideology, was fuelled as much by patriotic fervour and a profound historic resentment of western colonialism. In Vietnam, Australian troops had confronted the will of a nation, and one of the most effective guerilla movements in the history of modern warfare.

By the time Kennett was posted to Malaysia, public support in Australia for the troops abroad was evaporating. The death toll was mounting. Many of Kennett's generation were politicised by their opposition to the use of conscription for what they regarded as a dubious, if not immoral, military cause. As a result, many would become lifetime supporters of the Australian Labor Party, which opposed conscription and the war. Kennett, however, had taken a different path. Not for the last time, he adopted a less fashionable view of the rights and wrongs of the debate. It was not that he could not accept the arguments of those who were strong critics of Australia's role, more that he could never come to terms with the notion of undermining the foreign policy stance of the government of the day. 'I was obviously aware of the protests and rallies, and of the number of people who were claiming to be conscientious objectors. I didn't believe myself to be out of sync with my generation. I did what I did because I felt it was my duty. My number had come up so I did it. I was just bitterly disappointed at the attitudes of some others enjoying the luxury of living in a democracy in Australia. The government involved us in Vietnam because they thought it was morally right, and to follow the old domino theory of fighting our battles offshore. I can understand those who opposed that stance, but I don't agree with them. Ultimately, the democratic process worked and we changed the government and the new government came in and ended conscription and ended our involvement in the war. Whitlam did it in the first week. I don't resent them at all. I just had a different view and fundamentally did as I was told.'

Kennett's ethos of saluting the uniform verged on blind loyalty. It was to become a governing principle throughout his public life, sometimes to his cost. In the first instance, however, Kennett came into this military milieu purely by accident. A numbered marble plucked out randomly in a lottery, according to the date of birth, was the system for determining whether or not young Australians were compelled to don the uniform. Once drafted, Kennett sought to make the most of it: 'There was no point just doing time. I might as well do the best I could. Working hard at it, I got selected for officer training. And I made sure I graduated well. High in the class.'

Jeff Kennett had known there was a high probability he would be called up for national service. Both his father and his maternal grandfather had distinguished themselves as soldiers, and Jeff was determined he would not be found wanting. For the six months before his number was called he voluntarily increased his physical exercise, determined to get his fitness levels up.

The fact that Kennett excelled at the Scheyville camp says something for the doggedness of his character. It was a training regimen designed for the fast-tracking of young officers. He was not gifted athletically, and only the most strong-willed survived the arduous, often brutal mental and physical tests. For the first 30 days there was no quitting the course, and recruits were not permitted to walk anywhere. In every waking moment they were forced to either run or jog. Sunday was the only day off, with Saturdays reserved for work in the morning and compulsory team sport in the afternoons. Says Kennett, 'In the first three months, you were treated like dirt. Bastardisation, as they call it.' The system of rewards and penalties imposed shared responsibilities, based on a 'father and son' calculation. Each junior trainee was paired with a more senior partner. If the junior was unable to meet the standards required, the senior assigned to him would receive the same punishment whether he failed or succeeded. The sins of the son were visited upon the father. 'If we made mistakes, there was a high price to pay. You would have to do more physical work. They worked you so hard: you were up before dawn and through to end of the day. It was physically exhausting. On the other hand, it was exhilarating, as you watched your own fitness levels rise and began to understand what they were on about. As you got towards the end of the first period, if you were any good, you were given management tasks.'

Within three months, Kennett was elevated to the rank of company sergeant major. This meant he was spared the bastardisation by senior trainees. Instead, he was bastardised by regular army officers. 'It was very gruesome at times,' Kennett admits. 'But it was all part of the process. It was very tough. If you were not able to mix it, you were failed at various stages during the course. It was always a great pity when people didn't make it. These young men had worked their butts off and you could see them break down when they realised they were not going to get there.'

One of Kennett's fellow trainees at the camp was Graham Cornes, later to become a football legend in South Australia and the first coach of the Adelaide Crows Australian Rules football team. Cornes arrived at Scheyville in the intake after Kennett. He remembers a strict hierarchical system, in which Kennett was his superior. 'The position he held was given to those with the most potential. He had a certain arrogance and aloofness, but I don't mean that as a negative thing. He had an officer air about him. In any other field of employment, this might have been seen as a negative. Some thought he was a pain in the arse. But the thing that has to be said is that this was one of the most intense and physically demanding courses; you either embraced it or you were severed.' Cornes succumbed in the final days of the course after a nightmarish 11 days of sleep and food deprivation, culminating in a 50-kilometre march. Even for someone who was to become an elite athlete the demands were too great, and he was culled from the course. Cornes admired Kennett, not only for the fact that he battled through, but also because, amid the rigours, he managed to maintain some irreverence throughout. 'He would have had an enormous sense of achievement in having made it through. The thing I always respected was that he wasn't crushed by the army system. He always had that twinkle in his eye that showed he had a sense of humour.'

At the end of the six-month crash course, Kennett had not only survived the elimination process – an average of half of each intake failed – but finished third in a graduating class of 68. He, too, confirms it was a matter of pride to have mastered the course and defends the brutality of the process. 'They crammed stuff into you. Given you were going to end up as an officer in the army, you had to perform. At the end of the day you were going to be making decisions that were going to put at risk other people's lives.'

Former deputy prime minister and National Party leader Tim Fischer was another graduate from Scheyville. He left for a tour of duty in Vietnam just as Jeff Kennett was arriving at the training camp. Fischer, too, recalls the experience of Scheyville as arduous and demanding yet providing valuable lessons in the pyschology of man-management: 'It was terrific in that sense. I was in the intake before Jeff Kennett so I didn't come across him. But you can see how it contributed to his success. That black-and-white style of leadership.'

Kennett was posted to Malaysia soon after graduating. Four years after visiting as a teenager, he was back in Asia. His garrison at Terendak included New Zealand and British soldiers, and represented the vestiges of the mopping-up operations that followed the so-called armed communist insurgency of the Malayan Emergency. In the early 1960s, when the newly independent Malaysian Federation faced the aggressive opposition of Indonesia's Sukarno during the period of Confrontasi, the garrison's strategic value was reaffirmed. After the overthrow of Sukarno in Jakarta, however, the military presence of the Five Power nations on the Malay Peninsula lost much of its imperative. But with Asia seized by political upheaval, the troops were maintained as a stabilising influence. The garrison came to serve as a staging post for Australian troops on their way to and from the war zone in Vietnam. Kennett appears to have relished the experience: 'If you speak to anyone about their time in the military, whether in a war zone or not, it is important because it is so comprehensively different from anything else you experience. You are taken out of your natural environment, you have to relate to people around you regardless of their education, background, status or economic position in life. You are all basically equal. At the end of the day, you know your life depends on his work, and his life depends on yours. You develop very strong bonds.

And also you develop a strong sense of man-management. You might disagree with the person, but you saluted the uniform because often it was the only way you could achieve sensible outcomes.'

In charge of a platoon, Kennett struck up friendships with soldiers from far more diverse backgrounds than he had come across in Melbourne's genteel eastern suburbs. 'I'd had no contact with people from the bush or from Footscray. But in the army we were all together and you started to understand that, although people might express themselves differently, everyone's very similar. So it was very important in giving me exposure to different perspectives on life.' He also developed a strong sense of solidarity with those who had served in Vietnam. Many of his own infantry had seen action there, and were stationed in Malaysia before their return to the theatre of war as reinforcements.

Kennett admits he was daunted by the notion that, as a fresh-faced junior officer, he should have command of men hardened by war. 'I was a newly graduated officer in charge of a platoon where just about all of the men had come back from Vietnam, and I was supposed to be training them for a return to the war zone. Some had been wounded. Some had seen mates die. I remember sitting in the officers' mess and we had a very strong electrical storm. The first peal of thunder and lightning shattered the sound barrier. The guys from Vietnam sat there as if nothing had happened.'

Many of Kennett's attitudes in adulthood were shaped by his military service. It also contributed to some of the peculiarities of his lifestyle. First, his unconventional sleeping patterns: starting work before dawn each day and retiring after midnight. Although this is not unusual behaviour for people with hyperactive minds – former British prime minister Margaret Thatcher adopted a similar routine – Kennett was able to learn in the army how to conserve his energy in the downtime of his day: 'I enjoyed getting up early. I found that training period exhilarating. I never slept in late. As I got older, I realised anyway that I have lived two-thirds of my life, I have only one-third to go. What's the point of spending it horizontal? The army taught me how to nap very quickly. I can go to sleep just like that. I can get in the car, put my head back, go to sleep for 5 minutes or 10 minutes, and get out at the other end refreshed, and keep going.

'I suppose the other aspect of life it taught was that you should never take your problems into tomorrow. Before I go to bed at night, I run through my mind what I have done. I go to sleep. The alarm goes off at 4.55 every morning, and I have this explosion of celebration of life. I am still here, I have got another 24 hours, and then I get on with the day.'

Even today, Kennett has a phobia about being in confined spaces, especially aircraft. Like his sleeping patterns, this can be attributed to an incident during his overseas service. 'I was on a helicopter over the jungles of Malaya that hit some turbulence. It dropped 400 feet in no time at all. I don't know how it happened. We dropped to just above the canopy of the trees and the pilot got enough air to get the rotors churning again. We all thought we were gone.'

But doubtless the aspect of his military service that had the most far-reaching impact related not to anything that happened on his tour of duty but rather the mood in Australia when he came home. Kennett flew into Melbourne in 1970 to find a deeply divided community writhing in upheaval. The future Labor deputy prime minister and leader of the anticonscription movement, Dr Jim Cairns, had called a series of moratorium marches demanding an end to Australia's involvement in Indochina. At least 70 000 anti-war activists took to the streets and converged on the steps of Parliament House in Spring Street. It was a popular movement that had captured most of the baby-boomer generation. On the strength of their support, the Whitlam Labor government would surge to power nationally in 1972, breaking a conservative stranglehold on the politics of postwar Australia.

Jeff Kennett was with his contemporaries at that march 30 years ago, but as a perplexed bystander rather than a willing participant.

He knew intimately fellow soldiers who had been wounded, physically and emotionally, by their experiences in Vietnam and
watched in disgust as an elderly protester collected donations for
Ho Chi Minh's National Liberation Front. 'I could not understand
it,' Kennett would recall. 'We were committed to Vietnam, yet here
were Australians actually raising money to send to those firing
bullets back at Australians. It was awful. Incomprehensible. Then
someone came along and knocked this elderly gent over, objecting
to what he was doing.' Kennett watched as the old man fumbled to
recover the coins he had collected. He didn't help. 'I was just pro-
foundly annoyed. It didn't make sense. People were giving money
to provide bullets to maim Australian soldiers.'

Kennett's distaste for the protest movement sprang mainly
from solidarity with his mates in the army. More fundamentally,
though, it provides a window into a mode of thinking that would
dictate his life and career. Kennett forever struggled with the distinction between robust criticism of those in authority and the
notion of betrayal. He had been brought up on the importance of
loyalty and service – saluting the uniform above all else – and his
officer training had left him with a near-obsessive yearning for
hierarchical orderliness and military efficiency. He expected others
to abide by a strict code of obeisance to the leader. Decisions taken
for the right reason were to be respected, even if they sometimes
seemed ill considered or difficult to defend. He demonstrated a
rigid intolerance for those who were unable to conform to this
creed. Throughout his career in public life, Kennett showed a
quick-tempered impatience with those who were unable to do the
same. As many of his colleagues would attest, it was a code he
enforced with all the subtlety of a sledgehammer. As he would roar
down the phone at one Liberal in 1991, 'You know I cannot abide
fucking disloyalty.'

Kennett's anger over the anti-Vietnam marches put him at odds
with the mood of the day: in the streets, on the campuses and in
the opinion elites. As student radicalism and the youth revolution

took hold in Australia, Kennett, although barely into adulthood and liberal in many of his instincts, found himself defending conservative values. Notwithstanding those conscientious objectors who went to jail rather than serve a cause in which they did not believe, Kennett developed a strong sense of distinction between those he saw as assuming individual responsibility for making difficult decisions and those who merely postured. It was the difference, as he saw it, between leaders and followers.

The episode stirred his latent interest in the debate over the nation's identity and its future directions. At the age of 22, he joined the Liberal Party. An activist was born.

CHAPTER THREE

YOUNG MAN IN A HURRY

'I was fundamentally a nobody'.

JEFF KENNETT, ON HIS ARRIVAL IN PARLIAMENT IN 1976

In May 1970, friends of Jeff Kennett hosted a welcome-home party to celebrate his return from overseas service. The party was held at the home of Michael and Angela Rodd. Michael, a real estate agent, was an old schoolmate of Kennett's who had married one of the Kellar sisters from Lauriston and moved with her to the swish establishment suburb of Toorak. A guest at the party was Angela's younger sister Felicity, a 20-year-old trainee kindergarten teacher. This was the girl who, on the tram home from school five years earlier, had laughed at Jeff's hairstyle and poked fun at his kneecaps showing from beneath the kilt worn by school cadets. On this night, however, they struck up a rapport. Tall, vivacious and sharp-witted, Felicity shared Jeff's sense of fun, love of good-hearted banter and propensity for plain speaking. As she would later tell columnist Doug Aiton, she also admired Jeff's steadfast and strong-willed ways.

In December 1972, they married. Felicity was only 22. As she would reflect many years later, 'I have a complete understanding for people who just don't make it in marriage, because it is bloody hard. But we still do it. We can't stop ourselves from putting on the white dress.'

By this time Jeff was 24, and eager to raise a family and buy a home. He had big plans for the future and was thirsting for an opportunity to get out on his own. Returning to work at Myer, he quickly became impatient and restless about his career progress. He had already learnt that the nation's weariness with an unpopular war meant there was not much sympathy for the welfare of returning troops. 'They didn't recognise my service in the army, which was really a bit of a culture shock. I went back on the salary I had two years before. They said, "You've been away for two years. You've learned nothing, so you have to go back to where you were before." It was very, very difficult.'

Accustomed to a leadership role in his military life, Kennett was straining for operational control of a business. With two colleagues from Myer, Ian Fegan and Eran Nicols, he began plotting the establishment of a new, independent advertising agency. None of them had the capital to start a business from scratch. Nevertheless, in June 1971 KNF Advertising came into existence, essentially as a moonlighting operation. Nicols had responsibility for the servicing of clients, Fegan did the artwork and design and Kennett had responsibility for management and billing.

Later that year, Kennett resigned from Myer to take up a job as a designer with the locally owned advertising agency Clemenger's. They had approached him on the strength of his experience in retail advertising, and knowing he was a protégé of O'Donoghue. Kennett was assigned to the prestigious Kmart account; it appeared his talents were respected. He claims to have been miffed that he was never, as an employee, introduced to the directors of the agency. It is more likely still he was peeved at the level of salary he was earning: 'These guys were making a fortune out of my time compared to the pittance I was getting fortnightly in my pay packet.' At this time Kennett and Nicols were subsidising the income of Fegan, who had also resigned from Myer to see if he could get their joint business up and running as a viable new entrant in the advertising industry.

Jeff and Felicity's 1972 wedding heightened Kennett's anxieties that he was not fulfilling his ambitions quickly enough. He would, in the not-too-distant future, have responsibility for a young family. He decided it was time to take the plunge.

Early the following year, Kennett went to see the chief executive at Clemenger's, Peter Rankin, and stated his case bluntly: 'Look, I really don't think I'm getting my just deserts here. I think I am worth double what you pay me.'

Rankin did not agree. 'All right,' said Kennett, 'let's call it quits.' Rankin called his bluff, and Kennett left the St Kilda Road building that night by the back stairs.

Perversely enough, this is where he had his first chance encounter with a senior company executive. Kennett could not resist a parting word: 'Sir, I am Jeff Kennett, I have been working here for a year. How do you do? Now, having introduced myself, I'm on the way out.' Leaving a bemused executive in his wake, Kennett set off on his much-anticipated venture into the competitive world of small business.

The economic conditions were not propitious for a fledgling company. By 1973 the nation was heading for recession, and the Whitlam government had unnerved business, big and small, with its rapid expansion of the welfare state, across-the-board tariff cuts and tax-and-spend policies. In its early months, business for KNF dawdled along slowly. The company's eastern-suburbs headquarters began as a meagre two rooms on the top floor of a builder's office in Canterbury Road, Surrey Hills.

Kennett still rejoices in the memory. 'We existed in this tiny space. When we got in a new client that we wanted to impress, we wanted to look like we had a lot of staff. So we would contact the local Commonwealth Employment Service office, and they would send out this lady, Doris, who was very senior to us, to sit at the reception desk. In the front room, we had three drawers. In the top drawer were the invoices we had sent out. In the second were the invoices we had received. In the other, we put everything we didn't understand.'

Fegan had the first success, bringing in an account from Crittenden's, the wine merchants. Kennett then secured the business of Surrey Motors, a local car retailer. 'Somewhere, I still have that first account. It was for $13, which included the costs of taking space in the local suburban newspaper.'

As the business grew, the partners often worked from 7 a.m. until well after midnight. Kennett could sometimes be found taking downtime naps on the office floor. Felicity Kennett went to typing school so she could help with invoices and the presentation of advertising copy. But there was trouble among the partners. That same year, after only two years in business together, Fegan and Kennett bought out Nicols after a dispute over discounting to favoured clients. In 1973 the Kennetts also bought out Fegan's share, although he continued to work as a paid employee for KNF for another four years. As the company steadily became more profitable, Kennett finally possessed what he had so long hungered for. In the tradition of his forebears, he had built from nothing a successful business the Kennetts could call their own. The company moved into larger office accommodation in Canterbury Road, and Jeff and Felicity bought a rambling Edwardian family house in a neighbouring street. Their first son, Ed, was born in 1975, followed later by Amy, Angus and Ross.

In addition to growing his business, Kennett had been active – but unsuccessful – in local politics throughout the early 1970s. He had failed in two attempts at election to the Camberwell council. 'The first time I got beaten on preferences. The second time I stood outside of my ward, which was a bit silly.' Invariably, he presented himself as a candidate for the small-business community, focusing on local issues and building up networks. But Camberwell council politics were not partisan. The ALP had only a minor presence in these rock-solid conservatively voting suburbs, and conflicts were about personalities, not political ideals.

Within the local Liberal Party branches, however, Kennett was also making his presence felt. 'I was pretty outspoken and, like most other young people in the Liberal Party, I found myself in a branch where most of my colleagues were three times my age. They wanted volunteers for jobs. "You're it," they told me. I had youth on my side.' He went onto the executive of the Surrey Hills branch.

With his aggressive and sometimes abrasive style, Jeff was not afraid to cause offence. His gimmicky advertising approach to events such as fundraising functions appalled many Liberals. Nor was he fussed about trampling over the unwritten rules of protocol within the party. He was told more than once by party colleagues that his conduct was considered 'terribly rude'.

Undaunted, Kennett made his first run for state preselection in 1975, nominating for the seat of Burwood. A newly created electorate as a result of a redistribution, Burwood was nestled in comfortable blue-ribbon Liberal territory. Kennett's nomination confirmed his reputation as an audacious upstart. By standing for Burwood, he was putting in jeopardy an attempt by senior Liberal politician Haddon Storey to make the transition from the Legislative Council to the Legislative Assembly. An erudite lawyer, Storey not only outranked Kennett but was a soulmate of the state's Liberal premier, Dick Hamer.

'I didn't consider myself any chance originally,' reflects Kennett. 'I don't know whether I declared myself a candidate before Haddon Storey nominated or not. I realised that Haddon was the premier's choice but I was already into it by then, and we are, after all, a party of competition. I had to work very, very hard. Haddon was known in all the branches. But I was a young man, maybe overly confident. I produced a pamphlet on myself. I used my advertising background to produce this little booklet. I went around to every delegate and spoke to them and gave them a booklet. The

last people I went to visit were Haddon Storey's upper-house electorate committee chairman and his wife. There was not a chance
they were going to vote for me, but I wanted to be able to say I went
to everyone.'

There were 13 candidates in the preselection field. All but six
were eliminated in the first ballot. Storey led after each count. But
on the final ballot, Storey and Kennett were tied. 'We didn't know
this at the time – we were all locked up in our rooms. The chairman of the preselection committee was Graeme Harris [later the
federal MHR for Chisholm] and I thought if he had exercised his
casting vote it would go against me. But whether it was in the
Constitution or not, Graeme didn't exercise the casting vote. He
put it back to the people. I think we were both called back to make
short speeches. I said, "I respect Haddon Storey, he is a very good
man, he has a lot to offer, and he is going to be a minister. But you
people here today have the opportunity to preselect two members
of parliament. You can decide to retain Haddon Storey for the
upper house and to introduce a younger person with different
ideas, fresh ideas, into the lower house. It gives you a wonderful
opportunity."'

It was a persuasive argument. On the recount of the final ballot,
Kennett won by six votes. However, such was the backlash over
his use of campaign brochures in a preselection contest that the
party rules were subsequently changed to preclude candidates promoting themselves in this fashion. Kennett remains unapologetic.
'All I had done was use my professional experience, and I had
listened very carefully to all of the delegates I visited. The speech
I gave to them was essentially an amalgam of all the things I had
heard. It would have been hard for them to reject these ideas and
arguments.' In essence, Kennett had quite brazenly told the preselectors what they wanted to hear – not a characteristic that
would typify his political style later in life. Also, he had used a very
powerful emotional trigger, insisting the preselectors could get two

MPs for the price of one by leaving Storey in the upper house. 'If Haddon was upset, he never held it against me. He became an important friend and confidant. Terribly honest, constructive, generous; great integrity. His wife, Cecily, on the other hand, was furious. She was calling me everything under the sun.'

On Australia Day 1976, Kennett's nascent career in politics very nearly ended tragically. Driving along Old Dandenong Road on his way to Mount Eliza on the Mornington Peninsula, he swerved his old Volvo to miss an oncoming car and veered into the side of a garbage truck: 'The *1812 Overture* was still going on the cassette player and the windscreen wipers came on and I realised I was alive and terribly lucky.'

Kennett survived without serious injury – but claims the near-death experience changed his outlook. As he would insist for many years to come, the trauma of that event had drilled into him the importance of living each day as though it were his last. Kennett determined he had no time to waste.

The Hamer government was returned comfortably in the March 1976 state election, and Jeff Kennett became the first member for the seat of Burwood. He had come into politics by portraying himself as a rallying point for the concerns of small business. He had an influential power base in the Victorian Employers' Federation and through the networks of the prominent and outspoken small-business activist Peter Boyle, head of the Australian Small Business Association. Through his involvement with a lobby group known as Survival for Business – set up in 1974 to protest the economic policies of the Whitlam government – Kennett had developed a vocal cheer squad, not so much among Melbourne's business establishment but among the thousands of self-employed tradespeople and shopfront businesses in the city's outer suburban stretches.

The small-business philosophies Kennett brought into politics were not dissimilar to the trends towards neo-liberalism gathering momentum in America and Europe. But, as ever, Kennett was not interested in grandiose intellectual debates. His charter on entering state parliament was simple and straightforward: in an era when 'big government' was the height of fashion in Australia, he saw the nation's economic opportunities being retarded by excessive union power, unnecessary bureaucratic red tape and high taxes. He saw a political process trapped in the corporatist model of extensive consultation and dialogue between the main centres of power in government, industry and organised labour. With the advance of the welfare state in the Whitlam years, he saw dangers in the rise of a dependence culture in Australian society, a belief that government had all the answers, and that government, rather than individuals, should assume all the responsibility. He also saw politicians who were too intimidated by fear of defeat to challenge the electorate's assumptions about the role of government in their lives. In his speeches and private discussions, he railed against cave-ins to lobbyists and handouts to 'noisy minority groups'. Such attitudes conspired against the engines of economic growth, the risk-takers in small commercial enterprises who had 'invested a dollar of their own' – people like Jeff Kennett and his ancestors.

The touchstones of the thinking that would govern his conduct through much of his political career were evident in Kennett's maiden speech, delivered to the Legislative Assembly on 13 April 1976, just six weeks after his 28th birthday.

> Tremendous pressures for change have been placed on society, the most dramatic of which is the change in human expectations. For instance, prior to formulating policies, political parties are highly conscious of their popularity at the polling booths, and the result is that too often one sees policies that opt for short-term popularity instead of responsible government aimed at developing a secure, sound Australia for future generations. At no time, to my knowledge, has small business or the free enterprise system

generally called out for, or expected, charity or handouts . . . what business does request, if it is to remain viable and provide employment for 75 per cent of the workforce, is a stable political and economic environment in which responsible planning and budgeting can take place and where a reasonable profit return on capital, labour and initiative invested can be expected.

CHAPTER FOUR

INTO THE FRAY

'He was a doer, a goer. If I was to say, "Jeffrey, see that brick wall?
For the good of Victoria, we've got to go through that at 9 a.m.",
he would want to know "What's wrong with 8 a.m.?".'
FORMER VICTORIAN PREMIER LINDSAY THOMPSON

By the time Jeff Kennett entered state parliament in 1976, his business, KNF Advertising, was a small but successful player in the advertising industry. Kennett's relentless energy had resulted in the company poaching some big retail clients: the Westfield shopping centres and, ultimately, even Myer. The agency was ambitious and aggressive. Its non-unionised staff worked frenetically, and often well into the evening. Kennett paid his employees above award rates. Sometimes, he would take them to lunch at the Peninsula Golf Club in Frankston as a reward for the more hectic weeks. On Friday afternoons there were staff barbecues. Almost inevitably, the agency came to the attention of the unions. It was to prove a ferocious test of strength.

In the early 1970s, the powerful Printing and Kindred Industries Union (PKIU) had launched a campaign to bring the advertising industry into the union fold. Casting a nervous eye to the future, the union was alarmed by the growing trend among advertising agencies to use emerging new technologies – such as com-

puter typesetting – to send final prints of their advertisements into
the major newspapers. The practice was seen as putting at risk the
job security of printing compositors, the core of the PKIU's membership. The union decided that those workers employed by agencies to prepare the final versions of advertising copy should be
required to enlist as union members.

Most of the major advertising agencies were fatalistic about the
union campaign and eager to avoid a confrontation. They believed
an element of unionisation of the industry was probably inevitable.
Predictably, Jeff Kennett disagreed.

Within six months of entering parliament, Kennett's decision to
portray himself as a small-business champion was put to the test.
His confrontation with the PKIU would take KNF Advertising to
the brink of financial ruin. Jeff's first great battle with the union
movement would shape his future attitudes towards the role of
organised labour. Indirectly, it would also leave him bitter over the
failure of big business and Melbourne's media to back him.

A week before Melbourne Cup Day, 'Fiery' Fred Nelson, the
Victorian state secretary of the PKIU, called on the offices of KNF
and told Kennett that those KNF workers responsible for typesetting should be employed under the Graphic Arts Award. Under
federal law, the union was entitled to enter the workplace to sign
up relevant employees. According to Nelson, Kennett insisted the
staff had appointed him as their spokesperson, and that they had
no interest in joining the union. Standing with a cup of coffee in
his hand, he left the union leader in no doubt he was unwelcome.
'I would offer you one of these, except you're not going to be here
long enough, I wouldn't think.'

Nelson, in turn, warned that unless Kennett was prepared to
allow the union to speak to his staff, he would ensure that none of
the agency's ads were handled by union labour. 'We'll see about
that,' Kennett snarled back, and then all but threw Nelson out of
his office. Later that same morning, Kennett received a phone call
from management at the *Herald*, Melbourne's evening broadsheet

newspaper. The newspaper's composing room staff would not accept further advertising from the agency unless the work had been carried out by union members.

Kennett was apoplectic. He phoned Nelson, to no avail. He tried to enlist the support of the newspaper's senior management, including Herald & Weekly Times managing director Sir Keith Macpherson. Bill Hoey, a senior HWT executive at the time, recalls running into Kennett that day in the office lift. Hoey sought to calm him down, offering the reassurance that the newspaper organisation would ensure ultimately that his agency's advertising copy was published. Kennett, though, could not be pacified. By this time, it seems, he was a man on a mission. At one point he even threatened to sue the newspaper if it refused to carry his ads. Yet in that afternoon's first edition, an advertisement Kennett had booked for Westfield did not appear. He marched straight to his lawyers. An urgent meeting of the parties was called. 'I remember being in my lawyer's office and saying to them, "Look, this is ridiculous, what are you going to do?" And they said, "We are going to ban all your work from tomorrow." That would have put us out of business.'

That same afternoon Kennett, in the company of his senior counsel, future federal court justice Alan Goldberg, QC, walked into the Supreme Court and applied for an interim injunction against the PKIU. 'Well, that really started the second world war,' says Kennett. 'If I couldn't place my ads in the paper, none of my clients would stick with me. It was life or death. We could have given in to the unions and got all our stuff in the next day, but it was very strongly a matter of principle. Not ideology. Principle! What right did they have to unionise my staff? None of them wanted to be unionised. But here they were, threatening our very existence. They were going to black-ban our advertisements. Nothing would be touched by a PKIU worker.'

Three days later Nelson received a summons to appear at the court hearing, where KNF Advertising would seek a permanent injunction. Meanwhile, Kennett sought industry backing for what became a historic test case. 'None of the big agencies supported us. Particularly the American ones. We were nothing, and all they were interested in was repatriating dollars back to home. They didn't want a brawl. In the end, though, we took the union to court and we got a section 45(d) [the restraint of trade provisions of the *Trade Practices Act 1974*]. We were the first people in Australia to get it.'

In the court's finding, the PKIU was ordered to pay costs of $17 000. Nelson, despite the urgings of his federal office, refused to sign the cheque. Kennett sent in the sheriff, applying successfully to the court for a sequestration order over the union's assets. 'They put stickers on all the union's stuff. I remember getting a call from Ken Stone [former PKIU official and secretary of the Trades Hall Council] saying, "What the hell do you think you are doing? Who do you think you are?" I said, "Ken, if you don't resolve this and pay up by the appointed time, I will have these guys come in and start selling off your stuff." Within an hour, I had the cheque.'

For Kennett, the victory was complete. To this day, though, he remains unimpressed by the lack of publicity for what was to prove a landmark case. 'It was quite a profound decision, yet the Herald & Weekly Times and the *Age* would not print our material. They were still in hot metal, and beholden to the PKIU. They gave little or no coverage to the case. Once we had won, of course, people were eager to congratulate us because they all did very well out of it.' Kennett's failure to achieve celebrity as a result of the case did not devalue his sense of personal vindication. The union movement had suffered a major legal setback, and Kennett had proved his preparedness to back his convictions. 'You hear politicians talk about reforming the industrial relations system. Very few of them have been in a position where they have put at risk their own assets to bring about change. That's what we did back at that time.'

In Australia's industrial relations folklore, it was the Dollar Sweets case in 1985 that marked the resuscitation of the common law to protect the rights of small-business employers against the power of trade unions. This landmark case became famous not just for the legal precedent it established – that is, to make union-imposed secondary boycotts punishable by civil damages – but also because it was seen to mark the resurgence of the New Right in Australia. It announced the arrival in public life of two new torchbearers of the free-market creed, solicitor Michael Kroger and barrister Peter Costello, who litigated on behalf of a Melbourne-based confectionery manufacturer, Fred Stauder. In fact, Kroger, Costello and the senior barrister – again Goldberg – were able to call on a precedent established in 1976 by another Melbourne small businessman who had gone to the Supreme Court to protect his business against a trade union black ban. Given how they would later cross paths in public life, it remains hugely ironic that Costello and Kroger were the beneficiaries, in part, of the pioneering work of none other than Jeff Kennett.

A year after his historic victory, the Trades Hall Council sought meetings with Kennett in the hope of having him lift the injunctions still in force against the PKIU. Kennett had the upper hand, but he was left in no doubt of the hostility he had generated. 'When I arrived, Ken Stone said, "Just be careful what you say and do because they're pretty stroppy." He got me in a bit of a fever. I was on my own, and I was very shaky. I went into the meeting, sat down and we had this discussion. Fundamentally, it became an argument. As I was leaving, I put my hand out to shake hands and one of the unionists spat on it. When I got out of the building, Ken said to me, "Whatever you do when you leave here, don't run. Just walk straight to your car and drive away quickly. Don't dawdle." Well, that really put the shits up me. Between leaving the door of the Trades Hall and getting to the car, I was petrified. I got in, put the key in the ignition, the engine started, and I put my foot down. I got up to near the Exhibition Buildings and had to stop. I was a nervous wreck.'

Kennett had established his reputation as a man of action. Soon he began to make an imprint on political life as a raw and radical right-winger. Senior Liberals took note of Kennett's sharp mind and self-confidence. From the start, he spoke assuredly and eloquently in parliament, undaunted by the atmospherics of the bearpit. Kennett began to distinguish himself as one of the up-and-comers among the Liberal MPs who entered state politics at the 1976 election. But for how long would his extroverted and ambitious nature be satisfied with the relative anonymity and impotence of the backbench?

Jeff Kennett befriended a powerful political ally. Andrew Peacock was Minister for Foreign Affairs when Kennett entered politics, a pivotal figure in the Victorian division and routinely tagged as a prime-minister-in-waiting. Kennett's electorate of Burwood fell within the boundaries of Peacock's federal seat of Kooyong. The two would see one another at municipal functions in Camberwell, and they struck up a rapport despite their very different public personas. Peacock was suave and urbane, a soft-centred Liberal in the Deakinite tradition and a jetsetting sophisticate. Kennett, nine years his junior, was restless, driven, even manic; hungry for power and red of tooth and claw.

'The local councillors would want to meet with state and federal MPs,' recalls Peacock. 'We came into contact through that and just got closer and closer.' Despite their outward differences, the friendship has remained rock-solid through 25 years. 'There are not many close friendships in politics and ours is a very close friendship. It's one of complete and utter trust. I know when I talk to Jeffrey, unless I indicate otherwise to him, it is not going to go anywhere else. I know when he is going to say something critical of me, or that will hurt me, I can say to him, "I disagree with you, I disagree", and he will listen and think,' says Peacock. 'We've been through a lot of tribulations.'

Early in the new parliament, some among the 'class of '76' began agitating for the regeneration of the cabinet. Kennett was foremost among them. Another was Lou Lieberman, a barrister from northern Victoria. A former senior backbencher explains, 'What occurred in 1976 was close to the biggest majority in history. There was a fair bit of talent there, and the majority were young men. Hamer's cabinet was aged and I believe Hamer made a mistake in not bringing younger people into the cabinet. Here you had a young group of enthusiastic people, they had their offices out in the back shed. They threw parties out there, there was a fair bit of grog out there, and there was a fair bit of activity out there. They looked on the ageing cabinet with disdain. Kennett was an enthusiastic young man, involved in all the mischief in the shed out the back. People like he, Lieberman and others were looking at their parliamentary life and wanted to make a contribution as soon as they could. But because of this ageing cabinet, there was no role for them at that time. By the time they got to the 1979 election, they thought they knew the game. So out of all the boozy parties, and some of the sensible discussions, they determined to get behind several of their own and push them forward after the '79 election. They mainly did not succeed.'

Kennett, however, benefited from the activities of his cohorts. After his re-election in 1979, he became chairman of the parliamentary committee on economic development. This gave him a platform within the party room to cut a profile for himself, and to criticise shortfalls or drawbacks in government policy. He did so loudly and consistently, and became a constant irritant to ministerial colleagues. In 1980, when a vacancy arose in cabinet, Hamer decided to give Kennett a chance to put his words into action.

'Kennett was an energetic, problematic young fellow; obviously with a brain,' recalls a senior backbencher. 'Dick saw him as one of the leaders of the pack, and put him into the cabinet. There were others who had the ambition but didn't have the talent. Dick wasn't stupid about it. He picked the brighter ones and put them into the cabinet and got rid of the noisiness by picking one or two who were not dickheads.' Some colleagues, however, saw it as an attempt to rein in the Liberal Party's squeakiest wheel – a reward for Kennett's grandstanding and publicity-seeking. The decision was not greeted with wild enthusiasm by media commentators either. 'Why Mr Kennett?' the *Age* winced in an editorial.

At this point, Kennett had to recant his publicly stated insistence that he intended to stay in politics for six years only. 'When I came in I always said I was only going to stay two terms. I would come in, do the job to the best of my ability and then go back to the private sector, to small business. To be honest, I didn't think I would have a career in politics. I thought I would be too outspoken, in terms of the clubby atmosphere, that nobody would want me. So I had set myself for two terms. As it happens, Hamer appointed me to cabinet, against my expectations.'

However, when Kennett learned of his portfolio responsibilities, he was not entirely sure he was not being set up for a fall. Hamer gave Kennett the housing ministry at a time when the department was entangled in a royal commission over suspect land deals undertaken by the Housing Commission. Kennett had inherited a scandal. At the press conference announcing his elevation, journalists asked Kennett whether, at 32 years of age, he felt he was sufficiently experienced. As Kennett recalls, 'Hamer turned to them and said, "He will either sink or swim". Here's me, sitting at this press conference and thinking, "Jesus Christ, this is the end of me."'

Hamer's decision to give Kennett his opportunity was equally part of a wider strategy to freshen the government's image. The Liberals, after a quarter of a century in power in Victoria, appeared to be at the fag end of a prolonged cycle of success. The party was seized by internal instability. Two backbenchers, Doug Jennings and Charles Francis, QC, had openly rebelled. The land deals controversy was sapping the government's morale and Hamer was under siege. Having succeeded Sir Henry Bolte 10 years earlier, Hamer, a scholarly lawyer, had led the Liberals to successive election victories. Under him, Victoria had become known as 'The

Garden State'. Urbane, articulate and liberal in instincts, he had revitalised the party with an agenda more attuned to the thinking of the 1970s, bringing in a softer policy focus on issues such as conservation and the arts.

'My greatest memories are of sitting somewhere near Hamer, hearing the other MPs talking to him about a whole range of issues, and watching the breadth of his knowledge and the way in which he expressed himself,' recalls Kennett of his first year in cabinet. 'I just sat there lapping it up. So I was a supporter of Dick's but I was very worried that we had lost touch with some of the basic issues.' The fact is that by 1981 the Hamer government was confronting its own mortality, and everyone in the government knew it. As one of Hamer's confidants says, 'He could see the water was going out.'

Kennett, though, was determined to make his mark. He was forever out in the public arena, fists flailing. In his other portfolio responsibility, as Minister for Aboriginal and Ethnic Affairs, he fired off an open letter to the Returned Services' League accusing its controversial Victorian branch president, Bruce Ruxton – perhaps the one public figure with more talent for attracting headlines than Kennett himself – of an 'un-Christian' attitude towards migrants.

However, Kennett's activism got the better of him when, in May 1981, he set in train a strategy that he now concedes was one of his gravest miscalculations. Not only did he type and send a letter to Hamer criticising the premier's decision to make a trip overseas at a time when the state was wrangling with the Fraser government over its share of Commonwealth taxes, he copied the bombshell to his ministerial colleagues. Inevitably, it was leaked.

Not surprisingly, Kennett, then and since, has been under suspicion for having undermined his leader deliberately. 'I very much regret having sent that letter. I guess it's one of the learning experiences in life. If you have some advice to give somebody, don't put it in writing. But I could see us losing touch, and it was doing a great deal of damage. The party was going down the gurgler.

I spoke to him about it, but he didn't seem to comprehend. So I put it in writing and sent copies to other cabinet members. I regret very much that that letter was leaked by one of my colleagues. I was a contributing factor to Dick's retirement.'

Kennett's indiscretion followed a mutinous incident earlier in the year when Ian Smith, the social welfare minister and another of the 'young turks', had breached cabinet solidarity over the government's decision to block proposals for a casino in Melbourne. Hamer sacked him. But as one ministerial colleague recalls, 'Smithy then stood there and cried in the party room, saying he would never do this again. And Dick, the magnanimous man that he was, put him back in.'

Party discipline, though, had collapsed. In an interview with his local newspaper, the *Warrnambool Standard*, shortly after Kennett's letter had been made public, Smith was quoted as saying the party was 'numb with fright' about Hamer's leadership. This, for Hamer, was the last straw. Kennett recalls, 'He came back from overseas. He had a haircut in Hawaii. He looked 50 years younger and he told us all he was going to resign. You could have blown the stuffing out of me. He was head and shoulders above anyone around the cabinet, but he'd had a gutful. It was a very sad day for all of us. It's one of the things you learn. It becomes very difficult to run government when you cannot write things to each other because an honest expression of opinion might become tomorrow's headline.'

Hamer's resignation signalled that the government was doomed. Lindsay Thompson, the education minister, was sworn in as his successor after beating fellow minister Bill Borthwick by one vote in a leadership ballot. However, he inherited a demoralised party. At one point, the Liberals even considered offering funding to the Right-to-Life organisation to prevent them campaigning against Bill Borthwick in his seat of Monbulk. 'That's when I knew we were finished,' says Kennett.

Even so, Jeff determined that he, for one, would not go quietly. He was a ferocious supporter of Thompson's campaign to confront the unions over a ban of milk supplies. And, in a tactic favoured by Bolte whenever there was a need to deflect the public focus away from the government's woes, he launched a blistering attack on his Liberal counterparts in the federal government over housing policies. Even Peacock was startled: 'He was giving us a belting, making a lot of noise.'

Kennett's actions compounded anxiety over his precociousness among colleagues in Canberra. He was summoned to the national capital for talks. 'Victoria got a particularly lousy deal in public housing and I was the public housing minister. I was articulating the case for Victoria against a prime minister who was bigger than Ben-Hur,' recalls Kennett of his meeting with Malcolm Fraser. I would have spent half an hour – three-quarters of an hour – in his office arguing, and I thought I was getting somewhere. I really did. Then he said, "Hold on a moment, I'll be back in a few minutes."'

Fraser left the room, unhappy that the young housing minister had refused to back off and determined that he would bring him to heel. The prime minister returned with every heavy-duty Victorian Liberal he could find. 'He came back with Phil Lynch, Margaret Guilfolyle, Tony Street, everyone else. He had rounded them all up and briefed them, and the whole lot of them got stuck into me. At one moment I was arguing with Fraser and doing a bloody good job for Victoria, and I thought he was about to give in – he was obviously having difficulty dealing with this whipper-snapper – but then he gets out the whole bloody artillery. Once they all started, I knew I had lost. But it took all these senior people to send me packing.'

As the 1982 Victorian election neared, Kennett again proclaimed publicly his impatience and disenchantment with the constraints of public office. He spoke yet again of contemplating an early exit from political life at the 1982 poll. Few of his colleagues believed him. They suspected he would stick around, even in Opposition, to see what opportunity arose next. Kennett now says his decision not to leave politics came down to a calculation about what sort of signals his departure would send. 'I realised that if I resigned, that would have been seen as terribly disloyal to Lindsay, who is himself a very loyal fellow. For the youngest member of the cabinet to resign just when the party was seen to be going down the gurgler, it would have been seen to be terribly disloyal.'

CHAPTER FIVE

THE WAITING GAME

'I said "Kennett's the man." She nearly fainted.'
TOM AUSTIN, FORMER LIBERAL MP, 1987

'I represent risk,' announced Jeff Kennett to an astonished media on his election as leader of the Victorian Liberal Party in October 1982.

Kennett's elevation to the leadership came when the party was at its lowest ebb. Indeed, the 1980s were to prove the most barren years in Liberal history. Both federally and at the state level, conservative governments were exhausted of ideas and energy, outwitted and outperformed by a new generation of professional and pragmatic Labor politicians. In 1982, Victoria, the birthplace of Liberal Party founder Sir Robert Menzies – and held up in party mythology as 'the jewel in the crown' – fell to Labor after 27 years of continuous Liberal rule. By March 1983, the only surviving right-wing administration on mainland Australia would be the idiosyncratic National Party government of Joh Bjelke-Petersen in Queensland, governing courtesy of an electoral gerrymander. The federal Coalition government led by Malcolm Fraser had been trounced by a rampant and hugely popular Bob Hawke, completing Labor's domination of the political landscape. In Melbourne, traditionally the powerhouse of Liberal politics, the party leadership was left to ponder how long Labor's cycle of success would run.

The victory of the Victorian ALP carried unusual symbolism. Labor was led into government by John Cain, an earnest middle-class lawyer whose father had been premier in the previous state Labor government. John Cain senior's government had imploded in 1955 as the Labor Party tore itself apart in intense hatred and factionalism. It had taken the Victorian ALP almost 30 years to reconstruct itself as a credible political force. The repositioning of the party as a moderate and modern left-of-centre political organisation was typified by the emergence of the younger Cain as leader seven months in advance of the election. As one of his senior ministerial colleagues, David White, commented, 'The one thing that can be said about John Cain is that when the public woke up in the morning, whether in Box Hill or Monbulk, they knew the world would not have been turned upside down. You were dealing with a reliable, stable person. Predictable. They knew where he came from, what he stood for, and this was the key to winning the Maroondah Highway seats in the eastern suburbs which are basically the key to government. They understood John Cain.'

For the Victorian Liberals, rivalling the New South Wales Right of the ALP as perhaps the most formidable and successful political tribe in the nation, the defeat was soul-destroying but inevitable. Chided by their opponents for exuding a 'born-to-rule' air of superiority, the party had receded gently from power, debilitated by the scandal of the Housing Commission land deals and unable to match the excitement generated by a new Labor team infused with fresh ideas and led by an eager, talented and ambitious front bench. Such was Labor's ascendancy, commentators were predicting the Cain government could expect a decade or more in office. They began to speak of the ALP as 'the natural party of government'.

How was a stale, bickering and psychologically shattered Liberal organisation to respond? What could the party do to counter the perception that only the ALP was offering new ideas? In the mournful aftermath of the state election defeat, Lindsay Thompson, the vanquished premier, agreed to serve on as leader until a proper succession could be planned. First elected in 1954, he was the only Liberal MP with dim recollections of the demands of Opposition. Inevitably, the party would need to embrace a new and more vibrant generation of leadership, but its stocks had been severely depleted by electoral defeat. 'We were very short on talent at that time,' recalls Liberal veteran Tom Austin.

One crucial casualty had been Bill Borthwick, the former Minister for Lands. At the time of Hamer's retirement, Borthwick had lost the leadership ballot to Thompson by a single vote. As an articulate and highly capable frontbencher, Borthwick's intellect was respected across the party. He was the logical frontrunner for the leadership. But the voters of Monbulk put paid to Borthwick's ambitions, and he disappeared from political life.

'It was hopeless,' agrees another senior Liberal, remembering the post-election party-room meeting. 'Guys would get up and make a statement and the head table was inert. I was absolutely devastated by the lack of action. Lindsay was such a lovable fellow, but he was old and tired. In that six months, there was nothing forward-looking, nothing in policy. It was just inert.'

Tom Austin had someone in mind. A shocktrooper. Someone with the no-nonsense streetfighting approach of Austin's friend and hero from Bamganie, Henry Bolte. 'I had been a great mate of Bolte,' Austin, a ruddy-faced and plain-speaking farmer from the Western District, recalls. 'Henry was a fair bit older than I was, but we set up the first branch of the Liberal Party in Meredith. We did a lot of things together: shootin', fishin' and drinking beer. When Bolte first got into politics, he couldn't string two words together. But he was a quick learner. We ran him and he won. Not by a lot, but he never won by a lot. I saw in Kennett the same qualities. He was there for the right reasons: to make a contribution to the state, to make it better than it was when he got there, and then get out.' At Austin's urging, Jeff was appointed by Lindsay Thompson to the Opposition's management team.

Kennett knew he was being positioned as the Next Big Thing in Liberal politics. His only rival among the younger Liberal MPs was Lou Lieberman, from east Gippsland. Among the veterans who survived the election, his main rival was frontbencher Robert Maclellan, who was rated as the best brain on offer. A brilliant scholar at Melbourne Grammar and Melbourne University, Maclellan had come to parliament with an eclectic background as a gentleman farmer, a stint as a schoolteacher and formal training in the law. Although noted for his eccentricities, he had acquired a reputation for his searing intellect and shrewd grasp of parliamentary tactics, and was credited with being among the most creative and forceful contributors to policy debates in the Hamer and Thompson cabinets.

The electoral defeat of Borthwick, whom Kennett had never admired, had certainly removed a formidable obstacle to his ambitions. But even with the standout candidate no longer in parliament, Kennett, at 34, was not convinced that he was the leading contender. 'Lindsay stayed because of his opinion, and that of the elders of the party, that he could take us through this healing process and allow the senior members to look around to see who might succeed. They took me into the management group, which included the four leaders of the party plus Lou Lieberman and myself. I think at the time we expected Rob Maclellan would have taken over. But his personality was such that in most of the party meetings after our defeat, Rob was seen up at the back of the room, lounging about, asleep or feigning sleep. That didn't endear him to the members because he didn't seem to be expressing much interest in wanting to take over. So my number came up.'

Austin, was always confident Kennett would be anointed. Quietly he and the Ballarat MLC, Rob Knowles, worked to muster support. 'I remember a journalist coming to me in Queen's Hall saying, "Tom, who do you think is going to get the leadership?" I said, "I know who's going to get the leadership. I am not going to tell you, but I trust you. So I will write it down on a bit of paper and put it in your inside pocket." I wrote JEFF KENNETT. The guy couldn't believe it.'

In the upper ranks of the party there was also a degree of incredulity. Austin remembers paying a visit to the South Yarra home of state president Joy Mein to discuss the choices on offer for the leadership. 'She said, "Come on fellas, what do you think?" I said, "Kennett's the man." She nearly fainted.'

In October 1982, Austin went to see Lindsay Thompson to argue that there was sufficient support for Kennett to take the reins. Thompson agreed and, on 26 October, the youngest MP in the parliamentary Liberal Party defeated Maclellan to be elected to the Opposition leadership. Typical of the brash self-confidence that would become his trademark, Kennett never considered he was too raw or inexperienced for the task. 'I had a fair bit of experience at 34,' he recalls cockily. ' I had my education, I had travelled overseas, I had served in the army. I had run my own business, and been involved in some community work. I had a lot more experience than most people at that age.'

Although steered into the role by Tom Austin, Kennett came to the leadership as a suburban middle-class Liberal without patrician pretensions. He had very few political debts to repay, and assumed for himself carte blanche to renovate and reinvigorate the party's profile. At the party-room meeting after his election, his colleagues were given their first taste of the style and approach he would bring to the leadership. Kennett immediately imposed his military style of discipline and devotion to punctuality.

'The meetings would start at 10, and you could count him down . . . 5, 4, 3, 2, 1 and he would walk through the door right on the stroke of 10 o'clock,' remembers one backbencher. 'So he opens this first meeting with a bland statement that he wants all members to turn up on time and expects everyone to participate in the meetings. One of our senior backbenchers, Cec Burgin, had a chair up against a window in the party room. It was his practice to open up the *Age* and read it from front to back while the meetings proceeded. He was a long-term, solid, sound and respected member of parliament, but he was probably weary of listening to some of the trivial debates we had been having. Jeff says, "Mr Burgin, do you intend to participate or not? If you intend to be here, would you put the paper down. If not, leave the room." There was a very interesting 45 seconds or so. They were eyeball to eyeball, in dead silence. It seemed to go on for hours. Then Cec folded the paper. In that one event, Kennett imposed his mastery on the party room. All of a sudden, it was invigorated. People were given jobs to do. Committees were formed and were expected to produce, both bill committees and policy committees. Many of us appreciated the discipline he put into it. It may have come from his army training. Most of us, once we knew the rules, were happy to work hard within those rules. In the first six months, there was quite a dramatic injection of energy.'

Kennett's bold, brash management style was welcomed by traditional Liberal supporters in Melbourne's business community, anxious to see the Opposition get itself back into the political contest quickly. A coterie group, known mysteriously as 'The Citizens' Committee' and including the abrasive small-business activist Peter Boyle, was to meet Kennett frequently, acting both as a sounding-board for Liberal policy development and as a vehicle for fundraising.

Kennett also attracted the support of a younger influx of Liberals eager to prod the sclerotic organisation to embrace a more forceful, forward-looking agenda. Among them was Ted Baillieu, an architecture graduate and a member of one of Australia's most prominent corporate dynasties, who had become active in Liberal affairs in 1981. 'Everywhere I went I was staggered at how bad things were. But Jeff impressed me as someone energetic who wanted to change things. So I was on side from the start. In the early 1980s Gerald Ryan, Richard Balderstone, Ian Castles and I set up the Melbourne branch. These were younger people, working in the city, and prepared to do something different. Jeff gravitated to them. We went around the whole state stirring things up. He was the one who had energy and grabbed your attention. I have never been fazed by anything he has done, despite other people seeing these things as an outrage. He is a larrikin, but he has his own value system and he has the courage to be himself.'

By the end of 1983, Kennett had made no significant impact on electoral sentiment. Opinion polls in November showed his personal popularity at 29 per cent compared with 66 per cent of voters approving of John Cain as premier. The new Labor government was enjoying an extended honeymoon. It won praise for progressive reforms in licensing hours and the introduction of a freedom-of-information regime. There was strong employment growth as the national economy recovered. Popular decisions included several minor but symbolic social reforms, such as legalising nude bathing at selected beaches, banning the segregation of women and men in the members' enclosure at Flemington racecourse, and insisting that the Australian Rules football grand final continue to be held at the sporting temple of the Melbourne Cricket Ground, not at the league's own stadium at Waverley.

Although Labor had increased taxes to fund growth in the public sector, and was drawing up an ambitious but ill-fated blueprint for economic development, its general approach to government was cautious and judicious. Under Cain, stability became the watchword as the ALP sought to escape the memory of the chaotic last months of the Whitlam Labor government in Canberra in 1975. Cain's dour and ascetic style set up a sharp contrast with Kennett, who was proving himself the archetypal risk-taker.

The Opposition leader continued to provide ammunition aplenty to his critics in the government, in the media and among party colleagues. His antics included squirting a soda siphon at an ALP member and arriving at a parliament house Christmas party dressed as a waitress. He ran the risk of being tainted forever with his legendary 'foot-in-mouth' reputation. Among Jeff's most notorious gaffes was his 1985 response to a talkback caller who was defending the achievements of the Cain government. 'It won't be any worse than when we were under you,' she snapped, to which Kennett replied, 'You were never under me, madam.' Then there was his impromptu redefinition of public transport: 'It would be cheaper to close the railways and buy everyone a car. I'm serious.'

Perhaps the most controversial incident came in September 1985, as he officiated at a ceremony for the Miss Italian Community beauty contest. At a boisterous formal dinner to crown the new queen, Kennett and the officiating party were heckled by protesters. Jeff sought comic relief. Turning to the disappointed finalists, he promised he would see them all backstage, 'because I've got a prize of my own to give you.' To this day, Kennett insists the subsequent furore was a Labor-inspired media confection. There was a public holiday three days later, a slow news day. A Labor source – Kennett suspects one-time ethnic affairs spokesman Peter Spyker – contacted the *Herald* to tell them about Kennett's remarks. Community leaders were reported to be highly offended by the Opposition leader's behaviour. Kennett says, 'The media took it out of context. What I said was quite deliberate. I was on the stage. We had been invaded by all these protesters. Tensions were very high. I was at the microphone, I had to somehow take the tension out of the room. So I made a reference which I thought was humorous. If you listen to the tape, everyone laughed. But what I said was interpreted later as being a sexual thing.'

Kennett's defence of his role in the incident did not persuade his colleagues then and some remain unconvinced. Tom Austin remembers his embarrassment. 'He did some terrible things. The Italian girls. He was so brash. I thought one of the weaknesses in our party, in our society, was that people were too terrified to do or say anything, so nothing happened. They waited for the world to tell them what to do or think. He was certainly not that. But when he started making those bungles, the party room and the back bench went mad. "It's all your bloody fault, Tom," they said to me.' Kennett was also roundly condemned for his claim during his first election campaign that Cain was 'not the sort of man you would trust your daughters with in a fit'.

These serial indiscretions were to confound and exasperate colleagues. One seasoned backbencher says, 'Although I became a strong supporter of Kennett, we used to despair at some of the stupid things he did. I think it was inexperience. He had come in from a small business background to run a big business. His energy is incredible, but it sometimes manifested itself in youthful exuberance.'

Sometimes Kennett's indiscretions were deliberately exposed by parliamentary colleagues unhappy with his leadership style. One of the most embarrassing incidents of his career resulted from a dinner held by Rupert Murdoch's Australian newspaper group, News Ltd, for state Liberal leaders. On this occasion Kennett decided to amuse his hosts and colleagues with a joke. He told the story of three of his constituents who belonged to a religious order. They had visited a zoo and watched apes masturbating. One of the nuns had got too close to the cage, was dragged in and raped. She was rushed to hospital. According to the story, Kennett went to visit and was told by staff that the nun was distraught and refusing to communicate with anyone. So Kennett gave her a pep talk. 'You've got to put it behind you and get on with your life . . .' Oblivious to the disbelieving hush that had descended at the table, Kennett blithely delivered the punchline. 'She sat bolt upright in bed and cried, "How can I get on with my life? He hasn't called, he hasn't written . . ."' An account of this incident appeared in the *National Times* a month later, and dozens of copies were circulated to Liberal MPs with a typed message: 'Wake up, Liberals! Do you really expect to win with this offensive man? Sent to you by a disenchanted Labor voter, looking for somewhere to go.' Few, if any, Liberal MPs believed this was the work of the ALP. The arrival of the mysterious message was seen instead as a strong signal from National Party MPs of their concern at Kennett's leadership.

For newspaper cartoonists, notably the *Age*'s Ron Tandberg, the early years of Kennett's leadership were to produce some of the industry's most enduring images of caricature: the Opposition leader, his mouth cavernous, spouting a succession of indiscretions and ill-timed quips.

Although Kennett's tribulations were a gift to the ALP, some of Labor's hardheads admit to sharing an understanding of his frustrations. As Labor frontbencher David White says, 'There are no good days in Opposition. You are floundering around trying to draw attention to yourself. If you are a personality like Jeffrey is, from time to time you are going to drop a clanger. This is all part of his make-up. We knew enough about him and we believed at the time the electorate knew enough about him that we could beat him. But you don't take anything for granted.'

Another prominent Labor frontbencher, Ian Baker, had a sneaking regard for Kennett's refusal to be swayed from his affable, bon-vivant approach to life. 'He was a great pubster. He was interested in ideas and enjoyed debate.' In hindsight, some colleagues believe Kennett was sometimes unfairly pilloried. One comments, 'I thought Jeffrey was a much better leader of the Opposition than people gave him credit for. The job involves constantly treading the line between being noticeable and not being irresponsible. I think he did a magnificent job. The so-called "foot-in-mouth" incidents, if you look back at them, were flippant. Or he was indulging in his sense of theatre. Or sending a message. The important thing is that it was never Jeff Kennett simply doing things in the heat of battle.'

Indeed, there was at times an element of strategic calculation in some of Kennett's more extravagant public pronouncements, in accordance with the time-honoured ploy of 'throwing a dead cat on the table' to keep a name and profile in the headlines. Kennett hinted at this in 1984: 'The media uses me as a whipping-boy. But they get my name right.' Looking back many years later, he elaborated on this theme. 'These things were not necessarily calculated to gain attention. But I don't believe you achieve anything in life without running some risk. That's not to say everything comes off. While often some of those things were described as gaffes, most of them were delivered after a lot of consideration. They were interpreted as gaffes, but in most cases they were risks I was taking that didn't come off.'

More widely, though, Kennett struggled for credibility amid media and public perceptions that he was too intemperate and adventurous for his own good. Whatever he achieved behind the scenes in revitalising policy and personnel, in the public arena he was portrayed endlessly as a buffoon, a court jester. A collection of pejorative soubriquets was heaped on his head – among them the Boy Babbler and Calamity Kennett. To this day, Kennett insists the media ridicule was to his long-term advantage. 'I think I was underestimated. When we did well, we exceeded people's expectations, including the media. This left them muttering and grumbling and spluttering. They only looked at the 10 per cent of froth and bubble. They didn't understand the character and the professionalism.'

Despite the bad press he received, Kennett in his early years as Opposition leader remained indefatigable. 'They won't change me,' he vowed. 'We're running a long race but we'll win. It's just a matter of timing.' Rather than change his style, Kennett complained endlessly that people expected politicians to be 'a lot less humorous, a lot less normal, a lot less approachable than I am. John Cain hasn't got a sense of humour. He's deadly earnest whereas I like to work hard and play hard. There's nothing wrong with a bit of fun. When my party wins government, I want to see much more fun in politics. It doesn't hurt and I think it will make parliament seem a lot more relevant to the community as a whole.' Kennett was to come under intense pressure from Liberal Party image merchants to refine his party animal persona. 'The PR people told me to change my hairstyle, make it softer or something. So I went down to the barber, spent an hour in the chair and bought combs and brushes, all sorts of crap. When I was walking back, I looked in a window, saw it, and messed it all up again.'

Yet for all the media taunts that he was a political lightweight leading a party bereft of ideas, Kennett and his colleagues began to build a coherent strategy to attack the Cain government's economic management and to mark out a longer-term policy posture. Despite their clash over preselection in 1976, Haddon Storey had become one of Kennett's most senior and trusted colleagues. As the Liberals' deputy leader in the Legislative Council, Storey began exploring the radical new directions undertaken by right-wing governments in the USA, Canada and Britain. He produced a policy for reform of the public sector that was to serve as the template for Liberal Party thinking over the next 10 years. He assembled this platform under the rubric 'Restraint in Government'. Kennett went on the attack over Labor's recruitment of an additional 9000 public servants onto the state payroll in its first two years in power. He insisted this would drive budget pressures that would lead inexorably to increases in state taxes and charges, including gas and electricity prices and public transport fares.

At the same time Kennett pursued his pet subject: the extension of weekend shopping hours. He saw this issue as a litmus test of leadership within the party, declaring, 'In the old days, we would have been scared to act against the vested interests of some of our supporters. But we are going to win by basing our policies on commonsense, and not by buying support. What we lose from the small traders we will gain by winning the common-sense argument. We will pick up the support of working women, the elderly and those who no longer live within the traditional family unit and can't shop inside the standard hours.'

Tariff protection was another significant issue where Kennett chafed against the conventions of the Victorian Liberal Party.

The manufacturing lobby, which wielded substantial political clout in Melbourne and in regional centres such as Bendigo and Seymour, was infuriated by the Hawke government's decision to bring down tariff walls in line with international free-trade sentiments. Kennett could best be described as a gradualist on the issue of winding back tariff protection. But at the risk of offending some of the party's longest-standing supporters, and despite Victoria's reliance on manufacturing, he was blunt on the need for Australian producers to prepare themselves for global competition. Although he believed manufacturers – who for almost 100 years had benefited from some of the highest tariffs in the developed world – could and should be given time to adjust, he warned there would be no reprieve. 'You need to remove protection to industry over a 10-year period [but] it is absurd to say you are going to increase protection.'

Kennett also began to articulate the Liberal Party's commitment to the privatisation of state-owned enterprises. In March 1984 he was forced to back down after suggesting that parts of the State Bank of Victoria, the state's biggest home lender, might function better if sold into private hands. 'I think that to sell off the State Bank would be very, very difficult but, if you look at it honestly, it is an option any government has,' he told a press conference. 'Philosophically, I think the policy of the Liberal Party is that we would like to move towards selling off all those areas that compete with private enterprise.'

Knowing that the bank had an almost iconic status as a bedrock of financial security, Labor went for the jugular. Cain warned that Kennett was 'threatening the home loans of thousands of Victorians'. Treasurer Rob Jolly went further: 'What will be next? It will be the SEC or the Gas and Fuel Corporation, because they compete.'

In the media, the clash was treated as yet another in the catalogue of Kennett gaffes. Commenting in the *Age*, David Broadbent argued that Kennett's subsequent attempt to retreat from the controversy demonstrated 'doubts about his ability to sustain a complex policy argument against the government's best performers, in this case the Treasurer, Mr Jolly.' At the time, it appeared Labor had scored a handsome victory. Six years later, as Labor unravelled amid financial scandal and was forced to surrender state ownership of the State Bank, the ironies of that early exchange would not have been lost on Cain and Jolly – or Kennett.

Like all Opposition parties, the Liberals were to succumb frequently to populism. One example was their opposition to Labor's proposals to force amalgamations among almost 250 local councils across the state. A pamphlet was prepared secretly by two Liberal MPs, urging the electorate to 'vote against the ALP policy of compulsory council amalgamations'. It was pulped after only a few dozen were distributed, not because the Liberals had reconsidered their policy position but because the Cain government, fearful of the issue becoming a scare tactic in the 1985 election campaign, backed down on its local government reforms. Seven years later, local government amalgamations would become a centrepiece of the Kennett government's agenda.

Through 1984, Kennett's approval rating edged into the 40 per cent range. Dismissed so readily as a political oncer, he was unexpectedly making up ground on the Cain government. Slowly the Opposition leader began to develop credibility in the public policy debate, although his aggressive, bulldozing approach provoked increased animosity among special interest groups.

John Cain called a state election for Saturday 2 March 1985 – Jeff Kennett's 37th birthday. Kennett was finally to get his chance to test his standing in the wider electorate. It was an opportunity to disprove his critics. Indeed, Kennett in this campaign would demonstrate an unconventional talent for pushing the right buttons in the electorate.

Only three years after returning to power, the ALP in Victoria remained firmly in the ascendancy, as it did across the nation. The Cain government received an endorsement from the *Age* newspaper in its election editorial. 'No doubt the state's economy would have recovered no matter who was in office, but there is no denying the Cain government's policies and attitudes helped to create a favourable environment for economic development, business confidence, industrial peace and job prospects. Like the Hawke government in Canberra, the Cain government in Victoria has also changed public perceptions about the fitness of the Labor Party for political power.'

Contrasting the styles of the rival leaders, the editorial continued: 'Vivacious in personality he may not be, but the premier is widely seen as a decent, cautious, earnest and competent leader, with a clear grasp of what counts in this community. Such characteristics are reassuring in a basically conservative electorate.'

In its assessment of Kennett's leadership, the editorial carried echoes of the 'bull in a china shop' theme of the ALP's campaign commercials. 'Liberal policy has become sharply ideological and experimental, suggesting that what is mainly needed is to get government off the backs of business (through lower taxation and less interference), to reduce labor costs (through a controversial employment scheme and some provocative proposals for breaking with the prices and incomes accord), to trim the public sector (by pruning administration and contracting out some government services) and to offer some practical incentives for industry and investment.' In summary, the newspaper dismissed Kennett's 'quaintly old-fashioned faith in laissez-faire liberalism' and said it could see 'no sufficient reason to gamble on a change of government. Mr Cain deserves a second chance.'

Out on the electoral battlefield, however, Labor strategists had begun to wonder nervously whether the voters might just be prepared to take a punt on the upstart Opposition leader. Kennett's bullocking attacks on Labor's 'tax-and-spend' policies appeared to be finding resonance in the community. David White admits that Kennett's election campaign gave the ALP a scare. 'When Jeffrey became leader, we thought we could beat him because he was a very rough diamond and we didn't think he provided the sort of stability as a person that would assist the Liberal Party in Opposition. But in 1985, he actually outcampaigned us. We did not conduct as good a campaign in 1985 as we had in 1982. Although we were in a very strong position, our position should have been better at the end of the election than it was. He campaigned on a very simple proposition – more jobs, less taxes. Basically, our record got us over the line rather than the campaign. People felt it wasn't time to contemplate a return of the Liberals at that stage.'

On election night, the Liberal candidates exceeded all expectations. The Cain government, the odds-on frontrunner to return to power, clung to office by a mere 1100 votes spread across four seats. The narrowness of the defeat was something of a personal vindication for Kennett. 'I'm here to stay,' he proclaimed to the media. But his attempts to sound upbeat were bravado. In truth, he was devastated. The prospect of another four years – 'four more bloody years' – in Opposition was almost too much for Kennett's impatient and ambitious temperament to tolerate. When he emerged to concede the result formally, he was the worse for wear. He had been drinking heavily and, as the reality of defeat sank in, had even contemplated announcing an immediate exit from politics. Solace was sought in more beer and whisky.

Andrew Peacock, always one of Kennett's companions on election nights, finally cornered him in a hotel bathroom, settled him down and persuaded him not to make any rash decisions. Peacock recalls, 'He wanted to sit down with me. He was a bit depressed. So I took him into the bathroom, shut the door and told him we had a huge regard for him. We had invested a lot of time and energy in him so he had better repay that by sticking with us. He said, "You're right, mate."'

A report by Michael Gawenda in the *Age* captured Kennett's mood that night. 'There were, said Jeff Kennett, 1460 days to go before the next election. He was standing behind the bar up in his suite at the Southern Cross Hotel, pouring drinks for his guests, and he looked at Andrew Peacock who was smiling the smile of a man who understood where Mr Kennett's pain was located . . . When Jeff Kennett finally made his way down from his suite to confront the television cameras in the Sigma Room, his face, as he stepped out of the lift with Felicity at his side and Andrew and Margaret Peacock just behind him, looked like it was fashioned from a sheet of thin glass which could at any moment shatter into a dozen pieces. His eyes were red and half-closed and the smile, despite his best efforts, was really just a hurt grimace.'

A Liberal insider recalls, 'By the time Jeffrey went to concede, he was feeling no pain at all.' None of the euphemisms in the world could hide what everyone could see for themselves. As Gawenda reported, 'Mr Kennett managed to sound coherent. His tie was straight and his hair neatly combed. He did not stay long.'

In fact, it was almost 15 years before Kennett actually gave true insight into the depth of his despair. At a rally in the Yarra Valley township of Lilydale during the 1999 campaign, Kennett admitted to his audience that he had 'curled up like a foetus' after that defeat, such was the agony of coming within a hair's breadth of a historic and unexpected revival for his party.

The next day, with cameras and reporters on the lookout for any hint of emotional fragility, Kennett told the media he could – and would – wait for the next opportunity. But the question being asked in Liberal circles was whether his own parliamentary colleagues, many concerned by his hit-and-miss approach, would allow him that luxury.

CHAPTER SIX

WILDERNESS YEARS

'If you work for me, you will never be bored!'
JEFF KENNETT

Tom Austin, fearing an internal backlash after the Liberals' 1985 election defeat, urged Kennett to moderate his insistence on revolutionising political management within the shadow cabinet. 'We used to talk about who ought to be in, and how it should be structured. At one stage, Kennett decided it would be a good idea that instead of just 18 shadow cabinet positions, there should be at least 26. I said, "Kennett, you are off your head." He said, "No, the only way to find out if they are any good is to put them in the shadow cabinet." I said, "Who do you think is going to support you once you decide to get rid of them?" It shows you the nature of the man that it didn't worry him. I was more pragmatic. "If you sack one of these bastards they will be your enemy for life."'

Other colleagues and friends, too, observed Kennett's approach with dismay, knowing it would leave him vulnerable in the wake of the party's defeat. As one of them says, 'He was a person who wasn't prepared to hold back for political gain. He would say his piece anyway, and then wait to cop the flak later. That was one of his problems in his first term as leader because he didn't quite focus on the political damage that could occur. Rather he pulled the gun out and fired and waited for it to richochet. He had a tinge of arrogance about him, mainly because of his army service. He tended to treat a lot of his shadow ministers as under-officers rather than as equals. This from time to time incurred their ire. Of course, after he lost the first election, much of the blame was put on his shoulders.'

Kennett's own assessment at the time was equally candid. 'People really like me or they loathe me,' he told the *Age*. 'For a long time, I couldn't understand why that was, but I have come to realise that I'm the sort of person who comes on so strong with people that they are either repelled or attracted. I have to accept this. I also have to accept that I will always drop a clanger every now and then and the media will pick it up and make a big deal out of it. I don't resent that any more.'

Austin sought to persuade Kennett to seek the counsel of former Liberal premier Henry Bolte on the practicalities of party leadership. 'Kennett was always thinking up a different idea: let's not do it the way it's always been done. I would say to him, "Why don't you go and have a few whiskies with Bolte? I saw him the other day and he asked how you were. It may be a good idea if you went and had a few drinks with him." Kennett replied dismissively: "He's yesterday's man."'

Although he may not have realised it then, the new Opposition leader would pay a price for his surfeit of self-confidence. The next four years were his most precarious. He would face four leadership challenges in as many years – an annual springtime ritual, along with the Melbourne Cup – as his enemies combined in relentless plotting to engineer his departure. The experience would teach him formidable powers of resilience. It would also leave him wary and unable to bestow trust readily on others. Kennett would decide to leave nothing to chance, asserting his authority bluntly, even crudely.

Not everybody, though, was put off by Kennett's aggressive and impetuous approach. His electoral performance had also gained him new allies, foremost among them Alan Stockdale. The industrial lawyer had arrived in state parliament directly at Kennett's urging. Their partnership was to have a profound influence on the future direction of the Victorian Liberals. Stockdale had been active in the Liberal Party since 1964, particularly through his association with Melbourne University's Liberal Club, where he came into contact with the Kemp brothers, David and Rod, both future federal ministers. Stockdale recalls, 'David provided intellectual stimulation for a whole generation of Liberal students. I emerged with a fairly strong philosophical commitment to the Liberal Party. I stood unsuccessfully for preselection in East Yarra and in Hawthorn, and I was in two minds about whether I would try again. I got an approach from Geoff Connard [upper-house member for Monash Province and secretary to the parliamentary Liberal Party]. This led to a meeting with Jeff. He asked me whether I was interested in Brighton. It was a branch known to be very jealous about only preselecting locals. I don't think Jeff was able to help that much. Several other candidates spread around the story that I was the favoured one. Jeff made it clear he couldn't support me directly. He was in favour of my coming into parliament, but I would have to win the preselection under my own steam.'

In 1984 Stockdale was preselected as the Liberal candidate for Brighton, one of the party's most secure seats. 'Almost immediately, I got a request to come and speak to the leadership team. My wife, Doreen, and I had a discussion about whether it would be realistic for me to become shadow minister for industrial relations. When I got home, I went to her and said, "Guess what? If I'm not mistaken, I think they are going to offer me the job of shadow Treasurer." I was looking at the steepest learning curve in human history.'

After the election, as anticipated, Stockdale was appointed shadow treasurer – the second most important job in Opposition after the leadership. He took the job before being sworn in to parliament. His rapid elevation caused disquiet in the Labor Party, where Stockdale's aggressive pursuit of union rorts through the industrial tribunals was well known to the trade union leadership. At the first question time in the new parliament, Labor went straight on the attack, portraying Stockdale as a zealous right-wing ideologue. 'John Cain spent most of question time pointing his finger at me. The back bench regarded me very favourably after that. The government was noting the fact that I was there. Cain was reflecting the antagonism of Trades Hall, in particular some of the more left-wing unions like the Food Preservers, who hated the idea of this "industrial hawk" going into parliament. The unions had said to Cain, "This guy's a real bastard. You need to jump right into him." It helped to lift my profile immediately.'

Stockdale came into politics convinced that the Liberals had to adopt a less timid approach in the economic management debate, particularly when it came to relations with the trade union movement. 'I thought the Opposition had not been really focused on being an alternative government . . . They had a belief that you had to undertake any change incrementally, one issue at a time. I came in arguing strongly that . . . what a Liberal Government should do was to tackle as many issues on as broad a front as it could possibly manage. This would confuse the forces of opposition. I think Jeff Kennett readily accepted that view. It might already have been his view. I think that became a very important tactical approach.' Stockdale has been credited then and since with providing the intellectual force that drove the Liberal Party's shift to a neo-liberal economic philosophy. But he argues that Kennett and Storey had already set the course for a far-reaching policy reappraisal. 'Thatcher showed you could do it. But Jeff had his own ideas. Anything he regarded as impractical or inappropriate had Buckley's chance of getting up. His intellect is grossly underestimated. It was as if he could absorb a briefing paper by putting it under his pillow at night.'

Within four months of the 1985 election, the Liberals were to get a second, unexpected opportunity to test electoral sentiment. A by-election was called for the upper-house seat of Nunawading, where the Liberal and Labor candidates had tied at 54 281 votes each. The seat lay in the heart of the eastern suburban electorates that almost always decided government in Victoria. Labor again chose to run a campaign of personal ridicule, depicting Kennett as a 'spanner in the works'. But in their eagerness to secure the preferences of minor parties, ALP members printed a bogus how-to-vote card purporting to be from the Victorian Nuclear Disarmament Party, directing voters to give their preferences to Labor. When the scam was uncovered, the Electoral Commission, on the advice of the solicitor-general, chose not to lay charges. A furious Kennett demanded a judicial inquiry, claiming the Cain government had behaved like the Marcos regime in the Philippines in tampering with the electoral process. At the second ballot the Liberal candidate, Rosemary Varty, won comfortably. Kennett was triumphant. 'It is certain that the Liberals will win the next election.'

So thrilled was Kennett that he sought to persuade party headquarters to run an advertisement thanking the voters of Nunawading. He was told that the by-election campaign had already far exceeded the budget, and that the cost of his gesture would run to $3000. When the then state director, John Ridley, vetoed the plan, Kennett hit the roof. But emboldened by his first electoral success as leader, he soon turned his aggression back to the Cain government's failure to act in the face of this electoral irregularity.

Kennett's euphoric mood, though, was short-lived. His refusal to adopt a more staid and conventional approach was a constant source of irritation to his senior colleagues. In September 1984 another former Liberal minister, Ian Smith, returned to state parliament after a two-year absence. Kennett was put on immediate notice he had a rival in the ranks. Credited with bringing about the downfall of Hamer, Smith made no secret of his ambitions.

The son of a wealthy farming family and a product of the nation's most exclusive private school, Geelong Grammar, Smith had been nominated in his mid-twenties as a potential future leader. Bolte had liked his brusque approach and dubbed him 'young Smithy'. He became the youngest state minister since Federation, awarded the water supply portfolio by Hamer in 1976.

Back in state politics after an unsuccessful attempt to run for federal parliament, Smith began to stake his claim. Austin, who knew Smith well through family connections, was in no doubt: 'He thought Kennett was an absolute disaster.' Amid the controversy over his comments at the Miss Italian Community function, Kennett's personal approval rating had slumped to 29 per cent. On Tuesday 10 December 1985, in the hope of exploiting the sentiment that the leader was an unguided missile, Smith made his move. Kennett was ready and waiting with a shrewd counterploy. 'Ninety per cent of the time Kennett already knew what was happening. His information network was terrific,' says a former backbencher. On the morning of the scheduled party-room meeting, Kennett launched a pre-emptive debate in shadow cabinet. He invited the criticism of his colleagues. They responded deafeningly, accusing the leader of being too abrasive and careless. Although chastened, this pressure-valve release worked to Kennett's advantage. Come the full party-room meeting after lunch, much of the heat had evaporated, and Smith's spill motion proved a fiasco. Some MPs were to claim later that Smith and his supporters did not even bother to contact them. Fewer than 10 MPs voted in support of the move against Kennett.

Two days after the challenge, and despairing of the 'bitching and moaning', Kennett acted ruthlessly to reshuffle his front bench, banishing four of the most outspoken dissidents to the back bench. Smith was dumped as transport spokesman. Lou Lieberman lost education, and was soon to depart state politics to pursue a parliamentary career in Canberra. The member for Forest Hill, John Richardson, and Bruce Reid, who, like Lieberman, went on to a federal career, were also removed. By punishing his opponents, however, Kennett created a cluster of inveterate enemies in his party room. In a fascinating bridging manoeuvre aimed at bolstering his numbers, Kennett also promoted another potential rival, Phil Gude, to the frontline role of shadow minister for employment and industrial relations.

Although Kennett survived the challenge comfortably, the view in Liberal circles was that he was merely buying time. This was reflected in the postmortems. Commenting in the *Age*, Tim Colebatch pointed to Kennett's opinion poll ratings, which ranked him as the most unpopular party leader in Australia. 'Jeff Kennett is the local equivalent of those fanatic Shi'ite teenage girls in Lebanon who drive truckloads of explosives at high speed into Israeli and American targets. True, unfortunately he destroys himself on impact, but he certainly damages the targets, too. Without Mr Kennett, Labor probably would have won the Victorian election easily. His relentless attacks made the government's popularity fade prematurely – even if his own credibility has been an even greater casualty. The Liberals probably need to replace Mr Kennett, but at the right time and with the right person.' Possibly feigning contrition, Kennett assured his supporters he would adopt a less strident role in future. It was a promise he was temperamentally incapable of delivering.

In May 1986, Kennett generated fresh controversy by suggesting that people receiving unemployment benefits should be required to do community work in hospitals, schools and local councils. They should work for most of their week, with time off to attend job interviews and training. The proposal was howled down by the ALP. Kennett was attacked as heartless and uncaring by the welfare lobby and civil libertarians. Ten years later, a work-for-the-dole scheme was implemented nationally amid much fanfare by the Howard Coalition government. It was in line with the 'reciprocal obligation' approach to welfare adopted in the late 1990s by the Blair Labor government in the UK.

Kennett was gaining in confidence, reasoning that the Coalition was finally proving itself capable of taking the policy fight to the government. Writing to backbenchers at the end of the parliamentary session on 11 May, he said, 'Thank you for your support and contribution to the last session. I feel it was the best session since 1982. Now we have just got to keep it going and the party will do well . . . I am sure we have more than made up the ground the party lost [during the leadership manoeuvres] last December.'

Beneath the surface, however, a more profound structural issue was dividing Opposition MPs: the poisonous relations between the Victorian Liberals and the smaller rural-based conservative party, the Nationals (formerly the Country Party). Although the two parties had served harmoniously in Coalition governments in Canberra and New South Wales through much of the postwar era, there was a long tradition of hatred and bitterness between the two in Victoria. On the surface, it seemed the Liberals and Nationals should form a natural anti-Labor alliance. However, the Liberals had never forgotten what they saw as the treachery of the last months of 1952, when the Country Party under John Gladstone Black McDonald (later Sir John) had governed with the support of the ALP. The jousting between the conservative cousins had destroyed the government of Tom Hollway, and poisoned relations between the two parties. Through all the Bolte and Hamer years, the Liberals had neither sought nor needed the support of the National Party. Their electoral ascendancy allowed them to govern in their own right, and they treated the Nationals with disdain.

Jeff Kennett had inherited this contempt for the Nationals and what they had come to represent. The feeling was mutual, and the National Party's wily and long-serving leader, Peter 'Possum' Ross-Edwards, was never reluctant to give a running commentary on Kennett and his failings. In the 1980s, as distinct from earlier decades, Ross-Edwards could engage in this gainsaying from a position of strength. Through all but six weeks of the Cain government, the conservative parties held a majority in the upper house, a powerful strategic weapon with which to frustrate and harass the ALP. But it also meant that the Liberals always had to rely on the National Party to deliver the numbers. Given the fraught dynamics between the two parties, there was no guarantee that the Nationals would play the game. Indeed, Ross-Edwards and his colleagues had the disconcerting habit of dumping on Kennett and the Liberals at crucial moments, notably by pointing out their capacity to veto major policy proposals advanced by the Opposition. Many Liberal MPs came to regard this situation as the single biggest impediment to the Liberals regaining power, and a strong push began within the party to strike a peace deal with the Nationals. For the first time in 40 years, some Victorian Liberals were eager to reach a Coalition agreement. But the lingering en- mity between Kennett and the Nationals persisted, leading to all manner of intrigues.

In October 1986, the debate about the use or abuse of the anti-Labor majority in the upper house reached an inevitable flash- point. In a turbulent fortnight, Kennett was to come within one vote of losing the leadership over an arrogant miscalculation on the extent of his freedom to dictate parliamentary strategy within the Opposition parties. Strolling down the esplanade in the bayside suburb of Williamstown on a Saturday-morning meet-the-people walk, Kennett was approached by a constituent who asked why the Opposition had handicapped itself tactically by pledging never to block supply in the Legislative Council. This – as Malcolm Fraser had shown in 1975 – could force the government to an early poll. Kennett's ears pricked up. The most recent Morgan poll had shown his popularity falling two points to 31 per cent, and the Liberal Party floundering at 36 per cent. He needed a circuit- breaker. The next day, 5 October, he told a reporter from the *Age* that the government should not count on a tame Opposition, and floated the possibility of using its powers in the upper house.

Kennett would have known such talk would be controversial. Fraser's use of the Senate to obstruct supply in 1975 had set off a constitutional crisis which left deep wounds in the nation's political psyche after the Governor-General, Sir John Kerr, had dismissed the Whitlam government. Kennett was playing with fire. He himself was a signatory to constitutional reforms, agreed in parliament in 1984, requiring that state governments serve a fixed minimum of three years of a four-year term. The next day, as the controversy flared, Kennett took a step backwards – albeit momentarily – issuing the reassurance that he did not envisage an early election. But on Wednesday 8 October, media reports appeared to confirm he was still flirting with the strategy. In parliament the following Thursday, in the face of taunts from a government backbencher, Kennett lapsed into crass boastfulness. 'Get ready, fella, get ready, because I can tell you there is going to be an election in this state. I'm ready, Mr Speaker, I have never been more ready in my life.'

The first the Liberal Party's leader in the Legislative Council, Alan Hunt, heard of these events was in a news bulletin on his car radio while driving home to Mornington. Kennett had not consulted Hunt – a party elder who felt he could serve in the role of mentor to the young leader. Hunt had for months been privately complaining of Kennett's refusal to heed his advice on parliamentary tactics and bemoaning his infuriating tendency to make policy on the run. Hunt considered the supply threat out-rageous: the last straw. He phoned Kennett as soon as he arrived home, demanding the leader leave the chamber to take his call. Hunt would later tell the *Australian Financial Review* that Kennett showed 'a lack of judgement beyond belief' and that, at home in Mornington, he had been inundated with calls from angry MPs. 'The troops were disappointed with Jeff's performance and his failure to consult with them on a matter of such importance. He was warned not to go in on this supply issue but he did, and it went off like an unguided missile.'

On the very night of this confrontation Kennett flew out of Melbourne for a family holiday at Orpheus Island, a luxury resort

off Queensland's far north coast. Whether or not it was a calculated delaying tactic to buy time for his supporters to shore up
his numbers, it effectively cancelled a proposed shadow cabinet
discussion the next Tuesday and the party-room meeting that was
scheduled to follow. But Hunt continued to plot his strategy for a
showdown. It was time, he told colleagues, 'to end the charade
with a leader we eventually wanted to depose anyway'.

On Thursday 16 October, Kennett phoned Hunt from his
island retreat to demand his support. Hunt rebuffed him, bluntly.
There was a heated altercation. Kennett told Hunt his purpose in
raising the threat to supply was purely tactical: 'What we were
doing was changing the agenda. You bastards are too wimpish to
play the tune.' Hunt replied that Kennett's attitude was unforgivable, and pointed to two key flaws in the strategy. First, any
genuine move to block supply would require the support of the
National Party, which held the balance of power in the upper
house. Ross-Edwards had stated explicitly that his party would
only consider blocking supply 'in the most extreme of circumstances'. Second, it was constitutionally impossible to force an
election before March 1987, when the formal appropriation bill
came before the parliament. 'He hadn't done his homework,'
Hunt complained. 'He may have panicked the government for a
while but they would have done their homework and realised
pretty quickly it was all bluster.'

Next evening an angry Kennett phoned again, attacking Hunt
over his refusal to accommodate Kennett's game plan and accusing
him of 'a gross act of disloyalty'. The terms for confrontation had
been set. On Monday 20 October, Hunt announced his resignation
as upper-house leader. Although portrayed as a protest on a matter
of high principle, it was also an essential and calculated element of
Hunt's strategy to bring about Kennett's downfall. Hunt could not,
as a member of the leadership team, move a spill. His resignation
signalled that a challenge was imminent. Kennett's support team
went into overdrive, with Kennett phoning many MPs personally.

Tom Austin, Kennett's numbers man, was enraged. 'Henry Bolte didn't like Hunt, and I didn't like Hunt. He had a good brain, but Bolte never trusted him and nor did I.' Kennett and Hunt swapped insults publicly. The Opposition leader accused the upper-house elder of being 'a messenger of the Labor Party', adding bitterly, 'He can never be trusted again by anybody in any walk of life. He has disgraced himself.' Hunt's retort was equally impassioned, insisting his move against Kennett had nothing to do with a personal vendetta. 'The only question is his loose tongue and his continued tendency to say things without thinking.' Hunt claimed an 'avalanche' of resentment surrounded Kennett's leadership, and that a substantial majority within the Liberal Party did not believe he could lead them to an election victory.

Curiously, however, Hunt chose not to nominate an alternative leader. Although both Smith and Gude were seen as possible starters, the strategy to topple Kennett was undermined by the lack of a compelling candidate to succeed him. Nonetheless, Kennett's leadership was close to terminal. One of his erstwhile allies in the upper house, Geoff Connard, phoned the leader at home on the night before the ballot with disquieting news: 'If you are counting on my support you do not have it.' Connard was wrestling with a divided loyalty. He was both an admirer of Kennett and a long-time friend of Hunt. As he was later to explain, 'These were two men I respected.' The vote on Hunt's spill motion was tied 24–24. Kennett was compelled to use his own casting vote to bring into effect a technicality which forced the failure of the spill.

In an interview with Paul Chadwick in the *Sun* on 6 December, Kennett offered a revealing insight into his narrow escape. 'Felicity has a theory she has had ever since I got this job four years ago. The only time anyone will want this job is when they know you can win government and they'll get rid of you before the next election. That's always a possibility, but I don't see myself as a stop-gap leader.'

In his Christmas note to backbenchers, Kennett wrote, 'This year has been a good year although as far as the public is concerned it has been overshadowed by the Orpheus [Island] incident.' Kennett also issued a six-page end-of-year statement, in which he said, in an unusually sheepish tone, that he had learned important lessons from the challenge. Upper-house Liberal Reg Macey, who had supported Kennett against the spill motion, says he remembers admiring Jeff's self-deprecating sense of humour at this time of inordinate stress. A chortling Kennett had told fellow MPs, 'This was my Elba. I got away in time. But Napoleon only got away once. I am not going to the island again.' In fact, Kennett did go to another island retreat in Queensland at the same time the following year. It was to carry the same repercussions.

As everyone knew from the narrowness of his survival in 1986, it was inevitable Kennett's opponents would regroup. Indeed, a few short weeks later Smith and Gude were seen dining together, prompting renewed speculation of a joint ticket to roll Kennett at the first opportunity. Meanwhile, Kennett strove desperately to shift the debate onto the Opposition's performance in the public arena. He reminded his colleagues of the gains made in exerting pressure on the Cain government and began to pinpoint the issues that five years later would bring about the demise of Labor. 'We'll inherit a huge debt burden from Cain and it's not going to be easy to make this state great again,' he told a press conference. 'We are in dire straits and it's going to take a decade of good, responsible conservative government to steer us out.'

Early the next year, the Victorian Liberals held their state council meeting at Geelong and Michael Kroger was voted into power as the party's new state president. It was a bolt out of the blue. He was only 31, and surprisingly defeated a senior BHP executive, Alan Castleman, for the job. A forceful, eloquent and charismatic lawyer, Kroger was a product of campus politics through his leadership of the Australian Liberal Students' Federation and a belligerent campaign to wrest control from the left-wing National Union of Students. Although he was a policy hawk on issues such as industrial relations reform, Kroger revealed a ruthless pragmatism about the means of achieving political change. In a speech to students at the Australian National University, he had outlined his position. 'Politics is a career like no other. It is a fascinating and intriguing occupation. It requires so many skills that no institution teaches. Governor Thomas Kean, the current governor of the state of New Jersey, wrote a book recently in which he expounded upon one of the virtues of a successful modern politician. It is the ability to verbally extricate oneself from difficult situations. In his book, he tells the story of a legislator in New Jersey who, after arguing passionately for a bill for twenty minutes, was informed during his speech that his party had decided to oppose the bill. And so, without pausing, he simply said to the Speaker, "Those are the arguments for the bill. However, there are even better arguments against it" and he then proceeded to denounce the bill for a further twenty minutes.'

A protégé of former prime minister Malcolm Fraser, Kroger had established a strong network of Liberal connections across the country. His closest mate was Peter Costello, a brilliant barrister three years his junior. Despite his youth, Kroger had earmarked Costello as a future Liberal prime minister. He also coveted a future role in federal politics for himself. Exploiting the deep self-doubts within the Liberal Party about the lack of electoral success in the 1980s, Kroger set about a personal and provocative crusade to change the method of preselecting candidates for parliament.

'There is still much to do by the Liberal Party in establishing a career path structure but such a path is quite meaningless unless those who obtain a political education can put their desires into practice by winning party preselection. Under current preselection procedures, nothing is guaranteed. In Victoria, preselections are determined solely by the branch members in the electorates in question. Naturally enough, a parochial view will prevail. Electorates will often choose a member who best suits that electorate rather than look at the state or national interest. It is almost impossible to encourage outstanding Australians on the conservative side of politics to nominate for a preselection where there is little or no guarantee of them winning. If the president of the party or the parliamentary leader seeks to influence delegates they are accused of interfering or being heavy-handed.'

Kroger argued that Labor had established a professional edge over the Liberals by providing, through the organisational skills of its trade union base, a superior training ground for potential MPs. This background taught Labor politicians the value of political research, involvement in political and ideological debates, experience in articulating progressive and differing viewpoints, agenda-setting and kite-flying. 'They all add to an understanding of how important discipline is within the political framework.'

Importantly, Kroger also came to power with strong views on relations with the National Party in Victoria. 'Disunity is death,' he insisted. 'The Liberal and National parties must recognise that it is one of the prevailing reasons why electoral success has not come our way this decade. The finger is pointed by the Labor Party apparatchiks at any sign of disunity and division between our own party and the Nationals.' He frequently cited a 1986 plebiscite which showed over 80 per cent of the Liberal Party branch membership wanted to merge with the National Party. 'So where does the problem lie? It lies, in fact, in the membership of the National Party in many rural areas who still wish to cling to their party as the separate and different representative of country people.'

Kroger's forthright stance on these two fundamental organisational issues were ultimately to set him on a collision course with Kennett. Kroger had derided the Liberal organisation as 'Sleepy Hollow'. Kennett, in turn, was suspicious of Kroger's motives and chary of the implications for internal stability.

Any upheaval within the state division could not fail to have implications for Kennett's precarious hold on the leadership. Kroger, like Kennett, was energetic and driven, anxious to make his mark quickly. And as one senior Liberal noted, 'One change merchant in town was quite enough for Jeffrey.'

Part of it was a personal dynamic: both were strong-willed, ego-tistical and determined to have their own way. Kroger was also a well-known supporter of John Howard, Andrew Peacock's bitter rival in Canberra. This immediately put Kroger at odds with Kennett. Within the strange and shifting constellations of power in the Victorian division, the two men would invariably find themselves in opposing camps. 'Too many bulls in the paddock' would become the favoured analogy within Liberal ranks for describing this clash of heavyweights. Indeed, through the 1990s the feud between Kroger and Kennett would become one of the most vexed relationships within the Victorian party.

Nevertheless, in the revivalist excitement of that historic state council meeting in 1987, old enemies and cautious new team-mates came together over drinks in a room at the Ambassador Hotel in Geelong to toast Kroger's elevation. Ted Baillieu, elected a vice-president on the same weekend, recalls it was a boisterous occasion. 'We were having a drink at the end of the day. Vinnie Heffernan [MLA for Ivanhoe] was there, and Pescott [Roger Pescott, MLA for Bennettswood] and various others. Vinnie was lying on the bed. Jeff was sitting on the windowsill. All the Ambas-sador's windows opened onto the street. This was five or six floors up. Jeff overbalanced and started to go out backwards. I can't remember how he saved himself, but I thought, "Shit, the leader nearly went out the window."'

The new state president had a whirlwind effect on the party. Kroger's arrival intensified efforts – at both organisational and parliamentary levels – to add a sharper edge to the party's per-formance. David Kemp became state director, and set up a new management system for administration and campaigning. The party began the process of challenging Labor's supremacy in modern campaigning techniques, market research and marginal-seat strategies. Petro Georgiou, a former senior adviser to Fraser and a political science academic, was appointed to head a policy unit similar to that created under Sir Keith Joseph prior to the

Jeff Kennett was raised in modest affluence. Here, his parents, Ken and Wendy Kennett, join the premier and his wife, Felicity, at a garden party in the grounds of the Victorian parliament.

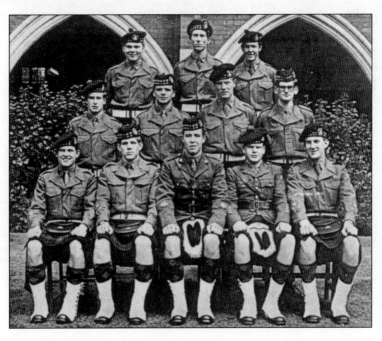

'A splendid sergeant major'. Jeff (front row, far right), here aged 17, excelled in school cadets at Scotch College.

Training for far-off wars. A strong-willed youngster (middle row, centre) graduates third out of 68 at the gruelling Scheyville army camp.

Officer Class. Second Lieutenant Jeff Kennett (front row, far left) of the 1st Royal Australian Regiment.

*KNF Advertising, the Kennetts'
25-year business venture, hangs
out its shingle in Canterbury
Road, Surrey Hills.*

*Taking on the unions: Kennett's
nemesis was 'Fiery Fred' Nelson,
the print union official who
threatened to black-ban KNF.*

*The Next Big Thing. At 34, the youthful enthusiast is elected to lead the
Victorian Liberal Party. Beaming admirers of Kennett in the leadership
team include (from left) Lindsay Thompson, Rob Maclellan and Alan
Hunt. It would not always be thus.*

Here's looking at you, kid. Jeff and Felicity celebrate his elevation to party leader.

Mentors and mates. Kennett works the crowd with former Liberal premier Sir Henry Bolte (top) and former federal Opposition leader Andrew Peacock.

Kennett on his infamous car phone: 'and the poor little fella didn't know whether he was Arthur or Martha'.

Narrow defeat in 1985. Kennett, the worse for wear, had sought solace in a few drinks.

Dynamic duo. Michael Kroger and Peter Costello announce their arrival in Liberal politics with a landmark legal victory in the Dollar Sweets case, thereby establishing their New Right credentials.

Portrait of the leader as a young man. After facing his second leadership challenge, Kennett, like Napoleon after Elba, would pledge never to be stranded on an island again. He was, the next year.

election of the Thatcher government in Britain. In turn, Georgiou recruited Peter Alford, a gruff and gritty business journalist, and long-serving party worker Helen Morris. The unit established an office on the seventh level of Alcaston House, a historic Collins Street building across the road from the parliamentary precinct.

Kennett's personal office was also bolstered, by the arrival of two key men who were to forge a lasting relationship with the leader. Dr Peter Kerr, a gregarious, chain-smoking former lecturer in politics, became Kennett's chief adviser, and David Wilson, a seasoned state political reporter, his press secretary. The two men began the task of translating Kennett's natural exuberance into a more calculated and sophisticated approach. Peter Poggioli, later to succeed Georgiou as Liberal Party state director, was also brought in. 'I met Jeffrey in July 1987. I was recommended as a prospective staffer because I knew Petro. I was doing research at Melbourne University, and Petro thought this would be a good opportunity. He got me to meet Kerr. Then Jeffrey walked into the office and said, "Well, if you work for me, you will never be bored!" I think he kept his promise over the years.'

Poggioli was assigned the role of making sure Kennett was consistent in his speeches and statements. This was conceived by Peter Kerr as a strategy to minimise the 'foot-in-mouth' headlines. 'The aim was to harness Jeffrey's enthusiasm. I don't know how much reining-in Peter did. But I would be brought in sometimes and Kerr would say, "The leader wants to say this. Can he say that?" and I would say no and he would say, "Why not?" and I would say, "Well, he said the opposite two weeks ago." Kerr would go to Jeff, who would say, "I did not", and my job was then to go and find the press clipping and take it to him and say, "Yes, you did." He would say, "Oh, well, yeah I did", and then we would move on to something else. Then I went on to writing speeches but I wasn't particularly good at writing Kennett-speak. He usually knew much more about the subject. He was a very quick study, very careful with what you gave him, and always added value. At the end of the day, he would usually know enough about the subject to absorb it naturally and not read the speech from notes. There was one instance where he actually made a show of not reading the speech. He put the notes in his breast pocket and gave the speech almost verbatim. He's very good, especially with an oral brief.'

Poggioli says Kennett's enthusiasm was infectious. 'He had the capacity to bring his team along with him. You were working for him, and you wanted to work for him because he put a lot into it himself and he gave you a lot of good feedback. Part of that was Peter Kerr, and the way in which the two of them interacted. Kerr was the conduit. He was a feisty, very bright person who used to jolly people along. He probably found me a bit less blokey than he liked. I probably didn't drink enough. I smoked heavily at that time, but not as much as he did. He was the person with whom Jeffrey could have his fights, get stuff out of his system and keep on working with. They were soulmates. I don't think anyone had a relationship with Kennett in the way Peter had.'

Despite the increasing professionalism of the Liberals as a fighting force, a clash between the strong-willed Kennett and Kroger was inevitable. Kroger's push on preselections initially targeted three federal MPs in safe seats: Ian Macphee, Roger Shipton and David Hamer. Three close Kroger associates – Peter Costello, Julian Beale and David Kemp – took their place in a startling purge conducted with brutal efficiency. Kroger's fingerprints were all over it. The putsch caused massive upheavals within the branches, and friction at the highest levels of the party in Canberra and Melbourne. But as Ted Baillieu argues, the process of introducing a central panel to counterbalance the vote of the local branch members was crucial to injecting greater energy and accountability across the party. 'There were a lot more people involved in preselections; there was a rise in activity across the party which probably helped produce a public awareness, a sense that the party was engaging in a serious process.'

For Kennett, naturally on guard against the potential for future leadership challenges, the process would ultimately mean seeing some of his rock-solid party-room supporters coming under threat, notably Geoff Leigh in the seat of Malvern. Leigh had embarrassed the up-and-coming Kroger by defeating him in a preselection in the early 1980s. Kroger had Leigh forever in his sights.

As the shockwaves of change rippled through the party, Kennett found himself facing another leadership threat. In September 1987, Labor launched an attack on him for taking a trip to Hamilton Island for a sojourn with his family despite parliament sitting. It was a deliberate exercise in hardball politics. Cain had recalled parliament early; this would inconvenience the Opposition leader and fuel anti-Kennett sentiment in the party. Although Gude was quietly staking his claim, the challenge was ultimately brought on by Roger Pescott, a former diplomat elected to parliament two years previously. Former Speaker Jim Plowman acted as his numbers man. Elsewhere in the party, Smith was widely suspected as being the prime architect. Says one upper-house Liberal, 'The plotters like Plowman thought themselves very clever, but in my mind they were always manipulated by Smith. Smith was quite brilliant at playing these games, cajoling MPs with the line that, "We can't let this fellow keep doing this or that, railroading us." Pescott was just a pretty face. Gude was on the periphery, being very careful, wanting to play two sides and ending up not being really trusted by either.'

With the party in revolt, Kennett was forced to abandon his family holiday for the second year in succession. He returned to Melbourne fuming over Cain's politicking, incensed by the disloyalty of colleagues and mortified by the *Herald*'s publication of an unflattering front-page photo of him lying on a beach. The paper had sent its 'On the Spot' columnist, Bruce Dover, to the Queensland resort. He was briefed to ask for an interview and a photo. When Dover knocked on the Kennetts' door, he was told bluntly by the Opposition leader to leave them alone. The newspaper, however, already had pictures of the family frolicking on the sand. The story began: 'While his colleagues were busily counting numbers at

Spring Street, Jeff Kennett was grinning and baring it on a Queensland beach.' The accompanying picture depicted an Opposition
leader not at the peak of fitness, his midriff poking out over his
shorts. Kennett would complain privately for years that they had
made him look like 'a beached whale' and would hold Bruce
Guthrie – deputy editor at the *Herald* – responsible for the story's
treatment. Says Guthrie, 'He was obviously upset by the interrup-
tion of his holiday. But I think vanity was also part of it. Some of his
colleagues had told me never to underestimate the vanity of the
man, and I suppose no young family man wants to be featured on
the front page of the afternoon daily looking out of shape.'

Such was the dark mood in the Liberal Party that a delegation
of MPs came to see Tom Austin, pleading with him to switch
allegiance and back Pescott as the new leader. 'Digby Crozier [a
long-serving rural-based Liberal] was with them. He was a decent
straight-shooter. He said, "Tom, we can't have this."' Austin
refused, and warned the plotters that Kennett would not be abandoned by his supporters. 'I knew him better than they did. I knew
of the inner part of Kennett, I knew he was basically still sound,
although some of these stupid things that were public and very
embarrassing should never have happened. But it was the nature of
the guy that he was always having a go. He was trying to be funny.
He didn't think. He spent a lot of time not thinking.'

Was Austin tempted to dump Jeff? 'They thought I would.
That amazed me a bit. I had absolutely no hesitation in working
to shore up his leadership.' Austin mobilised support from his
home in George Street, East Melbourne. He set up a bridge table
beside the telephone with a checklist of Liberal MPs, for and
against. 'I sat there from four in the afternoon until four in
the morning calling parliamentarians, business people, anybody
I thought was a bit of a Kennett supporter. I got them to use any
bit of influence they could on anyone in their electorates or wherever.' Ted Baillieu, by this time a rising force in the organisation,
also exerted influence on Kennett's behalf. 'When there was the

challenge to Jeffrey, I thought I might ring around a few people I had met. I was stupid enough and cocky enough to think I could ring up members of parliament. About a week later, I got button-holed by a member of the Prahran branch, a large Hungarian character called Peter Frankel. "How dare you ring people and tell people how to vote? It is not your position to tell people which way to vote on the leadership." I was still learning how to do things myself.'

On 6 October, Liberal MPs gathered in the party room. The spill was moved by the party's longest-serving parliamentarian, Tom Evans. Reg Macey, who seconded the motion, recalls, 'Nobody else would do it. Tom Evans had nothing to lose. He was planning to retire. He hated Jeff. I didn't. But I supported the spill, even though I was going to vote for Kennett. If I hadn't done it, it wouldn't have happened and I felt the failure to reach a Coalition arrangement was harming us and would contribute to defeat at the next election.' It was a four-and-a-half-hour meeting. Kennett told the MPs that he might be entitled on a constitutional technicality to delay the meeting, given that one of his closest supporters, Dick Long, was on a Commonwealth Parliamentary Association trip to Vanuatu and was unable to be notified of the meeting in time to return. However, he said he was prepared to allow the vote to proceed. 'Let the cards fall where they may.' When the ballot was completed, Kennett survived by a single vote. However, Austin's loyalty to Kennett came at a price. He lost the deputy leadership to Alan Brown, a quietly spoken small businessman from Victoria's south-eastern coast.

Macey claimed this was precisely the outcome some MPs were seeking. He and others in the party believed Austin was obstruct-ing any moves towards a Coalition with the Nationals. 'Tom Austin was one of the haters of the National Party. That's why he went. I wanted Brown as deputy leader. I thought he could get in Jeff's ear. He was in a position to influence him without changing the leadership. Kennett was the better leader but we needed to do something about the Nats. Brown was a very good deputy, with a capacity to bridge the divide between country and city.' Austin, for his part, believes there were ulterior motives. 'They failed to get Kennett by one vote so they got me instead. It wasn't really necessary to do that. Alan Brown before that had come to me and said, "Tom, when are you going to retire from parliament? When you do, I would like your job. I need your car."'

After a third failed leadership challenge, leading figures in the party organisation demanded that those responsible appear before the party's electoral committee to explain their actions. At the following party-room meeting, Joy Mein warned MPs that the party, its supporters and the general public were losing patience with the constant infighting. 'She pleaded with us not to do it again,' recalls one MP. 'She said supporters were ringing up and threatening to withdraw their regular financial support. They were saying if Kennett wasn't there, nor were they.'

Kennett's mates believe the challenges were instrumental in toughening him up for the years to come. 'They would write him off and challenge him every time he went on holiday. With that sort of experience, you soon find out who are your friends, and who are your enemies.'

The following year, the Liberals began to make up ground strongly. A Morgan poll in May revealed that although Kennett still trailed Cain as preferred leader, the Liberals could easily have won a state election held in April. Behind the scenes, the big end of town was gathering behind Kennett's leadership. In early May, more than 600 Liberal supporters gathered at the Hilton hotel in what Elders-IXL chief and federal Liberal president, John Elliott, described as 'a sort of launch' of the campaign to win back Victoria. Sir Henry Bolte, celebrating his 80th birthday, attended. So did Dame Pattie Menzies, widow of the party's founder. And John Howard, the federal Opposition leader, flew in from Sydney for the event. Kennett finally had momentum running his way.

Within days, however, Kennett's veteran backbench enemy, Tom Evans, announced his retirement. His departure brought on

a by-election that threatened to reignite tensions with the National
Party over the need for tighter gun control measures. The government had introduced tighter controls after two crazed gunmen
had gone on murderous shooting sprees in Melbourne's streets.
Never a popular cause in rural and regional Australia, the recent
reforms had been heavily opposed by the Nationals. Kennett, on
the other hand, held the line in support of the broad thrust of the
reforms. National Party leader Ross-Edwards immediately pointed
out that the Liberals under Kennett had lost the confidence of
country voters.

Once again, Kennett's enemies in the Liberal Party were circling.
Says Poggioli, 'Tommy's bailing out in Ballarat North was certainly
designed to damage Jeffrey. All of those things were hurdles. You
got the sense his colleagues were saying, "Well, if you don't win this
with a big swing, you're out, boyo."' The Liberals retained the seat
with a modest margin. Although unsuccessful, the Labor candidate, a local Ballarat boy, Steve Bracks, was marked down by Labor
insiders as an up-and-comer. Kennett, however, survived to contest
the next state election.

Kennett ran the 1988 campaign by focusing on the economic
mismanagement of the Cain government, and what was later to
unravel as one of the state's greatest financial scandals. He worked
furiously in the crucial southern and eastern suburbs, and was
credited with exercising far greater discipline and restraint. Accustomed to Kennett's sometimes self-destructive exuberance, some
critics complained he was spoiling the fun. But Kennett was unable
to convince the media to focus on the serious failings in the Cain
government's industry and investment policies.

Labor kept strictly to the strategy of playing up the contrasting
styles of Cain and Kennett. It also produced a highly effective
spoof on John Elliott that was scripted by Don Watson, later to
become speechwriter to prime minister Paul Keating. The television commercial generated widespread mirth in the community, and distracted from the Opposition's claims of government

mismanagement. 'We anticipated Kennett could win in '88 and in fact we campaigned better,' recalls Labor frontbencher David White. 'We were more focused in the sense that we started the campaign at about 47.5 per cent, we took it through the Grand Final period when there were a lot of distractions and it was much harder for the Opposition to get on the noticeboard. And we were very, very aware of the needs and expectations of the key voters in the half-dozen or so marginal seats we had to win to return to office. At that time, we had a better grasp of the key marginals than he did.'

The centrepiece of Labor's re-election strategy was a 'family package' pledge to hold down increases in the cost of basic house-hold bills such as gas, electricity, public transport, water rates and motor registration charges over four years. The Liberals, campaigning under the slogan 'Life will be Better', matched the pledge on gas and electricity through to 1990 and promised reduc-tions in payroll tax, land tax and stamp duty on home purchases. There was the customary bidding war on police numbers. Kennett believed he had Labor on the run. But he was unsettled by a visit to his paternal grandmother, Dagmar, who was dying of a tumour in hospital. 'She said to me, "Jeff, dear, you are not going to win this next election." You could have bowled me over. She was non-compos mentis most of the time. But she came to and said, "Jeff, dear, you are not going to win the next election," and then just drifted away again.'

In the last days of the campaign, with the Government and Opposition running neck-and-neck, the National Party leader, Peter Ross-Edwards, entered the fray and proved to be a godsend to the ALP. 'Mr Kennett will need to negotiate with us to get any of his proposals through,' he said. The failure to negotiate a Coali-tion agreement created an air of unease and uncertainty about the Opposition's plans in the final hours of the contest.

The *Age* editorial of 30 September 1988 commented: 'For many voters, it will not be an easy choice. Mr Kennett has campaigned with spirit and much enthusiasm. The policies he propounds and the promises he has made indicate that the Liberal Party has emerged from the political doldrums. In the past three years, he and his party have worked hard to rebuild a rickety platform.' Of the government's performance, the editorial observed: 'Too often it has indulged greedy unions in order to complete important projects. Sometimes it has tolerated sloppy administration or poor financial management or rash decision-making.' With those reservations, however, the newspaper's verdict was the same as three years earlier. 'The government has succeeded in setting the state back on the road to development based on Victoria's distinctive strengths and potential. It has kick-started the economy. It has constructed an administrative and strategic environment in which individuals and business can operate with energy and with the hope of future rewards. We believe the state and its people would be best served if the Cain government were given another term to maintain the momentum.'

On the night of 6 October John Cain was re-elected, although the result was in doubt for many days beyond. For Kennett, it was again an excruciating case of so near and yet so far. He waited with Felicity, family and staff – and Andrew Peacock – in an upstairs suite at the Southern Cross Hotel, avoiding the press. He remained there as the count came in, consoling his chief-of-staff and close mate, Peter Kerr, who had been reduced to tears by another narrow defeat.

The following night, party officials gathered gloomily at the Liberal Party's headquarters in Exhibition Street to sift through the ashes of dashed expectations. 'Jeff was doing the numbers on the back of a drinks coaster or a how-to-vote card. He strung it out for 10 days, never conceding the result. It was a really smart tactic. It was deliberately intended to make sure everyone understood this was bloody close,' recalls Ted Baillieu. Close, certainly – but as events were soon to prove – not close enough. The Liberals had won two seats, and a majority of the two-party preferred vote. Labor would govern with a four-seat majority. Tom Austin knew the implications for Kennett were perilous. 'The bottom line was that he lost the '88 election, an election we thought we should have won.'

As soon as the Liberal party room convened after the 1988 defeat, Jeff Kennett was confronted again by the endless ritual of leadership manoeuvring. Roger Pescott brought on an immediate challenge, which Kennett survived by seven votes. He returned to his duties matter-of-factly. By this time, he had faced more leadership challenges than any Liberal leader.

Victor Perton, a former president of the Young Liberals who arrived in parliament as the new member for Doncaster, remembers being confronted on his first day by the spectacle of ballot papers being carefully counted and cross-checked on the billiard table in the Opposition rooms. 'Pescott came to visit me and asked me for my vote. Kennett didn't ring me at all. Not to congratulate me for winning the seat, nothing. Mark Birrell, who was an old friend, rang me and said, "This is what's going to happen" et cetera. Birrell was saying, "Kennett's very good," and I said, "Well at least he could talk to me." My recollection is I voted for him anyway. Kennett won by a few votes but I don't think he rang me to thank me afterwards.'

It was almost universally accepted in the party that the anti-Kennett forces would strike again. And, after two successive election defeats, Kennett had learned to be fatalistic. For his opponents, there were only two questions to be resolved: when to make the next run, and who they would put up as their champion to topple Kennett. Smith, Pescott and Gude continued to garner support, but none individually could ever achieve the critical mass necessary to clinch the ballot. Says one backbencher, 'Smithy was always having lots of coffees with MPs. One day he rang me and said, "Why don't you go for me?" He was puzzled that I didn't support him even though he knew I admired his abilities. So there was always this ambitious and mischievous group there.' Poggioli recollects, 'Kennett's style with his colleagues was somewhat abrasive. I'm not sure

that he and John Richardson are capable of having a civilised conversation. There are some people who are completely beyond the
spectrum. It wouldn't matter if Jeffrey walked on water, they would
be out to get him. I don't know what the cause of animosity between
Kennett and Pescott was, but it was palpable when I got there and
nothing you could do would actually change them.'

By May 1989, Kennett's enemies in the party were rising as one
against him. Kroger had been approached by MPs saying, 'We've
had enough of Jeff. He's been there two terms. He's never going to
win. We need a change.' Kroger's advice to the rebels remains a
matter of historical dispute and one of the reasons for the continuing bad blood between Kennett and Kroger over the next
decade. It is understood Kroger did not counsel against a challenge,
but rather insisted the onus was on the MPs and they would have
to live with the consequences if they failed. This was always seen by
Kennett as the party president having given his imprimatur to a
challenge. Certainly, the chances of success in removing Kennett
had heightened. All his rivals, with the exception of Ian Smith, had
begun to coalesce around a single candidate: the cautious, unas-
suming figure of Kennett's deputy, Alan Brown.

A coalminer's son from Wonthaggi in south Gippsland, Brown
had come to parliament 10 years earlier as a self-made man. From
the age of 14, when he subcontracted the delivery of newspapers to
other children in the neighbourhood, he had demonstrated an
entrepreneurial bent. After serving an apprenticeship as a cabinet-
maker, he had set up his own joinery business and studied for
his matriculation by correspondence classes. He then expanded into
hardware, signwriting, plumbing and a half-share in a car dealer-
ship. He spent eight years in local government, three as mayor
of Wonthaggi. Although his father, Glen, had been a Labor Party
member for 45 years, Brown came to the view during the early
1970s that the policies adopted by the Whitlam Labor government
were disastrous for the nation's economic future.

Brown did not have a reputation for political passion. Nor was he an ideologue. He styled himself as 'the quiet achiever' and was uncontroversial, verging on bland. In confronting the divisive forces tearing apart the Liberal Party, his instinct was to seek compromise and consensus. His affability and readiness to work with all persuasions of the party had established his reputation as an able and much-liked deputy. However, his colleagues needed Brown to become more ambitious in his aims. Explains Reg Macey, 'Brown didn't chase the job. Pescott delivered it to him. What you had was a whole range of people wanting the same outcome for different reasons. Some of those reasons might have been in opposition to each other, but still required the same outcome.'

Many of Pescott's colleagues – even some close to him – believed his support for Brown was driven by longer-term personal ambition. 'He saw Alan as not being strong. With Kennett gone, he might get his chance,' recalls one MP. However, Pescott was also strongly in favour of a Coalition agreement. His family had significant forestry interests in the state, and he had more empathy with the Nationals than many other Liberals. The imperative of bringing the Nationals into a united Opposition had become a crunch issue. And Alan Brown had never attacked the National Party publicly. Colleagues reasoned he might be the one to deliver a Coalition agreement. Perton was another to swing his support behind Brown, despite his initial support for Jeff. 'Kennett had begun to treat me with contempt, really, and I had a general dislike of the way he chaired the meetings. I had joined a team, I wanted to be given some creative tasks to do and he treated me with disdain. There were a lot of people like that.'

On 9 May, however, the focus of the Liberal Party shifted dramatically to Canberra, where federal leader John Howard was rolled in a breathtakingly efficient coup by supporters of Andrew Peacock. While Kennett's mate was back in the leadership and positioned for a second tilt at the prime-ministership, the pro-Howard forces, among them Kroger and his supporters in Victoria, were left seething. One of the reasons cited for Howard's defeat was his refusal to intervene to stop Kroger's preselection campaign aimed at removing the 'dead wood' in the federal parliamentary ranks. These preselection purges were seen as a fight-to-the-death struggle between the party's right wing led by Kroger and Howard, and the Liberal moderates or 'wets', including Peacock and Kennett. The instability claimed Howard's scalp. It also proved ominous for Kennett. His opponents pencilled in 23 May as the day they would strike.

By Friday 19 May, Kennett and his supporters were acutely aware that another challenge was afoot. Geoff Connard, by now a Kennett ally, was in London. He was phoned by backbencher Geoff Leigh with the news, 'There is going to be a revolution.'

'I said, "Right, I will be home."' But within the space of a few hours, Connard was phoned again, by Rob Knowles, Kennett's closest colleague – and this time the news was even more dramatic. 'Don't come home. He hasn't got the numbers. It will be a waste of time.'

Austin and others had been keeping a close check on party sentiment over the preceding six months. It had taken only a few phone calls to establish there was no means by which Kennett could survive this challenge. A petition had circulated, in which a majority of the Liberal MPs had registered their support for a spill. Brown was shown this, and agreed to stand for the leadership. After four previous challenges and two election defeats, it seemed Kennett's career was over.

That Monday, Kennett gathered his staff together. 'There might be change,' he warned them. 'I want you all to consider working for the party.'

The next day, the spill motion passed comfortably. Brown nominated for the leadership. So did Ian Smith. Kennett, to the surprise of his enemies, said he would not be putting his name forward as a candidate. In the vote that followed, Brown gained 30 of the 51 votes. Kennett told his colleagues he would not be standing for the shadow cabinet. Pescott was rewarded for his persistence by being elected deputy, defeating Alan Stockdale for the job.

Many MPs were horrified at Kennett's decision to opt out of the shadow ministry. 'Of course, we didn't think Jeff would refuse a portfolio, do what he did. I thought he would always be there,' one says. At one point, during a spiteful party-room meeting, his enemies attempted to censure his behaviour. 'Even some of his former supporters got up and said how hypocritically he was behaving after demanding loyalty himself,' says one backbencher. 'Now he was undermining Alan Brown. Alan kept saying he would not allow it to go to a vote. He was a peacemaker.'

For the first time in a decade, Kennett was reduced to being a minor player in state politics – he was 'yesterday's man', as he had once said of Bolte.

The Cain government launched into an immediate parliamentary attack on the new leader – accusing Brown of being a puppet of Kroger and the 'New Right' in Liberal politics. Meanwhile, Kennett hosted farewell drinks for his staff and close colleagues. He was, he told the media, philosophical about his defeat. 'I have done my best. I feel no pain whatsover.' The private postmortem extended into the early hours.

'It was a very long and emotional evening,' recalls Poggioli. 'I kept on being sent out for bottles of Scotch. I woke up next morning, got to work, and realised that Kerr and others had resigned. I was left the senior staff member, so I was the acting chief of staff.'

Kennett, for his part, had been driven back to his family home, his career apparently in tatters and with no reason to suspect he would return to the leadership any time soon. Having claimed so often in the past that he would gladly return to running his own business once he had finished with politics – or once politics had finished with him – there was much speculation that he would give the game away. Instead, he chose to style himself as a 'middle-bencher', a menacingly ambiguous description. Was this a soft landing before he drifted gently from public life, or a convenient staging-post while he awaited the next opportunity? If the latter,

why on earth persist, having absorbed so much ridicule and punishment over his years as Opposition leader?

Close friend Ron Walker, a prominent business leader and
former Lord Mayor of Melbourne, with whom Kennett often
sought counsel at the low points of his life, says, 'He was cast into
political purgatory. Both Andrew Peacock and I stood shoulder to
shoulder beside him to encourage him not to give up the fight
because we believed he had such talent and leadership qualities. It
would be a shame for him to fall onto a political scrapheap and
then become so dejected, eventually to retire hurt. It was all very
destructive.' Peacock admits, 'There was a time in politics when he
had only three supporters, two in the state parliament and one in
the federal parliament: Knowles, Austin and Peacock.'

On the outside, Kennett remained typically upbeat. 'He had an
office on the third floor. A few of his mates would occasionally go
up and see him. He seemed quite happy, it didn't worry him. He
almost enjoyed it,' Austin recalls. Baillieu agrees. 'I think he got
a life for a while. He had a good time not having to carry all the
responsibility. In Opposition, the leadership responsibility is a
heavy burden.'

Kennett, though, remained hyperactive. His public profile did
not stay in eclipse for long. He was offered, and accepted, new
outlets for his views. The *Sun* newspaper commissioned a regular
column on political affairs. Brown, sensing the dangers of the
column becoming a forum for second-guessing the Opposition leadership, asked that he 'use the column wisely'. Kennett also hosted a
summer fill-in talkback slot on commercial radio network 3AW.

Inevitably, Kennett's high-profile media activity prompted speculation that the leadership remained very much a 'live' issue in his
mind. Kennett was not an innocent bystander. In one particularly
mischievous broadcast, in January 1990, he devoted part of his
radio segment to an interview with himself, in which Jeff (the radio
host) probed Kennett (the former leader) on whether he still harboured ambitions for the top job. Was he plotting a move in secret

against Brown's leadership, Jeff the radio host asked. Kennett, the former leader, reacted savagely to the questioning and stormed out of the studio leaving Jeff the radio host to deliver the following post-interview analysis of the leadership speculation: 'Mr Kennett denies it and I – not knowing Mr Kennett as well as I could, perhaps – accept his word.'

As Kennett must have known only too well, the mere fact he dared to toy with this piece of vaudeville was enough to persuade many he was merely biding his time. Elsewhere on 3AW, they played the song 'Nowhere Man' to accompany an interview with Alan Brown as doubts began to surface about the Liberal leadership.

But if Liberal policy under Brown appeared to be drifting aimlessly, nobody could question his diligence in unifying the non-Labor forces. In July, he announced the crowning achievement of his leadership. Together with Kroger, he had been involved in prolonged negotiations with the National Party. Now, Brown delivered as promised on his undertaking to forge a Coalition agreement and end the long-running and destructive feud between the two conservative parties. Kroger was a co-signatory. The deal locked the parliamentary and organisational wings of the Liberal and National parties into a formal agreement on how they would govern in unison. A new shadow cabinet was formed, including, for the first time, the four most senior National Party MPs. In a ceremonial announcement at Parliament House, Brown boldly pronounced the agreement as the end of the instability that had haunted the Opposition. He told the media the Liberal and National parties were officially united on one objective: to rid the state of its socialist government.

Brown secured another important strategic victory when Pescott resigned as deputy leader to seek preselection for a federal seat. The party room selected Alan Stockdale, well known as one of Kennett's keenest supporters, as Pescott's successor. The emergence of Stockdale as deputy was seen as bolstering Brown's sometimes insipid leadership with greater gravitas and intellectual horsepower. If ever Kennett had prospects of rekindling his leadership hopes, they appeared to evaporate on 7 July 1990, when Stockdale stood alongside Brown as part of the team that would embark on the campaign to return to government.

'For Jeffrey, it was a bit of a disaster,' says one former staffer. 'If the political challenge for him was to work to get back, his linkage with Stockdale was a crucial ingredient. If he didn't have Stockdale, what did he have?'

As Brown grew steadily more accustomed to the leadership role, Melbourne's business community, so important a constituency for the Liberal leadership, began to dismiss Kennett as a spent force. Most of the business hierarchy – including prominent and influential chief executives such as Stan Wallis of Amcor and Tom North of Coles-Myer – were expressing doubts openly about whether Kennett would or should return as a major player. Although Ron Walker, Kennett's good mate in big business, continued to praise his capacities as 'head and shoulders above the rest', his audience in the corporate cliques of Melbourne appeared to have moved on. 'Many of the business leaders started to give up and accuse Andrew [Peacock] and I of backing the losing candidate,' says Walker.

But Brown was to make a series of damaging miscalculations, notably the limited front-bench reshuffle he carried out after Pescott's resignation. Significantly, he chose not to invite Kennett back into the shadow ministry. Although the Opposition seemed outwardly to have become more settled and stable, there were too many talented and ambitious potential ministers sitting on the back bench with time on their hands: Rob Knowles, Vin Heffernan, Ian Smith. Kennett was the most dangerous of all. Making the most of his free-ranging role as part-time politician, media commentator and leader-in-exile, he proved a constant irritant.

With more time on his hands, Kennett also made regular trips to visit former premier Sir Henry Bolte on his farm at Bamganie. Peacock had joined Austin in urging Kennett to take full advantage of the veteran's knowledge and experience, and now he was heeding their advice. Later, in government, Kennett would pay tribute to the guidance of the old master, putting on prominent display in his office mementos of the Bolte years, including a portrait of the former premier and his original desk. Bolte, too, had been dismissed as a bumpkin and a stopgap leader, and yet had gone on to rule for 17 years. This was, for Kennett, a valuable lesson in the powers of endurance and plain rat cunning. At Bolte's farm, often in the woolshed, the two discussed the internal politics of the party and how to keep one step ahead of predators. Kennett always took a bottle of Scotch with him. Over a drink they would chew the fat, Bolte offering his thoughts and insights on the events of the day. Kennett listened. And learned. But for the moment, he remained anchored on the sidelines. Although publicly supportive of Brown's leadership, he was known to complain bitterly and repeatedly in private of the failure of his fellow state Liberals to drive home their political advantage.

A few months after the death in January 1990 of Bolte, Kennett suffered a body blow. His great mate and trusted adviser, Peter Kerr, died of a heart attack while playing tennis. Kerr was only 41. Kennett was devastated. Nevertheless, through these volatile and difficult years, influential figures in the Liberal Party continued to watch closely as Kennett absorbed the punishment. Said one long-serving cabinet minister, 'He didn't reinvent himself. He grew. Through the 1980s you were aware of someone growing faster than the speed of light, and learning a million lessons.'

CHAPTER SEVEN

THE PATH TO POWER

'Stockers! Something's going to happen, mate.'
TOM AUSTIN, 2 MAY 1991

In the days before Christmas 1990, Jeff Kennett sent out his usual batch of goodwill greetings to his Liberal parliamentary colleagues. Stranded on the back bench, with no apparent means of resurrecting party-room support for another tilt at the leadership, Kennett penned a note in sorrow to his old rival Roger Pescott. Pescott too was in limbo after resigning as deputy leader to make an unsuccessful run for federal preselection. 'It's a shame things didn't turn out differently,' Kennett wrote.

In the years before their ambitions clashed, Pescott had been an admirer of Kennett. He had even told colleagues that Jeff's fresh and aggressive approach had, in part, inspired him to enter politics. By the end of 1990, however, both were on the scrapheap, discarded and dispirited. Both were nursing wounds. Both were still nursing ambitions. Pescott replied to Kennett's Christmas greetings tentatively and enigmatically, but with a strong hint that they should mend their fences and abandon their policy of mutually assured destruction. This return mail was to be the genesis of Kennett's comeback.

Public sentiment about the former Opposition leader had shifted dramatically. In January 1991, Kennett spoke rousingly at a 'Save Australia' rally. This public demonstration had been organised by rural communities stung by the collapse of the Pyramid Building Society, which the Cain government had publicly endorsed. Fifty thousand angry Victorians hit the streets of Melbourne. Kennett was accused of rabble-rousing, but opinion polls demonstrated strong and rising support for his forthright approach. In contrast, the earnest but unobtrusive Brown had by now acquired the soubriquet 'Mr Beige'. By the early months of 1991, the forces who had spent years undermining Kennett's leadership had come to the view, that, whatever Jeff's failings, he was the more substantial figure to lead the party into government.

In March 1991, Pescott invited Kennett to lunch at the exclusive Melbourne Club. An imposing 19th-century edifice, the club sits grandly at the top of what was once called the Paris end of Collins Street. Since the 1870s, it has been the members-only meeting place for the city's bluebloods – captains of industry, the squattocracy, old money. Although it began to lose its mystique as the fulcrum of Melbourne's power elite as early as the 1970s, the club's elegant dining rooms and picturesque private garden remain a favoured retreat, where people of influence, primarily in commerce, can network over lunch or a drink. Pescott had run into trouble in a preselection battle for the state seat of Bennettswood with a Kennett ally, Geoff Coleman. He was looking to reach an accommodation. In a bid to rescue his flagging career, Pescott would become part of a covert operation to restore Kennett as leader.

The political circumstances were propitious for the Liberals. The state's balance sheet was haemorrhaging, with debt and unfunded liabilities soaring towards $60 billion. Once a triple A state, Victoria's credit assessment had been downgraded to A1. The cause of the crisis was the Labor government's grand plans to reconstruct the state's industrial base. Cain and his treasurer, Rob Jolly, had believed that the government should take an interventionist role in setting signals for investment. Accordingly, they had borrowed heavily to finance business start-ups in select industries. Through the State Bank, easy credit was offered to entrepreneurs with the Victorian taxpayer carrying some or all of the risk.

The Victorian Economic Development Corporation (VEDC) was one of the creatures of Labor's intervention industry policy. Already, by 1988, the Liberals under Kennett had uncovered unnerving reports of its bizarre lending practices. Details of the loss of $130 million in bad loans would ultimately force the resignation of deputy premier Rob Fordham.

According to Peter Poggioli, the Opposition knew they were on to a scandal of major proportions. 'It began with an interesting collection of bits and pieces. It all started with loans to Wallace International, a pharmaceutical group. We had been poking around, and we knew something was wrong. Then again, it could have been a one-day story. But Jeffrey . . . knew the right people to talk to and where he could dig for more. While there were a lot of people doing the digging, he was doing the driving . . . I think it was probably a parliamentary campaign that was one of the best moments in the history of the Opposition. We actually took control of the parliament. You could see it in Fordham's eyes. You could see it in Cain's eyes. We knew we were on a roll. We knew we had them in August 1988. They took one or two days of questions, and then they called a snap election. We knew we had them. Had they given us three weeks of questions, we would have killed them.'

Kennett has blamed sections of the media ever since for not grasping the full ramifications of the VEDC scandal: 'Don't forget, they ran to an election in 1988 because they knew we had the VEDC stuff. We tried to give it to the *Age* and they were just not interested at all.'

Its electoral victory in 1988 was sweet for the ALP, but the celebrations were illusory. As senior figures in the government knew only too well, the adventurous economic strategies of Jolly and his advisers were beginning to self-destruct. The pump-priming policies employed to kick-start the economy, boost public-sector capital works, employ more teachers and nurses and stimulate business investment had involved the government borrowing heavily to fund its programs. Now the Hawke government in Canberra was beginning to tighten monetary policy severely, in a bid to temper consumer demand and rein in the nation's current-account deficit. Interest rates were climbing steeply. The Cain government's gamble on Keynesian strategies was to prove catastrophic. Labor in Victoria had won one election too many.

Within weeks of beginning their third term, a tabling of a report on the VEDC showed that the state-funded investment scheme was technically insolvent. There was $112 million in outstanding loans, $70 million of which was unrecoverable. An investigation by leading city accountant Fergus Ryan revealed inadequate board supervision of loan approvals, inadequate ministerial and departmental oversight, and the absence of appropriate financial controls. On 31 January 1989, after six weeks of persistent Opposition demands for his sacking, Rob Fordham resigned. Although nobody knew it at the time, Fordham was to be the first domino in an utter collapse of the Cain government's credibility.

By 1990, the government was unravelling. During the federal Labor government's election campaign in February and March that year, Bob Hawke defended publicly the competence and integrity of his Victorian colleagues. Privately, however, senior federal ministers were appalled. Labor's support in the state had gone into a tailspin. In February, a crippling public transport strike over attempts to introduce automated ticketing had embarrassed the state during Melbourne's bid to host the 1996 Olympics. But this was as nothing compared to the emerging horror story of Tricontinental.

Hard on the heels of the VEDC scandal, Cain's sober and cautious image was emasculated by the multi-billion-dollar losses of Tricontinental, the state-owned merchant bank. By 1989 it was known that the bank had lost at least $800 million, and that its parent, the historically staid and sturdy State Bank, would need a $750-million bail-out simply to service its debts. The financial mayhem created a crisis of confidence.

Suddenly Cain, for so long the unimpeachable cleanskin, began to feel the blowtorch of public odium and party dissent. His personal approval rating, which had once soared above 70 per cent, plummeted to a record low of 25 per cent. In a by-election that year, Labor suffered a mortifying 20 per cent swing in the rock-solid Labor constituency of Thomastown. In Canberra, there were fears that Victoria could prove the Hawke government's 'valley of death'. Party heavyweights exerted pressure on Cain to take decisive action to placate a surly and embittered electorate. In vain they urged him to force the resignation of the one-time wunderkind, state treasurer Rob Jolly, over the Tricontinental disaster. The losses incurred by the State Bank's merchant bank subsidiary were staggering even by the global standards of the day. By the time of the federal election on 24 March, the bank was known to be carrying bad debts of more than $1.3 billion. Inside the Cain government, however, the secret expectation, kept carefully hidden from the electorate, was that total losses would spiral to double that amount. It was to become the single greatest corporate loss in Australia's history. The debacle led to a royal commission investigation and would ultimately produce the unthinkable: the forced sale by a Labor government of the State Bank.

Throughout the federal election campaign, however, the Cain government worked feverishly to shift blame onto the State Bank's board of directors. Jolly told reporters the government could not be held accountable for the commercial decisions of an independent board, although he stressed that the bank would no longer be permitted involvement in 'entrepreneurial banking'. The premier also moved to adjourn parliamentary sittings to preclude debate on the fate of the bank. Alan Stockdale, who spearheaded the

Opposition questioning of the role of both Cain and Jolly in the debacle, maintains to this day that both Tricontinental and the VEDC were symptoms of a flawed understanding in the Labor government of how markets work. 'They were totally out of touch with what was going on. They were not held to account for the deliberate policy initiatives that ended in the collapse of the State Bank. Jolly set out as a matter of deliberate policy to dramatically grow that bank at a time of rapid expansion of credit in the economy, so the market automatically selected them the higher-risk business. They tried to turn the State Bank and the Triconti-nental brand into a full-service international bank, at a time of booming conditions in the global markets. I don't know that they ever understood the risks they were taking. Their VEDC initiative, also, was totally nonsensical. It was supposed to operate under commercial principles but fill gaps in the capital markets by lending to people who could not borrow from the established institutions. How can you lend money to people on commercial principles on that basis? They actually got off lightly for the absolutely stupid policies they pursued. Cain had no real under-standing of how the business world works. He sought to expose us to ridicule when we were saying things that subsequently proved to be spot on.'

David White, a cabinet member at the time, concedes that the VEDC acquired a reputation as a 'lender of last resort' and became an easy target for often dubious business proposals. He also regrets that the Cain government chose not to sell Tricontinental when there were rumours in 1987 of an offer from private interests to buy the merchant bank for $100 million. 'The point about all these issues is that you are dealing with taxpayers' money and you need to be extremely circumspect about what you do with it. I was part of a cabinet decision where we took 100 per cent equity in Tricontinental. We should not have. We should only have taken 25 per cent. In any event, we should not have held on to it as a necessary part of government. It may have had some advantage at some stage, but we should not have continued to hold it. The same applies to the lending program of the VEDC.'

The perfidy attached to these financial disasters, and public alarm over the ramifications for the future prosperity of the state, were to prove crucial factors in delivering Andrew Peacock nine Labor-held seats in Victoria at the March 1990 federal election. It pushed the Hawke government to the edge of the precipice. The federal Liberals under Peacock won a majority of the two-party preferred vote but fell short of winning sufficient seats to claim power. Peacock's enemies immediately began circling, claiming, in what has become a familiar mantra, that this had been the 'unlosable election.'

Kennett was alone with Peacock and his daughters when the federal leader was forced to grapple with the realisation that he had exhausted his opportunities to become prime minister – the office which for 25 years had seemed his destiny. For both men, it was the nadir of their years in public office. Briefly, the two looked at going into a business partnership, in preparation for life after politics. Given their media talents, they considered a bid for the Melbourne radio station 3AK. 'We needed to find about 20 grand. We were going to call it 3PK – the station you can chew on. It was going to create havoc on the airwaves,' says Peacock. 'Thank God we didn't get it.'

Although Labor had survived the closest of federal elections, the scale of the party's losses in Victoria prompted Cain to seek to circumvent the inevitable moves against him by offering his resignation. But his Socialist Left deputy, Joan Kirner, who would later succeed him as premier, backed away from a challenge, unsure of her numbers. Jolly's political career could not be salvaged. He was forced to resign on 2 April, within weeks of the federal poll.

But it was too late to stop the rot for Labor. High interest rates imposed by the Hawke government to dampen consumer demand had sent the nation plummeting into recession. Victoria, already struggling to cope with the impact of economic restructuring and reduced tariff protection for its manufacturing industries, descended into gloom and pessimism. Unemployment soared. Compounding the crisis, government reforms to workers' compensation laws had created a $5 billion blow-out in unfunded liabilities. To cap it off there was yet another financial collapse: the Pyramid Building Society, a mortgage lender based mainly in Geelong and western Victoria. In February Labor had recklessly assured depositors that 'they should feel very secure about funds invested in Pyramid Building Society'. By June, the building society – a private financial institution – had ceased trading. Depositors blamed the government, which, under intense pressure, agreed to a partial guarantee of funds still frozen, hoping to appease the many thousands of small depositors whose life savings were at risk. An unpopular surcharge was imposed on petrol taxes to cover this liability.

The Labor government was disintegrating by the hour. Cain's leadership was under siege. All attempts to impose public sector spending restraint met with the trenchant opposition of the trade unions. Amid the descent into chaos, factional leaders began to look to self-preservation. Cain was crippled, indeed paralysed, by malevolent forces over which he had lost all authority and control. The demands from the Hawke government in Canberra for the Victorian ALP to clean up its act became ever more shrill. The smell of blood was in the air. In August, some of Cain's closest supporters decided they could resist no longer. The premier was a liability. If Labor was to prevent annihilation at the next election, there was no choice but for Cain to go. On 16 August, after a failed attempt to shore up his leadership at the party's state conference, Cain announced his resignation. Labor's first premier in 30 years – and a three-time election winner – retreated ignominiously to the back bench.

Joan Kirner was sworn in as the state's first woman premier. She suffered an immediate setback when Melbourne lost its bid in Tokyo to host the 1996 Olympics, running fourth behind Atlanta, Athens and Toronto. Then, on 26 September, she announced to parliament the sale of the State Bank to the Commonwealth Bank, in a deal negotiated with the Labor government in Canberra to relieve Victoria of the crushing burden of the bank's losses. The transaction came at a huge symbolic cost to Kirner and her colleagues on Labor's Left. It was the first significant landmark in the privatisation of government-owned enterprises in Australia. The ALP had opened the door to a precedent that would be taken up with alacrity by future Coalition governments in Victoria and elsewhere.

Although the State Bank sale was another shattering blow to the morale of a city and state, Kirner handled the process with efficiency and a measure of poise. Yet as all of her colleagues knew, the surrender of 'the people's bank' was another nail in the coffin. The collapse of self-esteem in Victoria was palpable. So were the anger and dismay over the government's incapacity to arrest the slide.

Victoria's woes had become a major national story. The state was being widely depicted as a 'rustbucket' and had become the butt of national jokes: 'What is the capital of Victoria? Not very much.' 'What is the definition of living in Victoria? An optimist.'

Through all of this, the Liberals surged in the opinion polls. But doubt raged about Alan Brown's capacity to exploit the chaos. The Opposition's credibility as an alternative government became a pressing issue. The *Sydney Morning Herald* commented: 'Many people believe that the only hope for Labor is that an election is not due for two years and it is up against a poor Opposition led by Alan Brown, an ineffectual leader who has made little apparent impact.' Around this time, Poggioli left his job as Brown's chief of staff to take up a new strategic role at party headquarters. 'Brown was not dynamic. Although Cain got really old, really quickly, you didn't get the sense it was Brown driving it like Kennett had driven the VEDC issue.'

Kirner, as premier, was likeable and respected, and the Coalition frontbench adopted a policy of not engaging in personal taunts. In contrast, Kennett, the headkicker, ridiculed her incessantly, describing her as 'a tragic figure' for whom he felt sorry. 'My natural instinct is that I want to protect her. I see her looking tired, I see her looking depressed, exhausted . . . But I have to say to myself, "Hang on, don't feel sorry for her, she's the premier." She sought this office and she should be treated accordingly. She must realise it is her position, not her person, which is under attack.'

The *Herald Sun,* the state's mass-circulation tabloid, strongly supported Brown as the next premier, but within the Liberal Party itself, the atmospherics had shifted. Disaffection with Brown had reached critical mass. Despite holding an unassailable lead over Labor in the opinion polls, the party had come to regard Brown's leadership as a profound disappointment. 'There was a sense of panic in the community about where things were going, and there was a perception the Opposition was sitting on its hands. Kennett had been out there, articulating some of the frustrations. He had picked the public mood,' recalls a senior Liberal colleague.

Brown's office had introduced a rule that unless otherwise authorised, only the leader would speak on the issues of the day. However, Brown and his staff had adopted the safer course in which the Opposition leader kept his head down. After all, the Liberals led Labor by more than 30 per cent in the polls. The effect of this, though, was to vacate the field to Kennett, the only Liberal around town prepared to be outspoken. Recalls one backbencher, 'I think people like Birrell and Gude and others blew their chance at that time. If any of them, seeing the collapse of Brown, had worked to take over, they would have taken over.'

Publicly, Kennett continued to pledge his loyalty to Brown's leadership. Nonetheless, he maintained his high media profile, and the contrast between his self-assured and forthright worldliness and Brown's timidity and lack of charisma had become stark. In December 1990, the two men lunched with leaders of peak business groups, including Peter Boyle of the Small Business Association. The lunch at Bamboo House – a favoured Chinese restaurant of the Liberal and business elites in Little Bourke

Street – was not a pleasant affair for the Opposition leader. He was amongst avid Kennett admirers. Brown was left on the outer as Kennett took command of the dialogue. 'Brown was a nice bloke, meant well, but he was bound to be swamped by Kennett,' one participant was reported as saying.

Three months later, on 6 March, the same business leaders, among others, were invited to 'peace talks' in the Liberal party room. On his way into the meeting, Boyle – a fiery and aggressive lobbyist – threw a grenade in Brown's lap, telling a waiting reporter that 'Kennett's return is inevitable'. It set the tone for yet another difficult meeting for the Opposition leader, who was forced to confront Boyle over the incident, insisting his leadership was secure. Boyle snapped back, 'Alan, if you are so confident of your leadership, why do you feel you have to confirm it here?' Brown's authority was haemorrhaging by the hour. As Geoffrey Barker was to write in the *Age*: 'Poor Alan Brown. He never understood. A political leader has to project his personal will to lead convincingly. He has to reward and protect his supporters. He has to crush his enemies. He has to cultivate the constituencies vital to his party's electoral success.'

The Labor Party, watching from the sidelines, had also assessed Brown's leadership as terminal. As David White recalls, 'He didn't seem to be making any headway at all. One of the characteristics you have to have in these jobs that endeared both Hawke and Cain to the Labor Party was that they were passionately hungry about winning. That didn't seem to be part of Brown's make-up. He may have desired to be premier but that's different from being desperate and prepared to do anything required. If you are desperate about it you will go beyond what you might reasonably think you are capable of doing because the party has asked you to.' Nobody doubted Brown could win the election. But what sort of government would he lead? No one wished for a repeat of the fag end of the Hamer–Thompson years, in which the Liberal Party had meandered aimlessly into mediocrity.

Tom Austin decided it was time to act. The crucial conversation that proved the catalyst for his final power play came over lunch with Petro Georgiou.

AUSTIN: 'How do you think Alan Brown will go?'
GEORGIOU: 'Oh, we'll win the election.'
AUSTIN: 'But what will we do about after the election?'
GEORGIOU: 'Let's just win the election.'

'That's when I became absolutely determined,' remembers Austin. 'First of all, I had to get out of the shadow cabinet. Two or three people had come to me and said, "I think we ought to try and get him out." I said, "You can't. I can't. None of us can because we're part of his team."'

Austin, in the knowledge he would retire at the next election, chose to resign his front-bench position. This freed him to engage in the clandestine head-counting that was gathering momentum within the party. 'It's like running a coup when you know you have to keep it absolutely under wraps. There were only four people who knew precisely what was going on. Kennett wasn't told. People still don't believe it. He knew there was something on, but he didn't know when or how or why.'

Austin's resignation from the front bench should have signalled to Brown that an ambush was imminent. Certainly, he appeared to anticipate there was trouble ahead when he ordered another minor reshuffle aimed at securing the support of a younger core of MPs. He promoted Denis Napthine to the shadow ministry and appointed Victor Perton, Michael John and Robert Clark, a Kroger ally, as assistant shadow ministers. But back in harness as Kennett's chief numbers man, Austin was soon conducting secret negotiations with the serious powerbrokers within the Liberal Party. For the Liberals, a return to government had become a matter of when, not if, and none of those coveting future ministerial positions wanted to be left on the outer when the new government was sworn in. Austin offered guarantees to some of Kennett's erstwhile enemies that they would not be overlooked. 'I don't think many people realise that Kennett didn't really instigate or negotiate getting rid of Brown. Most people don't believe that. They think I'm having them on. But it was people like myself who knew that Brown would not make it as premier. We got on board. People like Smith and Pescott could not stand the idea of Brown either.'

By this time, Kroger was urging Liberal MPs not to engage in the constant intrigues. Among Kennett supporters, this was interpreted as an attempt by the head of the party organisation to circumvent any moves against Brown. But Poggioli, for one, takes the view that the state president was entitled to be uneasy. 'My view from where I stood was that Michael and the organisation were much more vocal in their support of Brownie probably because Brownie needed that support.' Was it a propping-up exercise? 'Well, Brownie was never as dynamic and self-sufficient as Jeffrey was. And there was the issue of instability. You have to remember this was in the context of almost annual leadership challenges. From the organisational point of view, there could have been a legitimate case to say, "OK, we're in the run-up to an election campaign, we look like we're going very well, and we want to be unified." I remember Michael basically came out and said, "Well, if you want to knock him off, go ahead. But if you don't, there will be consequences." I don't think this is a particularly exceptional statement to make in the context.' In fact, Kroger's stance was counterproductive. The party president had turned his attention to influencing state preselections, and many MPs feared another purge. Brown was seen as too compliant to the Kroger agenda, and this added to the urgency of looking for a leader who might offer some protection against the predations of the party president.

At 10 p.m. on Monday 22 April, three Liberal MPs – Rob Knowles, Geoff Connard and Ian Smith – arrived at Austin's East Melbourne home for the final council of war. One of them phoned Kennett at home. 'Kennett knew something was afoot but he didn't expect the revolution,' Austin insists. Their discussion centred on the tactics for the party-room meeting the following day. A few close allies were contacted and told to prepare for a spill motion. The four adjourned after midnight, but reconvened at Austin's home at 4.30 a.m. They hit the phones in a frenzy, carefully accounting for each MP on whose vote they believed they could rely when the party room met at 10 a.m. Phil Gude could account for a crucial parcel of five votes, and his support became critical. 'We needed to get Gude's five. The only way was to offer him the deputy leadership,' says Austin. 'Stockdale was a very good friend, and I hated doing it. But as a means to an end, that was it. Of course, people in the party room could not understand why they were being told to vote for Gude. "I want to vote for Stockdale," they were saying. As we walked into the party room, I said, "Stockers! Something's going to happen, mate."'

The four had laid down elaborate plans for the timing of the spill motion, and by whom it should be moved. Tactically, it was imperative that Brown be caught completely off guard. Says Connard, 'It became important to the small group there that we didn't want the spill motion moved immediately. Brown was presiding, and could easily have said, "Well, the meeting isn't full and we will have this vote next week." It was part of my trivial job to convene each meeting, read the correspondence. I had to keep this going for about 20 minutes. There was only so much filibustering you could do. So I read through the minutes and I read through the correspondence and tried to get a debate going and didn't succeed. Then we had a stroke of luck. One of the members demanded to know how we had selected the members to go on a parliamentary trip to Lithuania. He wanted to know how the people were picked and by whom. This was a classic opportunity to speak for well over 20 minutes. We then had the room full of people and Tom Reynolds [MLA for Gisborne and a future cabinet minister] got up – in a fairly brave act – and moved the spill.'

The motion was seconded by Mildura MP Craig Bildstien. Says Austin, 'Brown had the option of getting on with it, or putting it off for a week. But because Tom Reynolds wasn't seen as a very powerful guy, he thought it was just some stupidity. He couldn't believe what he was hearing. There was no inkling of it happening.

'How could anyone be so ridiculously stupid? Didn't the colour in his face change when the bloody thing was carried? There was disbelief at the top table. It was a complete shock to him.'

The Opposition leader was not the only one shocked. Stockdale, who was sitting alongside Brown, says, 'The fact it happened then was a total surprise to me. They knew the value I attach to loyalty. Out of respect for that, they made damned sure I didn't become involved. It would have been known outside the circle of Alan Brown, myself, and those who were the immediate support base of Alan Brown.'

Victor Perton was also perplexed. 'It was a complete bolt from the blue. Clearly, there was masterful organisation, by Austin and others. I hadn't a clue until Tom Reynolds stood up in the party room. In my most stupid political decision, I got up and spoke. I just couldn't understand why this motion was being moved. We were 33 points in front in the polls, we would win as long as we were united. That was basically what I thought. I thought it was the right thing to do. But a lot of people said to me later, "Victor, that was your greatest political mistake ever."'

In Alan Brown's office, there was also disbelief. His staff were notified by Gude that there had been a spill. They waited tensely in their office for word of the outcome. Then Alister Drysdale, Kennett's right-hand man, sauntered into Brown's office. 'You're gone,' he told Brown's advisers.

Kennett was apparently taken aback by the coup. 'Kennett wasn't all that confident we had done a good job,' Austin recalls. 'I was certain we had, but he was very nervous about having his reputation ruined if this failed. He said to me afterwards, "Mate, you might have told me." I said, "You've got to be joking." Anyway, they reckoned it was the best spill ever.'

The shock waves of the morning's events travelled quickly around the party. Kroger arrived at Parliament House and sat on a bench in one of the Legislative Council corridors, in awestruck conversation with Liberal MPs. He broke from the group occasionally to make calls on his mobile phone. Ted Baillieu, Kroger's vice-president, was sitting in Petro Georgiou's office when the news came through. 'We exchanged the usual profanities, then Petro called Michael. Michael must have gone up to parliament, and done all the right things. He appeared to be a bit unknowing and caught off guard. I think they did it extremely well.'

Brown, for his part, was gracious in defeat. He agreed to accept a shadow ministry. His conduct in the midst of the tumult earned him the respect of many of his critics in the party. 'He went with great equanimity,' recalls Austin.

Stockdale, although he lost the deputy's job as part of Austin's deal with Gude, was philosophical about the outcome. 'I could work well with either Jeff or Alan. I have never been the slightest concerned about losing the deputy's position. Under either leader I would have a level of influence. I am close to both of them, and I thought either would lead well. But I was well and truly known as a strong supporter of Jeff. Alan would not have been under any misapprehension about my view. I thought Jeff was a much better leader of the Opposition than people had given him credit for.'

As government and Opposition MPs trooped into the Legislative Assembly and Kennett resumed the leader's seat, a government member sidled up to Tom Austin and whispered teasingly, 'Who killed Cock Robin?' Laughs Labor frontbencher Ian Baker, 'Tom didn't like it one bit.'

Jeff Kennett's return to the leadership was the last link in the chain for the Liberal Party's revival. In his absence, the policy development process had continued virtually seamlessly. Now Kennett urged his policy-makers to lift to another gear. Tania Price, who would serve as Kennett's first press secretary in government, recalls, 'He basically said we were going to review everything the Liberal Party had ever said. It was never challenged by anyone. Birrell came in talking about money from a casino licence that could pay for this square, or that sports centre, or a new museum. It was a cauldron of ideas, quite radical ideas. Kennett said, "I don't care. Just give me policy."'

In keeping with the agreements struck by Austin during the plot to oust Brown, Kennett appointed Smith and Pescott to the front bench, along with Rob Knowles and Vin Heffernan. Jim Plowman and other long-standing critics of Kennett kept their jobs. The deal brought into the shadow cabinet all the warring elements of the party. Kennett played statesman with the media. 'I have tried very hard to forget the past. Whatever has gone on in the past in terms of relationships between individuals to me is no longer important.' In fact, Kennett had serious misgivings about the longer-term viability of the arrangements. Although he wanted Stockdale to remain as deputy, Smith, Pescott and Heffernan had insisted on Gude. They did not want power concentrated in a clique that could potentially lock them out in future. When Kennett warned his supporters he might not want to carry through on all of these com- mitments if and when the Coalition won government, he was told in blunt terms that there could be no rescinding of the arrange- ments. 'The deal is made in your name and you will honour it.' Kennett could not pretend he had no prior knowledge whatsoever of the deal-making – after all, he had lunched with Pescott – and was persuaded that any backsliding would be an unacceptable breach of faith. Such was the price of unity, a precious commodity for the Opposition as it prepared for government.

Meanwhile, at ALP state headquarters in Drummond Street, Labor strategists were staring bleakly at a potentially massive defeat at the next election. The beleaguered Kirner government came under pressure from the Hawke government in Canberra to go to the polls at the first opportunity, no matter the risk. The series of financial crises in Victoria was giving the party a bad name nationally. Says David White, 'It becomes a question of what do you do to keep your head above the water, if you can. And how do you manage this when the federal government is screaming from the rooftops for you to go to an election? They were begging us to clear the decks, and give them a chance. They said they were being contaminated. They were all saying it. If they had any differences among themselves, there was one topic on which they were agreed: bagging us. All you can do in that environment is make the best of it, to present yourselves as best you can. At one point, our primary vote had dropped to 24 per cent, according to some polls.'

Nevertheless, Joan Kirner was attracting positive remarks from surprising quarters. In a television interview, trucking magnate Lindsay Fox praised Kirner's performance as premier. When asked what he thought of Kennett, he said the jury was still out. Coles-Myer chairman Solomon Lew was also reported as being impressed by Kirner's grace under pressure.

Kennett was riled. He was determined that Labor should be seen to have no credibility at the top end of town. He contacted both business leaders to complain, and was soundly rebuked. 'That was one of the things that hurt him most during that period of time,' says one of Kennett's big-business mates. 'They just reckoned Joan Kirner was doing a good job in the circumstances. He was not very amused. Not very amused at all.'

On 13 May Kennett upped the ante, issuing a warning that business should think of the public good in its dealings with the Kirner government. He threatened that a future Coalition government would not look kindly on any companies or business leaders seen to 'get into bed' with Labor by signing deals that would undermine the state's future interests. Ostensibly, the threat was inspired by suspicion within the Opposition that some banks and businesses were entering 'fast buck' arrangements of leaseback contracts on public assets and interest-swap deals to take advantage of a government desperate for cash. Although this concern was legitimate, the tone and temper of Kennett's warning sent another tremor through business circles about his impetuosity.

Kennett returned to the leadership insisting that the Coalition had to become more aggressive and harass the Kirner government into an early election before the end of 1991. At a press conference soon after resuming as leader, he was asked whether he would reconsider blocking supply to force the government to the polls. 'Stay tuned,' he replied, mysteriously.

Inexplicably, Kennett then threw Labor a lifeline, as part of a 'five-step plan' he had conceived to force an election before the winter recess. On 7 May, he announced that unless Kirner issued writs for an election, the Coalition in the lower house would oppose a supply bill allowing the government to fund its budget through to October. Predictably, the government dismissed this ultimatum. Next, on 16 May, Kennett sought amendments to the Constitution providing for upper-house reform. Again, the government ignored his browbeating.

Kennett had briefed senior National Party MPs and his Liberal leadership – Gude, Birrell and Storey – on the broad outlines of his strategy. None had demurred. For the rest of the party, however, Kennett's game plan remained a mystery. As he unveiled each element of it, backbenchers and party strategists grew ever more nervous. Kennett's close mate Rob Knowles warned him bluntly, 'I hope this is not going to lead to a blocking of supply.'

On Thursday 23 May, with many of his trusted confidants in China on a parliamentary trip, Kennett launched into a strategy which was to become notorious as the 'quantum leap'. He faxed the following letter to Labor MPs: 'If the government has not caused a state election to be announced by midnight, Wednesday 29 May 1991, then all sitting Australian Labor Party members of the Victorian parliament who retire from parliament after that date and prior to the next state election, or who stand as a candidate at the next election and subsequently lose their seat, will

be denied any access to the taxpayer-funded component of their parliamentary superannuation entitlement.' Kennett flagged the surprise
tactic on a radio interview on the Thursday morning, telling 3AW's
Neil Mitchell he had briefed only a couple of his staff members.

> MITCHELL: 'Is it the most dramatic thing in Victorian politics for
> some years?'
> KENNETT: 'Yes.'
> MITCHELL: 'How long?'
> KENNETT: 'I can never remember anything as dramatic as this ever
> being done.'

He told the party room of his tactics at 4 p.m. The threat provoked an immediate uproar. As debate raged in parliament over
succeeding days, Labor's treasurer, Tom Roper, called it 'an act of
thuggery'. 'As members of this house, we are faced with one of the
most fundamental assaults on parliamentary democracy we have
seen in this country or in any other civilised countries with which
we prefer to compare ourselves,' Roper cried. 'Our parliamentary
and democratic society does not expect parliamentarians to be
threatened with reprisals or punishment if they exercise their
consciences and decision-making powers . . . Who will work for
the Crown if their salaries and superannuation can be cancelled at
the whim of the political party in power at the time? He wants to
overthrow the Westminster system with the politics of retribution
and revenge.'

For almost a week, Kennett sought to defend his stratagem. On
28 May he told Labor MPs in parliament, 'It should not be forgotten that we are employed by the public. It is not your money,
and it is not my money – we are talking about the public's
money, and the public is entitled to hold us all accountable. What
is so extraordinary about being accountable? Most people in the
community are accountable. Further, the Opposition has given
the government and its members until midnight tomorrow night

to rearrange, if they wish, their financial affairs. What could be fairer?'

The media commentary was scathing. In an editorial, the *Australian Financial Review* accused Kennett of descending to 'the politics of the lynch mob'. The *Age* was also horrified. 'The Opposition leader's obsessive pursuit of premature power has led him and his colleagues to commit an act of political blackmail so vindictive as to raise grave questions about their political judgement and stability.'

Kennett's threat was not only grotesque politically, but possibly dubious legally. Labor threatened to censure Kennett through the privileges committee. Labor frontbencher Steve Crabb raised the possibility of criminal charges. Kennett stood his ground defiantly: 'Put me in the dock.'

It was not only the ALP and the media that were appalled. Kennett's own party room was dismayed. Several of his upper-house colleagues insisted they would cross the floor if he attempted to put the legislation into parliament. At party headquarters Petro Georgiou was furious, as were most of the political professionals. None had been told of the plan, which cut across the election strategies they had been carefully putting in place. From Canberra, two senior Liberals joined the chorus of condemnation. Peter Costello, by now the federal Opposition's spokesman on corporate law reform, said the threat could be seen as an affront to human rights. 'Singling out people for punishment because of the political party they happen to represent is not what one would expect in a society that values freedom of political opinion.' Former leader John Howard described the tactic as 'unorthodox' and urged the Victorian Liberals to look instead to develop credibility as 'a strong, orthodox, reliable, stable alternative government'.

Labor could hardly believe its good fortune, and seized on perhaps its last glimmer of opportunity to fight its way back into the contest. The superannuation gambit was seen to confirm all the old prejudices about Kennett's lack of self-control. Labor's attorney-general, Jim Kennan, told parliament, 'Two weeks ago, there was a bubble aura around this man that has burst . . . He represents high risk. He represents instability, secret strategies, divisions and, above all, mindless populism.'

On the morning of 30 May, Kennett finally relented. Petro Georgiou and his political adviser, Alister Drysdale, had confronted Kennett over the stupidity of his stance. Georgiou, as ever, had the party's internal polling close at hand. It showed that well over 90 per cent of the electorate thought Kennett's tactics ridiculous.

Initially, Kennett responded contemptuously, arguing that a backdown would suggest a lack of stomach for tough strategies. Georgiou, in gruff and explicit terms, explained that in the face of widespread public and party opposition, Kennett had a choice between retreat and annihilation. Drysdale urged the chastened leader to move quickly. Most of the senior press gallery reporters were in Canberra for a premiers' meeting. Kennett could sneak his backdown past the junior reporters, without being subject to intense questioning. At the Coalition party-room meeting that morning, the Opposition leader acknowledged to colleagues that his ploy had backfired. He then issued a public statement officially renouncing the tactic. It was an abject and humiliating backdown.

The bungled strategy forced Kennett into a dramatic tactical switch: rather than politicking through newspaper headlines and TV news bulletins, the Opposition leader would now give priority to getting back onto the streets and into the electorate, talking directly to voters in the meet-the-people style of campaigning at which he was a proven performer. This came at the urging of party headquarters, and was aimed not only at stabilising the party, aghast over the superannuation debacle, but also to get the Liberals back onto the strategy they had laid out months before. Politically, Kennett had no choice but to pull his head in. For a time, he left Kirner to make the running. It left him less visible – the only time in his career he was persuaded to adopt a 'keep small' strategy –

allowing the main political focus to remain on the premier and her government. For the first time as Opposition leader, Kennett was not constantly seen or heard. In hindsight, Labor could have dashed to the polls to capitalise on Kennett's miscalculations. In fact, it was at this time that Kirner's popularity peaked. 'But she wasn't going to win,' says White. 'It was never sufficient to get us back in front, or even into a competitive position. It might have reduced the loss relative to the one we had.'

The debate became academic by the end of 1991. By this time, the Liberals had conceived perhaps the single most effective political campaign pitch in 20 years. An advertising team had put together a series of hard-hitting television and print advertisements entitled 'The Guilty Party', which identified and vilified individual Labor ministers for their role in the state's economic demise. With a stentorian voice-over, the text and images created a virtual reality where ALP frontbenchers were effectively put on trial for crimes against the state. The campaign resonated across the community.

Labor did its best to ignore the fuss. It hoped that, come the official ban on all electronic advertising by official parties during an election, no one would remember 'The Guilty Party'. Again, the ALP was out of luck. The ban was overturned by the High Court the following August. By this time, 'The Guilty Party' had already entered the political lexicon.

'I always thought their strategy of letting the Guilty Party be out there for 10 months, virtually with no response, was odd,' says Peter Poggioli. 'It became part of the language. I remember somebody in the *Sunday Age* writing about Carlton losing a game, and a reference being made to "The Guilty Party". It got into people's minds. And they wanted retribution.'

Ian Baker, who has famously described his role as a minister in the crumbling Labor government as akin to having 'a ringside seat at the last days of Pompeii' believes the Kirner government let Kennett off the hook. 'He was entitled to a bit of good luck after all the misfortune. But he got lucky because he got Kirner. Cain would have treated him with contempt. People didn't want to vote for Jeffrey. What they wanted to do was get rid of the Kirner government. Kennett has always had the intuition and the nerve and the verve to go on the offensive. But let's take the philosophers' position and say, well, what would have happened if he had confronted a good Labor government? Would he have won? I believe the answer is he would not have got his chance. They would have dumped him. People thought he was a joke.'

In contrast, David White is convinced Labor was never in a salvageable position, no matter whether Kennett performed well or badly. 'We knew we were in a lot of trouble and we were hoping – as you always do – that you can get a marginal improvement of your position, but we didn't expect we could win. We knew we were gone. I realised that basically once I had been informed about Tricontinental and Pyramid. I knew that we were on borrowed time.'

In mid-August 1992, Kirner announced a 50-day election campaign. She had deferred the poll until one of the last possible weekends available to her, Saturday 3 October. This was more in hope than expectation that some event – a 'Jeffism' perhaps – would come to Labor's rescue.

At Liberal Party headquarters at 104 Exhibition Street, electoral preparations were well advanced. Sitting in his cluttered third-floor office in the quaint 19th-century office building which serves as the nerve centre for the Victorian Liberals, the gruff, chain-smoking Petro Georgiou, who had taken over as state director in 1990, had been devising a strategy not just to win an election but to annihilate the government on a scale that would devastate Labor for a decade to come. The strategy had been set out clinically in a confidential internal document as far back as 12 July 1991. Its contents provide rare insight into the ruthless planning and execution of a landslide victory. A meeting of the party's administrative committee had agreed to do what the Liberals had never before attempted: to take the fight to the besieged ALP machine in electorates that Labor had held unchallenged throughout the 20th century.

'Our voting support is sufficiently strong to pursue a strategy of fighting hard in all Labor seats right down to Footscray,' the document said. 'We now have the capacity through telephone canvassing, direct mail, central planning and organisation to fight strong grassroots campaigns in areas where our local organisational structure is limited or non-existent. We will be fighting, in electorate terms, the most extensive campaign in Victoria's history. The object is to win strong Labor seats in which we have not previously mounted substantial campaigns; wipe out a future generation of Labor leaders; and win sufficient seats to establish a Liberal hegemony in Victoria for the next twelve years by making the ALP in the following election and the election after that expend its diminished resources on recapturing its "natural seats" before attacking our marginals. By making the ALP fight everywhere with an inferior organisation, we will be drawing the ALP back into defending their safe seats, thereby limiting their ability to concentre their strength in the marginals. By threatening key ministers in their seats, we will systematically undermine those ministers' capacity to focus on the central campaign . . . we will fight hard in every seat they hold.'

The document also set out the disciplines the party would impose on itself to ensure leaders and candidates stayed in step with the strong central direction of the strategy. Significantly, it insisted the party's schedule must operate to a strict 33-day timetable. No more, no less. This was aimed at reducing the one significant tactical advantage Kirner still had at her disposal: the timing and duration of the election campaign.

Labor had sought to postpone the inevitable for as long as possible. In June 1992, this strategy provoked an astonishing attack on the premier by one of the city's media institutions, the *Herald Sun*, which demanded that Kirner take her government to the polls forthwith. The newspaper devoted a full front-page editorial to this cause – an unprecedented intervention by the tabloid – that drew howls of protest from the ALP. The newspaper argued, however, that the state's precarious condition could not tolerate further delay by the premier. 'She must show real leadership and go to the people for judgement. A rule must be drawn across the accounts of the state, blocking any squandering of our remaining assets.'

When, ultimately, the election was called, Kirner chose a seven-week campaign, unusually lengthy and apparently conceived in the hope that Kennett would come under greater pressure over a longer period to explain his policies. Labor was still holding out hope that Kennett would implode, committing an act of indiscretion that might just give the ALP some momentum on which to build.

The ploy failed. When Kirner announced the campaign, the Liberals simply refused to engage in battle. The Opposition kicked off its campaign precisely at the moment it had decided more than 12 months earlier – not one day sooner. As the campaign document pointed out, 'We have systematically undermined our ability to fight effectively in the campaign period by firing off our bullets too early . . . between now and the election we should basically allow reality to mug the ALP while very strongly exploiting opportunities that are in the public domain and/or cannot be stored up.'

Peter Poggioli, who had left Brown's office in 1990 to take responsibility for marginal-seat campaigns at Liberal headquarters, explains: 'We had learned a lot from previous campaigns, where you would take your policy out early and they would pick the eyes out of it, take the good bits without any of the difficult bits. The campaign had been mapped out but Kirner stretched the campaign to seven weeks or eight weeks. Our campaign would start only 33 days out. Nothing happened for the first two weeks, to Labor's frustration. We put in place the campaign we already had. Every day was mapped out. Jeff fronted in the morning, we would do all the appropriate media analysis and he would do the things that were mapped out for him. He kept calm, did what was required.'

In Ted Baillieu's eyes the increased levels of professionalism between 1988 and 1992 proved crucial. 'I came onto the administrative committee with Kroger in 1987. We went through the '88 election. It was all conducted on the first floor at 104. Fifty or sixty people in that one room. It was chaotic, a case of hope over experience. It was well intentioned, but just didn't work: a shotgun, scattergun approach. I remember some of us going around to a storeroom at the Liberal Party, getting some old brochures from the 1985 campaign, chopping off the corners which identified the '85 election, and distributing those. There wasn't a discipline. It was an organisation that had gone into decay and wasn't sure how to get itself out. Everyone in the influential positions recognised it was in decay. Petro put the strategy together to which everybody else consented. It happened whether they consented or not, really. They liked what he was doing in the marginal seats.'

'We had a very good idea we were in for a big win in this state. Into 1991, we knew we had real chances in safe Labor seats. They looked good for a while, and the campaign was much more extensive than the ultimate result indicates. We were out looking at seats like Geelong North. Had Labor gone [to the polls] in 1991, we could have won a few more,' Poggioli confirms.

A week after Kirner announced the election, the Liberals held their state council. At the meeting, Kroger stood down after five years in the presidency and was succeeded by Baillieu. By this time, Georgiou and the strategists at Liberal headquarters had fine-tuned the strategy mapped out a year earlier to take the battle to safe Labor seats. The Liberals also resisted government pressure to unveil their policies. Ominously for Labor, the Liberals' qualitative research had produced an extraordinary finding: 'The Guilty Party campaign is not regarded as negative advertising by swinging voters. They regard it as "the truth". They want to be reminded.'

The Liberals also decided against unveiling new policies in a glitzy, showbiz environment. The party's profile had to be business-like and methodical. 'People want sobriety and real leadership and that's what they are going to get.' Doubtless, it was a message intended in part for Kennett. Against his nature but in accordance with his better judgement, he would be required to curb his exuberance and adopt a more subdued, low-key profile. Labor was to be given no leverage whatsoever to shift the dynamics.

'Frankly, he was still the person who had lost two elections, and hadn't put any runs on the board. I thought he performed exceptionally well as the front person. He stuck to his own message. Joan was absolutely frustrated because she had actually underestimated him. The Labor Party usually did. In their heart of hearts, they like to think he is a dickhead. But every day we had something newsworthy to say, and the advertising made sure it all fitted into the theme,' recalls Poggioli.

'I worked full-time during the campaign,' Baillieu remembers. 'We started every day at 7 a.m. meetings. Jeff was calm, organised. There was none of the 6-a.m.-at-the-railway-station stuff, throwing pamphlets at people who didn't want to know. This was the most sophisticated of Jeff's campaigns: it was well managed, coordinated, statesmanlike. "On-message" stuff. We achieved just what we were trying to do.'

Kennett, however, was snowed by his advisers on one occasion. 'We were preparing for the launch at La Trobe Uni. We were doing the preparation on a Saturday morning. I was doing events coordination. Jeff came out to check on the arrangements. We had to choose some music for his exit. We had discussed three alternatives. One was a version of "Waltzing Matilda". Another was "Do You Hear the People Sing?", which he used on his radio program. But the song we thought we should play was the third one, "Open for Business". It was an upbeat sort of thing . . . We knew Jeff would want to have the final say about something. If we played him our preferred song first, and made it our suggestion, he wouldn't want to use it. So I played "Waltzing Matilda" first, and he said, "No, we have to get something more upbeat." Somebody said, "Well, what about this one?" He said, "That's better, that's what we'll do." Afterwards, he said, "Yes, that worked well."'

The 1992 election saw the smallest amount of pork-barrelling and spending initiatives promised by either side of politics for a generation. Kennett relied largely on aspirational rhetoric, the politics of revivalism: 'It will be our responsibility and goal to regain the spirit of Victoria. We intend to rebuild a state in which the community is again proud to be Victorian, where this state is not the butt of jokes by other Australians but a community confident and excited by the future. We will create a foundation for the next 50 years of growth and development. We will create the base that will give to our children during the next 50 years the same opportunities, the same security and the same rewards that we, the postwar baby boomers, have enjoyed. That remains the great responsibility of our generation, the next government, and the next parliament.'

In the final fortnight of the campaign, Labor unveiled proposals for a $2 billion capital works program for schools and hospitals in a last-gasp bid to turn around public sentiment. In contrast, the Coalition said as little as possible about its budget plans. Throughout the campaign, senior Liberals were careful not to deny explicitly the claims that they planned significant public sector job-shedding, yet they were never pinned down on the precise numbers. They made the point repeatedly that they did not accept Labor's budget documents as reflecting the true nature of the worsening financial crisis. This distinction, they would later claim, entitled the Kennett government to go far beyond what anyone had anticipated in its budget cuts. All attempts to bait Kennett failed, although accusations by David White that Kennett was deceiving the electorate by not releasing his policies prompted a defamation writ against the Labor frontbencher.

At about 6 p.m. on election night, Kennett, accompanied by Felicity and his parents, arrived at the Southern Cross Hotel, opposite Liberal headquarters in Exhibition Street. The party hunkered down in a private suite on the hotel's 15th floor. At the other end of the corridor, there was a dinner for 100 influential Liberal

Party supporters. 'I was the host,' recalls Baillieu. 'I got there at six and went straight upstairs. I stood at the door of this function and greeted people. We had a couple of TVs going before we sat down for dinner. Kroger called the result at 7.20. Jeff was in his suite. He was being very calm about it all. We had grown up.'

For Ron Walker, who had backed Kennett for more than a decade through the many vicissitudes of Opposition, it was a shared sense of vindication. 'The electorate said, "We have seen the worst of this bloke, and he's not as bad as they said. He won't eat my children."'

In a ground-level ballroom, the rest of the party faithful had gathered to celebrate a historic victory. The media was waiting, too. The Liberals had won a 34-seat majority in the Legislative Assembly, the second-biggest landslide in the state's history. It had secured a two-to-one ascendancy in both houses. As Labor crept into the shadows to count its dead (five ministers lost their seats), Kennett emerged to claim victory. With Felicity at his side, he spoke for 10 minutes. He was measured, businesslike. There was no delirium, no rancour. He promised a 'new beginning' but warned that Victoria faced a daunting task of reconstruction.

'The time for fighting is over,' he proclaimed. 'What we clearly need now is four years of community commitment to restore the values, to restore the employment and to get our debt under control.'

Midway through his address, there was a slip of the tongue. He transposed the word 'victims' for 'Victorians' then laughed self-consciously. 'I guess in part that is what I meant.'

CHAPTER EIGHT

SHOCK OF THE NEW

'In Victoria, we are a fast people – we walk fast, ride fast, talk fast;
we sleep fast, eat fast, and drink very fast indeed; we make money fast
and spend it even faster still . . . He who would succeed in Victoria
must not let the dust settle beneath his feet.'

THE ARGUS, 1859

On 10 November 1992, an estimated 100 000 Victorians poured onto the streets of Melbourne in the biggest public demonstration since the Vietnam War. The target of the deafening protest peered through the window of his office at state parliament in Spring Street, less than 50 metres away, as demonstrators set fire to a cardboard effigy of the newly elected premier. The leader asked his staff whether he should go out to speak to the crowd. 'Don't be stupid,' his chief of staff, Alister Drysdale, told him bluntly. 'They won't listen to you.' Jeff Kennett had been elected to lead the state of Victoria only four weeks earlier. He had embarked on a blitzkrieg of reform that stunned his critics and brought on an upheaval the likes of which had not been seen in Victorian politics for 40 years.

The mass protest, one of three staged through the government's first year in office, had been called by Trades Hall secretary John Halfpenny and was backed by the Australian Council of Trade Unions. It was the labour movement's first fitful reaction to the shock of the new. This was a newly elected Liberal leader whom they had come to regard as a fool. Yet here, in the conservative state of Victoria, he was prescribing solutions to the state's financial embarrassments that would challenge the assumptions of more than two generations of electors about what to expect of government. The declared aim was to address Victoria's debt/interest spiral and rehabilitate a discredited state in the eyes of investors. In truth, it was a policy revolution.

Kennett's transition-to-power strategy was set in train the moment Labor conceded defeat. Indeed, it had begun on election night. The head of the premier's department, Dr Peter Kirby, had arrived at Kennett's suite in the Southern Cross Hotel shortly after 9.30 p.m. He brought with him the transitional documents prepared for the new government by senior public servants. The 'blue books' carried detailed briefings on the budget position, the government accounts, and the Treasury's costings of Coalition policy proposals. Kennett went into a room by himself to study the documents. Alan Stockdale, the new treasurer, joined him later. The books confirmed the awesome nature of the budget challenges they faced. Despite the raging celebrations downstairs, Kennett remembers feeling strangely subdued.

'I wasn't in any way euphoric,' he says. 'It would be true to say we were expecting to win, but I wasn't expecting a win of that size. I got the blue books. I had told Kirby I wanted the books the moment I had accepted victory. That wasn't very late. I remember sitting in the hotel room about 10 o'clock actually going through the blue books. There was no champagne. Didn't have a drink that night. We got the blue books, we sat down. I went home relatively early. Had half a dozen friends at home. Not political people, although maybe Rob Knowles was there. Got up early next morning and came in to have further meetings with the public servants. From that moment on, it was nose to the grindstone.'

Within days, in an emergency mini-budget, the new government embarked on a ruthless program of cost-cutting across the state bureaucracy – slashing the size of the state's public sector, closing and merging schools, cutting country rail services, withdrawing almost $400 million from the state's public health system and introducing an industrial relations reform agenda that provoked a withering backlash from the entire Labor movement. The program contained strong traces of Thatcherism, albeit on a smaller canvas. Kennett, for his part, insisted voters would understand and accept the need for cost-cutting. He now concedes he was also testing the limits of public tolerance to an unprecedented degree. 'It was all very severe. But it had to be done. It's like a splinter in the hand. You either pull it out straight away or you let it fester. We did what we did knowing the pain would be sharper but shorter. We had made the intellectual decision on how we would proceed well before the election. It wasn't an easy task for anyone but there was no alternative. I would argue we had spent all those years in Opposition preparing for this. We had been elected and we had to perform.'

The political adventurism in this strategy was typified by a $100 across-the-board impost on all households: a poll tax, in effect. The revenue gains were significant but not indispensable. Kennett and Stockdale reasoned that the action was a crucial signal to the community that nobody would be spared sacrifice. By the normal conventions of politics, this was risk-taking of a different order. In a community scarred by recession, haunted by unemployment and resentful of the taunts that the state was confronting inevitable structural decay, the mood was a mix of anger and anxiety. Yet the government explicitly imposed a penalty on each household, almost as though voters, not governments or bureaucracies, had been responsible for the deterioration of the state's economic health. With only a few exceptions made for cases of 'genuine hardship', every household in the state had to contribute, through a direct cash payment, to the plan for financial reconstruction.

No community interest group was to be left untouched. Some

of the constituencies that had enjoyed significant political leverage under the previous Labor government, particularly the public-sector trade union leadership, suddenly found the institutions that guaranteed their power base under siege, their government funding slashed. This was the first broadside in an inevitable ideological battle. Kennett and his senior colleagues were out to redefine the corporatist power relationships that had governed Victoria for much of the postwar era: big government, big business, big unions. As Stockdale had long argued, they reasoned that the only way of maintaining forward momentum was to launch the assault across as wide a front as possible. 'I had warned the party room that we were in for a lot of flak. We had decided to address all these issues at once. That was the best way to split the union movement, so they could not coalesce around any one issue,' Kennett confirms.

In its budget cuts and its unilateral stripping of a series of state-based industrial award entitlements, including the cancellation of holiday leave loadings for state employees, the government antagonised a third of Victoria's workforce. It was audacious risk-taking and, on that turbulent day in Melbourne, it seemed to have backfired dramatically.

Throughout the morning of that first demonstration, Kennett's fellow ministers and senior party officials called by his office to survey the spectacle of this massive backlash. Mounted police lined the steps of Parliament House. 'I looked out through the window at this crowd. They were screaming for my head, and every other part of my anatomy,' Kennett recalls. 'But it didn't worry us. We had to withstand it.'

In fact, there were genuine fears about security. Both Kennett and Stockdale had been receiving death threats. Several of Kennett's staffers wondered whether some of the more hot-headed protesters might try to invade the building. Although the organisers of the demonstration had set in place strict crowd-control procedures – knowing the fight for public opinion would begin

with the images captured on the television bulletins that night –
this was a vast and unruly body of the disenchanted and politically
dispossessed. Among them were those who had emerged for this
day of protest from an early start in the city's bars. The parliament
building was by no means impenetrable. It had been stormed by
students only two years earlier in protests over compulsory university tuition fees.

Out on the streets now was the combined might of the state's
trade union movement, grassroots members of the Australian
Labor Party, teachers, nurses, other public sector workers, and the
hard men from the construction industry unions. Even some
church activists had joined the rally. All felt threatened by the
government's agenda. Kennett's aspirations to prove himself a
'conviction politician' were about to be put to the test of popular
anxiety. Stockdale, as he gazed out the window of Kennett's office,
sought to downplay the scale of the revolt. In what constituted
a pep talk for those around him, the treasurer, with a measure of
bravado, observed, 'There might be 100 000 out there, but there
are 4.5 million Victorians who are not marching.'

The pressures on Kennett to retreat to a more cautious strategy
were immense during those early months of his premiership. Quite
apart from the widespread community anger, the Keating Labor
government in Canberra, under pressure from its trade union base,
passed overriding federal legislation to frustrate Kennett's attempts
to reform Victoria's workplace culture. This, in turn, created pressures within the Liberal Party nationally for the Kennett government to moderate its hardline agenda in order to give the Coalition
a better shot at the 1993 federal election. But Kennett would not
relent. The advice from Bolte had been explicit. 'Jeff, you just get
in there, and if it's right, you do it, mate.'

Those helter-skelter first months of government – 'the 100 days
that shook Victoria' – cast the mould for the Kennett style: bulldozing, in-your-face, unapologetic and way outside the comfort
zone of political convention. 'He didn't blink. It was inspired

leadership,' says Ted Baillieu. Says Drysdale, 'He stuck. If he hadn't, he would have been gone as premier.'

The philosophical underpinnings for Kennett's approach lay in the belief that Victoria would not be able to reverse its structural decline unless the government could reignite a more vigorous competitive ethos in the community: an enterprise culture. It was an attitude that carried echoes of the state's vibrant early history in the goldrush years. It also reflected Kennett's personally held view that government should be less intrusive, that it should set the conditions for private sector expansion and innovation without the encumbrance of high taxes and red tape. But when Kennett arrived in office, there were genuine and well-founded doubts about the extent to which this culture would be embraced by the wider community. Victorians had voted out of office an incompetent government, but had they given any meaningful endorsement to the alternative vision put forward by Kennett? Other than the general desire for a government with the strength and commitment to 'fix things', the answer was probably not.

Undeterred, Kennett declared Victoria 'open for business'. The government promptly set in train an eight-year timetable to reposition the state in a range of strategic industries – from food processing to high-tech manufacturing – capitalising on its strengths as a research base and trading hub, its skilled industrial workforce and its low-cost energy reserves. Yet as the Coalition began to work towards this vision, there were two mountainous speed humps standing in the path of its reform agenda. The first was cultural and historical: from the Depression years onwards, Victorians had become accustomed to the practice of governments and bureaucrats making decisions for them. The state had more local councils than any other. It had bigger and more powerful state-owned enterprises than elsewhere in the nation. A higher percentage of its workforce was on the public sector payroll than in either New South Wales or Queensland. If not a culture of dependence, there was in Victoria an attachment to the notion that governments and their agencies should play a paternalistic role across the full spectrum of economic and social activity.

This, in part, had contributed to the second major hurdle confronting the Coalition: Victoria had become a debt junkie. As far back as the Bolte years, the state had borrowed heavily to finance infrastructure: power stations, water reservoirs, railway rolling stock. Under the Cain and Kirner governments, the state's debt profile had ballooned as Labor borrowed to expand the apparatus of the state. Since the mid-1980s, the growth of the bureaucracy in Victoria had been at double the rate of other states. State expenditures had grown from $6 billion in 1981–82 to $14 billion in 1991–92. By 1992–93, the state was running a $2.2 billion budget deficit. Victoria's public sector net debt stood at $33 billion, and budget sector debt was over $16 billion.

Public finances were groaning under intolerable stresses. Net interest payments had climbed above 20 per cent of total revenue. The more the state's debt accumulated, the greater the proportion of revenue siphoned off to meet interest costs, the less money available to provide services. As Kennett put it bleakly, it was like a cancerous growth. Moreover, unlike the federal government, the states were severely restricted in their ability to raise revenue through taxation. After handing over income tax to Canberra during World War Two, the states had come to rely on a narrow, inefficient and distortionary tax base. They could levy a payroll tax – or a 'tax on jobs' as it was widely condemned; administer monopoly charges for gas and electricity; collect a range of stamp duties on bank transactions and property transfers; charge motor registration fees; and impose a land tax on the wealthiest householders. Finally, there were the so-called 'sin' taxes – franchise fees on tobacco and alcohol, and the government's share of the take from the gambling industries. The states' revenue base was then topped up by a significant one-fifth share of federal government revenue – distributed each year through the mechanism of the Premiers' Conference. But the states themselves had an extremely

limited capacity to extend their own tax base, given the constitutional constraints of not intruding on the Commonwealth's tax-
raising efforts.

There were also basic political impediments to raising the level
of existing taxes. Most of the state taxes fell directly on individual
households or small businesses, and hence were highly sensitive to
politicking and populism. Indeed, since the late 1980s the Labor
government in Victoria had borrowed funds to cover the blow-out
in spending rather than risk electoral disaffection by imposing
higher taxes and charges. In effect, it had simply deferred the ever-
spiralling cost to subsequent generations. As interest rates soared
in 1988, international credit agencies became increasingly wary
of the state's capacity to repay its debt. Soon Victoria – with a
downgraded credit rating – was paying a premium whenever and
wherever it borrowed. On every additional $100 million in debt,
it would be required to repay $1 million more each year in inter-
est than would the Commonwealth, or its rival states of New
South Wales and Queensland.

The Kennett government came to office facing what it believed
was the unprecedented risk of a state actually defaulting on its
debt. The financial crisis, and the imperative to tackle it quickly,
meant the Coalition had to rework much of the policy it had
brought to office. Ultimately, the Kennett government's answer to
Victoria's long-term structural debt would be to sell off the state's
gas and electricity industries in the biggest privatisation program
by any government in the nation. But this would be a lengthy and
complex process, involving more than $30 billion in assets. The
first and more urgent priority was to arrest the state's debt/interest
spiral by containing government spending, raising more taxes and
getting the budget back into balance.

There were no politically palatable solutions on offer – or at
least, none that had any prospect of lasting success. The government could begin an incremental process of budget repairs but
that would represent the public policy equivalent of a finger in the

dyke: the debt would continue to climb, albeit at a slower pace, and interest costs would creep ever higher. The other option was draconian. The government could launch an aggressive campaign of reform to tackle the financial crisis head on. It could slash spending, raise taxes and charges, reduce the public sector work-force and get the budget into surplus as quickly as possible, in order to contain the impact of interest costs.

Such a strategy would necessarily involve austerity measures the likes of which had not been seen in the prosperous postwar era. The burden would fall heaviest on government employees. Wages and salaries accounted for more than two-thirds of the state budget. It was a certain recipe for industrial confrontation. There would be strikes and disruption to industry. There would be rancour and dissent. There would be panic and uncertainty in the wider com-munity. No matter how necessary or unavoidable the spending cuts and tax increases, there was no way of judging the level of com-munity tolerance for such upheaval. How great was the appetite for change? Kennett felt he had no choice but to find out.

He had two factors working in his favour. The first was a wide-spread recognition in the electorate that Victoria was in a parlous condition. People were despairing that the state, once the nation's political and industrial powerhouse, had been condemned to a dwindling significance in the years ahead. In a climate of grudging acceptance that tough decisions would be necessary, Kennett set about demanding more of his electorate than any other premier in the country.

His second, immeasurable advantage was that people under-estimated his capacities and resolve. The miscalculation of his enemies was to assume that the Jeff Kennett who led the Liberals to power in 1992 was of the same freak-show variety ridiculed in the 1980s. Kennett's exercise of power would be measured against this low base of expectations, which gave him a good deal more latitude in the public mind than more orthodox politicians might reasonably expect.

Well before the election, Kennett's policy-makers had been putting plans into place. Leading accounting firms in the city had been asked to advise on strategies for reform to the public hospital system, the state education system, the water authorities and the public transport system. For months shadow ministers had been crunching the numbers with financial advisers from private industry, eager to ensure that, on coming to office, they would not be 'snowed' by bureaucrats keen to stifle the government's reform agenda with technical arguments about the financing or resource implications of policy proposals. The Coalition had done its homework. Kennett had already sounded out senior New South Wales bureaucrat Ken Baxter, a tough and astute administrator, to take over as the new head of Victoria's public service, a pivotal position given the breadth of public sector reform the government had in mind.

On election night, the premier-elect spoke at length to the outgoing head of the Department of Premier and Cabinet, Peter Kirby. 'He was wonderfully supportive; not politically, but professionally. He didn't want to go on, but he helped us manage the transition. Although he didn't necessarily want to leave the public service, he told me that if I felt I needed someone else he would not stand in the way. I had Ken Baxter down here already. I had been training with Ken for some weeks before.' Kennett had first approached Dick Humphreys, the head of the New South Wales public service and subsequently chief executive of the Australian Stock Exchange. When Humphreys declined, Kennett said, 'Well, if you have done your job properly, there should be a very good 2IC.' This was Baxter. 'I was able to get him down here to start a lot of preplanning,' Kennett explains.

Tall, lean and conservative in dress, Baxter comes across as almost donnish in demeanour. Yet he is street-smart and sometimes sharp-tongued, with an impatience towards humbug and posturing. He had spent almost 20 years as a senior public official in Canberra and Sydney, working initially in the Whitlam government. Baxter had heard on the grapevine about the collapse of budget discipline under

Labor in Victoria, but when he began more intensive inquiries he was appalled by what he found. 'Not only had the Kirner government mortgaged just about everything, the cabinet processes had unravelled,' he says. 'It was not unknown to have senior Commonwealth Treasury officials down in Melbourne, having to closely supervise anything that was done. They might not have been physically sitting in on meetings, or approving every cheque paid, but they were certainly taking a very close and active interest. It needs to be understood that Victoria was facing the equivalent of an IMF situation. Had it continued, or unless there was some miracle, the Commonwealth would have been forced to intervene directly, or there would have had to have been a massive increase in taxation. While we had not reached the stage where we could not pay wages, we were certainly getting very close to the stage where if we had experienced a number of retirements from the public service, we would have been pushing things uphill to meet the full superannuation entitlements.'

Kennett's first task after being sworn in as premier on the morning of 6 October was to clear out the top ranks of the bureaucracy. The Coalition had drawn up a hit list of Labor appointees. Not all were removed, but it became tantamount to a purge of the top ranks of public service advisers. 'We moved very quickly,' Kennett recalls. 'Pat McNamara [the National Party leader and deputy premier] and I interviewed all the permanent heads, one after another. We didn't beat around the bush. Those we didn't want we thanked very much, and told them we would not be requiring their services. We got rid of 11 before lunch.'

In fact, only five department secretaries were actually dismissed. Eight more were reassigned to other duties within government. But the message was out. The incoming government was working to a strategic plan, and was prepared to be ruthless in ensuring it was implemented.

The reshuffle of senior bureaucrats served as the precursor to an announcement that same afternoon of an unprecedented shake-up of the public service structure. The 22 existing departments were streamlined and amalgamated to emerge as 13 'mega-departments'. By week's end, the government had foreshadowed the repeal of the *Public Service Act 1974* and abolished the Public Service Board, the agency responsible for setting wages and conditions and for managing the cumbersome and elaborate process of determining promotions and job classifications. Corporate management principles were introduced, aimed at achieving greater efficiency and accountability. For the first time, departmental heads were given broad-ranging management prerogatives, including the right to 'hire and fire'. This ended the long tradition of the Victorian public service as a protected species, where promotion was dependent on length of service according to rigid and arcane formulas, and where security of tenure was virtually guaranteed irrespective of competence. The senior bureaucrats themselves were put on performance contracts similar in tone and style to those of private industry chief executive officers. They became subject to dismissal on four weeks' notice.

Three days later, on 9 October, the new government appointed an audit commission to trawl through the public accounts line by line. It would not present its final report until nine months later, but both Kennett and Stockdale knew they could not await the outcome before launching their assault on the financial crisis. Indeed, on 15 October Stockdale produced a Treasury update revealing that the state's budget deficit was running at more than $2 billion, not $1.35 billion as had been claimed by the Kirner government. This prepared the ground for the introduction of the Kennett government's emergency mini-budget less than a fortnight later. Here, Kennett and Stockdale forced their colleagues to undertake perhaps the most gruelling expenditure review process in the history of the state. 'We went through a collaborative exercise. The whole cabinet worked together,' Stockdale says. 'There was a strong understanding of the general approach we were going to take, but I was also known to have Jeffrey's personal authority.

No treasurer could have done the job without the leader's absolute, unqualified support. All heads of department were brought in and told what savings they would need to make. They were each asked to return with a detailed plan for spending cuts.'

An early casualty of this process was the head of the department of justice, Alan Neave. 'He didn't take it seriously,' says Stockdale. 'We had asked for their plan. He had delivered a plan, but said he did not think it was possible to achieve the savings target. He specified a few possible targets for cuts, but not much else.' Stockdale reported this to Kennett. Baxter then spoke to Neave to warn him formally.

'Justice, health and education were by tradition the departments that always said it couldn't be done, and they were able to get all the bleeding hearts out of the cupboards very quickly,' says Baxter. 'We wanted $40 million out of justice but what Neave was trying on, in my view, was to string it out long enough so we would get near the end of the financial year and nobody would be game to push it. There was no control at all over [senior law officers] who thought they had a bottomless pit of money to spend. I told him bluntly, "Look, you have to understand this – we don't have the dough. You need to take this very seriously." Ultimately, Kennett hauled him in. "Get your stuff and get out," he said. "Tell your deputy to come and see me."'

The appointment of Warren McCann as Neave's replacement as head of justice – the first non-lawyer ever to assume the role – sent a shudder through Melbourne's legal establishment, and not for the last time. The public service was also mortified by the spectacle of Neave's removal. Legal action was taken on his behalf. 'Down through the ranks, they didn't like what we were doing one bit,' recalls Stockdale. 'But some of the more senior bureaucrats were less hostile. They were relieved in a way to have a government which at least knew what it wanted. The ministers were totally driving the agenda. Normally, the bureaucracy has its own agenda and bowls things up to ministers. But the ministers were incredibly demanding, and drove the departments to implement our program.'

The imposition of 10 per cent savings across almost all departments over a two-year period was an awesome discipline. Grandiose plans for spending initiatives had to be recast or simply dumped; new capital works were out of the question; vision and ideology had to give way to the hard grind of finding ways to spend less money more effectively. As Rob Knowles, the junior health and aged care minister in the first Kennett cabinet, admits, 'For a lot of us, at the start, it meant having to fly by the seat of our pants.'

The introduction of casemix funding to the public hospital system was one such example of necessity being the mother of invention. The new funding formula meant hospital administrators could no longer rely on the old system of open-ended block grants, a guaranteed flow of funds regardless of how their hospital performed. Now, they could only increase their resource demands on the basis of fulfilling their required quota of surgical and medical services: in other words, payment for services rendered. If they overran their budgets, they had to show why. The effects were dramatic. In the human services portfolios, the productivity gains approached 30 per cent over the first four years.

Even within the cabinet, however, there remained strong reservations about the impact of the cost-cutting proposals. This manifested itself passionately in the debate within government over the fate of the state school system. Victorian taxpayers had been spending more on state education than their counterparts elsewhere in Australia. The state had the best-paid teachers and the smallest class sizes in the country. Student–teacher ratios were the lowest of any state, and Victoria had the lowest population per school (263 on average) despite being the most compact and high-density mainland state. There was a state school for every 1512 Victorians, against a national average of one school for every 2372 people. However, the cost of putting a student through school was $380 a year higher than in New South Wales, and $1700 a year higher than in Queensland. Moreover, Victoria's schools were open to students 11 days fewer per year than in New South Wales. Under Labor, spending on schools had increased an average 2 per cent in real terms over its decade in power. This was despite demographic trends showing an overall fall in the school-age population.

The reason for the education system's huge claim on resources was never seriously in dispute. As former ALP education minister Ian Cathie had confirmed publicly, Labor governments had become beholden to the lobbying pressure of the teacher unions and parents' organisations. The teacher unions were among the most powerful industrial forces in the state, and wielded enormous influence within the ALP and its branch membership. The 'education club', as it became known, had achieved the dominant position in the policy debate over all the key areas of philosophy, syllabus and re-sourcing. The system had become 'teacher-driven'. The unions had even negotiated industrial agreements guaranteeing that teaching periods would drop from 22 to 21 hours a week. In effect, less than half a teacher's working week would be devoted to direct instruction of students. Labor, enfeebled in its final months, had been unable to withstand the demands for perhaps the most generous 'sweetheart deal' for public employees in the state.

The Kennett government came to power knowing the teacher unions would constitute a formidable obstacle to any cost-cutting process. Under Labor, the unions had come to expect that any significant changes in working conditions, staff numbers or fund-ing for schools would be subject to their prior consent.

Don Hayward, a former senior executive with General Motors-Holden, had been made education minister. Silver-haired and amiable, Hayward had arrived late in politics. An avid supporter of Kennett, he was in his sixties by the time the Liberals came to government. A self-made man from the world of business, with an energetic interest in community organisations, he had succeeded in winning and retaining the marginal inner-city seat of Prahran, with its eclectic mix of yuppies, Housing Commission estates, trendy shopping strips and a lively arts community. Hayward's strategy aimed to introduce dramatic changes to the structure and culture of public education – the devolution of greater authority to school principals; the creation of salary incentives for teachers to encourage a breakaway from what the Liberals saw as a culture of sameness and mediocrity flowing from industrial agreements; and the opportunity for certain schools to specialise in fields of excellence. The aim was to escape the confines of a monolithic lowest common denominator' approach to state-funded education. But Hayward's plans involved medium-term targets, a phasing-in model that would allow time for adjustment. 'There is nothing confrontational in my make-up,' he had said prior to the election.

Yet in the very first budget meetings, it became apparent immediately that the education sector, as the second-biggest spending portfolio behind health, would have to tighten its belt along with the rest. Hayward had to find more than $150 million worth of savings in a year. Fifty-six schools were targeted for closure or amalgamation. These included the Ardoch-Windsor school for students from broken families and those trapped in the inner-city drug culture. Northland Secondary College, a school specialising in the problems of Aboriginal youth, was also targeted. Hayward was distraught. According to back-bench colleagues, he returned from one budget meeting visibly shaking.

When confronted with the scale of the cuts demanded of his department, especially the apparent death sentence on the Ardoch school catering to problem teenagers living in or near his own electorate of Prahran, Hayward's emotions got the better of him. Says Stockdale, 'Don Hayward fought to reduce the savings required of education. If there were tears, they were tears of frustration.'

'I don't remember him being in tears, but Don's a very volatile chap from time to time. He gets excited. It wasn't an easy task for anyone but there was no alternative. It was all very severe. But it had to be done,' adds Kennett. Despite Hayward's misgivings, the government persisted with its controversial closure of the Ardoch and Northland schools.

Although the police force had been quarantined from budget cuts, Kennett was not prepared to allow any other department to exempt itself from the rigours of finding and implementing budget savings. Along with the powerful education lobby mobilising its campaign of opposition, there would be public distress and alarm over the fate of local schools. But any concessions on the fate of schools could compromise the broader strategy. In describing how his cabinet was steeled for this process, Kennett slips into a lexicon that evokes the discipline of his army years. 'This is what we had been trained for. I would argue we had spent all those years in Opposition preparing for this. Certainly, this was true in the last 12 months before the election. While there was a lot of personal abuse and acrimony from sections of the public and the unions, it was just the start of the rebuilding process.'

On 29 October, two days after the new parliament had assembled, Stockdale delivered his mini-budget. It sent shock waves through the electorate. The budget provided for the loss of 15 000 public sector jobs (almost 5 per cent of the public payroll). It abolished a 17.5 per cent loading for holiday pay under state awards and imposed 10 per cent increases in gas, electricity and public transport charges. Motor registration fees were increased. There were cuts to country rail services. Although the state's health budget was left intact in the first year, it was earmarked for almost $400 million in cuts over two years.

The showpiece of the mini-budget – the ultimate virility test of a government determined to ensure that every Victorian was acutely aware of the sacrifices being demanded of them – was the $100 levy on each and every rateable property as a contribution towards restoring the budget to balance. The budgetary impact of this measure was relatively modest: $220 million in 1992–93. But it made it far more difficult for sectional interests to claim that they were somehow being singled out for unfair treatment.

Ken Baxter, who had worked at close quarters with various government leaders across the country, admits to being impressed by the instinctive political skills Kennett brought to the job. He says, 'Kennett had the capacity to put down on a piece of paper exactly where he wanted to be. It wasn't a political wish list; it was a forward-looking strategic plan. He impressed as a man who, despite very little formal education, was able to wrap his mind around incredibly complex policy issues and distil them into simple propositions. I had worked closely with Greiner [the former New South Wales premier], who was an extraordinarily good vertical thinker, but he couldn't always link the intellectual and political arguments. Kennett was lateral. He could see how to maximise opportunities by changing policy simultaneously. A classic example was when we were doing the reduction in the number of schools. This was a major series of closures, and the politics were going to be very difficult. There were enormous protests. I was woken up one morning by Rob Maclellan, who phoned me to ask whether I had heard the premier on radio that morning. I hadn't. "The premier has just announced that all the taxis in Melbourne are going to be pink."'

On arriving at Treasury Place, Baxter found Kennett barely able to contain a smirk on his face. 'I know, I know,' Jeff reassured him. 'But you realise what is happening today. Every taxi driver is on his mobile phone jamming the airwaves. None of them will want their taxis painted pink.' All that morning, the taxi issue dominated talkback radio. It had taken some of the heat out of school closures as the foremost issue of public debate.

'Now what we are going to do,' Kennett told Baxter later that day, 'is to call a meeting of all the taxi drivers out at Tullamarine. I will announce that the taxis will not be pink. They will all be yellow. The drivers will all wear uniforms. There will be an increase in fares as a quid pro quo, but we will get for that a very significant improvement in operating standards.'

Baxter was impressed by Kennett's guile: on a day when the government was fully expecting widespread public condemnation over a difficult policy decision on schools, the premier had managed to roll a second reform into the equation and achieve his desired result almost painlessly.

Yet the government still faced an arduous task in persuading the public sector workforce of the necessity of the government's actions. 'I went out with the heads from each department and we conducted a series of slide shows,' says Stockdale. 'We went out to see the teachers. On the change of shift, we addressed staff at the hospitals. We spoke to the police force, the departmental workforce. The presentation explained that interest payments were squeezing our capacity to deliver services, and forcing us to increase taxes. We communicated the strategy underlying the budget and we showed people why it mattered. In the end, our objective was to improve our capacity to deliver services.'

It was a battle for hearts and minds. Although the government invited a delegation from the Trades Hall Council to attend one of these briefings, the government knew the backlash from the union movement would be tempestuous. For not only had the government carved into public sector spending – threatening the jobs of union members – but it was also introducing workplace reforms that challenged the very concept of organised labour. On 18 October, Phil Gude, as Minister for Industry and Employment, had announced plans to replace the state's industrial tribunal with a new Employee Relations Commission. The government had also drawn up a radical employee relations bill, effectively providing for the scrapping of the state awards system. The state would legislate for minimum employment standards, including hourly pay rates, holiday and long-service entitlements, and sick pay. It would then set a 'use-by date' on state industrial awards, and employers and workers would be given the option of negotiating enterprise-based agreements or individual job contracts. The tenor of the legislation, however, appeared overly prescriptive, putting the onus on workers to 'opt in' to the awards system rather than 'opt out'. In fact, it invited workers to turn their backs on union membership. Compulsory unionism under the 'closed shop' would be declared illegal, strikes in vital service industries would be outlawed and, more dramatically, the notion of criminal sanctions for unauthorised industrial action, regarded as unthinkable within the labour movement since the 1960s, had been reintroduced. This was compounded by union anger over the government's overhaul of the state's financially strapped and heavily rorted workers' compensation scheme, to be replaced by a new model called WorkCover.

These changes put the Kennett government on a collision course with the Trades Hall Council in Victoria and the powerful Australian Council of Trade Unions (ACTU) nationally. With union membership declining across Australia, the ACTU spoke for less than two-fifths of the country's workforce. Even so, it remained a hugely influential ally of the federal Labor government, and had served as a career springboard for one Labor prime minister, Bob Hawke, as well as several federal frontbenchers. ACTU secretary Bill Kelty, a close confidant of prime minister Paul Keating, was not likely to stand idly by and watch the trade union movement's authority and influence be undermined by a state leader. In fact, Kennett's actions in Victoria appeared to give the union movement a shot of adrenaline. Gude did himself no favours when, in a throwaway line, he appeared to confess to drafting the radical industrial relations agenda over a bottle of whisky.

Despite such gaffes, Kennett and his senior colleagues were anticipating a sustained public campaign of opposition from the union movement. Indeed, they were half-hoping for it. Much like the execution of a military strategy, the Coalition's reform timetable was deliberately and heavily front-end loaded, almost as if the government actually went looking for fights. 'We moved on as broad a front as possible,' explains Stockdale. 'We tackled every issue at once. I actually thought the union movement would pick Work-Cover as the great issue to mobilise people around. I thought that was a good thing for us because, in the end, we were winning that

debate decisively. As it turned out, the union movement could not
coalesce around any one issue. We were retrenching some of the
teacher workforce, bringing in budget cuts right across the community and bringing in legislation in relation to WorkCover and
a whole lot of other things as well. In the end, the union movement
was not effective in handling any of these issues.'

With its two-to-one majority in both houses of parliament, the
government was able to pass all of its controversial legislation without hindrance. There were to be two further union-led rallies in
the city – albeit with each successive march attracting fewer
participants – and ugly clashes between police and protesters outside
the gates of Richmond Secondary College. The city's opinion elites
expressed apprehension about the potential for social unrest. Within
three months of handing down its first mini-budget, the Coalition
was plummeting in opinion polls. The sense of panic and alarm in
the electorate saw support for the government drop from 56 per cent
at the time of the election to 43 per cent by March 1993. Kennett
and his ministers feigned indifference. They could not afford to
admit any suggestion of a government having second thoughts about
its agenda. The merest hint of vulnerability would send the unions
and other hostile community groups into a frenzy of campaigning
to force the government to change its ways.

Then the federal politicians entered the fray. In the run-up to the
next national election the federal Coalition, under the leadership
of Dr John Hewson, had produced one of the most adventurous
and comprehensive packages of policy reform ever conceived in
Opposition. Initially, the 'Fightback!' agenda was well received by
the electorate. As a charter for change, it set up a striking contrast
with a dispirited Labor government, drained of authority by its
own internal tensions and the hard slog of defending the country's
bleak economic conditions. But by late 1992, prime minister Paul
Keating had rediscovered his streetfighting talents and was beginning to demolish Hewson's grand vision. Apart from proposals for
an all-embracing 15 per cent goods-and-services tax, the Coalition

package also provided for an overhaul of the welfare system and dramatic changes to the industrial relations system. The Kennett government's shock tactics in introducing its own radical labour market reforms provided Keating with additional ammunition to use against his opponents in Canberra. The federal Liberals were spooked. On 30 October John Howard, then the Coalition's industrial relations spokesman, flew to Melbourne for talks with Kennett. He urged his Victorian colleague to adopt a more measured approach in keeping with the broad outlines they had taken to voters in the election campaign. Kennett would not relent.

But if Howard was unable to convince Kennett to moderate his ways, Keating could use coercion. With an election looming, there were intense political pressures on the Labor government in Canberra to bring Kennett to heel, particularly over his rough handling of Labor's constituency in Victoria. Through the application of the Commonwealth's superior constitutional powers, Keating could do much to make life difficult for the Victorian premier.

On 2 November, Kennett and Stockdale flew to Canberra to meet Keating and the federal treasurer, John Dawkins. It was a cap-in-hand visit. Kennett says, 'Alan and I went up there, laid out in front of them what he had found, expressed our concern, and told them we wanted to go to the Loan Council to borrow so we could start reducing staff.'

The federal government had veto power over state borrowings – and Victoria needed $1.6 billion in initial loans to act on its mini-budget provision for large-scale redundancies in the public sector. At a time when national unemployment verged on 10 per cent and job insecurity was taking hold in the community, it was a hard-headed pitch to be putting to a federal government looking to shore up its own electoral support. The tense meeting took place close to midnight in Keating's Parliament House office. Perhaps surprisingly, the prime minister proceeded to give Kennett and Stockdale a lecture on fiscal rectitude. 'Get your house in order,' he told them. The Victorians were left with the distinct impression that there would be no Loan Council latitude given to the state unless it proved itself able to rein in its own purpose spending.

But the Keating government was in a compromising position. Unbeknown to the Coalition, Labor in Victoria had borrowed $1.26 billion without Federal Loan Council approval. The state's debt profile was in fact somewhat worse than Kennett and his colleagues had been led to believe. Revealing this news to Kennett and Stockdale, Keating and Dawkins were embarrassed. The tone of the meeting shifted. Says Kennett, 'They were very critical of what had happened in Victoria, both Cain and Kirner, but particularly Cain. They said they would do what they could to help us. They didn't put any extra cash in – they didn't actually do anything – but they allowed us to borrow that extra billion or so. That started the process of getting our finances under control. We developed a good relationship very quickly.'

Keating gave Kennett and his treasurer a confidential understanding that the Loan Council would sign off without demur on all the borrowings they'd inherited from the Labor years. It soon became clear, however, that for political purposes, they would have to be seen to beg for it. As Stockdale recalls, Keating and Dawkins 'would always have agreed to what we were proposing, but they wanted to make their point in front of the assembled multitude that they were bailing us out. We didn't want that image put around.'

The public posturing between the two governments intensified as the federal election approached. Keating was eager to fight on just about any issue other than the spectre of unemployment, which had risen above 11 per cent. The two treasurers, Stockdale and Dawkins, clashed heatedly on radio over the Loan Council affair. In a major defeat for Kennett's reform agenda, the federal government played its industrial relations trump card. It signalled that it would allow Victorian unions operating under state awards to protect their conditions by transferring their members to federal awards. This effectively cut Gude's labour reforms off at the knees.

Meanwhile, Labor strategists sought to capitalise on the uncertainty generated by the helter-skelter approach to reform in Victoria. ALP party officials spoke confidently of the 'Kennett factor' as a major plus for the Keating government as it sought to discredit Hewson's radical reform proposals. Much of this jousting was a sideshow to the central preoccupation of the 1993 federal election – Hewson's controversial proposals for a tax revolution, which failed to find voter support.

At the 4 March election, Labor was returned with an increased majority. In Victoria the ALP achieved a spectacular turnaround, reclaiming almost half the seats it had lost to the Liberals in 1990 and achieving a two-party preferred swing of 4.6 per cent. This was the biggest anti-Coalition swing of all the mainland states. The Victorian ALP rushed to proclaim the result a crushing repudiation of Kennett and all he stood for. 'There is no doubt there was a Kennett factor. Victorians have told us they do not like a divided society,' announced former premier Joan Kirner. 'Mr Kennett will now have to be more cooperative.' But Labor strategists conceded privately that by far the most potent force at work in the 1993 campaign had been their exploitation of community fears of a goods-and-services tax. The banner draped around Trades Hall on the eve of the federal poll said nothing of Kennett. Its message was short and snappy: 'No GST'. Nonetheless, Kennett's opponents looked eagerly for signs that the defeat of the Coalition federally would force the Coalition in Victoria to swallow its pride and adopt a more pragmatic approach to government.

Kennett did his best to feign ambivalence over the fact that his government's workplace reform agenda had been rendered virtually redundant by the Keating government's counterploy. The federal government held the whip hand on the issue constitutionally, leaving the Kennett government powerless to respond. The premier did, however, issue a warning to the trade unions: 'The obstruction of the industrial relations reforms is not as serious as many people would like, because it is forcing a lot of people into the federal award net. The fact that all these people are captured in that federal net will make it easier for a future government – be it Labor or conservative – to actually change the rules. There will be nowhere for those people to go.'

At the time, it seemed like the sour grapes of a politician who had been outmanoeuvred. Four years later, however, with the advent of the federal Coalition's *Workplace Relations Act 1996*, Kennett's remarks would prove prophetic.

Within a fortnight of the federal election result, those looking for any softening-up of the Kennett government believed they had concrete evidence. Alan Brown, as transport minister, succeeded in negotiating a deal with Victoria's notoriously militant public transport unions to accept reduced cuts of 6500 jobs, the introduction of automated ticketing machines, and a union-controlled timetable for the removal of train conductors and guards. Given the unions' capacity in the past to cause havoc within Labor governments, Brown's deal was widely portrayed as a significant victory for the path of negotiation rather than confrontation. Brown was hailed as 'the Minister for Getting Things Done', and his measured and consensual demeanour was spoken of approvingly by union leaders.

The truth was somewhat more complex. The transport unions were under no illusion about what would happen if they refused to cut a deal. Brown had threatened to close down the entire system. Given the government's conduct to date, the unions had no reason to doubt this would indeed happen. They knew Brown had to deliver budget savings. Rather than risk an indefinite lockout, the unions negotiated for a result which would satisfy Brown's bottom-line requirements while still maintaining significant union control of the public transport system. It was as close to a win-win outcome as any union achieved in the early years of the Kennett government. But was it a sign that the government was beginning to wilt under pressure?

Certainly, to the Victorian Labor Party, it seemed the momentum was finally beginning to edge back towards it, albeit at a pace measured in millimetres. Enthused by Labor's federal victory, the state ALP took the opportunity to attempt to recraft its image. On 22 March, Joan Kirner stood aside as leader to be replaced by her deputy, Jim Kennan, a polished and pragmatic politician from a legal background. The relaunch of the Opposition under a new-look leadership was aimed at building a platform from which it could sensibly plan its revival.

However, amid factional disharmony and the party's refusal to embrace a meaningful policy review, Kennan took almost no time at all to decide that he was not the man for a job that would require unusual levels of patience and commitment. The federal election victory had been a significant, if temporary, morale-booster to the ALP heartland, but nobody – least of all Kennan, a talented and experienced parliamentarian – was underestimating the challenge faced by the party in hauling itself back into the political contest. He stunned colleagues by announcing his resignation in June, after only 92 days as leader.

By now, the Victorian Labor leadership was attracting the scornful title of 'the worst job in Australian politics'. The party had to scramble quickly to salvage its credibility. State ALP president Greg Sword noted pointedly that it was also crucial for the party to 'confront the demons' of its past. Only by presenting a new face to the electorate – and promoting to prominence a younger breed of Labor MPs not tainted by the years in power – could the Opposition hope to persuade sceptical and unforgiving voters that the party had truly changed its ways. As Labor sought to leapfrog to a new generation of leadership, the person to emerge as the 'renaissance man' was 40-year-old John Brumby.

Although having served in federal parliament as a Labor MP, Brumby was the closest the state ALP had to a genuine cleanskin.

He had not served in the Cain or Kirner cabinets. He was not party to the mismanagement that had brought the ALP into such disrepute. Brumby's emergence as leader represented a chance to begin erasing the images of 'The Guilty Party'. As if to stress the importance of cutting links with the past, one of his first public statements was a seminal declaration on the party's behalf. 'We the Victorian ALP accept we made some mistakes, we accept we got a drubbing in the election, and we accept we have to produce policies that are focused on the future.'

There was no question Brumby could talk the talk, but his most formidable challenge would be to move beyond the rhetoric of repentance and persuade a party still clinging to the nostrums of the past to accept policy shifts that would allow it to present itself as a credible and forward-looking alternative.

Any suggestions the government was losing its nerve in the wake of the deal with the transport unions should have been dispelled when Stockdale handed down his April economic statement a month later. Far from relenting on its austerity program, the Coalition raised the heat and tempo. A second round of harsh spending cuts was announced. Departments were ordered to find extra savings totalling $731 million over two years, bringing the budget cutbacks to 9 per cent over the six months since October. Another 100 schools were listed for closure or merger. A further 19 000 public sector jobs were to go. Additional revenue-raising measures of $112 million were imposed on the state's taxpayers. It was the political equivalent of shock therapy.

The aim was to restore the state's budget to surplus by 1994–95. No postwar government in Australia had ever attempted such a dramatic turnaround over such a compressed time frame. At the same time, the Coalition chose to launch a fresh assault on the state's unfunded liabilities. Finance minister Ian Smith ventured into a political and legal minefield with plans to overhaul public sector superannuation schemes, which had threatened to become a significant long-term drain on the state's revenues.

It remained for the government to coerce and cajole a recession-fatigued electorate to accept that all this hardship and upheaval was necessary. While the rest of the nation appeared to be increasing in buoyancy after the economic slump of the early 1990s, Victorians were to remain on a strict diet of bread and water. Indeed, the ALP portrayed the Victorian strategy as a threat to the national economic recovery. Labor was not alone in its viewpoint. Columnist Geoffrey Barker, writing in the *Age,* argued that the Kennett government was confecting a crisis which did not exist. The state debt per capita was no higher than at the end of the Bolte era, wrote Barker, and interest payments constituting 14 per cent of all outlays could actually be considered modest. According to Barker, Kennett and Stockdale were jeopardising Victoria's tentative recovery, and had made a 'basic value judgement [that] the welfare of Victorians has less immediate priority than the judgement of financial markets. In this sense at least, they are straiteners and punishers.'

Given the climate of resentment and resistance, the political risks were immense. Every political convention strongly suggested that voters would make the Coalition pay dearly for imposing such privations when next given a chance to have their say. Such austerity measures were unheard-of in Australia. The very fact that Stockdale had to deliver a slide-show presentation explaining in detail to his own back bench the need for the second round of spending cuts and tax increases was an indication of the scale of the challenge the government had set itself. But Kennett remained insistent on toughing it out. His fellow Liberals, whether friend or foe, had little recourse but to join him for the wild ride. Even some of his most ardent internal critics, such as former upper-house Liberal Reg Macey, were impressed by his fortitude: 'I don't know anyone else who could have led the government in Victoria the way he did, and defended the tough decisions that had to be taken.'

Curiously, by the middle of 1993, after months of confusion and upheaval, a mysterious phenomenon began to take hold. In the middle of all the tumult and shouting, it appeared the electorate was beginning to come to terms with Kennett's resolute if unorthodox leadership style. A steady revival in both the government's popularity, and that of its leader, began to make itself felt. Doubtless, this was partly explained by the skittishness of the ALP in Victoria, which had embraced two new leaders in the space of a few months. But evidence that a majority of voters were actually locking in behind the government's strategy was becoming incontrovertible. By August, according to Newspoll, support for the Coalition was back to 53 per cent. For the first time, Jeff Kennett's approval rating was higher than at the time he was elected. Significantly, the percentage of voters expressing dissatisfaction with the way he was performing in the job fell below 50 per cent. Less than a year into office, Kennett was beginning to win the argument where it mattered most of all: out in the electorate. The mainstream community, having witnessed at first hand a new and highly adventurous approach to politics and policy-making, were signalling, at the very least, that they were open to persuasion that the Kennett style of leadership might just pay off.

By the end of 1993, Victoria was beginning to emerge from deep recession. Economic growth was patchy, but the government began to take heart from a stronger performance in exports, a small surge in vehicle registrations and retail turnover, and higher-than-average growth in job advertisements. Growth in gross state product had begun to skip ahead of national trends, albeit off a much lower base than in other states. The unemployment rate remained the second worst in the nation, well above 11 per cent, but the business investment climate was beginning gradually to improve.

Kennett and Stockdale had been infuriated, however, by the federal government's August budget, which signalled an increase in sales tax on manufactured goods, notably cars. With a heavy concentration of Australia's manufacturing industry based in Victoria, they saw the imposition of additional costs as an impediment to the industry's incipient resurgence. 'We have the beginnings of a recovery in Victoria,' fumed Stockdale. 'We cannot afford to have it flattened by a classic Labor budget which only adds to the cost of people investing and doing business . . . We cannot afford for Mr Dawkins to make it tougher than it already is.'

His attack reflected the Kennett government's frustration with its limited capacity to kick-start business growth in the state. For cabinet minister Rob Knowles, it was a classic quandary. 'You had to get the state's finances back into a sustainable position but, within that constraint, how did you actually get some economic development happening? We didn't want to operate like company receivers, where you're there just to wind up the business. The challenge was how to get some vibrancy back into the economy at the same time as fixing up the budget.'

In its early budgets, the Kennett government had made a concerted effort to lower business costs in the state – companies had been spared tax increases, and the reform of workers' compensation offered the medium-term prospect of lower insurance premiums for employers. But there seemed little else a cash-strapped state could do proactively to generate new investment. This was illustrated when the government announced its industry policy in September 1993. The financial incentives available to attract new business to the state came to only $10 million in the first year. It was modest to the point of verging on minuscule. In dollar terms, it was less than a third of what Canberra had paid in export bounties in the early 1990s to keep just one manufacturer, Eastman Kodak, in Melbourne.

Whatever the pressures to restore Victoria's standing as an industrial powerhouse, the Coalition had to live with the realities. The Cain government's disastrous experiments in venture capital funding had intensified dramatically the 'moral hazard' argument about states and their agencies attempting to pick winners. In addition, financial and constitutional constraints imposed severe limits on the capacity of any one state to make itself more seductive to outside investors. None of the states had the wherewithal to significantly outspend its rivals on industry incentives. And Victoria, facing its debt management and budget repair challenges, was probably the least able to play that game.

Confronting these obstacles, the Kennett government decided to promote the fast-tracking of project approvals and the removal of regulatory barriers by introducing a 'one-stop shop' process. This was potentially important to industries such as pharmaceuticals, where as many as 2000 separate licences could be necessary to operate one major plant. The government's industry policy also announced small, targeted assistance packages, such as the forgoing of payroll tax in the start-up phase, for those companies in the strategic industries the government had nominated as having significant growth potential. These included information technology, telecommunications, food processing, aerospace engineering, downstream minerals processing and scientific instruments. The long-distance aim was to reinvent Victoria as something of a Switzerland of the south – a small but sophisticated, high-quality producer. But for all the enthusiasm within the Kennett government about the state's industrial potential, it was an agenda on which the Coalition was compelled to hasten slowly.

Going into 1994, it seemed that Victoria's economic outlook would remain tied to the painful and painstaking task of getting the state's finances back under control. Yet Kennett knew that more – much more – would be needed to revive the state's shattered morale. Through the 1980s, Melbourne had decisively lost ground to Sydney as the nation's largest city, its international gateway and a thriving cultural and business hub. The negativity about Victoria was making it harder for the state to attract investment and was resulting in significant internal migration to the go-getter states to the north. The government had to find ways to overcome the 'psychological recession' and generate a sense of dynamism and optimism.

With all of this in mind, Jeff Kennett unveiled his agenda. A big agenda. One plank of his revitalist creed was a policy revolution that would change fundamentally the role and reach of government in the state.

CHAPTER NINE

REINVENTING GOVERNMENT

'We were doing something inimical to the
traditional model of government.'
ALAN STOCKDALE

Shortly after first being elected premier, Jeff Kennett paid a
visit to the health department. Health minister Marie Tehan
was overseas on official duties. Kennett, as was the case when any
of his senior ministers were away, had assumed for himself the
role of acting health minister. He walked out of an elevator onto
the 12th floor of the department's Collins Street headquarters and
strode up to the office of the director-general. Its official occu-
pant, Dr John Paterson, was attending a meeting on the other
side of town. With barely time for formalities, Kennett barked an
instruction, 'Get me some people up here. Two from each floor.'

'I'm sorry, Premier?' replied a bemused receptionist.

'Invite some people up here for a chat. And if you would organise some tea and coffee, please.'

Abandoning the usual protocols, Kennett opened a direct line of
communication with departmental staff – without the imprimatur,
and in the absence of, the department's chief executive officer. As
public servants drifted warily into the room, Jeff questioned a clerk

closely on what his job entailed and how things might be improved. The premier took notes. Thirty minutes later, the phone rang. It was the receptionist. 'Premier, Dr Paterson is able to join you now.' Kennett fended her off. 'No, we're OK. We'll be about another 30 minutes. He can have his office back then.'

As the new premier, Kennett sought to make clear from the start how the hierarchy would work under his hands-on leadership. He would take a personal interest in the running of each department. Senior public servants were there to do the bidding of cabinet, not that of the interest groups, client agencies or union officials in whichever field of administration they were operating. There were to be no rival power centres. It was a new structure – defined as a 'whole of government' approach – in which Jeff the premier was indisputably the boss.

Kennett's first public service chief, Ken Baxter, admits to being taken aback when he walked into the cabinet office only days into the new government's term to find the premier sitting at a desk and discussing the fine detail of cabinet processes with a relatively junior official. 'She happened to be the expert in the field in which he was interested,' says Baxter. 'It ran contrary to Westminster traditions to let him loose in departments like this. But I believe what emerged was the most mature set of relationships between elected politicians and the bureaucracy anywhere in Australia. Once I reassured people, and once Kennett had demonstrated by his own behaviour that there would be no recriminations when people disagreed with him, it became a very valuable exchange of ideas.'

Public sector management reform was the cornerstone of the Kennett agenda. It was the essence of his 'small government' philosophy. The aim was to produce a leaner, more efficient and more flexible bureaucracy, and to either sell or contract out to the private sector those functions that were viable as commercial enterprises. The transfer of economic activity from the public to the private sector was the signature issue for the Kennett government. It accorded with its pledge to revive an 'enterprise culture' in the state, and with its belief that governments should 'steer, not row'. In other words, politicians should decide what services were to be provided and how, but invite private industry to step in actually to carry out the operational tasks that had traditionally fallen within the ambit of the public sector. By 1992, the commercialisation of government enterprises was in fashion across Australia. But few, if any, governments moved as quickly, or across as broad a front, in implementing fully fledged privatisation as did Kennett's.

On coming to office, one of Kennett's first tasks was to see for himself whether the extent of bureaucratic 'featherbedding' in Victoria was myth or reality. Along with Baxter and his senior adviser Alister Drysdale, he strolled unannounced into the offices of the planning department at 2 Treasury Place. As Baxter recalls, 'We walked into this mausoleum and here were all these guys sitting in an open-plan office. The premier strolled up to one of them and went to shake his hand. He was obviously startled but Kennett sat down with him and asked him what he actually did. "Premier, do you really want me to tell you what I do?" "That's why I'm asking," Kennett said. So the guy says, "Well, I'll tell you. Sweet fuck-all. I don't have a real job. When plans for new schools come to us from the Department of Education, I represent the Department of Planning in the design of the gardens, to make sure shrubs and trees are planted in the right place, and where paths are laid." The premier said, "You can't be serious." The guy said, "Well, there's no relation between what I say and what actually happens. The principals and the parents' and teacher's associations really decide these things. I've asked for a redundancy but they turned me down."'

That afternoon, Kennett phoned his planning minister, Rob Maclellan, and his education minister, Don Hayward. Maclellan, in particular, was appalled that Kennett would take it upon himself to interview public servants in another minister's department. But Kennett was insistent. 'Look there must be a lot of people like this, doing non-jobs. It can't go on.'

According to Baxter, word passed around the bureaucracy very quickly. As public service chief, he was invited by a fellow official to try his hand at applying for a transfer of his New South Wales driver's licence at the motor registry branch in Lygon Street. He stood in a queue for half an hour. He then watched his paperwork processed by no less than eight pairs of hands before his new licence was authorised. Later, he sat down with the bureaucrat who had alerted him to the problems. 'We have seven people doing the job of one, but they've been told they can't have redundancies,' the official complained. 'These people know they don't have real jobs, and that they're just shuffling paper. They are completely demoralised.'

Kennett's experiences, combined with Baxter's feedback and Victoria's budget woes, steeled the premier's resolve to pare back the state's bureaucracy and introduce private enterprise management principles. In total, 50 000 workers were removed from the public payroll in the government's first three years. Despite fierce institutional resistance, the number of government departments was slashed, and the Employee Relations Act and Public Sector Management Act were rushed through parliament. A cumbersome system of 120 different pay and grading structures was replaced by five broad bands, and performance-based contracts were introduced, initially at the level of the senior executive service. The government abolished the bureaucracy's complex system of internal appeals, under which individual public servants had been able to lodge complaints or grievances over issues of discipline or their rate of promotion as measured against their peers.

The emasculation of the public sector's privileged status infuriated the union movement, but their protests went largely unheard. Kennett effectively deflected their outcry by reminding the community how the Cain government had unravelled when it surrendered to the demands of the public sector lobby. Union leaders, fairly or not, found themselves lumped in with the Guilty Party, and unable to gain traction in their efforts to mobilise a campaign of public opposition. Indeed, to add insult to injury, the Coalition announced an end to arrangements under which government departments collected fees on behalf of unions through direct debits from workers' pay packets. Moreover, the government began contracting out to private companies myriad functions formerly performed by public servants: school and hospital cleaning, computer processing, catering.

Meanwhile, the government took structural reform a step further. It introduced a new bureaucratic superstructure that would become known as the 'Black Cabinet'. The Kennett model effectively cast the 18 ministers serving in cabinet as a board of directors. Alongside this, more or less as an executive management team, was the so-called State Coordination and Management Council. This was made up of Baxter, who as Kennett's senior bureaucrat served as chairman, all of his fellow department secretaries, the Public Service Commissioner and the Chief Commissioner of Police.

The principle behind this structure was to entrench among public service heads a 'whole of government' approach to the policy challenges facing the state, and to promote a sense of teamwork and shared purpose. In reality, it also enabled the premier to exert unprecedented authority across the full range of government functions. He could hire and fire permanent heads and, through the council, they reported directly to him on a weekly basis. Moreover, Kennett's fellow ministers were not briefed on the details of the performance contracts negotiated between the premier and department heads.

Curiously, the 'Black Cabinet' never figured prominently in public discussion, despite its mysterious status as an inner sanctum of senior ministers and bureaucrats. It became one of the defining structures of the Kennett government, in which there was never the slightest doubt about who, ultimately, was in control. The public sector unions remained enduring critics, claiming the new structures were unaccountable and secretive. 'Kennett will keep the rhetoric that this is a Westminster system of government, but it's not,' said Community and Public Sector Union secretary

Karen Batt. The former premier, John Cain, joined in the criticism, writing in his memoirs, 'Good government requires a robust public service that will give brave and fearless advice. A public service tenured by contracts that enable dismissal on four weeks' notice will not meet this requirement. The Kennett government line on the public service is arguably its biggest single long-term blunder.'

Ken Baxter, who worked under three prime ministers and four state premiers in his public service career, disagrees vehemently. In fact, he argues, the reverse is true. The whole-of-government approach ensured that cabinet's achievements and objectives were conveyed accurately and comprehensively throughout the government and bureaucracy. He says, 'The process was in disarray under Joan Kirner, partly through sheer incompetence. Kennett brought a return to the proper scheduling of cabinet submissions and considered intellectual input from both civil servants and the external community. He was also quite happy to get on the phone to academia or the business sector to get their opinions on policy issues when they were coming up. Each Thursday morning, before he went down to do his radio commitment, he would go through the submissions. He would work through the arguments in each of them. He was absolutely scrupulous about this. Contrary to his reputation, he had a capacity to step back from his own personal views to assess them on the merits of the argument.

'Cabinet sat on time, at 8.30 a.m. each Monday, and would run for four hours. Kennett was insistent it should not get bogged down in trivia. Where ministers could deal with an issue as an administrative matter, he would speak to the minister and ask, "Does this really need to go to cabinet? What's the major policy issue? Or are you shunting your ministerial responsibilities onto cabinet instead of being able to carry the can?" He eliminated a lot of the trivia. Then Rosemary Varty [the Coalition's cabinet secretary] and I would collate the minutes of the debate, prepare a note on the formal decisions and Kennett would sign off on these.

There was then a detailed reporting back to ministers and departments. It created a sense of certainty. All this had collapsed under Kirner, where there were often as many interpretations of cabinet decisions as there were ministers sitting around the table.'

According to senior ministers and bureaucrats who worked with Kennett, the 'one-man band' accusation is not sustainable. Likewise, they reject claims that the premier sought to politicise the bureaucracy. 'This is absolute bullshit,' says Baxter. 'It was put around by people with absolutely no knowledge of how things worked. I didn't come down here as some sort of apparatchik. In my experience, the involvement of politics in bureaucratic appointments was nowhere near what has happened at the Commonwealth level and in some of the other states.'

For instance, Baxter points to the appointment of Meredith Sussex as Kennett's head of the cabinet office. She was appointed despite having been an active member of the ALP at university. When it first became known she was being considered for one of the most sensitive jobs in government, two ministers went to the premier to issue a caution: 'Why are we appointing this woman?' Kennett called in Baxter. 'I would like to talk to her. If she stands up on merit, we will go ahead with the appointment.' Sussex went to the premier's office. Later that day, she was told she had the job. Kennett issued one proviso. 'Just don't let your politics interfere with your advice.'

Kennett's choice of public service chiefs through his seven years in office appeared equally apolitical. All three had close links to the ALP early in their careers. Ken Baxter, of course, had worked for the Whitlam and Wran governments but, as was the case with most professional bureaucrats, had proved himself able to serve under governments of either flavour. His successor, Elizabeth Proust, had worked as a senior adviser to Cain, and had even been credited with having coined the 'bull in a china shop' description of Kennett as Opposition leader. Born in the Labor heartland of Balmain, in inner Sydney, she once described her politics as 'Left-leaning

Catholic'. Kennett's third choice was just as controversial: Bill Scales, the former chairman of the Industry Commission, Canberra's chief structural policy adviser. Born in Footscray, in Melbourne's inner west, Scales left school at 14 to become a fitter and turner, then trained at nights for an economics degree at Monash University. After working his way up to a senior role in manufacturing, he was recruited by the Hawke Labor government to chair the Automotive Industry Authority, and was for a time a member of the ALP.

In his Industry Commission role, Scales gained a reputation as a fire-breathing reformist, leading the charge for further tariff reduction in the motor vehicle and textiles industries. Even Kennett blanched at his recommendations, warning that the likely impact on Victorian industry was 'almost criminal'. But Scales believed rationalisation of inefficient industry was crucial to Victoria's economic performance, and to its image among investors. The state had for too long endured a reputation as sluggish, slow-moving and inward-looking, when in fact it had just as many successful exporters as anywhere else in Australia, and perhaps the strongest high-tech base.

According to Scales, improving productivity was the key to Victoria's future success and prosperity. This applied just as much to government departments as to the private sector. There had to be greater accountability. Scales had signalled his brusque, no-nonsense approach as Industry Commission chief. 'We know that governments spend around $6000 per year to educate a secondary school student and $4000 for a primary school student. But we don't know, for example, whether there has been any improvement in the learning outcomes achieved by students in some states. We have no robust way of comparing the performance of education systems. We have no robust indication about the level of unplanned readmissions to surgery across our public hospitals. For most services, we don't know the amount of capital inputs used . . . it points to a lack of emphasis by governments about the performance of importance services to people. We are talking about a fifth of the economy here.'

The common thread in these appointments was that all three public service heads were tough administrators, prepared to push out the horizons of policy reform – to be 'first over the barbed-wire fence', as Scales put it – and unlikely to meekly accept commands from on high. As Kennett said of Scales, 'I wanted an individual at my side who was going to challenge me intellectually and give me fresh advice and fresh ideas. From time to time, Bill and I may disagree. But I wanted someone to challenge me from a policy perspective.'

Contrary to popular perceptions, those within the upper echelons of the government came to understand the decision-making and testing of ideas as a highly sophisticated process. Baxter rates the Kennett government, managerially, as the best he has seen in public administration.

When Baxter resigned to return to Sydney, the premier opened discussions with the other chief executives on the State Coordination and Management Council as to who his successor should be. 'Can you imagine that happening in any other bureaucracy or, for that matter, in any major company?' remarks Baxter. 'In my view, the fact it could be discussed openly around the table reflected the nature of the relationship. It wasn't sycophantic at all. Chief executives would regularly disagree with the premier, and there was never any hesitation in doing so. He would be more cranky if people began telling him what they thought he wanted to hear. He looked askance at the Sir Humphrey Applebys of this world.'

With its remake of the state's bureaucracy set in train by the end of its first year in office, the Kennett government turned to a much broader and potentially riskier battlefield. In April 1993, Kennett introduced the City of Greater Geelong Bill into parliament. The legislation created a 'supercouncil' by amalgamating eight councils and shires in the surrounds of the state's second-largest city. This was to be the precursor for a dramatic redrafting of the municipal map of Victoria.

Within two years, the number of local councils would be slashed from 210 to 78. Names that had been part of municipal life for a century disappeared. The cities of Port Melbourne, South Melbourne and St Kilda became the City of Port Phillip; the cities of Kew and Camberwell became Boroondara; the cities of Richmond, Collingwood and Fitzroy became Yarra. It was a revolution within the third tier of government, casting aside many of the century-old traditions of town hall politics in the state. Local fiefdoms and community power bases within the suburbs of Melbourne, and in the towns of rural and regional Victoria, were abolished overnight. Unelected commissioners were appointed to oversee the restructuring process. Much to their chagrin, former councillors were deemed ineligible to accept these appointments.

The government came under heavy criticism for having not spelt out the scope of its plans during the election campaign. It was also accused of trampling democracy at its most basic, grass-roots level. But just as it had restructured its own departments to operate according to business principles, so the Kennett government was insistent that the local government sector, with control over revenues of more than $3 billion, needed a shake-up. The boundaries for local government had been drawn in the nineteenth century, when much of the state's population lived outside Melbourne. There were no less than 120 rural shires. Yet by the 1990s, only two of these had a population of more than 10 000. There were a further 35 nonmetropolitan cities and boroughs, of which only Ballarat, Bendigo and Geelong had more than 25 000 ratepayers. In Melbourne itself, there were 55 local councils. The costs of maintaining this proliferation of government at the local level were formidable. In some of the smaller municipalities, administration expenses were as much as 50 per cent of total rate revenue. Local government in Victoria spent on aggregate 23 per cent above the levels of other states, and its citizens were paying 12 per cent more in rates, fees and fines.

The government sought a 20 per cent reduction in the cost of local government to the community. In August 1993 the Local Government Board was established, with a former mayor of Prahran (and a future Liberal frontbencher), Leonie Burke, as chair. In its interim report the following year, the Board recommended that 19 inner-Melbourne councils should be merged into nine.

Where the government did give councils new responsibility was in extending the contentious principle of competitive tendering within their bailiwicks. Within three years, 50 per cent of all service contracts were opened to compulsory competitive tendering. Again, it meant a loss of local government jobs, as private contractors swooped on the chance to pick up maintenance work, the tending of parks and gardens, street-sweeping and garbage collection. Especially in rural communities, where council work had been seen as 'jobs for life', this policy caused ongoing rancour and resentment. Councils were also required to produce business plans, customer satisfaction surveys and performance measurement data, in order that the state could keep their operations under detailed scrutiny. Rate caps were also imposed – a further constraint on their financial autonomy.

In March 1995, two years after the initial appointment of non-elected commissioners, the first municipalities went to the polls. But as democracy was slowly restored at the local level, the government entered a state of undeclared war with several of the newly elected councils, which seemed eager to recreate the status quo – the good old days of local government. The conflict typically arose from tensions between elected councillors and a council's executive management, which under amendments to local government legislation had been given far greater powers without requiring the imprimatur of a council vote.

In a league of its own was the City of Melbourne. Derided as 'Clown Hall' for more than 20 years, the seat of civic government in the state's capital had been in chronic upheaval. Council meetings were infamous for their factional warring, and elections for the lord mayoralty descended routinely into farce. Those who paid the lion's share of the rates – the big retailers, commercial offices, restaurateurs and boutique shopkeepers of the CBD – complained wearily of their interests being overlooked by council majorities that were often dominated by residents' action groups and party political activists from the inner suburbs. The Hamer government had suspended the city council's operations for a time. So did Kennett.

Ironically – given the criticisms of Kennett as being overly Melbourne-centric – groundwork for the City of Melbourne's revival was laid by his minister for local government, Roger Hallam, a National Party minister from Hamilton in the western district. Hallam told Kennett that the City of Melbourne deserved a more elevated status in the affairs of the state. 'This is our capital city. Right? It's our window to the world, it's our trade hub. We should not only have it up there as a source of pride for the local residents, but it should be recognised as the capital by those who live in Bairnsdale and Mildura. Why does our capital city not include all the major assets? Why do we give our railhead to the City of Footscray? Why do we give our docks to the City of Port Melbourne? Why doesn't the city include both banks of the Yarra, the arts precinct, Optus Oval?' Hallam's notion of extending the boundaries of the City of Melbourne to incorporate the full gamut of attractions and key infrastructure within the city and its surrounds was something approaching heresy within the Liberal Party. Only four years earlier, the Liberals had campaigned to circumscribe the powers of an incompetent and unpopular city administration by shrinking its boundaries even further. Yet here was Hallam proposing not only to maintain the existing ambit of the Melbourne City Council, but to extend its empire, drawing in the river, the port and the university precinct and 'knowledge centres' of medical and biotechnology research. Kennett was sceptical.

But the premier did agree to let Hallam try his idea out on 'the leadership group'. This was a common stratagem of Kennett's. In advance of controversial proposals coming before cabinet, he would test them out with senior office-holders of the Liberal and National parties in both the Legislative Assembly and the upper house. It meant, in effect, that Kennett and his most senior colleagues maintained political oversight – and collective responsibility – when major policy issues came before cabinet. It also translated into extraordinary cabinet discipline. The first cabinet leak did not occur until the government's seventh year. And rarely were ministers caught talking across each other in the policy debate.

Hallam immediately sounded out Pat McNamara, Phil Gude and major projects minister Mark Birrell. Kennett sat back and watched. The reaction was positive. But the premier remained reluctant to submit the proposal to cabinet: 'Let me take it to my round table first.' He raised the concept at one of his fortnightly breakfast meetings with the city's business elite and other influential figures, including the then vice-chancellor of Melbourne University, Dr David Penington. Almost immediately afterwards, Kennett phoned Hallam. 'I tried out your bloody idea. And you know what? They loved it. We will take it to cabinet, but on one condition. I want to include Albert Park as well.'

Hallam was mystified. How did this cluster of recreational ovals and rundown grandstands on the edge of Albert Park Lake in South Melbourne fit into the category of a major infrastructure asset? It was used mainly by joggers and dog-walkers. 'What do you want Albert Park for?' Kennett's attempted addition to the plan was ruled out before the submission reached cabinet.

Unbeknown to Kennett's colleagues, the premier was on the verge of signing a deal to bring the Formula One Grand Prix back to Melbourne. It was a tightly guarded secret, but Albert Park loomed large on Kennett's private agenda. At the time, however, he made light of his disappointment at the park's exclusion from the vision for a greater City of Melbourne. He and Hallam jumped in a car and drove around the city, mapping in their minds the revised municipal boundaries of a new and more expansive city which, for the first time in more than 150 years, would take the logical step of bringing both banks of the Yarra under one administration.

'I believe that helped generate many of the developments along the river,' reflects Hallam proudly. 'Of all the things done in my patch, that's possibly the one that is going to have the longest-term effect.'

Yet if there was any single policy agenda undertaken by the Kennett government that challenged the basic shape of government in Australia, it was the process of privatisation. Putting Victoria at the heart of an intense and often passionate national debate, Kennett's government accelerated the trend, as elsewhere in the advanced economies, away from the notion of 'big government' towards what neo-liberals would call a 'shareholder economy'. Between 1995 and 1998, $29 billion worth of government assets in the gas and electricity industries alone were sold to private investors.

The state's two great monopolies, the State Electricity Commission (SEC) and the Gas & Fuel Corporation, were each split into competing businesses, right down the chain of generation, distribution and retailing. Of the 16 separate assets sold, 13 were bought by foreign energy companies, the bulk of them US-based. The 11 electricity businesses sold for $23.2 billion, and the five major gas businesses for almost $6 billion. The proceeds helped reduce state debt to only $6 billion by 1999. Proponents of the sales would boast that the successes in Victoria served as a prototype for the privatisation models adopted by the World Bank and 15 American states.

The economic imperative driving the privatisation push in Australia was threefold: faced with a dwindling revenue base into the 1990s, governments across the nation confronted growing pressures to either cut back their own expenditures and trim the range and level of services they provided, to look for new and alternative income-earning possibilities (which produced some hair-raising results under Labor governments in Victoria, Western Australia and South Australia) or to borrow to fund their operations. Inevitably, as part of this debate, and because the experiments in state entrepreneurialism in the 1980s had proved to be dismal embarrassments, the efficiency of the public sector came under much closer scrutiny. Were government agencies doing what they did as well as they should, and with value for money for taxpayers? And, even if they were, how could future state governments, without the extensive revenue-raising capacities of Canberra, maintain the income necessary to service borrowings for major capital works and investment in some of the essential industries in which they were operating?

Australia was in the midst of a 20-year process of restructuring its industry base, by diversifying its exports beyond the traditional reliance on commodities, and by setting out to establish world-class service industries and high-tech manufacturing. In an ever more competitive global market, the demands on government to provide the infrastructure for this new growth would be onerous. Would the community be better off rationalising the range of government activity and ceding to the private sector the responsibility – and risk – of moving into some of the industries traditionally owned and operated by the state? By dismantling the state monopolies, creating contestable markets and leaving it to commercial operators to supply consumer needs, governments could aim to ensure that key services were delivered more competitively, without the public sector carrying the burden of attracting professional expertise, paying wages and overheads, and maintaining the ongoing investment necessary to modernise plant and equipment. The proceeds from the sale of major assets could help reduce government debt. Moreover, the removal of some of these industries from the public sector would serve to limit the distorting effect of pressure-group politics on commercial decision-making in areas such as pricing, the extent of subsidies (or what bureaucrats describe quaintly as 'noncommercial obligations') and decisions on what investments should be made, and where.

A fundamental criticism of government-owned enterprises was that they operated according to conflicting objectives, in which the issue of cost minimisation – to both the taxpayer and the consumer – was often relegated to a minor consideration. Prey to the special pleadings of parish-pump politicians, the union movement and other lobby groups, the state-owned businesses – with their tangle of cross-subsidies and their propensity to featherbedding – were seen as a hindrance to the Kennett government's objective of establishing a more efficient and world-competitive industrial base in the state.

One obvious consequence of the state vacating important areas of economic activity would be a reduced public sector workforce – or smaller government. Not surprisingly, this was anathema to many social democrats, and to the trade union establishment. The battle lines had been drawn in the 1980s. The Evatt Foundation, a think tank associated with the ALP, had captured the essence of the critique of the sale of public assets. 'The philosophy of privatisation ignores the positive role and methods of the public sector in combating social inequality and creating otherwise lost economic and social opportunities. In reality, the rhetoric of privatisation often functions as a blunt ideological instrument wielded by those not fully versed in the subtleties and complexities of government.' However, the new Victorian Treasurer, Alan Stockdale, had in his arsenal a ready-made and compelling rationale for his privatisation agenda: the need to wind back the state's crippling debt burden. Without apology, he exploited this ruthlessly, at the expense of the Cain and Kirner governments.

While the need to reduce Victoria's debt created a valuable climate of urgency within which to push the privatisation program forward, debt reduction was never the government's overriding aim. Privatisation was seen as essential for future economic efficiency in the state. The first statutory authorities targeted for sale were the Totalizator Agency Board – the highly lucrative state betting shop set up by the Bolte government 30 years earlier in a bid to eliminate illegal bookmaking – and the Grain Elevators Board, one of the great bureaucratic fiefdoms of rural Victoria. Then, in 1995, the government launched the major phase of its program with the

In their footsteps: Kennett's predecessors as Victorian premier were (from left) Sir Rupert Hamer (Liberal, 1972–81), Lindsay Thompson (Liberal, 1981–82), Joan Kirner (Labor, 1990–92) and John Cain (Labor, 1982–90).

Victory at last. Kennett triumphs in 1992 at his third attempt to lead the Liberals into power.

Hired gun. The street-smart and experienced Ken Baxter came to Melbourne from senior government duties in Canberra and Sydney to head up the public service under Jeff Kennett's premiership.

The double act. Treasurer Alan Stockdale lambasts his Labor opponents in the Legislative Assembly chamber while the premier looks on approvingly.

The 100 days that shook Victoria. In November 1992, the biggest protest march since Vietnam hits the streets of Melbourne, its participants burning effigies of Jeff Kennett.

In a moment of informality, the premier points out a thing or two to Labor leader John Brumby.

In the driver's seat. Prominent Melbourne businessman and networker Ron Walker takes the premier on a grand tour of the Phillip Island motorcycle grand prix.

On the Move: a motto for a mindset.

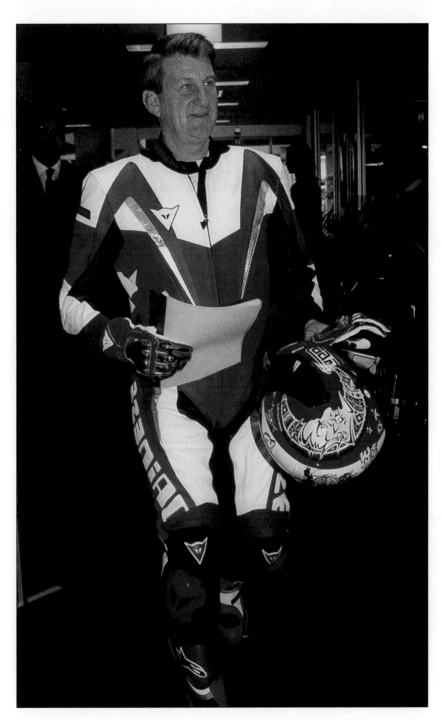

In the fast lane with the pop-star premier.

This will be the place for a major event. The two frontline spruikers for Melbourne and its attractions, Jeff Kennett and Ron Walker, sit by the seaside to contemplate their next big project.

High rollers. Amid ongoing controversy, Lloyd Williams and the premier officiate at the opening of the Crown citadel.

Jeff's Shed. The Melbourne Exhibition and Convention Centre on the south bank of the Yarra was one of the Kennett government's gambling-funded 'Agenda 21' projects.

The premier is jostled and jeered by Save Albert Park campaigners protesting the return of the Formula One Grand Prix to the inner-city circuit.

Despite the protests, the show must go on. At a pre-race test run, Kennett flags them home, watched by Major Events boss Ron Walker and Grand Prix chief executive Judith Griggs.

'*The Guilty Party*'. The Liberals' demolition job on their Labor opponents worked just as well at the 1996 election as it had in 1992.

Kennett, in familiar pose, rejoices in a second landslide victory in 1996.

disaggregation and sale of the state's energy industries. 'We had a very clear idea what we wanted to do, but people said it would take us several terms. The SEC would resist, and we would never be able to get it up,' recalls Stockdale. 'I was determined we would, but I admit the preparatory stages took longer than I would ever have imagined. To set up a competitive electricity market from scratch was immensely complex.'

Wary of the experience in Britain, where the existence of only two electricity generators in the privatised model had created the capacity for obscene profits, the Victorian government ensured four generators were competing in the market through the initial five-year phase.

The biggest obstacle, initially, was the bureaucratic streetfighting of the SEC itself. Victoria's state-owned enterprises were proud and powerful monopolies, representing some of the largest businesses in the country. In 1993, the combined assets of the SEC, the Gas & Fuel Corporation and the Melbourne Metropolitan Board of Works accounted for almost 2 per cent of the nation's gross domestic product. They had played an integral role in the state's economy and were crucial influences on the state's finances. Responsible for 13 per cent of the state's public sector, they were heavily unionised, and bankrolled a hefty raft of cross-subsidies – or 'community service obligations' – to rural consumers and other disadvantaged sections of the community.

They also had a long and prominent history as key institutions in the state's affairs, demonstrating clout and cunning in preserving their privileged and pivotal status. They had their own private golf courses, their own ski lodges. Their chairmen had become as powerful as any minister. Attempts to disturb the domain of these state monopolies inevitably met with stiff opposition from vested interests in the business community, influential pockets of the bureaucracy, and the rural lobby. As the government grappled with the harrowing task of budget repairs, the push for privatisation guaranteed further heartburn.

The sale of these assets into the private sector had enormous implications for regional policy, especially in the Latrobe Valley. Boasting one of the world's most extensive reserves of brown coal deposits, the area had become the natural hub of Victoria's power industry. Modernisation of the industry had been decimating the local workforce since the 1970s, and the power industry union – among the most active and militant in the state – was eager to protect what job security remained for its members. Stockdale says the government spelt out in stark terms to the union leadership the choices facing them: unless the industry became more efficient, the impending establishment of a national power grid, where states could compete as rival suppliers, would mean there might be no-body working in the region in 20 or 30 years' time. Stockdale notes, 'We were sensitive to that and we knew there would have to be investment by the federal government and the private sector in the Valley. But in the long term, the social impacts in the Latrobe Valley would be immensely greater if we drove hard to become the leading industrial centre for electricity, the leader in reform of the electricity industry nationally.'

Although accustomed to the taunt, Stockdale bristles at the accusation that Victoria's privatisation process represented a slavish mimicry of Thatcher's Britain. 'We were certainly doing something inimical to the traditional model of government. I had been to New South Wales and seen Nick Greiner's reform unit. I had been to New Zealand to see their state-owned enterprises unit. The British, I thought, had made mistakes. The entire process in the UK was all but discredited through the disastrous practice of issuing highly lucrative share options to executives of the newly privatised power companies. The options increased in value as profits increased. Inevitably, this created pressures for the new com-panies to raise their tariffs. It created the perception that the private takeover of public assets had been merely a ploy to line the pockets of the wealthy, at a cost to the general community and especially the poor. But in England I did take note of how they gathered around them a group of people to drive the reforms. I was convinced you would never counteract the vested interests inhibiting reform unless you took the agenda out of the hands of the government businesses and line ministers. The SEC said they should run the reform of the energy industry, that nobody else could sell the companies like they could. We said no, the SEC board's role would be to act under the direction of government. We indemnified them against acting under instructions from us. We effectively took control of the process into the Treasury and, to a large extent, into the hands of Jim Plowman and myself. We met the reform group two or three times a week. The SEC didn't have control. The tradition would have been for line ministers and particularly the bureaucrats to try to preserve their own positions. I don't think Jim Plowman was ever guilty of that. Some of the bureaucrats under him were. But in the end, it worked out to be a very good balance.'

Stockdale brought in outside experts – hired guns – to run his Electricity Supply Industry Reform Unit. Foremost among them was Peter Troughton, a former British Telecom engineer who had a lustrous – and ruthless – reputation in corporate restructuring, both in the USA and as the chief executive of New Zealand's Telecom Corp during its public float. Inevitably, downsizing was part of the equation. In New Zealand, he had cut the corporation's workforce from 27 000 to 12 500. Troughton's philosophy was blunt: 'I don't like inefficiency, I really don't. I think that if an industry is working extremely inefficiently, it's employing twice the number of people it should in a high percentage of non-jobs. That is essentially at somebody's cost. I think that has to be put right.'

Yet at a fundamental level, the core philosophy behind privatisation remained forever under suspicion. It represented perhaps the single biggest ideological division between the Kennett government and its Labor opponents. The ALP tapped into community unease when, with the electricity and gas sell-offs behind them, the Kennett government began extending the privatisation model to the construction of the CityLink tollway, the public transport system, the Latrobe Valley hospital and three high-security prisons. 'Privatising prisons is the depths of depravity,' claimed unionised prison warders.

Labor was able to exploit anxiety about the implications for the cost and reliability of essential community services. When there were power blackouts in the suburbs of Melbourne, for example, privatisation was commonly held up to blame. (When the same happened in Sydney's CBD, where the power industry remained in government hands, there seemed not to be the same intensity of reaction.) The scapegoating of the privatised industries reflected a natural conservatism in the community about changing the way things had always been done. Further, Labor was able to enmesh the debate in issues of accountability and transparency, attacking the Kennett government over the use of 'commercial in-confidence' clauses to prevent widespread scrutiny of contracts for these newly privatised activities. The perceptions of too cosy a relationship between the Kennett ministry and its privatisation consultants were to hound the government, even when the last of the gas pipelines had been sold.

Hallam, who became finance minister in the Kennett government's second term, concedes that the issues of confidentiality clauses became a rod for the government's back. 'We were at the maker's edge of this new territory for governments. We were trying to do the right thing, and we thought that unless we were able to persuade people that their souls would not be bared as a natural by-product of dealing with us we would find it hard to establish their trust and confidence.' In hindsight, Hallam argues it might have been better to make it explicit from the outset that companies tendering for major government business could expect to have details of the contracts thrown open to public scrutiny. 'If we had our time again, you would want it said from the word go: "Understand this: you are baring your soul."'

Stockdale, however, remains unyielding on the point of principle. 'The Labor Party behaved stupidly. They thought the businesses should be controlled by government, as if we had some god-given duty to deliver something inefficiently because it was important.' And, as Stockdale was ever eager to point out, if there was such a thing as an original sin of privatisation, that sin had been committed by two Labor governments who had agreed between them, back in 1990, to bring the State Bank of Victoria under the control of a partially privatised Commonwealth Bank. Given Labor's historic attempts at bank nationalisation – the ideological crusade that brought down the Chifley government in Canberra in 1949 – there could be no more emblematic philosophical somersault than that undertaken by the Keating and Kirner governments at the start of the decade. Like it or not, this was the end of the sacred status of state-owned enterprises, and it opened the door to the arguments for further privatisation in key industry sectors.

David White, as a senior economic minister in the Cain and Kirner governments, admits there was always a good case in favour of at least a partial privatisation of Victoria's power industry. 'When you looked at the debt-equity ratios of the SEC, I would have privatised 40 per cent because I realised the level of debt was unsustainable. You were borrowing to build a new power station before you had paid for the previous one you had built. There was no equity base. You could not sustain that forever.' But White sees the Kennett government's privatisation program as very much an ideological crusade driven by Stockdale. 'He had a strong ideological commitment. The rest are pretty well pragmatists. I knew he would privatise anything that moved . . . I would not have privatised everything. If you look at the model of full public ownership, your problem is twofold. One, the level of debt and two, the work practices are not as good as they should be. But the problem with privatised industry is you can create a setting where collusion can lead to prices going up. So I am a strong advocate of having a mix, so you can keep the private contractors honest.'

Inevitably, judgements on the ultimate success or failure of

privatisation in Victoria will involve elaborate calculations. How
does one define the criteria? Is price a criterion? Quality and reliability of service? Environmental impact? Industry competitive-
ness? Debt reduction? Or whether the public has received value for
money from the sale of the asset? The former auditor-general,
Ches Baragwanath, began wrestling with these issues in 1996, and
conceded in an official report in 1997 that it was difficult to make
a definitive call. He concluded, 'The success or otherwise of privatisation will not be known until well after the year 2000.'

Baragwanath questioned, however, the 'light-handed approach'
to government intervention through the Office of the Regulator-
General, the public official designated with the responsibility for
keeping watch over the activities of the privatised companies. His
scepticism may have been driven, in part, by the knowledge that
the Kennett government had his own office in its sights. The
auditor-general's department had been identified as a potential
target for contracting out a large slice of the audit responsibilities
to private accountants.

In reply to Baragwanath, the Department of Treasury and
Finance agreed that the benefits were not always obvious immediately. But, Treasury insisted, as early as two years into the privatisation program the community had already reaped significant
rewards. Claiming unprecedented efficiency gains, it cited a report
by Australia's Bureau of Industry Economics, which had found that
among the states, Victoria offered the cheapest basket of infrastructure services. 'Victoria's rapid productivity improvement in
recent years shows that a serious and well-targeted reform program
can provide tangible benefits quickly.' Moreover, by 1999, electricity privatisation alone had generated net savings for the state
budget of $1.5 billion a year.

What was never in dispute on either side of the political debate
was that many of the changes were irreversible. As business columnist Alan Kohler observed, the logic of Kennett's program was to
'permanently reduce government activity to an extent unprece-

dented anywhere in the world'. Kennett, for his part, understood perfectly the historical importance of what had been set in train. He believed his government's radical agenda had set new benchmarks, offering a different brand of leadership. 'What we have achieved, without being egotistical about it, can really be seen as a lesson for any group of political managers anywhere around Australia,' he would boast. 'We've released the reform genie out of the bottle.'

And there was more to come. As he embarked on his financial management and public sector reforms – a dour and demanding struggle that would test the community's appetite for change – Kennett knew he also had to produce a turnaround in the public's mindset. He needed a big, bold plan to salvage the state's tattered reputation and shift perceptions about its miscreant status.

Kennett put his marketing skills to work. The result was an ambitious and relentless strategy of turning Melbourne into a major events capital with a year-long calendar of sporting and arts festivals, high-profile business conventions, and a range of other cultural happenings that would attract interest not just around Australia but overseas as well. Kennett would run this campaign under the slogan 'Victoria – On the Move'. He sought to entrench this in the public consciousness by making it the official insignia on the state's number plates. The genteel days of 'The Garden State' were over.

CHAPTER TEN

———

THE CAN-DO CULTURE

'The public is getting as much of a buzz out of this as we are.'
JEFF KENNETT

J eff Kennett and Ron Walker, both towering men, crammed
their bodies into a converted dune buggy on Phillip Island. The
motorcycle Grand Prix had returned to Victoria, and the two had
ventured to the island resort at the entrance to Westernport Bay to
savour their triumph. Amid the squeal of engines hurtling around
the picturesque race circuit, Kennett and Walker visited the camp
sites where thousands of spectators – mainly bikers and bikies, in
beards, leathers and tattoos – were staying for the duration of the
sporting festival. They flocked to the premier.

'The air was thick with pot. They're all yelling and screaming at
him, as if the Messiah had arrived. They were offering him a drink
and a smoke,' Walker remembers. Did Kennett inhale? 'He wasn't
inhaling. But this was the heartland, and they loved him.'

Part of the Kennett phenomenon was his capacity to push the
right buttons in constituencies where previous Liberal leaders had
struggled to establish a foothold. Kennett's approval rating among
young voters became the equal of any politician of his generation.

While his reputation as a larrikin and a loudmouth was seen as a crippling liability in Opposition, as premier this sense of theatre – and his readiness to poke fun at himself and others – appeared to strike a chord with a new class of voters. His drive and enthusiasm, his talent for the unorthodox and quirky, his distinctive adaptation of the 'crash through or crash' theory of leadership, and his aggressive push to market Melbourne as a venue for major events, found resonance in the electorate. Kennett's Victoria became known as the 'Can-Do Culture' and the period from early 1995 to early 1997 was to represent its highwater mark.

By the end of 1994, the reconstruction of the state's finances was well advanced. Stockdale had turned the budget around in the space of only three years. Victoria's growth rate was outpacing the other states, and unemployment levels were finally trending downwards. The temporary casino at the World Trade Centre was contributing heavily to government receipts, and with the flow of gambling revenue into its Community Support Program, the government was pushing forward with its Agenda 21 construction program, a gambling-funded reconstruction of the state's prime cultural assets – $250 million for a new museum, $160 million for an expansion of the National Gallery of Victoria, $130 million for the Federation Square development in the heart of the city, $100 million to refurbish the State Library, and $65 million for a new sports and aquatic centre at Albert Park. At the start of 1995, big crowds turned out to see Kennett open the $130 million Melbourne Exhibition Centre on the Yarra banks, one of the first visible signs of a city's renewal. This vast building, part of the larger Southbank construction site, became known by the unofficial title 'Jeff's Shed'. Then there was the ambitious CityLink road project. Through a series of bridges and tunnels under and over the Yarra, it was designed to connect and widen the freeways running to the north, west and south-east, with the aim of cutting travel times for commuters and road freight and easing traffic congestion through the city itself.

Kennett was also twisting the arm of private industry in the city to commit investment to the $2.3 billion Docklands development in the old ports district. To buttress the mood of revival, the major events strategy that Kennett had hatched with his old mate Ron Walker was thrown into top gear. Apart from Melbourne's sporting staples of the Australian Open tennis, the Australian Football League grand final and the spring racing carnival, there was a major permanent addition to the fixture, with the Formula One Grand Prix to be staged at Albert Park from March 1996. Walker had also negotiated a string of one-off spectaculars, including the Three Tenors concert at the MCG; the Bledisloe Cup rugby union match between Australia and New Zealand, which attracted a world-record attendance for the code; and the Presidents Cup golf tournament at Royal Melbourne. This $15 million event had brought the best of the USA's golfers to Australia for matchplay against an international team led by Greg Norman. Some media commentators dubbed the extravaganza 'The Jeff and Greg Show'.

Ironically, the notion of an arts- or events-based recovery for Victoria had been the brainchild of Joan Kirner, when as premier she had groped for a means of restoring a semblance of credibility to the shell-shocked Labor government. To this end, in 1991 she had invited Ron Walker to be the inaugural chairman of the Melbourne Major Events Company, in an attempt to generate interest internationally in Melbourne as a sporting and cultural venue. One of the most influential corporate wheeler-dealers in Melbourne, Walker, like Kennett, was hyperactive, a workaholic and a supreme networker. The youngest-ever lord mayor of Melbourne at the age of 34, he had also served for more than a decade as the federal treasurer of the Liberal Party – the 'bagman' for party fundraising.

Kennett and Walker's friendship dated back to the late 1970s. 'I became a very good friend of Jeffrey's before he became minister for housing. Both of us were a bit loutish, and we always got on very well,' says Walker. 'We found a lot in common and the friendship grew. Both of us had a strong desire to achieve something in the state.' Like Andrew Peacock, Walker became a trusted ally, and a booster for Kennett's leadership. Kennett was known to be annoyed that Walker had accepted the Kirner appointment, which could be seen as something of a rescue mission for a dying government. But the business community in Melbourne was anxious that something – anything – be done to resurrect confidence in a community spooked by recession, financial insecurity and loss of self-esteem. Nor should Kennett have been surprised. In the late 1980s, Walker had helped John Cain in putting together Melbourne's beleaguered Olympic bid.

'Joan Kirner started it, invited me into the cabinet room at Spring Street and asked me to be the chair,' Walker says. 'It's interesting, though . . . we were so penniless that Margaret Jackson [a prominent company director] used to come in and do the books for us at night-time in an honorary capacity. She was a partner in Peat Marwick, but she didn't charge. Elizabeth Proust [then chief executive of the Melbourne City Council] also joined the committee and helped out. It was a serve-your-own-lunch, wash-your-own-glasses type of outfit.'

By the time Kennett came to power in 1992, he had put behind him his scepticism about the Melbourne Major Events Company. The organisation was to become one of the prime movers in his revivalist vision. As Walker tells it, 'Our annual budget at the time was $155 000. There was a chief executive and a girl to answer the phone. It was a do-or-die effort, a case of lifting the morale of the people. There was no strategy behind it. We didn't know if we would succeed. Kennett was amazing from day one. He was available to do anything. He got us to roll up our sleeves and get out and travel the world: "Let's harvest and get whatever we can." When he came into office, he gave it extra lifeblood and encouragement. He gave me an electric charge. He said, "Get out there and double your efforts, triple your efforts, if you have to." He kept saying, "No matter where you are overseas, you want decisions you can ring me any time of the day or night and, if it's feasible and your numbers are correct, let's do it."'

Before Kennett's arrival in office, Walker had identified their main target. In what became known by the codename Operation Vroom Vroom, Melbourne would attempt to wrest the Formula One Grand Prix from Adelaide and turn it into a showpiece of Australian sport. Walker flew to London repeatedly for negotiations with the Formula One chief, Bernie Ecclestone. It was a clandestine operation, and necessarily so. The Victorian strategy was brazen and predatory: to succeed would mean denying the struggling economy of South Australia one of its few headline events. The task was complicated by the election of a Liberal government in South Australia under Dean Brown in December 1993, by which time the Victorians had already reached a confidential agreement with Ecclestone. From London, Walker spoke daily by phone to Kennett.

'Three or four days before the deal was done, we had to speak to Brown and tell him the Grand Prix was lost for Adelaide. It was unfortunate. Mind you, a lot of the fault was on the head of the previous Labor government in South Australia. They took a lot of things for granted, they became sloppy, there was infighting in the Grand Prix office, and the Liberal Party in Opposition was having a field day over the costs.' To add insult to injury, Walker then recruited the chief executive of the Adelaide Grand Prix, Judith Griggs, a trusted former lieutenant of Ecclestone, to run the event in Melbourne. 'Judy had expressed the desire to become legal officer to the Sydney Olympic team because she knew all about television contracts worldwide and wanted to do something different. Then she said she would like to apply for the job of chief executive for our Grand Prix. That's how it all happened.'

Walker and Kennett's forward planning extended to a 10-year calendar, with the millennium conference of the World Economic Forum secured for Melbourne, and the two working assiduously to claim the rights to host the 2006 Commonwealth Games. None of this could compare with Sydney's coup in being awarded the 2000 Olympics but it represented an aggressive and determined campaign aimed at ensuring that Melbourne would not be side-lined. Apart from the influx of overseas visitors and the exposure of the Melbourne 'brand' in the national and international media, the underlying political motivation was to rebuild confidence within the state. According to Alan Stockdale, the importance of the strategy went far beyond the glitz and glitter. 'I remember talking to Haddon Storey and [former upper-house Liberal] James Guest about whether in a modern economy it is possible to run a regional economic development strategy. I was always a bit cynical about the extent to which you could fix outcomes away from the national pattern. I was wrong. Jeff Kennett restored confidence in Victoria and the fact that we made major infrastructure investments provided positive support for investment. It provided a good image of Victoria, which helped to attract investment here. Confidence is far more important than I would have imagined it to be. People like to feel they are associating with a winner.'

Stockdale believes another key benefit in the strategy was to create product differentiation for Melbourne in international markets where Australia's profile tended to be dominated by images of Sydney Harbour. 'People see Sydney as the centre of Australia. When I was in London, I turned on the television to see who had won the men's final of the tennis at the Australian Open. While they were waiting for transmission to resume, they superimposed a picture of Sydney over the picture of Flinders Park. At that time, we had been debating a change of name for the venue, from Flinders Park to Melbourne Park. Being a bit of a traditionalist, I was concerned about changing it – until I saw what the viewers in London were seeing. I instantly changed my mind. The name change guaranteed "Melbourne Park" would appear everywhere.'

The major events strategy was also important on the home front, as proof to voters that Kennett's game plan would bring dividends. Unless the Victorian community was persuaded that

there were tangible benefits to be had from reform and reconstruction, they would quickly lose their taste for Jeff's abrasive brand of
politics. The premier was up against a tight deadline to deliver
meaningful results ahead of his next election, in 1996. Any who
criticised or questioned the government's priorities were dismissed
as killjoys – even 'un-Victorian', as the premier was wont to declare.

This did not stop the criticism. Albert Park residents, fearful
of the impact on their lives, and on property values, of a major
motor-racing event on their doorstep, created a community protest
group, Save Albert Park. Over more than two years, until the com-
pletion of the track in March 1996, they engaged in a gruelling
battle for public sympathy, climaxing in the arrest of no fewer than
95 local residents for trespass during a protest over the construction
of a grandstand in the park. The arrests were subsequently ruled
unlawful, and the campaign of opposition persisted through the
1990s. Melbourne's inner-city elites regarded the Grand Prix
contemptuously as a loud, tacky and unwelcome addition to a city
known elsewhere in the nation for a slightly supercilious and over-
starched view of its place in the world. For all the critics, however,
much of Melbourne seemed to rejoice in the razzle-dazzle.

Labor sought to dismiss the 'events strategy' as a bread-and-
circuses diversion aimed at blunting public consciousness of the
impact of the government's economic and financial reforms. It was
undeniable, though, that the festive mood helped to lift the city
from a mood of defeatism and despair. Ron Walker believes an
element of middle-class snobbery was driving much of the criticism. 'The Labor Party can say what they like. They never achieved
this success. We were at such a low ebb in life. The bread-and-
circuses adage is a nonsense when you think about the hundreds of
thousands of Labor supporters who actually came to the circus to
have fun. It was a brilliant strategy. Kennett took over a state which
had been losing everything for 10 years. We lost the Olympic
bid. Everything we tried for we lost. There was low morale. There
was a lack of respect abroad. They referred to us in other states

laughingly as the rustbucket and Bleak City. Today, we are neither. Having spent the best part of a couple of years on the road, I know that you don't need a calling card for Melbourne any more. They know where Melbourne is. They see the tennis. They see the Grand Final on Sky Channel. It's the epicentre for sport in Australia.'

Walker, of course, remains one of the unwavering advocates for Kennett's entrepreneurial style of leadership. But the good vibes generated by the major events initiatives also began to register in the Liberal Party's private research. Kennett was building a positive profile among growing numbers of young adults from the 'battler' tradition of the suburbs, many of whom were to break with decades of solemn family ritual by switching from Labor to the Liberals. Qualitative research conducted for the Liberal Party at this time revealed that Kennett rated strongly among the young for his per-ceived capacity for 'getting things done'. This demographic became known to Liberal strategists as 'Jeff's people'. For Labor, which had been successful in politicising and recruiting virtually an entire generation of youth in the early 1970s, Kennett's appeal across a broad constituency was both a perplexing and threatening shift in the landscape.

Former Labor frontbencher Ian Baker was among those watch-ing enviously as Kennett seduced this new class of voters. 'He's not intellectually driven. He's driven by intuition. He's clever. He can smell it. That advertising stuff that we laugh at, once again, was all turned to his advantage. It may be fifth-grade advertising, but it works. Where it particularly worked was his intuition for finding Labor constituencies and pinching 1.5 per cent here and there. Young working-class men, for example. Kennett is not the sport-ing type. It's very difficult to ride a motorbike. He couldn't ride a motorbike if he fell over one. He will never be able to play ball sports as long as his bum points to the ground. Yet he had this image among them.'

On 5 March 1996, two days after the federal Coalition led by John Howard had swept into power in Canberra, Kennett called a snap election. The campaign would embrace the festivities and hoopla surrounding the return of the Grand Prix to Melbourne. In a political sense, too, the premier opted for a high-speed event: the election campaign would span only 25 days. Kennett would be the pacesetter; the ALP, needing a historic swing of 7.6 per cent, would start from a long way back.

But the strategy was not without risks for the government. What if the staging of the Grand Prix proved a flop or, worse, if protesters acted on threats to disrupt the race? Any loss of face for Melbourne on the second-last weekend of an election campaign could represent a wild card. This was cause for apprehension. More fundamentally, it had to be remembered that Kennett had led a government responsible for the most blistering attack on public expenditure, and perhaps the most dramatic reform agenda, of any government in postwar Australia. Nobody could be certain how the electorate would respond.

Unusually, there had been no testing of the electoral climate through the government's first term. There were no retirements or departures from the Coalition benches, which had allowed the government to avoid the potential pitfalls of unwanted and un-timely by-elections. This meant that the 1996 state election would be the first opportunity available to voters to pass judgement on those hectic and harrowing early years of Kennett's rule. Although Victoria had not produced a one-term government since the 1940s, this was an unconventional government with an unorthodox leader. What verdict would the community deliver?

Labor positioned itself from the outset as the underdog. John Brumby signalled his party's modest expectations by urging voters on day one to maximise the protest vote. Suspecting the ALP would need at least two elections to carve back Kennett's 1992 landslide majority, Brumby decided to run under the banner 'Restore the Balance', and launched into his campaign simply by inviting the electorate to 'give the government a whack'. For his part, Kennett pronounced the hard times over. From now on, he promised, the state would begin to savour the fruits of reform. The premier also deployed a large dose of hometown chauvinism, playing on the issue of Victoria's self-esteem. 'Three and half years ago, each and every one of us were the butt of jokes from other states,' he reminded the media at his press conference to announce the election date. 'Today, there are no jokes. Victoria is held up as an example of what a community can do when it works in partnership.'

Kennett's choice to run so soon after the federal poll was part of a calculated plan to capitalise on a demoralised and dispirited ALP. In the federal campaign, the Keating government had been swept out of office by a more ruthless and street-smart Liberal Party. John Howard had pitched at rural and regional Australia, claiming that Paul Keating's administration was concerned only with the pre-occupations of those in the triangle of power – Sydney, Canberra, Melbourne. Keating – obsessed by this time with the 'big picture' of Aboriginal land rights, the republic and closer economic inte-gration with Asia – seemed unable to come to grips with the reality that he was being mauled at ground level. After 13 years in power, the federal ALP, partly through the hubris of its leader, found itself dramatically out of touch with middle Australia. The party also mis-calculated in Victoria. 'Labor thought they could win the federal election here, on the back of Jeffrey; the so-called Kennett factor,' observes Kennett strategist Peter Poggioli. 'When we came back intact in Victoria at the federal election, that was bound to have serious consequences for Labor internally. The decision to run early in '96 was Jeffrey's and it was a good one politically. We had another six months up our sleeve but we had done well in the federal election, and there was the element of surprise – they would never expect us to do back-to-backs. And we knew from our own information that they didn't have a whole lot of money. We did. Over the longer term, we had been fundraising knowing that we would run a hard campaign taking nothing for granted.'

The disparities in the campaign resources were stark. After the federal campaign, the Victorian ALP had only $800 000 in its war chest. By the end of the 25-day campaign, glum Labor strategists calculated that the Liberals had outspent them by 13 to one. This threw a heavy burden onto Brumby to go headline chasing. It meant the campaign had to be kept flexible, with Labor always on the lookout for the next potential soundbite. As a result, it suffered for not having the underpinnings of a well-structured strategy. 'The strategy for the day became whatever Brumby and [chief of staff] Hulls decided as they sat in the car that morning on the way in,' recalls one party professional. 'We began to call their operation Air Force One.'

Meanwhile the Liberals followed the pattern of their 1992 campaign, releasing a new policy each day. Kennett remained earnest, if not subdued. The Liberals' advertising themes were a mix of the negative – 'Still the Guilty Party' – and the positive – 'Keep Things Moving'. A significant share of the budget was spent on FM radio advertising, aimed at the youth market: the Liberals were out not only to entrench their ascendancy, but to chase a new stream of support. Although Brumby would receive media praise for a feisty and accessible campaign, Labor was running publicity stunts; the Liberals were running strategy. In the second week of the campaign, while the ALP secured friendly free media coverage of Brumby chatting with schoolchildren and climbing aboard the Puffing Billy steam railway in the Dandenongs, Kennett announced $100 million in new funding to help care for the elderly, the disabled and the mentally ill. Labor desperately needed to shake up the chemistry. It took a high-risk gambit. Brumby announced that a Labor government would block the introduction of tolls on the $2 billion CityLink ring road.

Although CityLink was a pet infrastructure project of Kennett's, the government was determined that the state would not go into debt to finance this road system. Private industry would build, own and operate CityLink, with the asset reverting to state ownership after 34 years. The tender had been awarded to a consortium of Transfield and Obayashi. Contracts had been signed.

The companies would recoup the construction costs and turn a tidy profit by imposing electronic tolling: an income averaging an estimated $200 million a year over the 34 years. The project would be state-of-the-art both in engineering and in its introduction of a computer system, known as e-tag, to monitor vehicles as they entered tolling zones and then to bill the users.

Labor's stance against the tolls was not without a philosophical base. As a general principle the ALP remained opposed to privatisation, and this included the road system. Labor also took issue with the level of profits available to the private developers, which would bring estimated returns of more than three times the value of construction. But the ALP also had an eager eye on voters in the dormitory suburbs of the north-west, where the threat of road tolls might be expected to cause resentment among working families who had previously used the old two-lane freeway free of charge.

Labor was convinced its stance was a vote-winner. It warned that it was prepared to use all of the powers at its disposal to prevent tolls if Transurban, the CityLink project's private developer, refused to review the contracts and build a more modest alternative proposed by the ALP. It was a stance that diminished even further the ALP's meagre credibility in the eyes of the business community. Surely no incoming government would dare to renounce major construction contracts signed by its predecessors? Labor was seen as engaging in reckless and irresponsible posturing, flirting with the alarming notion of sovereign risk. Having worked painstakingly to rehabilitate its image after the Cain–Kirner disasters, Labor's tactics on the toll issue invited the accusation that it had learned very little. The Guilty Party was back in the dock.

Desperately Labor tried other tactics, including focusing attention on the government's handling of its proposed casino in Melbourne. But for all its attempts to inject greater intensity into the election campaign, and despite the beginning of rumblings in the Liberal Party about the premier becoming a control freak, the electorate seemed to be with Kennett. Opinion polls showed the government streaking ahead to a 12-point lead. Moreover, what-ever momentum Labor had generated came to a shuddering halt on Sunday 16 March, when all of Melbourne switched off to wit-ness the spectacle of the Grand Prix. Jacques Villeneuve, Michael Schumacher and the Formula One cavalcade had swept into town. Chequered flags decorated shopfronts across the city. Luxury vessels were moored in Albert Park lake. It was the biggest inter-national sporting celebration Melbourne had seen since the 1956 Olympics.

At the centre of this spectacle, in the spotlight, stood Kennett. Les Carlyon, one of Melbourne journalism's most gifted word-smiths, tracked Kennett's Grand Prix experience. Carlyon began by describing a motor race, and ended up grappling with a political phenomenon. The result was one of the most enduring portraits of Kennett at the peak of his popularity.

> For the Grand Prix, Jeff Kennett wears a navy blazer and fawn slacks. 'Look at the sky,' he says, smiling so intensely his blue eyes almost close. He is gladhanding, kissing, thanking people for coming. As he will later confess, in the next few hours he will know desperation, elation and, finally, euphoria.
>
> Right now, he's desperate. But wilful, too.
>
> He has always been that. And he is damned if he is going to let his nerves show.
>
> 'Look at that for a beautiful blue. Not a cloud.' He is proud of the sky. It is a Victorian sky. His sky. There is a hint he has arranged it.
>
> The Formula One cars are on the grid. Clive James had it right: they look like Marlboro packets with a wheel on each corner. Their engines scream. It is as if a hornet has flown into your ear and is about to do a kamikaze job on your brain.
>
> And somehow sensual, too: a furious foreplay that hints raw things are about to happen. And, straight away, they do.
>
> Martin Brundle's yellow car barrels through the air upside

down and the wheels fall off. With a tendency to suicide that is sublime, the English driver runs back for his second car.

Melbourne's big race has stalled in its first minute.

Jeff Kennett looks serene. Inside – and, again, he only tells us about it much later – he's dying, unsure of what has happened, wondering whether the threat to disrupt the race has been carried out.

Now the race is over. The overture to *Carmen* thunders over the public address: racy, urgent and triumphant. The crowd swarms onto the straight, a sea of denim and T-shirts, maybe 20 000 people, probably more, and they want a party. One of them notices Kennett looking down from his suite, emperor-like, his big jaw set.

The bloke in the jeans begins the chant. 'Jeff, Jeff, Jeff.'

Kennett allows a flicker of a smile. Hundreds take it up.

Jeff! Jeff! Jeff!

Kennett nods. Jeff! Jeff! Jeff! Louder and louder. Kennett finally gives the thumbs up, Tiberius with a 1947 haircut.

He's tired. His face is like porcelain, but he's enjoying this.

The chant goes on. No Australian politician has ever held so big a rally, or so owned a crowd, by offering nothing more than a slightly crooked smile.

The phenomenon described by Carlyon swept like a tidal wash through to election day. On Saturday 30 March, Liberal heavyweight Michael Kroger stood elbow-to-elbow with ALP workers outside a polling station in Tullamarine, the focus of Labor's anti-toll strategy. This was alien territory for Kroger. Here in the city's northwest, Labor had strong traditions and it was expected that the Liberals' Bernie Finn would struggle to hold the seat. Kroger watched intrigued as a man in his early thirties, clad in T-shirt and jeans, walked warily towards them. He wore tattoos. He also wore a cap, the peak swung around to the back in the style of American street culture. The man approached the Labor team and asked who they represented.

'David White for Tullamarine,' they said.

'Nah,' he told them bluntly. 'I'm for Jeff Kennett.'

Kroger stepped forward to thrust a how-to-vote card eagerly into the hand of this unlikely recruit. As the man turned towards the polling booths, Kroger noticed the logo on the back of his cap. It read, 'Grand Prix. Melbourne. 1996.' At that moment, there was at least one Liberal convinced the election result was in the bag.

CHAPTER ELEVEN

OPEN FOR BUSINESS

'It is his cavalier attitudes to the constraints of
public office that are cause for concern.'
SUNDAY AGE, MAY 1996

Jeff Kennett's election victory in 1996 defied all the accepted rules of Australia's political culture. Although the government suffered a 2.8 per cent statewide swing, this was mainly in its own safe seats and in rural electorates regarded for half a century as National Party strongholds. The Coalition was returned with a 32-seat majority: in effect, a second landslide. The result ran against expectations that Kennett would pay a high price electorally for pushing the community too hard, too fast. Amid boisterous celebrations at Melbourne's Hotel Sofitel, the premier had no doubts whatsoever about the significance of the win. 'This is probably the most profound election result in this country, state or federally, in the past 50 years,' he proclaimed. 'There has been no government in Australia since the war that has dared to govern in the way in which we have and, clearly, based on tonight's results, succeeded overwhelmingly.'

Sweetest of all the election results was perhaps Bernie Finn's win in the traditional ALP heartland of Tullamarine, for it brought with it the defeat of Labor's leader in the upper house, David White, who had been attempting to cross to the Legislative Assembly. In the late 1970s, White had been Labor's demolition expert in its attacks on the Hamer government's Housing Commission land deals. That scandal, which Kennett had weathered as housing minister, had debilitated the Liberal government. Since the Liberals' return to power in 1992, White had again taken the leading role again in the Opposition's campaign to discredit the premier. He brought to the task a combination of a sharp intellect, a phenomenal memory for detail, a strong dose of cynicism and a ruthless 'take no prisoners' attitude. He kept extensive files and was assiduous, if not obsessive, in chasing down all manner of rumours about Kennett, his family and his business activities. White, as a former cabinet minister tainted by the Guilty Party tag, was determined to turn the burden of proof back on his tormentors.

Jeff Kennett arrived in office precisely at a time when more rigorous standards of ministerial conduct were being demanded. This ensured constant friction between Kennett's entrepreneurial enthusiasm and community expectations that those in public office should stay strictly at arm's length from money-making ventures of any description. Kennett resented the constraints. For a man whose great-grandfather had been an original investor in BHP, whose grandfather had lost his fortune in the share-market slump of 1954, and who, in his own professional career, had gambled the livelihood of his family to build a $500 000-a-year business from nothing, it was like telling a fisherman not to bait his hook. Every instinct of Kennett railed against it. Through his years in politics, there would be endless controversy.

An early sign of Jeff's larrikinism came in 1977 when, as a back-bencher, he sought to offset the costs of a trip to South-East Asia by selling jade bracelets to his parliamentary colleagues. He did this in the surrounds of the Legislative Assembly, in what the *Age*'s Peter Smark ridiculed as Kennett's 'back-bench flea market'.

Barely weeks into his government's first term, the premier was under attack again for similar entrepreneurship. This time it was for selling, from his office, bottles of wine distributed by the Liberal Party for fundraising purposes. He had done so without first seeking a permit from the liquor licensing authority. Labor said this was an abuse of his office and Kennett, in a mock show of repentance, made his apologies and agreed to file the necessary paperwork. He was later fined $100 for selling wine without a licence. The story generated high excitement over the space of a few weeks and then drifted from prominence. But it set the tone for the tactics the ALP would choose in the hope of hauling itself back into the political contest. In Opposition, Labor would endeavour to make Jeff's leadership style – not the past sins of the ALP – the main issue in the public's mind. It aimed to keep Kennett constantly on the back foot by attacks on his personal integrity. This, in turn, would fuel doubts about the probity of decision-making within his government.

Kennett was sometimes his own worst enemy. At a personal level, the premier seemed forever frustrated at not being able to pursue business interests of his own. He worked long and punishing hours in a position carrying onerous responsibilities. Mingling frequently with the state's wealthiest citizens, there was doubtless an element of envy that they were free to amass fortunes while he was forced to settle for what, by corporate standards, was a modest, middle-rank salary. 'You will never be wealthy by being a politician,' he was wont to complain. Kennett was compelled by law to work within the constraints imposed by the principles of probity in public office yet, through his career, he chafed against the protocols barring him from exercising his own entrepreneurial bent; apparently unwilling or unable to come to terms with the potential for conflicts of interest. It was an issue that was to prove an enduring blind spot as money politics took on a higher profile in the affairs of the state.

As premier, Jeff Kennett would come under prolonged scrutiny over his stubborn belief that his job should not disqualify his family from pursuing financial ventures of their own. At times the criticism verged on the hysterical, with conspiracy theories in abundance. But the premier helped feed perceptions that he had a flippant disregard for rules and conventions. Throughout the early 1990s, the Kennett family dabbled in investments of one sort or another, suggesting a cavalier refusal to accept that politicians were subject to more exacting standards than the average citizen going about their business. The premier was tripped up more than once when revelations of private business dealings came to light. This became a constant source of ammunition for his enemies. As ever, Jeff spurned the criticism and chose to live dangerously.

Things came to a head in 1993 when White, who had been trawling through the operations of the Kennett family business, KNF Advertising, 'struck gold'. As Jeff celebrated his first anniversary in office, Labor launched a prolonged and bruising assault on the activities of KNF. In particular, David White called for an independent board of inquiry to investigate whether Kennett had breached the code of conduct for MPs. Section 3(1)(e) of the code specifies: 'A Member who is a Minister shall ensure that no conflict exists, or appears to exist, between his public duty and his private interests.'

Two months before winning office, Kennett had indicated that the running of KNF would be handed over to Felicity, although he would remain a part-owner through a trust, JGK Nominees. Labor's attacks were supported by a series of reports in the *Age* which focused on KNF's relationship with various housing developers in Melbourne's north-western suburbs. On 20 October 1993 White claimed in parliament that, by remaining a director and shareholder of JGK Nominees trading as KNF Advertising, Kennett stood to profit from the office of premier. He cited an advertisement that had appeared in the *Herald Sun* property guide the previous February in which Kennett had appeared in a photograph alongside a Mr Livio Mingot, manager of Mingot Homes. The premier had opened a display village for the developer at

Taylors Lakes. White then pointed to an advertisement for Mingot Homes which had appeared in a local community newspaper two months later. 'In the bottom right-hand corner, KNF Advertising is shown as placing the advertisement.' Argued White, 'Why is it that the premier has chosen to promote Mingot Homes? Is it not a fact that the only reason he promoted Mingot Homes is because he knows the company placed money in a pool . . . to pay for advertisements placed with KNF Advertising? The premier is sending a message to all real estate agents, builders and developers and to all businesses in Victoria that . . . if you want the premier to promote your company, your product or your service, become a client of KNF Advertising because the premier will use his office to promote your product, business or service.'

On the strength of White's findings, Opposition leader John Brumby taunted Kennett that this issue would make the premier 'bleed until Christmas'.

White would soon raise in parliament another advertisement lodged by KNF Advertising, this time for the Roxburgh Heights housing estate. This property development was funded in part by the Urban Land Authority, a government agency. If it could be proved that Kennett had received money from a government authority, thereby breaching the Constitution, Labor could force his resignation.

Kennett condemned White's attack as a 'cowardly' attempt to victimise his wife and cripple the viability of her business. He challenged the Labor frontbencher to repeat his claims outside parliament where he might be sued for defamation. At the same time, Felicity Kennett gave an interview to the *Herald Sun*, criticising what she saw as the media's obsession with her family's business. She wept as a photographer took pictures. But the following day, on 25 October, Jeff Kennett resigned his directorship of the family trust and transferred his shares to his eldest son, Ed. Kennett's staff insisted the paperwork had been prepared weeks before, and that the premier simply had not had the time to complete all the details.

Undeterred, Brumby continued the attack in the Legislative Assembly. That same afternoon, he asked whether Kennett had an ongoing role in KNF. In reply, Kennett said he had had no active interest in the management of the company since being sworn in as a minister in 1980. 'There was a short period when I had a couple of years off [having lost the Opposition leadership] and during that period there is no doubt I spent some time at KNF Advertising . . . I did not involve myself in any major way in the running of the agency but simply from time to time occupied an office that I went into.'

Brumby rejected this answer as a 'farrago of misrepresentation' – citing contradictory evidence from a former, aggrieved KNF executive, Peter Kolac. Once again, said Brumby, the honesty and integrity of the premier was in question. The Opposition leader then brought a motion similar to White's before the lower house. A surly premier granted leave for it to proceed. 'You are inaccurate and therefore your case flounders,' he told the Opposition leader, insisting that Mingot Homes did not have an account with KNF.

However, John Brumby had another matter to raise. He cited the grievances of two former directors of a company known as Ultrafine Pty Ltd, in which Kennett and his wife had invested $400 000 in 1991. The fate of this company was to become entwined with the debate over the activities of KNF.

Ultrafine was set up in 1987 by David and Josie Powers, and their business partner John O'Sullivan, a wool grower, to produce high-quality knitwear from the finest merino wool. The company began as a part-time operation, with almost no working capital, and by 1991 had foundered. The Powers went public with their plight and the Kennetts responded. They took a 60 per cent stake in Ultrafine, borrowing funds to do so, amounting to an all-up investment of $400 000. Quite apart from Kennett's innate enthusiasm for business ventures, the politics of the investment were helpful, to say the least. With Victoria in the doldrums, and

Kennett's eye on regaining the party leadership, what other prac-
tising politician would be willing to put their own money on the
line to sustain a value-adding export business? Ultrafine was
launched with much fanfare only weeks after Kennett returned as
Opposition leader.

Through 1991 Ultrafine's accounts, marketing and advertising
were handled by KNF, for which Ultrafine paid fees of $50 000.
In November, however, Kennett wrote to the Powers saying he
would have to sell his stake in the company to avoid any potential
conflict of interest. The Powers sought a loan from the Commonwealth to buy back the Kennetts' share in the business, which was
assessed at $430 000, and in January 1992 the sale agreement was
signed. In October, a week after Kennett's landslide election win,
John O'Sullivan wrote to Kennett seeking a meeting to tie up
some 'loose ends'. Under protective clauses in the sale agreement,
the Powers and O'Sullivan had the right to fully examine the
company's books and, having checked its accounts, the partners
wanted the Kennetts to refund $137 000. Threats of legal action
followed.

By the end of 1993, however, export orders were coming in
for Ultrafine's products, there were expressions of interest from
other investors, and the partners calculated that the negative publicity of pursuing a legal claim could damage the company at a
time when it was gaining in profile and profitability. For the
Powers themselves, though, the good times were short-lived. They
were soon trapped in another dispute, this time with O'Sullivan.
Although the company went on to be a success, they were not part
of it. Gallingly for the Powers, the new owners credited Kennett
with having introduced the fresh management approach that gave
Ultrafine a chance to survive. The Powers were left nursing grievances. As part of its attack on the premier's business activities, the
Opposition would cite in parliament claims by the Powers that
official parliamentary letterhead had been used for Ultrafine business, that a government car had delivered pay cheques to KNF,

and that a board meeting had been held in Kennett's parliamentary office.

In his formal response to the claims, Kennett accused Brumby of being 'White's lackey' and of proceeding with the motion against him even though 'half the Labor Party members believe there is no substance in the allegations'. Brumby persisted, needling Kennett with an accusation that as Opposition leader he had asked his government driver to collect artwork and bromides from KNF clients, only to subsequently bill those clients for transport costs. It was an accusation Brumby never sought to substantiate. Kennett reacted explosively. 'You are the most gutless politician,' he shouted. 'That's like me saying in this place I know you sleep with boys. Do you? Do you?' It was the first time Labor had rattled the premier in any parliamentary exchange for at least two years.

Kennett stormed back into his office, furious. His staff had witnessed flashes of rage before, but never an outpouring of anger such as this. When he had calmed down, a contrite premier told them he was annoyed with himself for his lack of discipline; he should have endured the taunts and not bitten back, he should not have said what he did. Kennett never apologised publicly to Brumby.

The KNF controversy did continue through to Christmas 1993. Labor persisted in its threats to challenge the premier's constitutional right to sit in the parliament, keeping the issue alive in the press. The negative publicity began cruelling the image of the agency, and to make matters worse, the Kennett family became the target of death threats. In the face of these pressures, the Kennetts made a decision that would leave them resentful for years to come. On 17 January 1994, they announced they were selling the business they had run for 20 years. KNF was dead and buried. It was a decision they believed had been forced on them by constant media hounding. Jeff would never forgive the ALP – or, for that matter, the *Age*.

The experience did not shake Kennett's view that the demands on him and his family not to involve themselves in ongoing commercial activity were unfair and unrealistic. And although he may have honoured the technical requirements for disclosure of private interests, it was a code of conduct he appeared to accept grudgingly. This is borne out by the fact that, at the very time the KNF furore was gathering steam, the Kennetts were making another controversial investment.

In September 1993, 50 000 shares in a Chinese corporation, Guangdong, were bought in the name of Felicity Kennett. The company was the investment arm of the provincial government of Guangdong in southern China, and was about to be listed on the Australian Stock Exchange. The Kennett shares were bought days in advance of a highly successful public float. When the stock made its debut, Felicity Kennett's shares jumped in value by $18 000. That night, the premier briefly joined a celebratory dinner held by Guangdong in Melbourne. He did not declare his wife's shares in his register of financial interests. He was subsequently to argue that she had bought them in a private capacity and that, as premier, he was in no position to influence the company or its performance. But over the coming years, allegations would emerge of his having taken a hands-on interest in the purchase of the shares. Indeed, he would at one point seek to justify the investment as having a totemic value for the state. Guangdong was the first company from the Chinese mainland to make a 'primary listing' on the Australian stock exchange. Kennett would claim that his family investment demonstrated as 'a matter of faith' the eagerness of Victorians to promote new listings by Chinese companies in Melbourne.

Details of the share transaction first emerged on the television current affairs program *Today Tonight* on the Seven Network, in circumstances that can best be described as bizarre. Before the program was due to screen, on 13 May 1996, Kennett received a hand-delivered letter from the station advising him of the allegations it was intending to put to air. Kennett read the contents and, as he would tell parliament, 'I had a little chuckle in my normal way.' Indeed, he contemplated issuing a writ for defamation, and told his staff not to respond. 'After all,' he advised them jovially, 'I have just finished one set of renovations at home, but I have not completed what I have in mind.'

When the program's executive producer, John Boland, phoned Kennett at 5 p.m., the premier warned that he was considering his legal options. The station would claim later that, on legal advice, management had decided not to air the report. This, in turn, gave rise to further drama. The program's presenter, Jill Singer, while announcing the decision on camera began to swoon, slur her words and slump visibly in her chair. She subsequently collapsed, and an ambulance was called to take her to hospital. Public reaction to this spectacle forced management into a rethink of its decision. The next night, the report ran in full.

The tip-off to *Today Tonight* had come from Stephen Mayne, a close friend of Singer's. Mayne claimed he had been present in Kennett's office when the premier placed a phone call to Sino Securities, the stockbroking firm managing the Guangdong float. A former media adviser to the government who had left to become business editor for the *Herald Sun*, Mayne was not interviewed on camera and remained a confidential source. But it was he who told the program's researchers that he'd heard Kennett speaking to Sino Securities director, Richard Li, who, in turn, had agreed to allocate shares in Mrs Kennett's name. This was despite Li having notified the stock exchange six days earlier that, due to overwhelming demand, it was unlikely any further share applications would be accepted.

As controversy erupted, an editorial in the *Sunday Age* voiced exasperation at the premier's apparent disregard for the distinction between public responsibility and private interests. 'Does he not understand, or does he not care? Either way, Jeff Kennett's political judgment is coming increasingly into question. His competence, energy and resolve are not in doubt. Rather, it is his cavalier attitudes to the constraints of public office that are cause for concern . . . it is unwise, to say the least, for the premier and his wife to engage in speculative share buying.'

Labor, for its part, seized on the episode as it sought to build evidence of the premier's abuse of office. The Opposition wrote to the Australian Securities Commission demanding an investigation into the Guangdong share purchase. In 1997, the ASC issued a statement saying it had found no wrongdoing by the Kennett family. But the point remained. An incapacity or unwillingness to acknowledge the dividing line between business and politics was to prove one of Kennett's ongoing vulnerabilities.

In fact, he had been warned explicitly of the dangers as early as 1988 – by none other than Michael Kroger. It is one of the untold stories behind their profound mutual suspicion and distrust. Kroger is understood to have become troubled when, at one point, Kennett began showing an interest in the stock market and mentioned that he was considering buying some banking shares. The state president had issued a caution: it was foolhardy for an Opposition leader to be buying and selling shares, given the level of contact someone in that position was likely to have with company directors and chief executives of major companies. Didn't Kennett understand the risk of private investments becoming a matter of public interest? And what of the insider trading provisions of the securities code, which made it illegal to profit from price-sensitive information about public companies not available to the market? It was a minefield.

'You should not be trading in shares. How often are you doing this?' asked Kroger anxiously. He left the conversation believing Kennett had no grasp of the implications and that 'if he got a tip on the market [he believed] it was no different from a tip at the racecourse.'

Kennett had a different view. As Opposition leader his income was relatively modest, and he told colleagues he felt he was entitled to play the market to 'make a quid'. Once in government, of course, the rules changed. As premier, he was persuaded by his private staff to put his investments into a trust fund. In 1994, in the aftermath of the KNF controversy and well before *Today Tonight* exposed Felicity's Guangdong share deal, Kennett had also ceased any share trading by his family. It was a commitment that lasted until 10 October 1997, when the ABC's *Four Corners* program re-examined the Guangdong share controversy – this time interviewing Mayne on camera as the primary source.

Kennett was furious. He attacked the program as 'irresponsible slime' and promptly went out and bought some BHP stock. He announced this on 3AW breakfast radio two weeks later, in a conversation with comperes Ross Stevenson and Dean Banks. As world share markets nose-dived momentarily in response to the Asian economic meltdown, Kennett blithely discussed the negative impact on his own investments.

BANKS: 'You've heard what's happening this morning from New York and anticipation as to what's going to happen on our markets today and, dare I say it, you've got a few shares. What's your reaction?'

STEVENSON: 'The question, I guess, is this: is Felicity on a window sill at the moment?'

KENNETT: '[Laughter] Felicity has no shares left. As you know, we were forced out of the market. I went back in about two weeks ago and bought BHP at what I thought was a very good price at $15.88 and obviously have bought them to keep for my retirement. I don't know what they closed at yesterday, but it was under 14 [and] I think we're probably going to have a bit more of a shake-up today. But if people are looking to make a good investment, pick the right stocks, there's probably, you know, very close to not being a better time.'

BANKS: 'What impact does this have on the state of Victoria?'

KENNETT: 'The likely effect, to the best of my knowledge, is that last year when you saw us record a surplus of about $900 million, part of that was unspent money on capital projects, part of it also the very good return we got on the equities market, that is where our super funds, Transport Accident Commission and others had invested, and

got a return of about 21 per cent. Now they're obviously not going
to get anywhere like that this year and that's why we've always said
it's better to be prudent in managing the public's money, as opposed
to how Jeff Kennett manages his own.'

This exchange provides a fascinating window into Kennett's
thinking. The state was a player in the global economy, its fortunes
tied to trends in international markets. So, in his eyes, was Jeff
Kennett, as an individual investor – stubbornly so. What he did
with his own money was his private concern; he would invest it as
he saw fit. If people didn't like it, they could vote him out. Just as
Kennett was a risk-taker on the markets, he was also ready to take
his chances with public opinion.

Yet if the Kennetts' share portfolio was to remain a matter of
lingering controversy, it was as nothing compared to the government's decision to grant Melbourne's first casino licence to the
Crown consortium.

CHAPTER TWELVE

HIGH ROLLER

'It's like a dead cat in the middle of the road –
stinking to high heaven.'
PAUL KEATING, ON THE BIDDING PROCESS
FOR THE MELBOURNE CASINO

On 8 May 1997, the Yarra River was the setting for a Melbourne spectacular. Fireballs leapt into the sky, and illuminated floats lined the river bank. As 1200 guests, including prominent business leaders, sporting stars and television personalities, were sitting down to a gala dinner, Kennett emerged in the spotlight. On a marble staircase in a cavernous and glittering five-storey atrium, he was handed a pair of gold-plated scissors with which to perform his ceremonial duties. As Crown chairman Lloyd Williams stood beside him grinning, the premier snipped a gold sash and declared open the permanent site of the $1.85 billion Crown casino – 350 gaming tables, 1300 poker machines, a six-star hotel, 40 restaurants: the biggest gambling and leisure complex in the nation.

Thousands of Melbournians turned out in drizzling rain to watch. 'It's been knocked and rubbished by some,' said Kennett of the casino citadel, 'but I think now we can all stand in awe of the final result.' The event was televised live across Australia and Kennett was at centre stage.

Also flanking Jeff that night was his good mate Ron Walker, a ubiquitous presence during the Kennett years. His role as chairman of the Melbourne Major Events Company gave him profound influence over the affairs of the city and state, and his close links to Kennett became the subject of intense speculation over whether, and to what extent, Walker's business interests stood to benefit from government decisions. Public perceptions of a premier too close to business would prove hard to shake, mainly because Kennett's links to the corporate world were often seen through the prism of his friendship with Walker. This was particularly true after Walker, in partnership with leading Melbourne businessman Lloyd Williams, had put together the Crown consortium's successful bid to own and operate the state's first casino. No single development in the Kennett years attracted more scrutiny, more headlines or more gossip.

It was an issue Labor would chase through both the state and federal parliaments. The essence of their case – never proven but never abandoned – was that Ron Walker and Lloyd Williams, as Kennett's business mates, had been given the inside running in securing a casino licence worth, conservatively, $200 million a year.

As early as October 1994, under protection of parliamentary privilege, Opposition leader John Brumby had identified Walker as one of 20 business 'cronies' allegedly given favourable treatment by the government. He went so far as to claim that some of these business people would end up in jail. It was an attack that severely damaged Brumby's credibility in the business community. His unproven allegations of widespread business malpractice were based on nothing more substantial than unconfirmed rumours.

Walker retaliated that Brumby's slight on his reputation was disgraceful and offensive, and he urged the Opposition leader to repeat the allegations outside parliament. 'I have been a friend of the premier for 22 years,' Walker said. 'I am very proud to have been his friend and if that's what cronyism is, then I'm guilty of cronyism. I have been coming to parliament house since the Bolte days so I don't know what Mr Brumby is on about. Perhaps when he gets some success in his life he might change his mind.'

Labor's eagerness to portray Walker as a Rasputin-like figure at Kennett's shoulder always had about it an element of overkill. For one thing, the very idea that a strong-willed individual such as Kennett would take riding instructions from anybody begs credulity. The perception that Kennett was a puppet in Walker's hands, or that Walker was the gatekeeper for business access to the premier, was known to infuriate Kennett. 'That's absolute rubbish,' he would insist. 'It is a popular myth that is totally inaccurate. I try and make myself available to business people, men and women. Here, interstate, overseas. I am only a phone call away. That's the way we do business.'

Walker himself offers this reflection on their relationship. 'Jeffrey's always had strong ideas. He takes advice from people. Then he makes up his mind on how to do things and he single-mindedly goes about them. I don't offer advice readily. But if there are certain things that I believe are in the interests of Victoria, and that he needs to know, I'll tell him. He and I are very strong personalities and we've had our differences over the years. A lot of people probably wouldn't believe that but we have had our arguments.'

Indeed, Walker's stature as a political mover and shaker was established long before Kennett came to power. His powers of advocacy and his capacities as a shrewd and skilful dealmaker were respected across party lines – and he had been employed by the Cain and Kirner Labor governments as well as by the Liberals. In the eyes of the ALP, however, Walker's achievement in securing the Grand Prix for Melbourne was merely the subtext to a bigger, far more lucrative game: the competition for the right to build and operate the state's first casino. Certainly, Walker and Williams knew before Crown lodged its final bid in August 1993 that the Grand Prix was returning to the city after a 40-year absence. As a result, Crown was able to factor into the price they were prepared to offer for the casino licence the potential revenue gains of up to 500 000 well-heeled visitors a year – an estimated extra annual profit of $18 million. Crown's competitor for the licence involved a joint bid by US-based multinational ITT Sheraton and their Australian-based construction group, Leighton. They were kept in the dark about the Grand Prix. As Lloyd Williams would boast later, 'Why should we have told Sheraton-Leighton? We were the catalyst for the Grand Prix, and the prizes in this life are for the people who want to march forward.'

Williams' somewhat smug assertion overlooked one important detail. Victorian taxpayers would contribute up to $10 million a year towards the staging of the motor-racing carnival. It was not an event to which Walker or Williams was entitled to claim exclusivity. And there was another significant issue surrounding the casino bid: was inside knowledge on the Grand Prix the only time Walker and Williams had access to privileged information?

Throughout Kennett's years as premier, Labor would claim there were irregularities in the crucial days between the lodging of the final bids for the casino on 16 August 1993 and the decision in favour of Crown three weeks later, on 5 September. In October 1994, the Opposition's bulldog, David White, asserted in parliament that cabinet ministers, including the treasurer, Alan Stockdale, were aware of the financial details of the competing tenders. He claimed that the premier had met with Walker prior to the lodging of the final bids. Had Walker and Williams been tipped off on the need to increase their final offer so they could outbid their rivals to win the licence? Labor would imply, if not prove, that they had. White called for an official inquiry to investigate whether Crown had enjoyed an unfair advantage over its rival, and whether anyone in government had communicated to Crown confidential details about the Sheraton-Leighton bid.

'Between June and September 1993, Crown casino increased its bid by $86 million, an increase in the upfront payment [to the state] from $170 million to $256 million, because it knew

its original bid would not succeed,' said White. 'The people of
Victoria have a right to know who told it to revise its bid . . . nobody suddenly finds $86 million within the space of a few months,
as the consortium did between June and September 1993, unless he
has to. We are making it clear that somebody chose to tell his mates
what was required to win the bid . . . What we are dealing with is
a corrupt government.'

White's claims were rebutted by the minister for gaming,
Haddon Storey. 'Mr White has given us a series of wild and unsubstantiated slurs. There is not a tittle of evidence in support of any
of the things he has said. He knows it is untrue. He knows he cannot prove it.'

As Storey and his colleagues would argue throughout the protracted casino debate, the conditions under which the casino licence
was awarded, the terms of the tender process, and the people who
would oversee that process, had all been determined by the Kirner
government. It was David White, no less, who had drafted the original legislation.

In February 1992, the Kirner government had set up a new, independent body, the Victorian Casino Control Authority (VCCA),
to decide on the 'preferred applicant' to build and manage a casino.
John Richards, a former president of the Law Institute, was
appointed as its inaugural chairman. Others appointed by the government included Paul Connelly, a former finance manager with the
resources company CRA, as chief executive; John 'Darcy' Dugan,
a former chief magistrate; and the former head of the Australian
Securities Commission, Henry Bosch. The aim was to assemble a
group of people unimpeachable in their probity, integrity and incor-
ruptibility.

The tender system to be used was a 'consultative evalua-
tion' – that is, the tenderers, throughout the bidding process,
would be in constant dialogue with the VCCA on the details of
their financial offers, the planning and zoning implications,
security and policing needs of their proposals, and the specifica-

tions of the gaming facilities, for example, the percentage of floor space devoted to poker machines as distinct from roulette or blackjack tables. The tenderers would be asked to specify the level of up-front payments they would make to government to secure the 12-year licence, as well as offer projections of the likely revenue stream for the state over succeeding years. In that sense, it was not a blind auction; the aim was for the government, through negotiations done via the VCCA, to maximise the financial return to the community within the constraints of ensuring a casino that met with the broad design specifications and gambling mix prescribed by the legislation.

The initial offers of the two final tenderers were to be submitted to the Authority by 30 April 1993, with the final bids to be lodged by 16 August. The competing consortia were permitted to vary their bids as they saw fit, while the VCCA, acting at arm's length from the government, was to keep the bidders advised through this period on the financial and legal parameters as laid down by the state. In order to guarantee a detailed flow of information between the tenderers and the VCCA through this process, the legislation provided for strict confidentiality on all aspects of the financial assumptions in the respective bids.

A month after the Kirner government came to power, the VCCA whittled down the initial group of 12 bidders to a short-list of three preferred applicants. These were Crown, Sheraton-Leighton and Jupiter's, the latter of which ran a casino on the Gold Coast in Queensland and had joined in a consortium with the US-based Conrad Hotels.

The new Kennett government embraced the casino proposal with enthusiasm. It would be emblematic of the premier's vision for the state's rebirth, and revenue from the casino deal would foot the bill for what Kennett, Stockdale and Birrell called Agenda 21. However, relations with the VCCA got off to a rocky start when Kennett demanded the resignation of Dugan over allegations that he had accepted a free flight to inspect Las Vegas gambling operations. Dugan departed the authority insisting that claims of wrongdoing were ludicrous. It was far from the last time conflict-of-interest issues would emerge in this debate.

In June 1993 the VCCA, acting on advice from its financial panel, eliminated Jupiter's from the contest. Crown and Sheraton-Leighton would compete in the final showdown for the licence. In their April offer, Crown had proposed an up-front payment to the state of $170 million. Sheraton-Leighton, apparently seeking to blow its competitors out of the race, was well ahead with an offer of an up-front payment of $305 million. It proposed spending $822 million building the casino, against Crown's more modest budget of $622 million. Sheraton-Leighton, believing Crown would struggle to provide financial guarantees if it significantly increased its bid, assumed that the contest was all but over. It seemed the rights to build and operate Australia's biggest casino were destined to go to the US giant. Crown began hastily restructuring its bid, but the talk around Melbourne was that the Sheraton-Leighton partnership was cruising to an inevitable victory and that the locals simply could not match its financial horsepower.

Hence the uproar in parliament about the whole casino licensing process. The final bids tell the story. Sheraton-Leighton had scaled back its offer to take into account higher than previously estimated construction costs, resulting in an up-front payment of $232 million. Crown's offer came in at $262 million. The local consortium had leapfrogged its rival, increasing its premium payment by more than $80 million. In its final assessment to state cabinet, the VCCA recommended Crown as the 'better bid' across all criteria. It was a stunning turnaround from the state of play only four months earlier.

According to senior ministers in the Kennett government, this was as much a surprise to those at the cabinet table on Sunday 5 September as to anyone else. They had gone into the crucial meeting to decide the winner of the casino licence expecting that the authority would recommend the Sheraton-Leighton consortium. Like the rest of Melbourne, they had heard the talk that Sheraton-Leighton's initial financial offer had blown Crown out of the water. In fact, senior ministers claim that the government, including Kennett, had plans for managing the politics if Sheraton-Leighton won the contest. Would there be a public backlash at the idea of this major development being handed to a US-based company in preference to the local players?

However, when Crown's success was announced, Kennett confronted a backlash of a different order. Almost immediately, Sheraton-Leighton denounced the 'hometown' decision, describing the bidding process as 'unbelievable'. Lloyd Williams, in his celebratory press conference, rubbed it in. 'Crown is Melbourne and places great pride in understanding Melbourne and its requirements. Crown will be the world's largest casino and will provide a huge boost for Victorian tourism. We simply understand what Melbourne's needs are, that's why the independent authority gave us the nod.' The managing director of Leighton Properties, Vyril Vella, said, 'We want nothing more to do with it; it's been a bad business and we are still licking our wounds.'

For Labor, ever on the lookout for any hint of scandal, the outcome of the casino bid threw up endless possibilities. The Kennett–Walker connection was as juicy a morsel as they come. White wasted no time, telling colleagues, 'We'll have a piece of this.'

Over the subsequent months, two other significant facts were to emerge. First, the Kennett government had cancelled a contract with an affiliate of Hudson Conway, the Walker–Williams property development company, to build new headquarters for the Gas & Fuel Corporation. Although there was a strong public finance case for the government to rescind the contract, the effect was to relieve Hudson Conway of a major capital commitment at the very time it was raising funds for its casino bid. Second, in early May 1993, the VCCA had sent a briefing note to an officer in the Department of Treasury and Finance outlining the financial offers it was considering from the casino bidders. Treasury had requested the information prior to formulating its budget, and government income projections, for the next financial year. Although the information had been coded – under the name 'bid A' or 'bid B' – so as not to identify either of the consortia, the implications were clear. If the resulting Treasury minute was circulating in government and could cross the desk of the minister, did this mean that Kennett and his senior colleagues had at their disposal an authoritative breakdown of the rival bids from Crown and Sheraton-Leighton? If so, was there a risk that this information could have been passed on? Stockdale denied ever seeing the so-called Treasury minute. But its mere existence created latitude for suspicion that the arms-length process prescribed by legislation was not watertight.

By October 1994 Labor was in full cry, alleging that the bid was rorted. In his call for a judicial inquiry, White did not mince words: 'This is a government that is corrupt at the core and at the highest levels.'

Storey's response was phlegmatic. 'During his contribution, Mr White named person after person who he claimed had been in-volved in some wrongdoing or improper behaviour in relation to the casino authority. Apart from implicating the premier and me, he implicated the rest of the casino cabinet subcommittee, com-prising the Treasurer and ministers for conservation and environ-ment, planning and police and emergency services. The bottom line is that Crown was the best offer, and it was so decided by the authority.'

Kennett also appeared unfazed. He claimed that Crown had simply outmanoeuvred Sheraton-Leighton, and that the losing bid-der's complaints were sour grapes. 'You would be a fool to put in your best bid early.' He insisted the bid process was clean, and that he could not have passed on details of the rival bid to Walker or Williams because he did not have the information.

Former public service chief Ken Baxter has since supported Kennett's insistence that the process was not compromised.

Throughout the tender process, Baxter sought to impose strict precautions against any hint of improper influence by insisting that any access to the premier by his mates in the business world occurred only in the presence of senior public officials. A full diary was kept of all meetings and phone calls were logged.

'I was well aware of these issues, and I was under instructions that under no circumstances was Ron Walker to be put through to the premier. Kennett was scrupulous in having no involvement. When Walker came into the office in his capacity as chairman of Major Events, there would always be a public servant present. Similarly, in the negotiations for the Grand Prix, I was always there and so was a solicitor from Arthur Robinson Hedderwick's.'

Baxter concedes that formal bureaucratic defences can never be impregnable against 'a nod and a wink' deal-making between governments and business. But, he insists, 'In New South Wales, when corrupt practices might be involved, the minister or the minister's political adviser would take it out of the hands of the bureaucracy. Kennett didn't do that. The checks and balances were there. In my view, the chances of corrupt behaviour were absolutely minimal.

'Given my previous experiences in New South Wales, I was certainly on the lookout. I was across the relationship with Walker and Hudson Conway, and I was also in no doubt that within Treasury and the premier's department there were any number of people quite prepared to blow the whistle. It was very different from New South Wales, where you might have property developers marching in and saying, "I have spoken to the premier, he told me this would happen, so why is it being held up?" Often, it might have been property developers gilding the lily, but that was the climate. I came to the view that Victoria was one of the states in the Commonwealth where I didn't think the corruption issue was justified in being raised. I certainly saw no evidence of the systematic corruption that had existed in New South Wales and Queensland.'

However, in October 1994, even Prime Minister Paul Keating had weighed in against Kennett. Keating was under close questioning himself over his purchase of a $2.2 million property in the salubrious inner-eastern Sydney suburb of Woollahra. The attacks on Keating were an extension of a campaign by the Liberals to embarrass the prime minister over his personal involvement three years earlier in a controversial investment in a piggery business. Sitting on the back bench after an unsuccessful challenge to Bob Hawke's leadership, Keating had turned a tidy profit of some millions of dollars from his rural investment. His decision to roll some of the proceeds into prime Sydney real estate resurrected the debate.

Interestingly Kennett, repeatedly the target of attacks over his own private interests, believed Keating was being unfairly pilloried. At one point, he even phoned the prime minister at home early one morning to express his sympathy. 'This is nobody else's business, and I am happy to say so publicly if you wish.'

Kennett is a notoriously early riser. And Keating may have been irritated at being stirred from his sleep to take the call. In any event, the upshot of that conversation was to give Kennett a lesson – if he needed one – about Keating's streetfighter instincts. It was not long before the Victorian premier would come to understand that the prime minister, as ever in his politics, would prove entirely unsentimental.

The sympathy call from Kennett counted for nothing. The prime minister, bristling over the slurs on his personal integrity, turned his guns on Kennett, Walker and Williams. In an extraordinary attack under parliamentary privilege on 13 October, Keating claimed the casino bid process in Victoria was 'like a dead cat in the middle of the road – stinking to high heaven'.

That same night, the prime minister flew to Melbourne for the opening of the Melbourne International Festival. The premier was also in attendance. The fur flew in public. In his opening address, Kennett accused Keating of 'skulking behind a candelabra' and denounced his remarks in parliament as 'gutless'. This public censure of the prime minister did not win the approval of the assembled guests, for whom Keating, through his interest in the subsidised arts, had become something of a darling. They jeered the premier. Socialite Sheila Scotter was said to have apologised to the prime minister privately 'for what that horrible man did'.

Keating had deftly turned his own discomfort into a story about Kennett's prickliness over claims of corruption. The story led all the front pages the following morning. The prime minister had engineered one of the great diversionary stunts of his career, and all at the expense of the Victorian premier. Jeff, however, was unrepentant. 'I am not going to allow a prime minister to make comments like that and then four hours later come down to the state that he's said is corrupt, to participate in a festival that the state government is a sponsor for, and just walk around, grinning from ear to ear.'

The result of the casino furore was an increasingly popular notion that the Kennett era somehow marked a loss of innocence in Victorian politics: a takeover of the political management of the state by big-business interests. When self-styled 'whistleblower' and former government adviser Stephen Mayne began his public campaign against what he saw as Kennett's unacceptable dalliances with Melbourne's business community, he claimed 'the Kennett government has had a more involved relationship with business than any other state government in Australian history'. All that can be said of this assertion is that history goes back a bit further than Stephen Mayne. As recently as the 1980s, governments in Queensland and Western Australia had been subject to extensive investigation over allegations of improper business dealings. And from its infancy, the Victorian parliament had been a magnet for men of money and influence, most notoriously the 'land boomers' who flooded into the parliament in the 1880s. The intersection of Collins and Spring streets allowed the ready conjunction of the city's business and political classes. With the possible exception of the Deakinite years of liberalism, Victorian politics became notorious as an unedifying tussle between the special pleadings of one private interest or another, with MPs often switching allegiances in accordance with whose interests they served. In 1920, Sir W. Harrison Moore wrote, 'The distinctive feature of Victorian political parties is their lack of a moral personality.'

The success of Menzies' reformation of the Liberal Party in the late 1940s was in broadening the party's base and shifting the focus of the conservative platform away from the express interests of big business towards what he characterised as 'the forgotten people' – the middle class of salaried professionals and the self-employed. While the Liberal Party remained vestigially the voice of capital – and the close connections between big business and the party were never more apparent than in the Bolte years – Menzies was known to have had a healthy distrust of the big end of town. It was a viewpoint that Jeff – coming from a small-business background – shared. Kennett came into politics as an anticorporatist, suspicious of deal-making between government, big business and organised labour. In turn, the business establishment saw him as an unguided missile.

Never was this more on display than in the early 1980s, when the Hawke Labor government called a historic national summit in Canberra aimed at debating and discussing the future directions of economic policy-making. Hawke, cannily, invited most of the nation's leading business figures to join senior ministers, state premiers, church speakers, welfare representatives and union leaders in a week-long debate, televised live from the chambers of the federal parliament. The prime minister subsequently did the same in 1985 with a tax summit, although with less success. These meetings represented the showcasing of Hawke's trademark style of consensus politics. Kennett, as leader of the Victorian Opposition, was appalled. 'The House of Representatives was used as the venue for Mr Hawke's version of the Grand Council of Fascists,' he told the media.

Kennett's pejorative attack on the process – and, by implication, those business leaders who attended – was overblown and counterproductive. Apart from the fact that he quite clearly misjudged the spirit of the times (Hawke, after all, was the master populist, and by 1990 would have four election victories to show for it), Kennett's outbursts also infuriated many in the business community. 'The man is an impetuous fool,' one of Melbourne's most prominent chief executives snarled privately.

There was further alarm in the business community in 1990 when shadow treasurer Alan Stockdale attacked prominent banker Bill Gurry in parliament, accusing him of being a Labor stooge. A Liberal Party source had seen Gurry chatting with John Cain at a street cafe in the Queensland resort town of Noosa, a favoured winter holiday destination for affluent Victorians. Stockdale later apologised publicly, but the episode compounded irritation in business circles that the Opposition was too ready to trash the reputations of business leaders as part of the thrust and parry of political debate at Spring Street.

It was not the first time senior officials at Liberal headquarters had heard these complaints. When he took over the state presidency in 1987, Michael Kroger was warned that business was uncomfortable with the 'ratbag' tactics of the Opposition leader. The same mutterings had reached the ears of the Liberals' state treasurer, Graeme Samuel. Letters of protest had also arrived on the desk of John Howard, then federal Opposition leader. Towards the end of 1988, with Kennett having lost a second election, Kroger and Samuel had gone to his office to issue a warning. Their message: 'Listen, we're getting a lot of flak from people who think you blokes are basically out of control.' It was to be a conversation that would ultimately poison relations between Kennett and Kroger.

At the time, Kennett and Stockdale were pursuing in parliament the activities of the state-owned Tricontinental merchant bank and, in particular, its managing director, Ian Johns. Kroger and Samuel had come to tell them that Johns was a loyal party supporter – code language for generous donor – and to impress on them the importance of not alienating the party's business constituency for the sake of political point-scoring. As events were later to prove, Kennett and Stockdale's suspicions were well grounded. Although Johns had been named young businessman of the year by the *Bulletin* magazine in 1986, within two years the merchant bank, under his leadership, had compiled a bad-debt portfolio of disastrous proportions. Although the scale of the Tricontinental debacle was not fully identified until the royal commission report in 1991, Kennett and Stockdale had sensed three years earlier that they were on to a major financial scandal. Kroger and Samuel, however, urged them to be sure of their facts. A group of prominent business leaders had approached the party to complain about what they saw as a campaign of vilification.

To this day, Kennett will not speak directly about the contents of that half-hour conversation with Kroger and Samuel. Kroger is known to have said, 'You guys are attacking a well-known businessman. Are you sure you know what you are doing? Is this all kosher?' Kennett had assured them it was: 'We know what we're doing.' Samuel had asked whether the party should get a major city accountancy firm to go through the financial dealings that were the subject of suspicion; there should be no guesswork or ill-informed assumptions when reputations were at stake. Where the conversation went from there remains the subject of dispute.

For his part, Kroger has denied vehemently claims by the ALP that he urged Kennett to 'go easy' on Johns. But significantly, at least in Kennett's mind, what Kroger did *not* say in that conversation was that he was a director of companies, run by his brother, which had taken out loans with Tricontinental. When Kennett discovered this, he took the view that Kroger should have declared this interest. According to his confidants, Kennett believed that this omission was unforgivable, and could have compromised the Opposition's pursuit of the Tricontinental scandal.

More than 10 years later, the implication left hanging over this incident is known to infuriate Kroger, who claims to have met Ian Johns only twice: once, briefly, at a cocktail party, and the second time at the frozen chicken counter at his local Safeway super-market. As Kroger has been at pains to argue publicly, Triconti-nental's loans to his brother's companies were repaid in full. There has been no suggestion of impropriety in these transactions. Indeed, the episode has spawned a prolonged public campaign by Kroger, driven in part by his hostility towards Labor head-kicker David White, against the rules permitting MPs to malign public figures under the protection of parliamentary privilege.

What Kroger is known to resent almost as much is the attempt by Kennett – or those around him – to use the episode as a 'moral justification' to explain their long-running animosity. According to the Kroger camp, Kennett has not once since raised the Tri-continental conversation with Kroger, privately or publicly. And if Kroger was not someone Kennett felt he could trust, why, in July 1992, when Kroger was poised to step down as party president, did Kennett ask him to serve on through the impending state and federal elections?

Kroger is understood to believe the emergence of aspects of their Tricontinental discussion can be linked to Kennett's own sensitivity about their other conversations during the late 1980s regarding Kennett's investment activities.

The ongoing rancour generated by these discussions highlights the sensitive nature of business alliances in Liberal politics, and their centrality. As state president, Kroger would meet regularly with Kennett to discuss the need for the Opposition leader to make himself available to the party's corporate support base. Kroger, together with Samuel, had responsibility for fundraising and, while protocol requires that the parliamentary leader never be told how much individuals are contributing, there is an expectation that financial supporters are entitled to have access to political leaders at fundraising banquets, boardroom lunches and the like. 'Access is the only thing they ever get,' insists one senior Liberal source.

Kroger's role was to advise Kennett's office to make room in his diary for dinners with various members of the party's coterie of business supporters. Both men mixed freely in these circles, and developed extensive corporate connections.

As premier, Kennett certainly consulted with business leaders. He appointed the billionaire boxmaker, Dick Pratt of Visyboard, to run the Victorian Arts Centre Trust. He held a monthly breakfast 'round table' with 16 of the nation's foremost chief executives, including former National Australia Bank chief and now BHP chairman Don Argus, Foster's Brewing Group's Ted Kunkel, Coles-Myer's Dennis Eck, Rod Eddington of Ansett and Arthur Andersen's Fergus Ryan. These business chiefs would join senior ministers, the state's top bureaucrats and the heads of Melbourne University and the Parkville medical and biotechnology research institutes for brainstorming sessions over muesli and toast. The premier also lunched at the Athenaeum Club with the Rumour Tank, a collection of prominent business leaders, lawyers and academics, including Tattslotto chief David Jones and soon-to-be state governor Sir James Gobbo.

In addition, he would host regular dinners on the top floor of the ANZ building in Collins Street for American, German and Japanese businesspeople based in Melbourne, inviting his guests to survey the impressive 180-degree views of the city skyline as he promoted the state as a destination for footloose capital. Sungrook Moon, Melbourne general manager of the Japanese securities house Nomura, said, 'We like Mr Kennett very much. He's very business-minded. More like an entrepreneur.'

Nor was Kennett averse to engaging in corporate intrigues: he opened a Victorian trade office in Dubai by poaching the Australian Consul-General, Peter Deacon. Visiting vice-presidents from US companies would be taken straight to his office as soon as their planes touched down. Kennett enjoyed dialogue with the barons of capital, and spoke their language: blunt, hard-nosed, assertive. Typically, he would offer free and usually forthright advice on how to run their businesses – whether they sought his opinion or not. There is little doubt that behind his determination to plug into the preoccupations of industry and investors was a legitimate public policy goal: Kennett saw it as part of his advocacy role to persuade major multinational corporates to set up regional headquarters in the state.

Ron Walker would argue pointedly that there was frequently a strong hint of the pot calling the kettle black whenever Labor launched its attacks on Kennett's links to business. Nobody seemed to mind too much when Hawke, Keating and the 'mates' of the New South Wales Right of the ALP, such as Graham Richardson and Stephen Loosley, entertained wealthy friends in the Sydney business community. 'They would wheel businesspeople into lunch with the PM at Kirribilli House and everyone was awfully impressed.'

Many of Kennett's critics argue that the premier's enthusiastic pro-business stance made his government captive to powerful interests 'at the big end of town', but Kennett, not unlike Menzies, had a healthy and long-standing scepticism about the preparedness of big business to back reform when it had a direct impact their company profits. In the government's first term, Stockdale had repeated run-ins with the aluminium giant Alcoa over a generous power subsidy deal it had made with the Cain government that would cost the Victorian taxpayer up to $200 million a year.

Likewise, when planning to privatise Victoria's electricity industry, Kennett and Stockdale engaged in a tense bout of sabre-rattling with the Business Council of Australia (BCA), the peak body for Australia's major corporations. In March 1995, a confidential briefing document prepared for the BCA's electricity taskforce was leaked to the press. It contained an explicit threat that if the government did not adjust its electricity reform model in the interests of the state's 50 major electricity users, 'much-needed investments may not take place, or may be directed to other countries'. The leak created anxiety in the marketplace at a highly sensitive time. Although senior BCA figures denied that the threat was or had ever been official policy, it sounded very much like an attempt to use

corporate muscle to bully the government into providing more generous concessions for business heavyweights.

To those in government, BCA's brinksmanship appeared eerily
reminiscent of Alcoa's success in the 1980s in securing its flexible
power tariff arrangement. This try-on aggravated Kennett. The
whole rationale for reform of the state's power industry was to
ensure it was stronger and more competitive in anticipation of the
new market that would be created through the national electricity
grid. Old cross-subsidies, which had benefited big business, were
one of the major hurdles to a more efficient industry. But the major
corporations were pushing for the right to sign direct long-term
contracts, circumventing pool arrangements for wholesale electricity supply. In short, big business wanted its power on the cheap.

In response, Kennett went on the attack. He warned a business
dinner in Melbourne that his government would view dimly any
sniping from the city's boardrooms about the electricity reform
process. In private, Stockdale was blunter still. The government
would not be cutting cosy deals on the side, irrespective of any
strong-arm lobbying tactics. The capacity to stare down one of its
own major constituencies was an important test of the virility of
the Kennett government's reform credentials.

That said, bringing a business ethos into the day-to-day operations of government became the credo of the Kennett years, and
the premier styled himself as the chairman of the board. He was
fond of comparing his role with that of the head of a major corporation, and he would speak of Victoria as a '$19 billion operation'
and 'the fifth-biggest business' in the country.

As he would tell his back-bench colleagues ritually, his government was not one made up of career politicians, but rather of
people with direct, practical experience of running a business. In
fact, this assertion greatly exaggerated the level of corporate know-
how in the Coalition party room. Certainly Kennett and former
Liberal leader Alan Brown had backgrounds in small business, but
both had been full-time politicians since the 1970s. Don Hayward

had served in the executive ranks of the Melbourne operations
of General Motors-Holden, Phil Gude had been executive director
of the Victorian Chamber of Commerce, and backbencher Tony
Hyams had come into parliament after a successful career in merchant banking. The deputy premier, Pat McNamara, had run
his own farming property at Nagambie, later converting it into
a vineyard. The Coalition team also included a pharmacist, a vet, a
handful of accountants and real estate agents, and two professional
broadcasters. Yet in the main, this was a government not unlike
most others, incorporating a preponderance of university graduates
in law and economics, all with long-standing career interests in politics and public administration. Nevertheless, it remained an article
of faith to Kennett that his government would look and sound very
different: it would bring a more brash and businesslike approach to
the exercise of public office. Kennett would exhort his ministers
and bureaucrats to be less intimidated by public service traditions.

In this attempt to create a more freewheeling business culture
within government, did Kennett ever understand – or accept – the
strict lines of demarcation between the worlds of business and
public life? The very philosophy of his government involved a blur-
ring of the boundaries. If ministers were to be running departments
as businesses or, in some cases, contracting out significant slices of
government activity to the private sector, this would self-evidently
require a greater level of consciousness of commercial practice and
a greater need to immerse government decision-makers in the attitudes and thinking of the business milieu. Although this might lead
ultimately to greater efficiency and effectiveness in government,
there were clear downside risks.

A notable example was the diminution of the public's right
to scrutinise all aspects of the behaviour of their elected leaders. It
is the very nature of competition that company directors bidding for government business do not want valuable commercial
information to fall into the hands of rivals. The introduction of
confidentiality clauses into government contracts was just one

example of how the Kennett model ran up against traditional public interest arguments for open and transparent government. Inevitably, this brought claims of excessive secrecy in government, and fed suspicions of behind-the-scenes deal-making. Through his years in government, Kennett's opponents would set out to exploit at every opportunity perceptions of a government, and a premier, rubbing up too closely to their corporate mates.

As demonstrated in his rebuff to Keating, Kennett's chosen strategy through much of this debate was to ride over the top of the criticism and to scoff derisively at any suggestion of backroom deals – no matter from whom they came. It proved surprisingly effective. By the time Crown opened, the premier appeared to have built up a 'teflon' quality not dissimilar to that for which former US president Ronald Reagan had become legendary. Kennett had about him an aura of invincibility, and there appeared to be unusually high levels of public tolerance for his indiscretions.

One reason for this may have been that for all the allegations of impropriety, there was never anything concrete to support the suspicions and accusations. Kennett characterised the attacks as mudslinging, and went on his way. Mostly, the tactic worked. For while discussion of conflicts between his public role and his private interests was good sport for politicians, journalists and lawyers, the ethics-based critique of Kennett's approach to government often came down to shades of grey about the protocols of public life. In the absence of hard evidence, the wider electorate seemed neither interested nor particularly fussed. What many saw instead was a city and state regaining confidence, the resurgence of growth in jobs and industry, major construction works under way, and events such as the Grand Prix and the opening of the casino. Kennett was a tireless spruiker for Victoria and, whatever his flaws, he seemed to get things done. As had been proven at the 1996 election, this go-getter image served as a powerful antidote to those who complained about the man and his methods.

CHAPTER THIRTEEN

RAISING THE STAKES

'A leader must be feared before he is loved.'
LEE KUAN YEW, BORROWING FROM MACHIAVELLI

In April 1996, a month after the state election, federal Labor MPs from Victoria began pressing for a full Senate inquiry into the circumstances of the Crown casino tender. It was an unusual step, constitutionally, on the part of the Labor senators. To push the federal parliament to appoint a select committee to investigate the affairs of a state government was unheard of. An infuriated Jeff Kennett saw it as muck-raking. Adding insult to injury, the Australian Democrats were supporting Labor's proposal. Rightly or wrongly, Kennett and his advisers saw this development as further evidence of 'the usual suspects' running as a pack in their attempts to cut him down.

As ever, Jeff went into battle all guns blazing. His denunciation of the Democrats' legal spokesman, Sid Spindler, however, went way over the top. Addressing a lunch in Melbourne, Kennett not only attacked the casino inquiry as a McCarthyist witch-hunt but turned on Spindler viciously. 'Sid Spindler was a member of the Hitler Youth, and I don't say that lightly, because he finishes his career in the same way as he started it . . . a campaign of, and a vendetta of, bitterness.'

As Kennett well knew, Spindler, like many thousands of young people in wartime Europe, had been an involuntary conscript. Spindler considered legal action. Two days later, Kennett apologised in public, claiming frustration over the casino inquiry. 'It was unnecessary to raise those issues, and I apologise to Senator Spindler for doing so.'

Jeff's strategy in politics had always been to confront his critics head on. Nobody was left guessing if they caused him displeasure or irritation. But in the aftermath of the 1996 election Kennett turned on his critics and tormentors with unusual belligerence. The premier had a few scores to settle, notably with the opinion elites in the media, academia and the law. Those who called for constraint in his leadership style were ignored – they'd been proved wrong at the election and he would aim to prove them wrong again. In what had become his trademark style, Kennett simply upped the ante. The privatisation push was thrown into top gear, his drive to lock in budget surpluses was unrelenting, and his impatience for reform continued unabated.

'Complacency must have no domain in Victoria,' he told his fellow Liberals. 'If we don't use these next two or three years, given the speed of change taking place, I'm very worried about where we might be. These are the good times in Australia: low inflation, very low interest rates. If we don't use the good times, we will have absolutely wasted this period of economic stability.' For any who sought to stand in his way, the warning went out: when Kennett confronted a speed hump, his first instinct was to put his foot to the floor and roll straight over the top. The first year of his second term was to see Jeff at his most ruthless and rambunctious.

Any sense of constraint on Kennett's part after his attack on Sid Spindler was short-lived. Only two days later, he referred again to being the target of a federal inquiry. Observing that 'this may or may not get me into trouble', he went on to compare his plight to that of former federal Liberal president John Elliott, targeting the long-running National Crime Authority investigation into Elliott's business dealings. As Kennett was aware, Elliott had been charged with theft, conspiracy to defraud and with giving false and misleading evidence to the authority. And, as Kennett should have known, the preliminaries to Elliott's trial were under way in the Supreme Court.

Not surprisingly, Jan Wade, Victoria's attorney-general, received a formal complaint a few days later. Justice Frank Vincent, who was presiding over Elliott's trial, wrote to her expressing concern that the premier's remarks could compromise an impending jury trial. Kennett was at risk of being in contempt of court. Wade referred the issue to the solicitor-general. On 28 May, the premier arrived in Justice Vincent's courtroom, accompanied by his Queen's Counsel. In a statement read by Counsel, Kennett made an unprecedented apology to the court, insisting his public comments had in no way been intended to reflect on the proceedings before the Supreme Court.

Justice Vincent made it clear he was unimpressed. 'It would seem that Mr Kennett asserted in his view the investigation conducted by the Authority was undertaken for the purpose of causing damage to a high-profile businessman who was associated with the Liberal Party. Had the reported remarks been made shortly prior to or after the empanelment of the jury, I think an application to discharge made by the prosecution would have merited serious consideration. Fortunately, this is not the position as it appears unlikely the trial will proceed for some time.'

Kennett received a humiliating scolding by one of the court's senior judges. 'To put it mildly,' Justice Vincent remarked, 'I was not appreciative of the utterings of the premier.' In an editorial the following day, the *Age* was scathing of what it saw as reckless behaviour. 'The premier, as the state's standard-bearer and chief lawmaker, must improve his behaviour and . . . watch his tongue.'

This was not the first time Kennett had run headlong into

the laws governing contempt of court. In July 1993, he had been drawn into making remarks on radio about the arrest of a suspect, Paul Denyer, wanted for a series of three murders of young women in the south-eastern suburb of Frankston. Denyer was later convicted. But the premier's public intervention infuriated the then Director of Public Prosecutions, Bernard Bongiorno, who warned publicly that he was considering whether to charge Kennett with contempt. The next month Bongiorno attended a two-hour meeting at Jan Wade's home, during which they discussed his threat to lay charges. The meeting was interrupted by at least two phone calls from the premier. By late August, Bongiorno had decided not to proceed with his threat.

The following October, Bongiorno resigned as director of public prosecutions, complaining that changes to the functions of his office had reduced the independence of the chief prosecuting officer. At a subsequent dinner for his colleagues at the Bar, Bongiorno was understood to have mentioned the evening he spent with Wade and the phone calls from someone he presumed to be Kennett. Wade, he claimed, had told him, 'The premier is very concerned about this.'

Bongiorno's colleagues were said to be aghast at the revelation. Had the government, through the attorney-general, pressured Bongiorno to back off from any action against Kennett? In the subsequent furore, Bongiorno would not discuss the issues publicly, but offered himself as a witness if the government was prepared to call a full public inquiry. The Victorian Bar Council and the Law Institute backed Opposition demands for an official investigation. Both Kennett and Wade flatly denied any improper conduct. They accused elements of the legal profession of orchestrating public controversy purely to undermine their reforms of the judiciary, sentencing laws and changes to the rules governing the legal profession itself. Certainly, a leading consultancy, International Public Relations, had been retained by the Law Institute to run a public campaign of opposition to the Wade agenda.

The Bongiorno affair became one of a series of run-ins between Kennett and Melbourne's legal community. It began with the abolition of the Accident Compensation Tribunal in November 1992, described by a senior bureaucrat as 'one of the great sinkholes of public spending'. The dismantling of the tribunal meant, effectively, the sacking of the 12 judges attached to the court. This was to become a running sore, with former judges such as Paul Mulvaney emerging as strident critics of the Kennett government's attitudes towards the judiciary.

Wade's decision to extend the talent pool from which the state's judges were selected added fuel to the fire. It meant senior barristers were no longer the sole claimants for elevation to the bench. Barristers immediately complained that this led to a diminution in standards and a higher frequency of appeals. There was also controversy when Wade appointed Nick Papas as chief magistrate, passing over several more senior magistrates. A former Crown prosecutor, Papas had been the architect of government changes to the office of the Director of Public Prosecutions.

Perhaps Wade's most threatening move was her appointment of a working party to investigate the self-regulating traditions of the legal profession itself. She was responding to long-standing grievances among regulators and the wider community over the restrictive practices and monopoly rights of what was regarded as an elite, self-managing professional club. Although the initiative appeared to have some support among legal heavyweights in the big national law firms, it gave rise to deep hostility among suburban and country solicitors, resentful that a government should seek to impose itself on the independence of the profession. They too became vocal critics of what they saw as government infringement on basic legal rights. Over the years, Wade and Kennett would be in a state of constant friction with influential groups in the legal community. In this context, the Bongiorno affair became a banner issue for a profession determined that the government should understand the need to keep a respectful distance.

The popular view in legal circles that Jeff Kennett was inattentive to due process also seemed to colour his relations with Government House. When the Coalition came to power, the incumbent governor was Richard McGarvie, a long-standing friend of John Cain and a distinguished jurist. As a former Supreme Court judge, McGarvie was a stickler for precision in the drafting of legislation. As the new government rushed its first wave of legislation through parliament, McGarvie developed a habit of sending some bills back to the cabinet office complaining they had been poorly drafted. He would make corrections, akin to a stern and scholarly schoolmaster marking an essay. McGarvie was no rubber stamp. Indeed, he demonstrated an unusual level of activism for the Queen's representative. Observed one senior bureaucrat, 'The poor man was bored witless.'

McGarvie's interventions became a source of endless annoyance to Kennett. The premier, though, was fastidious about keeping the tensions in-house. Unlike events in the famous row between Cain and Sir Brian Murray, or New South Wales premier Bob Carr's epic battle with Rear Admiral David Sinclair, during which the governor was all but evicted from his official residence, Kennett never pressured McGarvie to resign. Only on one occasion did their clash of wills threaten to become a public flare-up – and it arose over McGarvie's insistence that he would not wear a morning suit to the Melbourne Cup. As a matter of custom, it normally falls to the Governor-General to present the trophy to the winners of Australia's premier horse-race. In 1994, McGarvie had been invited to deputise. He agreed, but only on the condition he did not have to wear formal attire. Kennett, a stickler for certain traditions himself, was appalled. 'If he won't wear the suit, he's not bloody well coming.'

As the stand-off worsened, McGarvie's official secretary and Ken Baxter sought a compromise. Fortuitously, perhaps, a formal invitation had just arrived from a provincial governor in China, who had recently enjoyed a stay at Government House and was eager

to return the hospitality. A Victorian delegation, including prominent business leaders, had been invited to Beijing, and the official
party would be given access to the highest levels of the Chinese
government. Protocol demanded that the delegation be led by no
less than McGarvie himself. Unavoidably, the trip clashed with the
Melbourne Cup. Thus McGarvie went to China, and Kennett to
Flemington. Neither suffered a loss of face.

Perversely, perhaps, there is a view among top bureaucrats that,
despite the lack of personal warmth, Kennett and McGarvie in
fact complemented each other. Although Kennett brooded over
what he saw as the Governor's pedantic ways, McGarvie's close
scrutiny of the legislative fine print became a valuable tool in the
government's hectic early months. The Governor also became an
effective ambassador for Victoria outside of Australia, where his
official status was able to open many doors. Local business, in particular, benefited from the level of access he achieved. The premier,
of course, was all in favour of that. 'Kennett ensured the dignity of
the office was preserved, but they were never comfortable with
each other,' says Baxter.

More broadly, however, the premier's relationship with the legal
fraternity was one of undisguised hostility. Some of Kennett's
fellow Liberals believe that the government's clumsy approach to
issues of legal reform played into the hands of the profession. Any
attempt to force changes in the industry, such as the creation of
a government-run Legal Practices Board, could simply be characterised as government interference in the operations of the courts.
'Kennett liked to get in amongst it, but a lot of us could not see
the point,' comments a Liberal backbencher. 'We would be better
off having the legal profession working with us than against us.
The changes we made to the Legal Practices Act were not particularly good; but there was a group of lefties who were always going
to be against us, whatever we did. Kennett was never terribly good
at portraying the government as "small l" liberal, although, for
example, the changes we made to the Equal Opportunity Act were

all "small l" liberal changes. The effect of the changes to the DPP's act were inherently democratic, but we got portrayed as sacking this great independent person. We allowed the separation-of-powers argument to run away from us.'

That said, many backbenchers also believe the government was consistently gang-tackled in the public debate by an orchestrated alliance of like-minded opponents in the law, academia and the media. The idea of an anti-Liberal conspiracy in the opinion elites is a frequent lament within the Liberal Party, although Kennett, for his part, seemed to rejoice in the gruelling arm-wrestle to shape public opinion. Predictably, much of his venom was reserved for his enemies in the media.

The first major post-election controversy for the premier in 1996 centred on the revelations of the Kennett family's Guangdong share investment. Accompanied by press reports of Felicity Kennett's free use of a promotional BMW, the issue touched Jeff's raw nerves over the constant press focus on what he considered private family matters. His contempt for sections of the media exploded on 30 May. Opening the CityLink toll road site in a 'turning of the first sod' ceremony, Kennett took a shovelful of sand and hurled it towards camera crews filming the event. His audience laughed, albeit nervously. Kennett sought to make out later that it was all great sport, intended in jest. But on any measure, it was an undisciplined show of spite.

That day, the public witnessed for the first time the depth of Jeff's disdain for his media critics. It was a camera crew from the ethnic broadcasting service, SBS, that took the brunt of the shower of sand. But there is little doubt that had Kennett had the chance to take proper aim, his targets would almost certainly have been the *Age* and the Australian Broadcasting Corporation.

The culture of antagonism between Jeff Kennett and the city's broadsheet newspaper had been part of the fabric of public life in Victoria for the best part of two decades. Kennett's attitudes about the paper and its politics were probably influenced by his Liberal mentor, Sir Henry Bolte, who fulminated against the 'pinko rag'. Under the editorship of Graham Perkins, the *Age* had established a strong reputation for crusading journalism. It attracted and fostered some of the finest writing and reporting talent in the nation: Claude Forell, Les Carlyon, Michelle Grattan, Cameron Forbes, Terry McCrann. It ran campaigns, and it ran them hard. One of the most vociferous had been over Bolte's insistence on hanging convicted murderer Ronald Ryan in 1967. Bolte went ahead with the last state execution in Australia despite serious misgivings within his own government and in the face of a passionate community backlash, led by the press.

As it built a new readership among the Vietnam generation of tertiary-educated youth, the *Age* also became the voice of a new and more liberal social agenda, with issues of the environment, the arts, women's rights, Aboriginal land rights and the campaign to reform Australia's onerous censorship laws all becoming part of the mainstream political debate. The plight of state schools was another flashpoint. As a long-standing defender of the public education system, and with an extensive readership base among the state's teaching workforce, the *Age* found itself at loggerheads with the Bolte government over the school strikes of the late 1960s, when the ageing premier dismissed protesting teachers with the taunt, 'They can march up and down until they're bloody footsore for all I care.'

The *Age* was also to become an enthusiastic supporter of the sweeping social program proposed nationally by the Whitlam-led Labor Party. By 1975, when the Labor government was besieged by scandal and incompetence, the newspaper was at the fore in exposing its many foibles. Yet it took a hard line against the decision by the Fraser-led Liberals to block supply and force a constitutional showdown, and it became a trenchant critic of Governor-General Sir John Kerr's actions in dismissing the Whitlam government and commissioning Fraser to form a caretaker government pending a fresh election.

By the late 1970s, some senior journalists within the *Age* began to speak openly of the newspaper establishing a 'left-of-centre' tradition in the mould of the *Guardian* newspaper in Britain. This raised the curious concept of a newspaper and its editorial staff reflecting an official 'world view'. The reality, of course, was that the *Age* was never truly a monolith of left-leaning opinion. Even in the 1980s, it had too many good journalists who valued their professional objectivity too highly to be swayed by any suggestion of ritual support for one side of politics over another. Nevertheless, Liberal supporters, as a general rule, viewed the newspaper warily. Throughout the 1980s, without exception, the *Age* in its editorials supported the election of Labor governments in both Canberra and Melbourne – a defensible stance, in the main, with the exception of 1988, when it was painfully obvious (within the ALP in Canberra, if not the editorial offices at Spencer Street) that the Cain government had lost the plot and was a disaster waiting to unfold.

Kennett, of course, had his own reasons for questioning the *Age* and its motives. For one thing, the newspaper's response to his arrival in the ministry in 1980 had been less than welcoming. In an editorial that was generally laudatory of Hamer's cabinet reshuffle, the paper singled out Kennett for some rough handling: 'The strangest aspect of the reshuffle has been the rise of Jeff Kennett. A man of 32, who terms himself "an outspoken conservative", Mr Kennett has been selected for the ministry over more able contenders and then given the sensitive portfolios of housing and ethnic affairs. Mr Kennett is a man of energy who apparently has impressed some business leaders, even if he occasionally acts like a larrikin in parliament. But he would seem to add little to a ministry which is already short on intellectual talent and social concern. Let us hope we have misjudged him; for the jobs awaiting him will demand an understanding of society very much more sophisticated than that which he has shown to date.'

The editorial writer was Tim Colebatch, himself only in his twenties at the time. He would go on to become the newspaper's

Washington correspondent, and would serve for many years as an economics commentator based in Canberra. Almost 20 years later, Colebatch penned a confessional, revealing his authorship of the editorial and admitting that – yes – Kennett had in fact proved many of his doubters wrong. At the time, however, for a young minister with Kennett's ambitions, the newspaper's hasty judgement of his capacities and prospects must have hurt. Indeed, through the 1980s Kennett struggled to be taken seriously by many of the newspaper's opinion-makers – particularly its cartoonists, and especially Ron Tandberg. Despite the insistence of senior reporters covering state politics that Kennett was a formidable leader in the making, the general tone of political coverage in the *Age* through those years tended to pigeonhole the Opposition leader as a lightweight and loudmouth populist. He was good copy, good fun, but not a politician of substance.

This arrogance cost the *Age* dearly in 1988. In the months leading up to John Cain's decision to call a snap election, Kennett staffers provided reporters at the *Age* with an offer they thought was too good to refuse: a box of documents detailing irregularities in the operations of the Victorian Economic Development Corporation, including loans of government seed money to companies with dubious business credentials. The Opposition believed it was on to a genuine scandal. According to Kennett insiders, the *Age* could never be persuaded to run hard on the story.

Indeed, in the lead-up to the state election, most of the spadework on the emerging VEDC controversy was done by Brendan Donohoe, then state political reporter for the afternoon *Herald*. The editor-in-chief of the newspaper at that time was Eric Beecher; his deputy editor was Bruce Guthrie. Almost daily, the newspaper revealed new and embarrassing episodes in the lending practices of the VEDC. Beecher was subsequently to appoint investigative reporter Ben Hills to head up a team devoted exclusively to the pursuit of this bizarre saga in government financing. It was a campaign later described as 'the last grand roar' of an afternoon newspaper with a 150-year tradition in Melbourne journalism. The *Herald*'s sister paper, the mass-circulation *Sun News-Pictorial*, also chased the story tenaciously. But Kennett, entering his second election campaign as Opposition leader, was perplexed by the apparent lack of enthusiasm shown by the city's leading broadsheet newspaper for a scandal that would ultimately help bring down a government. Rather than focus on the evidence of serious failings in the Labor government's industry and investment policies, the *Age* drew attention to Kennett's leadership style. The late Robert Haupt, writing a campaign notebook in the *Age*, could not resist the temptation to mock: 'When the public meets Jeff Kennett, they laugh at him. Not with him, at him.' The concluding paragraph was brutal: 'In the end, you can only trust your instincts. Mine tell me that Jeff Kennett, life of the party as he is, won't be laughing on election night. But one thing is clear: if he is, I won't be.'

'He got a very rugged run from the journos,' recalls Peter Poggioli, at the time a Kennett staffer. 'They all seemed obsessed with the foot-in-mouth theme. Peter Kerr was keenly aware of it, Jeffrey was keenly aware of it, and we all worked to make sure whatever was said in public was sufficiently discreet. There was a letter of apology from the *Age* for the Haupt piece [specifically, over a derogatory comment on the shape and size of Kennett's ears] but it did not do us a lot of good because it wasn't made public. Everybody got angry but it was almost as if you expected it.'

Ironically, in 1992 Haupt was to write a hard-hitting column for the *Australian Financial Review* criticising the *Age*'s coverage. It was a journalist's lament over why a great newspaper that prided itself on the tradition of journalistic exposé had failed its readers during the collapse of Labor rule in Victoria. In the Cain–Kirner years, Haupt wrote sternly, the *Age* was 'the dog that didn't bark'.

By 1992, of course, the election of a Coalition government in Victoria was a foregone conclusion. The *Age* and the *Sunday Age* both supported the election of Kennett as premier, but not without qualification. A week out from election day, the *Sunday Age* ran a survey of voter attitudes under the front-page banner headline 'Kennett a risk'. As Labor warned of the Coalition's 'secret agenda', the *Sunday Age* ran lengthy analyses of Opposition policies and chastised shadow ministers for not releasing full details until the final weeks of the campaign. The Liberal organisation ignored the attacks; it would not be diverted from its campaign discipline. The reasoning of the paper's deputy editor, Bruce Guthrie, was that the Liberals were effectively a government-in-waiting, and ought to be treated as such.

After Kennett's victory, Guthrie took the view that a shambolic ALP would be unable to mount any effective opposition to the new government. Newspapers had a duty to step into the breach, and to ensure that the government was kept under close scrutiny. Guthrie also made no secret of the fact that he was unimpressed by Kennett's leadership style. The two had been butting heads from the early 1980s, when Guthrie was state political reporter for the *Herald*. He says, 'I don't think Jeff really understands the reality of the press. Deep down, I think he sees the press as the enemy of the state rather than an agent for good. Thinking back to when he was in Opposition, I don't think he understood the workings of the press at a practical level. Reporters come to work, they do their job, they don't play favourites. The simple fact is that when I was state roundsman for the *Herald*, Jeff's shadow cabinet leaked like a sieve. In contrast, Cain's was a first-term Labor government, and was very disciplined. I always thought that instead of beating up on the press, he should have looked at doing something about controlling his own people.'

Guthrie's judgements had been shaped predominantly by witnessing at close quarters the early impetuous years of Kennett as an Opposition leader, although it is probable that the two were always destined to clash. Both enjoyed the exercise of power, albeit in their different spheres. Both could be headstrong and wilful, and neither enjoyed taking a step back in an argument. Guthrie – tall, well dressed and wordly in outlook – could easily have been mistaken as someone from much the same milieu as the premier. In fact, he was the son of British migrants and had been brought up in the struggling north-west Melbourne suburb of Broadmeadows, a dormitory suburb for newly arrived workers in the massive immigration wave of the 1950s and 1960s. He had come up the hard way to a position of considerable influence in the newspaper industry. He had attitude.

Guthrie proclaimed it the role of the press to 'shed light in dark places'. This was a highly respectable journalistic stance, but for one niggling inconsistency. A newspaper organisation criticised for having soft-pedalled when it came to holding Labor governments to account was now going to redouble its efforts to ensure it would never again face that accusation, and this rigorous approach was being articulated by Guthrie, among others, at precisely the time a new Liberal government had come into power. In the eyes of Kennett and his supporters, however, this was not about journalistic fact-finding in the public interest; it was simply part of a pattern of pro-Labor bias dressed up in high-minded rhetoric.

Kennett's antipathy towards the *Age* intensified in 1993, when the newspaper led the charge against his family business, KNF Advertising. When the *Age* accused him of being 'thin-skinned' towards criticism and intolerant of debate, Kennett wrote a letter to the editor. 'My colleagues and I give generously of our time to Australia's media but the days when the media . . . dictates to the government are over.' Kennett was running the strategy he would employ throughout his years in government towards critics in the press. He would publicly confront them head on, and then attempt to ignore – and/or marginalise – those he regarded as chronically adversarial. This was payback politics. As premier, Kennett believed that they now needed him more than he needed them.

Jeff's preferred media outlet was commercial radio, where he could speak directly to his audience. As premier, he agreed to do weekly interviews each Thursday morning with 3AW's Neil Mitchell, the radio host with the biggest audience reach in the city. He was giving fewer press conferences and limiting the number of formal interviews. The newspapers had little choice when it came to reporting the premier's views on the issues of the day. They could either pick up what he said on Mitchell, or they could pretty much go without.

It was a strategy that angered and frustrated many of 3AW's media rivals. Jeff was playing favourites, ruthlessly. Yet there were few Thursdays in Melbourne when his hour-long session on 3AW did not make for prominent news stories the following day. Those who bemoaned his leadership style were reminded weekly of his value as a newsmaker and, despite the humiliation, were forced to run extracts from his radio interviews. As a media strategy, it doubtless worked to Kennett's advantage. However, it also guaranteed ongoing tensions with aggrieved journalists.

Kennett had particularly come to despise the *Sunday Age* under Guthrie's stewardship. An insight into the state of relations between the two can be gained from an interview I did myself at the end of 1992. The newspaper organised the interview to mark its decision to declare the new premier Victorian of the Year. Kennett's greeting in his office at Treasury Place was gruff and inquisitorial. 'All right. What's this about? What's bloody Guthrie up to?' When he learned that the Victorian of the Year was awarded to the person judged by senior editorial staff at the *Sunday Age* to have made the biggest impact on the state – for better or worse – he snorted, 'Typical.'

It was inevitable that sparks would fly when, in October 1995, the Fairfax management decided to appoint Guthrie as editor of the Monday-to-Saturday editions of the *Age*. Guthrie himself had misgivings about accepting the job, warning Fairfax senior management, 'Kennett will go feral over this.' He comments, 'You have to remember that I was among those who thought the *Age* had gone to sleep in the Cain years. I was determined we were not going to fall asleep on my watch. People interpreted that as an anti-Liberal thing. In fact, it was simply that I was not prepared to see the newspaper repeat the mistakes of a decade earlier.'

Guthrie succeeded business journalist Alan Kohler in the role of editor. Kohler's tenure had been part of a strategy to restore the newspaper's credibility at the business end of town and to broaden its perspective in areas of debate such as economic policy and market deregulation, where, as a general rule, it had tended towards a left-leaning critique. As one Liberal would complain: 'You take one look at *Age*'s consultative committee, and you see a list of people you would have at a Joan Kirner dinner party.'

Guthrie, however, saw the attempt at realignment as a serious misreading of the *Age* and its readership. He took the view that the paper could only prosper by defending what he described as its 'small l liberal traditions'. He pledged that the relationship between the newspaper and the Kennett government would never be comfortable. 'I thought in the early Kennett years many sections of the Melbourne media were intimidated and were eager to fall in behind him,' he explains. 'I felt the *Age* should remain true to its liberal traditions and the principles of fair and balanced journalism; unlike some, we should not become a cheer squad for the government.' As Guthrie assumed editorship the message went out. The new editor had a point to prove, and the newspaper would become more aggressive in its coverage of the state government. The dog that didn't bark would now bark often, sometimes hysterically.

Predictably, relations deteriorated rapidly in the weeks leading up to, and immediately following, the 1996 election. Through the election campaign, the newspaper ran hard on the issues surrounding the casino tender. Guthrie was filmed by the ABC in charge of an editorial conference, where he canvassed openly the likelihood of corruption within government. It confirmed Kennett's worst prejudices about the editor and his predispositions.

Moreover, the day after the Grand Prix carnival began in Melbourne, the newspaper chose not to feature the race prominently in its front-page news coverage. Rather, it led with the first serialisation of the so-called 'Baxter Diaries' – a collection of jottings and observations about cabinet meetings and ministerial conduct by Ken

Baxter. These documents had been leaked to the newspaper several months earlier. Their publication in the middle of an election campaign was seen within government as a calculated attempt to embarrass and damage the premier. Kennett attacked Bruce Guthrie on his regular radio slot that morning, calling his editorship a disgrace. Guthrie has since revealed he was phoned within minutes by the then chief executive officer of Fairfax, Bob Mansfield. 'What the hell are you doing? Jesus, I'm trying to repair this relationship with Jeff Kennett and you go and do this to me. The board is furious.'

Guthrie sought to reassure Mansfield that there were only a few days of the campaign to go. However, it was not the only time Fairfax management would take Guthrie to task for what was seen as the paper's negative and carping attitude towards the premier. In December 1996, when Conrad Black sold his controlling interest in Fairfax, two new directors from Brierley Holdings in New Zealand flew into Melbourne for an early-morning meeting with senior executives at the *Age*. As Guthrie delivered a presentation on the newspaper's achievements, he was cut short by a question from one of the new directors, Rod Price: 'Why are you waging war on a politician of international stature?'

Kennett, for his part, would not hold back in complaining to Fairfax directors about his treatment at the hands of Guthrie. Although Kennett's convincing victory at the 1996 poll strengthened his arm in his jousting with the *Age,* Guthrie remained insistent that the newspaper would continue on the course he had set. Bob Muscat, who succeeded Mansfield as chief executive at Fairfax, has retrospectively offered the boardroom view of events in Melbourne. 'I think there was a bit of a duel going on. My view was that the newspaper needed to reflect what Victoria was about. Jeff Kennett had brought about a sea change in Victoria, and I don't think the *Age* was giving him credit for that.'

In July 1997, Muscat appointed Steve Harris, the former editor-in-chief of the Herald & Weekly Times, and previously Guthrie's superior on the *Sunday Age,* as publisher of the *Age*. It was a title that combined responsibility for the financial management of the newspaper with the role of editor-in-chief. Guthrie would no longer have free rein in determining the newspaper's editorial direction. Resigning as editor, he accepted a job offer in New York with American publishing giant Time Inc. He left the newspaper believing he had been undermined at board level by Kennett and his business mates. 'I think Jeff Kennett was very shrewd at applying pressure in the right places. Politicians have been doing that to editors for decades, trying to get them removed or sacked. I thought the Fairfax board should have been committed to stand by me. Instead, he absolutely convinced them it was in their commercial interests to make a change.'

An interesting postscript to the tensions between the editor and the premier is that soon after leaving the *Age*, Guthrie was the target of an approach from the Victorian ALP. Through a third party, he was told there was enthusiasm at the highest levels of the Opposition for him to consider nominating as a Labor candidate. Although Guthrie rejected out of hand the notion of becoming a high-profile ALP recruit, as he did a similar offer from the Australian Democrats, the incident suggests that if Kennett misinterpreted the editor's motives, he may not have been the only one.

The Australian Broadcasting Corporation was another of Kennett's regular targets. Like most Liberals, the Victorian premier was convinced that there were strong pro-Labor sympathies among the staff of the national broadcaster. Moreover, he believed that the organisation, with many of its decision-makers based in Sydney, was increasingly reflecting the agenda of that city at the expense of Melbourne, the smaller capitals and its large regional audience. In 1998, prompted by the controversial axing of a major ABC arts production team in Melbourne, Kennett would announce a parliamentary inquiry into whether the ABC was diverting a disproportionate level of its $500 million taxpayer-funded budget to its Sydney headquarters. The ABC was to be cast almost in the role of a hostile alien.

The incident that permanently coloured Jeff Kennett's view of the ABC came during the 1992 election campaign. For the next seven years, Kennett would impose a ban on any of his ministers appearing on the *7.30 Report*, the ABC's nightly current affairs program following the national news. It was a decision based on the conduct of staff associated with the program. At one point during the 1992 campaign, an ABC camera crew had, in an act of stupidity, followed Kennett into a public toilet. But the flashpoint was an interview conducted at Kennett's Surrey Hills home by the anchor of the program, Mary Delahunty. Although Delahunty has since sought to defend her role in the incident, she in fact asked Kennett whether he had 'played around'. Kennett answered the question without hesitation, telling the reporter he had enjoyed his days as a young man before he was married. But when the interview was over, and the crew were packing up their gear, Kennett's press adviser, Tania Price, went to him and pointed out a provocative double meaning implied by the question. In effect, wasn't Delahunty asking Kennett whether he had cheated on his wife? According to Russell Skelton, then executive producer of the program, who dealt with the fall-out, Jeff flew into a rage. The Opposition leader all but forcibly ejected the crew from his home.

The tape of the offending segment of the interview never went to air. As Skelton was to write many years later, 'Why Delahunty asked such a needlessly antagonistic and irrelevant question remains a puzzle to me.' The incident left Kennett permanently jaundiced in his view of ABC reporting standards. His experience with Delahunty became legendary throughout the Liberal Party, and the ABC journalist was given the soubriquet 'Red Mary'. According to Skelton, what peeved Kennett most was that when his staff asked for the original tape of the interview, they were told by Jock Rankin, then the head of news and current affairs (and Delahunty's husband) that it was ABC property, and would remain so. Skelton wrote, 'It was not clear in whose interests Rankin was acting: Delahunty's, the ABC's, or both.' In 1998, Delahunty was preselected as Labor candidate for the safe seat of Northcote, and went straight to the front bench. In an article in reply to Skelton, she conceded she had asked a sloppy and ambiguous question, but insisted the controversy was largely confected: 'a minor Spring Street myth'. She argued that Kennett's ban on the *7.30 Report* had more to do with an attempt by a 'bullying' politician to use – or not use – the media to his strategic advantage. 'The premier had big plans for Victoria, much of it politically difficult or controversial. Why bother to risk it all by going on live TV when things might get difficult?'

Jeff Kennett's near-obsession with media politics was not unusual for a politician. Paul Keating kept files on particular journalists; Bob Hawke was in regular dialogue with media bosses; John Howard appointed one of his closest friends, Donald McDonald, to chair the ABC board. But as much if not more than these other leaders, and due in part to his marketing background, Kennett became a keen student of the media industry and a skilled practitioner in media presentation, especially on radio, where his relaxed and freewheeling style was well suited to the talkback format. Indeed, on several occasions during his premiership, Kennett seemed to be considering a full-time career in the media. Towards the end of 1997, there were informal approaches for Kennett to consider taking up a senior executive role at News Ltd. Likewise, in 1998 rumours circulated in Melbourne and Sydney that Kennett was being considered for a high-level management role at the Fairfax organisation.

Although Kennett now insists there was no serious ballast to these rumours, he would often choose to send the media into a flap by refusing to deny the speculation. Ron Walker declares that Kennett joining Fairfax was never a starter. 'He was bagging the *Age* every day. Unmercifully. Maybe people put two and two together. But it's easier to have a shot at a newspaper than run it.' The truth is that Kennett's overwhelming motivation in all of his posturing with the Melbourne media was the same as that of any street-smart politician: to get the most favourable coverage possible for his government and his policies. Where he differed from others was that if he believed organisations such as the ABC and the Age were unreasonable in their criticism, he would shout it from the rooftops to make sure everyone knew exactly where he stood. He was combative and confrontationist.

In an interview early in his second term as premier, Kennett sought to explain his refusal to relent on his hard-hitting approach despite persistent community and media criticism of his heavy-handedness. 'This is where people have so misunderstood me,' he said. 'I don't find governing tough. You know you are going to face opposition to some decisions, or have public campaigns launched against you. Naturally, some people are scared of change. But it's not a worry at all if you believe what you're doing is right. And when people see the benefits, the dividends of reform, they may not like us but they respect us. They know where we're going. We set goals, and we achieve them. They may disagree with the pace, they may not like the personal style, but there's only a few who would argue that the state is in a worse position than 1992.'

Amid the avalanche of criticism and controversy in media and legal circles in the months following his 1996 victory, Kennett's self-belief appeared undiminished. As retired Liberal veteran James Guest was to note wryly of the premier's daredevil demeanour at this time, 'Having walked a tightrope, he wants to do it in the dark now, without a safety net.'

CHAPTER FOURTEEN

CROSS-CURRENTS

'It is not for the government to send in thought police.'
JEFF KENNETT

In the last weeks of the 1996 election campaign, Jeff Kennett did an interview with *Beat* magazine in which he openly revealed the fact that three of his four children had experimented with marijuana as they entered adulthood. As the government awaited the recommendations of a report he had commissioned into the state's drug laws, the premier convened an impromptu discussion around the kitchen table at the family home. At the time, Ed was 21, Amy 20, Angus 18 and Ross 16. What would they think of moves to decriminalise marijuana use? 'It was interesting,' Kennett said. 'Three of them had tried marijuana, one had not. That in itself was a revelation. I said to them, "All right, if you were in my position, what would you do?" They said, "Don't decriminalise." I said, "Well why do you say that?" and they said, well, two of them had only tried it once and won't try it again. The third will – has tried it several times and may continue. What the fourth does, I've got no indication.'

Similar kitchen-table conversations might well have happened

in many households in middle Australia: the quest for understanding by parents of how their children deal with the issue of
illicit drugs. As Kennett went on to say, 'I don't think I felt disappointed. I was surprised and then educated by it.' Felicity Kennett would add later, 'Surely it's better to know what your children
are doing and have done than bury your head in the sand . . .
I need my kids to tell me stuff.' For a supposedly conservative politician in the final days of an election campaign, these were remarkably candid insights to offer to the public on how the Kennett
family was grappling with the drugs culture. Some other politicians, Liberal and Labor alike, might have feared a backlash from
any admission that their family members had engaged in drug use,
but Jeff Kennett, in his stance on many of the social debates of the
day, showed himself to be anything but a common-or-garden-
variety conservative.

Confounding his critics, Kennett had a perplexing habit of
adopting progressive, small 'l' liberal attitudes on issues such as
censorship, minority rights and individual freedoms. Americans call
this 'crossover politics'. Kennett's preparedness to range beyond
the predictable confines of public debate and to open his mind to
radical, 'out there' policy prescriptions was to become as much
a part of his persona as his controversial approach to economic
reform. It was doubtless an important factor in his formidable profile among younger voters.

In 1993, attorney-general Jan Wade brought to cabinet a submission seeking tougher enforcement of restrictions on the sale and
display of 'soft pornography' at newsagencies. This stirred Kennett's
libertarian instincts and he spoke strongly against it. 'It is the
responsibility of parents and newsagents to determine what children see. It is not for the government to send in thought police.' In
an attempt to remind his colleagues of the bad old days of onerous
censorship in the 1960s, when the vice squad would run raids on
booksellers at the urging of the former chief secretary's office,
Kennett said, 'I have no desire to see a return to Rylah's police.'

When Wade brought a submission for the introduction of mandatory sentencing for certain indictable offences, Kennett again voiced disapproval, fearful such a move would simply give rise to the overcrowding of prisons. But the 'tough on crime' initiative had the support of most of the cabinet and the legislation went ahead. The premier said nothing against it publicly.

In 1994, however, in the aftermath of an infamous police raid at Tasty, a gay dance club in inner Melbourne, the premier would not bite his tongue. The controversial police action happened at 2.10 a.m. on Sunday 7 August. As on most weekends, the club was full to capacity. Music was blaring and the dance floor was crowded with young gays and lesbians. Police swarmed into the club, some wearing baseball-style caps, some carrying batons. They were under instructions to carry out a drug raid after an anonymous tip-off that amphetamines were being bought and sold at the club. Turning the lights on, police ordered the patrons to place their hands on their heads or against the nearest wall. When some protested, one police officer called them 'faggots'. After a wait of 20 minutes as police questioned club members, an inspector then issued an astonishing order: all 463 patrons were to be strip-searched immediately. Told to file into a cloakroom, the males were ordered to remove their clothes and bend over to ensure they were not concealing drugs. Police refused requests from those who asked to be searched in private. Meanwhile, 130 women were being searched by female police officers in the club manager's office. The whole humiliating saga took more than three hours, and led to a lengthy series of civil actions against the police.

Prominent in the community reaction was the premier's apparent dismay. Widely portrayed as a law-and-order hardliner, Kennett had greatly bolstered police powers of investigation, including the right to demand names and addresses and the power to take fingerprints and blood and hair samples. Amid the debacle at Tasty, however, Kennett would not come to the defence of police – far from it. He described the tactics employed as 'extreme and disturbing' and would later accuse the police commanders responsible of going 'absolutely over the top' in their neglect of the rights of the individuals involved. Writing in the *Age*, columnist Claude Forell remarked on the paradox of 'as red-blooded, firm-wristed a heterosexual authoritarian as Jeff Kennett' joining the chorus of protest.

In similar fashion, Kennett's image as an 'alpha male' – loud, sometimes boorish, one of the blokes – sits at odds with his attitudes to women in high places. Kennett's inner circle over the years included a high ratio of women among his top advisers, from Nerida White in the 1980s to Tania Price after his return as Opposition leader, to Elizabeth Proust as his second public service chief and Anna Cronin as his senior adviser through the latter half of the 1990s. As one Labor MP concedes, 'He competes with men. He listens to women.'

Perhaps the most significant of Kennett's interventions in the broader social debate, however, was his attempt to kick-start a national debate on drug law reform. Heroin use had soared in Australia in the mid-1990s as the market was flooded by cheap heroin from South-East Asia. Almost 300 Victorians a year were dying of drug abuse, approaching the same number of deaths as occurred each year on the state's roads. Jeff decided the time had come for a reappraisal of the traditional law-enforcement approach to combating the drug menace. On 11 December 1995 Kennett commissioned the vice-chancellor of Melbourne University, Dr David Penington, to chair an inquiry into what options were available to prevent a more widespread use of hard drugs and target the heroin traffickers. Kennett also promised a special sitting of the Victorian parliament, which Penington would be invited to address, in order to debate at length the possibilities for drug law reform.

Penington's Drug Advisory Council reported soon after the 1996 state election. Its most controversial recommendation was a call to decriminalise the personal cultivation and use of marijuana.

South Australia had gone part of the way towards this reform, by reducing penalties for marijuana possession to monetary fines without convictions. Dr Penington urged the Victorian parliament to go further. He argued that most of the $500 million market in illegal drugs annually in the state was attributable to the trade in marijuana, and that prosecution of marijuana users was soaking up the resources of the drug enforcement agencies. Moreover, by treating marijuana users as criminals, the legal system was forcing otherwise law-abiding citizens to seek out illicit dealers. This exposure to criminal networks was heightening the risk of the 'stepping-stone' effect of soft drug users being tempted into buying heroin, amphetamines and other more deadly and addictive drugs.

'The efforts and resources of the police need to be redirected to hard drugs, to traffickers and to the important area of community policing activities,' Penington advised. The distinguished academic was under no illusion about the likely level of community resistance to a reform of this magnitude. In the weeks leading up to the special parliamentary sitting, many Liberal MPs in conservative electorates had taken soundings; there was widespread apprehension, and much opposition. When Penington came to parliament in May 1996, he had anticipated just such a response. 'I can understand decent people from any background, whether they be parents, journalists, police officers or members of parliament, being fearful of drugs and the drug culture and being apprehensive about change. Some still have a strong feeling that the law should remain unchanged in the hope that it will hold the line . . . the reality is we have not been able to hold the line. The 1995 household survey revealed that 388 000 Victorians said they had used marijuana in the past year. That includes 335 000 people between the ages of 14 and 34 years. Will we leave these young Victorians at the mercy of rapacious drug traffickers, inevitably to be exposed to the harder drugs over time, or will we make a realistic attempt to attack the vested interests, to break one link with traffickers where we can, and to put in place drug education programs which young people will respect, so as to curb their use and abuse of the drugs?'

In measuring his response to the Penington report, Kennett knew the proposal to liberalise the marijuana laws had split the Coalition. Although he had found no problem in admitting his children had experimented with drugs, he sensed that the preponderance of opinion within the Coalition was almost certain to be against change. The premier was also troubled by the advice from officers of his health department that a growing body of medical evidence suggested that excessive smoking of marijuana could trigger psychiatric disorders in some users. In receiving the Penington report in parliament, Kennett's response did not shut the door on the prospect of reform, but signalled his ambivalence. 'We must be mindful of the impact on our society of any changes we make, and where our society will be left if we make no changes at all.' In a significant pointer to his ultimate thinking, Kennett characterised the tabling of the report as only 'the first stage in the process of community consultation'. In the end, Kennett deferred to the majority opinion of his colleagues; and the government did not adopt Penington's key recommendation. The premier won considerable kudos in bringing the drug reform debate into the parliament. He also kick-started a broader, ongoing debate nationally. This time, however, his government would not be the pacesetter in challenging the established order. Even Kennett assessed the risks as too high.

Although the drug debate became the headline illustration of Kennett's activism on social issues, his government was also pushing out the horizons in other important, if less visible, areas of social policy. One field in which the government became a trendsetter – and not without controversy – was in mental health services. On coming to office, Kennett's health minister, Marie Tehan, stepped up efforts to turn a system functioning on 19th-century principles – and dependent on Dickensian asylums built 50 to 100 years earlier – into what many believed to be one of the most progressive policies of deinstitutionalised care in the world.

The theory of deinstitutionalisation had been pioneered by a Canadian, Wolf Wolfensberger, and had been adopted by the Nordic countries of Europe, in particular, as a more enlightened approach to mental health care. Labor ministers in Victoria, notably Jim Kennan, had begun exploring the possibilities for Victoria and laid the framework for a policy shift. These initiatives were taken up with gusto by the incoming Kennett government.

Over the next seven years, such oppressive and cell-like psychiatric hospitals as Larundel, Mont Park and Arandale would close their doors. They were replaced by separate and smaller community-based units spread through suburbs and country towns, each specialising in the care and counselling of adolescents suffering mental disorder, the intellectually disabled and geriatric patients. A majority were encouraged to live in the general community, calling on assistance from these centres or from mobile units only at times of distress. The switch to 'community care' was dramatic. By 1998–99, almost two-thirds of all funding for psychiatric patients was for treatment and assistance outside of the hospitals. It was a philosophy aimed at treating people with mental illness in the least restrictive and stigmatising way possible, encouraging them to socialise freely in the wider community.

The program was not without its critics. Within the industry there were complaints that too often the government's enthusiasm for deinstitutionalisation seemed to be driven primarily by the search for budget savings. Some parents and carers complained of the difficulty of getting access to acute-care hospitals when patients were suffering life-threatening psychotic episodes. In 1995, the Royal Australian and New Zealand College of Psychiatrists called for a moratorium on acute-bed closures, saying deinstitutionalisation was being taken too far. By 1999, however, the preliminary findings of a joint research study by Melbourne and Monash universities appeared to suggest that for the vast majority of those released from long-term care in mental hospitals, the alternatives in accommodation and community care units had been a success. Further vindication came when the Blair government in Britain sent a specialist team to Melbourne to investigate the approaches used in the treatment of mental health.

Kennett was to further elevate the issue of mental health on the national agenda by becoming the first leading politician in the country to speak on the need for a new approach to the growing incidence of depression in society. He proposed the establishment of a world-class research institute in Melbourne devoted exclusively to depression's causes and treatment. He focused particularly on the trends in youth suicide, especially among teenage boys in the bush.

As in the drugs debate, these were not issues of advocacy readily embraced by political leaders. They meant opening the window onto areas of social dysfunction that might once have been swept under the carpet, or tainted as criminality and therefore treated as taboo. In his readiness to confront these issues, Kennett proved himself eager to grapple with contemporary challenges beyond the sometimes drab routine public debate. For the most part, his libertarian streak enhanced his political reputation – with one glaring exception. His tolerance, if not encouragement, of the growing gambling culture threw him into a passionate public debate over gambling's impact on the city and state's social fabric. At one point in 1996, as church speakers raised their voices about the incidence of problem gambling, Kennett lashed out at them as 'yesterday's people'.

The saga of Victoria's wrestle with the social and moral issues associated with legalised gambling stretched back 20 years. In 1979 Federal Hotels, the owner and operator of casinos in Tasmania and the Northern Territory, was trying to gather political support for plans for a casino on the banks of the Yarra. Kennett, then merely a promising backbencher, was sent by Premier Hamer to discuss the proposal with Federal Hotels' chairman, John Haddad. Although

Kennett had seemed enthusiastic, the Hamer government was in fact deeply split on the question of liberalising the gambling culture in the state. Gambling, especially on sports, had always been an integral part of Australian culture. Victoria already had a thriving horse-racing industry and one of the first and biggest state-run total-isator betting agencies in the world. In and around the city and its suburbs there was also a robust illegal starting-price bookmaking industry, and a cluster of small, illicit gaming houses offering fan tan, Russian poker, baccarat and two-up for those willing to risk a run-in with the officers of the gaming squad. But there remained strong opposition among the Liberals' conservative, churchgoing constituency in Melbourne's eastern suburbs – the so-called 'wowser' tendency within the party – to the notion of the state being seen to endorse the spread of gambling. This opposition was fuelled by fears of the encroachment of organised crime into the gambling industries.

One of the first decisions of the incoming Cain government in 1982 was to set up an inquiry into the establishment of a legal casino in Victoria. It also set up a parallel inquiry into whether poker machines should be introduced into the state. Both inquiries recommended against the introduction of new forms of legal gam-bling. By 1991, however, the departure of the straitlaced John Cain as leader had removed from centre stage the most vehement oppo-nent within the Labor Party towards officially sanctioned gaming houses in the state. Tasmania had been operating casinos for almost 20 years, and the Northern Territory for more than a decade. South Australia, Western Australia and Queensland had followed their lead in the mid-1980s and New South Wales, already the home of 100 000 poker machines, was preparing for the establishment of a major casino in Sydney. Cash-strapped, desperate for new revenue sources and looking to create some impetus and confidence in the local economy, the Kirner government chose not only to proceed with the casino plan, but also to allow the introduction of poker machines into the state's hotels and licensed clubs. This was despite the recommendation of a second inquiry by Xavier Connor, QC, that the state 'would be better off without casinos'. Introducing the legislation in 1991, Kirner said it was time to acknowledge that 'Victorians no longer wanted a government telling them how to behave in terms of . . . gambling'.

This was a statement of principle with which Kennett fundamentally agreed. For him it was an issue of free choice in a free society. Adults could make up their own minds. This stance set Kennett at odds with an alliance of old-style prohibitionists, all the major churches and Melbourne's influential and well-organised networks of social welfare activists, who set up an interchurch gambling taskforce. In their view, the gambling explosion may have been delivering vast new revenue streams for state governments, but at horrendous cost to the poorest sections of the community who were among the most vulnerable to the gambling bug. No sooner had Melbourne's temporary casino opened in 1994 than the antigambling forces, led by prominent church figures, became active in lobbying. Among the protagonists was a Uniting Church pastor, the Reverend Tim Costello. His forceful involvement in the public campaign of opposition brought extra piquancy to the test of strength. First, Costello was a former mayor of St Kilda who had been sacked as part of local government reforms, and determined from that point on that the government would not silence its critics. Second, he was the older brother of one of Kennett's party enemies, federal Liberal deputy Peter Costello. Tim Costello's running battle with the premier always carried these various overtones, which virtually guaranteed him a prominent run in the media. His profile was helped by the fact that, like his brother, he was an eloquent and effective advocate who seldom minced words. 'We have the biggest casino in Australia. I think it's scarring the soul of Melbourne.'

Predictably, Kennett did not take the criticism lying down. Prior to the 1996 election, he fended off attacks by saying that he found the churches' critique 'incredibly boring'. Reaffirmed in victory, he went after his critics in typical blunt style, accusing church leaders of 'using the pulpit for political purposes' and adding the insult that the churches were facing the need to mount a revivalist drive to recruit new worshippers. 'Getting involved in the political field is almost to me an indication of failure in their primary purpose. Their flock has flown.'

In November 1997, however, the stakes were raised higher still when Kennett was caught up in a public scrap with no less than the Governor-General, Sir William Deane. In a pointed public address, Sir William defended the right of church leaders to speak out on political issues and said gambling addiction was placing strains on working families and their finances. In the midst of a by-election campaign in the conservative eastern-suburban seat of Mitcham, Kennett made no attempt to disguise his irritation. Questioning the wisdom of Sir William's intervention, he sent a shot across the vice-regal bow: 'It will not be long before people start responding in kind, and that will be unfortunate for the office. He is opening himself up to responses which, I think, if he is not careful could tarnish the role of the Governor-General.'

Despite his attempts to stare them down, the premier's critics would not retreat. In 1998, though, Kennett came under pressure from another front – and perhaps from where he least expected it. In Canberra, Prime Minister John Howard had been regularly expressing his concern over the rise of gambling in the community. With the federal election safely out of the way, Treasurer Peter Costello announced he would be ordering an inquiry by the Productivity Commission into the impact of gambling. In July 1999, as Kennett prepared for a state election, the Commission lodged its draft findings. They demanded tough new regulations, including stricter controls on advertising, the creation of an independent industry regulator in each state, caps on gaming machine numbers (the cap already existed in Victoria, if not in New South Wales) and requirements that casino and poker machine operators disclose the odds of winning. The report found that 'problem gamblers' were contributing one-third of the $11 billion in annual gambling industry revenue.

The gambling issue may never have become the heartbeat issue that decided significant shifts in voter affiliation one way or another, but it remained an important undercurrent throughout the Kennett years. Perhaps the greatest irony is that Kennett gave the churches the very platform on which they could attempt to revive their sense of relevance. As Tim Costello would note wryly, 'In my living memory, the Kennett years probably represent the period of greatest social influence for the church in this state.'

CHAPTER FIFTEEN

———

A LARGER STAGE

'He would love to go down in history as the
best prime minister Australia never had.'
A SENIOR VICTORIAN LIBERAL

In the first half of 1997, Jeff Kennett became the chief public
advocate for an overhaul of Australia's tax system. In his usual
blunt and bothersome style, the Victorian premier set out to generate a greater sense of urgency and adventure among his federal
Liberal colleagues in Canberra, going out hard in support of a
fundamental restructuring of the nation's tax base.

In mounting this campaign, Kennett was dragging the Liberal
Party into the danger zone. Australia's ramshackle and inefficient tax
system was the great unfinished business on the checklist of economic reform. The precarious politics of attempting to engineer
change had cowed and defied two generations of national leadership. It had cost the John Hewson-led Liberals the 1993 election.
As politicians of all flavours knew (but in some cases, dared not
admit), almost any meaningful genuine tax reform would almost
certainly have to include the dreaded acronym 'GST' – a broadly
based goods-and-services tax that would take the weight off income
tax and the cumbersome system of wholesale taxes on which

Australia had relied for 50 years. But the community had demonstrated a perennial scepticism about the impact of a tax shake-up,
especially on poor and low-income families. Now Kennett would
attempt to prod John Howard into tackling what the prime minister would later describe as an '800-pound gorilla'. Kennett, though,
knew Howard could not ignore him.

Kennett was at the height of his powers. He had become a national story. The Sydney newspapers began sending senior writers
down to Melbourne to report back on the phenomenon. The Canberra press gallery was also taking a much closer interest in what the
Victorian premier said and did. Political commentator Michelle
Grattan, writing in the *Australian Financial Review*, said, 'Kennett
has got Victoria on its feet again with a combination of astuteness,
innovation, audacity and brutal, sometimes obsessive politics . . .
business praise for Kennett's consultative and go-go approach
contrasts with some private sector doubts about the Howard government's mettle on reform. Kennett is galloping as fast as ever and
doesn't conceal his frustration with those who canter.'

Kennett's stunning second election victory and 'think big' reputation had stamped him once and for all as a leader to be reckoned
with: a conviction politician against whom others were measured.
Labor's Robert Ray – the former defence minister and factional
overlord – warned his colleagues that Jeff was fast becoming a
modern hero of the Liberal Party. The question for his opponents
was: how could this man's momentum be stopped? The question
for his Liberal colleagues was: would he be content to remain at the
helm in Victoria, or did he have ambitions for a larger stage?

Speculation regarding the possibility of Jeff Kennett making a
move to national politics began gathering momentum barely two
years after he took office in Victoria. Partly, it was a function of
the disarray in the federal Liberal Party after John Hewson's defeat
at the 1993 federal election. Out of power for more than a decade,
and having endured the shock of watching the electorate reject
the most ambitious policy agenda assembled in a generation, the

federal party was searching desperately for someone to lead them out of their deep malaise. The charismatic and single-minded leadership of Menzies had hauled the Liberals out of the abyss in the 1940s. Now, in the mid-1990s, Kennett had established himself as arguably the dominant conservative politician in the nation. Might he be the saviour?

In September 1994, Ron Walker, Andrew Peacock and federal Liberal Party president Tony Staley began sounding Kennett out about the possibility of him standing for the federal seat of Kooyong, held by Peacock and once represented by Menzies. It was the most sought-after prize in the Victorian Liberal Party. All three had known Kennett for 20 years. They knew his strengths; they knew his foibles. They also understood that this would be no easy sell. Kennett was careful and calculating: what would be the implications for his career, his family? Was an outside chance at the prime ministership worth the gamble? The three men knew Kennett harboured serious and perhaps insurmountable reservations: in blunt terms, he just wasn't all that interested. But they thought they should ask anyway. Walker and Staley went to see him. 'We'd like you to stand for the seat. We need you in Canberra,' Walker argued. Kennett listened, then imposed absurd conditions.

The premier wanted his treasurer, Alan Stockdale, to be found a federal seat as well. If he was going to Canberra, he wanted to take his senior advisers with him. 'We work as a team,' he told them. Kennett also made a demand which none of his colleagues, notwithstanding their influence in the party, could hope to deliver, either individually or collectively: 'Can you organise the numbers?' Was Kennett asking whether Peacock could ensure his preselection for the seat of Kooyong? Surely this was a given. Or was the premier hinting at a shortcut to the top? A guarantee of the federal leadership of the Liberal Party? If so – and Peacock, for one, insists that Kennett never laid down an ultimatum of this nature – it was either fanciful or mischievous. The federal parliamentary party at that time included two men who had led the Liberals to federal elections, John Howard and John Hewson; there was already a surfeit of senior Victorians in the upper ranks, among them two former deputy leaders, Peter Reith and Michael Wooldridge, and the shadow treasurer Peter Costello, a man earmarked as a prime-minister-in-waiting. Each had his own support base in the party room, and the federal party, as ever, was a cauldron of ambition. Walker and Staley knew Kennett was asking the impossible; so, they suspect, did Kennett.

'I discussed it with [Jeffrey] quite regularly,' Walker acknowledges. 'With the talents and success he had in Victoria, he would be a brilliant prime minister. But federal politics is a different scene altogether and the fact that Jeffrey had kicked a lot of federal heads along the way wouldn't have endeared him to them. Costello and Reith and Wooldridge and all the others would have seen him coming into their patch as objectionable. It was no easy task. And why would he leave his job as premier of Victoria and chance his arm at becoming federal leader when nobody could guarantee him the numbers? He said he and Stockdale were like Henry Bolte and Arthur Rylah; they were a winning team together, and it would be nice if both of them could be attracted to the federal party. But nobody could ever guarantee everything. I never thought Jeffrey was absolutely serious about it. He flirted with the idea for many years. But he totally understands the frailties of the federal party. And I don't believe being a prime minister suited his lifestyle. He doesn't like flying. He doesn't like overseas travel much. He loves his home, and his family. And the thought of living in Canberra would have been the opposite to what he believed he should be doing in life. The challenge would have been good, and the invigoration surrounding the job, but I just don't believe it was for him.'

Peacock is convinced that Kennett knew all along that a 'draft' was never a prospect, although he admits that, in informal discussions over many years, the two had discussed the logistics of the premier moving to Canberra. Peacock, for his part, believes

Kennett was never doing more than keeping his options open. 'There was never a moment when he said, "Yes, I'm going to do it." He just wanted to know about it in the event that a seat came up. You have to bear in mind that, in 1994, he had only been premier for a couple of years. He wasn't greatly attracted to it because he was loving every second of what he was doing. It would have meant he had to move base and depart the things he loved most in life. We had a number of discussions on the pluses and minuses. I even put some examples down on a sheet of paper for him, listing the considerations on either side of the ledger. We were talking more about the personal and intimate elements – frankly, more practical issues – not the sort of things he would ask of people he didn't know that well. What is it like to go away on Monday and not come home to see the family until Saturday? How do you restrict the functions at the weekends when you come home? How would this sit with a wife who had a career of her own? And what about the kids? You have to remember the sort of guy he is. At this stage, he was ironing the shirts every Sunday evening – his shirts, the kids' shirts. He would stand there and iron them all. That was part of his routine.'

Through all this, says Peacock, he cannot recall any commitment being sought or given that Kennett could be fast-tracked into a leadership role nationally. 'Look, there was no guarantee he would go into the shadow cabinet. He probably would, but he would certainly not have been elected leader straight away. In that sense, you were asking him to make a serious change in his professional as well as personal direction. I didn't push him on that at all, and I don't recall him making any definitive proposition to me. He might have to others.'

Nevertheless, throughout his premiership Kennett's enemies within the Liberal Party remained ill at ease over his ambitions. Although Jeff invariably scoffed at the speculation, the 'will-he-or-won't-he?' guessing game remained a constant in Liberal politics in the 1990s. Senior colleagues could never be sure he did not

have his sights set on the glittering prize of the prime ministership. After all, throughout his career Kennett had demonstrated an
often obtrusive eagerness to make his voice heard in national
affairs.

Kennett's presumption that he was entitled to have his say in
national debates was partly personality-driven but also a function
of the history and tradition of the Liberal Party. The Victorian
Liberals have long regarded themselves as the dominant state division in the organisation. Postwar premier Tom Hollway was once
warned by one of his top bureaucrats, 'You can't run the country
from the Windsor Hotel.' Hollway ignored this advice, and so has
almost every senior Victorian Liberal since. Six of the 10 federal
Liberal leaders have been Victorian, including four prime ministers: Menzies, Holt, Gorton and Fraser. Even when the leaders have
come from other states, it is invariably with the say-so of the party
powerbrokers in Melbourne.

Indeed, in 1994 John Hewson claimed that agitation against his
leadership was being led by the 'old school tie establishment' in
Melbourne. This was nonsense, and calculated to extract sympathy
for Hewson from the other states. But it demonstrated the power
of a mythology which inspires imagery of cigar-puffing party
grandees gathered around an open fire in one of the city's genteel
clubs, anointing their chosen one. The Victorians, for their part,
would insist that their power and influence are purely performance-
based: the party emerged as a creature of middle Melbourne,
and over five decades, beginning with Menzies' role as the party
founder, the division has contributed more than its share of intellectual and organisational horsepower to the movement nationally.
The Victorian Liberals have also enjoyed the most electoral success of any state – often holding their seats in the face of massive
national swings.

Sir Henry Bolte, the former Victorian premier and the closest
thing to a Jeff Kennett role model, was notorious for throwing
his weight around on the federal scene. Bolte's persistent bad-

mouthing of his federal counterpart John Gorton became a critical factor in the vote of no-confidence that would ultimately cost Gorton the prime ministership. But no matter how deep the resentment elsewhere, the Victorian Liberals claim as their right the role of guiding the destiny of the party nationally – and the power to make or break federal leaders. Although this haughty tone of superiority has subsided somewhat in recent years, it took the young Jeff Kennett almost no time at all after entering Liberal politics to tap into this dynamic.

Barely a year after becoming minister for housing in the Hamer government, Kennett sensed the political kudos to be gained from the ploy of being seen to stand up for the interests of Victorians against those remote and uncaring policy-makers in Canberra. Demonstrating his early instincts for effective, if crass, grassroots politics, Kennett sent an open letter to the Fraser government demanding interest rate relief for homebuyers and increased federal grants for public housing. 'They're wrong in Canberra. They're so out of touch . . . people are destitute out there,' he ranted. This was seen in Canberra as a precocious, headline-grabbing stunt by a ministerial upstart. John Howard, then federal treasurer, sought to slap Kennett down publicly. Refusing to buckle, Kennett scoffed at suggestions that by risking the wrath of powerful Liberals in Canberra he could be short-circuiting a promising career in politics. 'I'm simply one cog in a huge wheel. What happens to me is irrelevant,' he told the media. He also claimed cheekily that his letter, published in five newspapers, had been misunderstood. 'What I was doing was thanking the federal government for being big enough and human enough to rethink their policy on housing,' he taunted.

Some months later, Kennett visited Canberra to present a submission directly to Prime Minister Malcolm Fraser. He lost the argument. Significantly, however, there was open dissent in the federal camp the following day. Andrew Peacock came out publicly in support of Kennett's proposal for mortgage subsidies for low-

Kennett works the airwaves in his regular weekly radio slot with 3AW's Neil Mitchell.

Here's one in the eye for my friends in the media. Kennett flings sand at media crews during the opening of construction on the CityLink project.

The challenges of parenthood. As he ponders drug law reform, Kennett relies on the relaxed informality of his family life. Calling his children to a conference around the kitchen table, he asks about their experience of drug use. Three out of four reveal they have experimented with marijuana.

An awkward coexistence. Kennett with former state governor Richard McGarvie: 'If he won't wear the suit, he's not bloody well coming.'

Dr David Penington addresses the historic drugs summit in the Victorian Legislative Assembly. Under back-bench and party pressure, Kennett later pulls back from major innovation.

Looking to distant horizons. Despite a looming election deadline, Kennett in 1998 continues to articulate his long-term strategy for the state.

As prime minister and premier, John Howard and Jeff Kennett grew closer – but were never close.

King of the kids: the premier plays ball with the next generation of voters.

On the national stage, Kennett uses his reputation as a 'conviction politician' to push hard for tax reform and combat the anti-immigration prescriptions of the One Nation movement.

Under the pump. Former health minister Marie Tehan faces fierce questioning in parliament over her role in the Intergraph affair. In private, Kennett has issued her a formal warning.

The hot eye of scrutiny: auditor-general Ches Baragwanath, the indomitable public watchdog.

Seldom the twain shall meet. But for one rapprochement, Jeff Kennett and Roger Pescott engaged in a feud lasting more than a decade. It climaxed in Pescott's fiery resignation speech, which precipitated the Mitcham by-election.

A moment to savour. Labor leader John Brumby (left) enjoys a day in the sun after Labor's Tony Robinson scores a spectacular victory in Mitcham.

The way we were: Jeff and Felicity Kennett in the best of times.

income home buyers. Peacock was at this stage a backbencher. Having resigned from cabinet in protest at Fraser's style of leadership, he was positioning himself to become the next federal Liberal leader, with Howard as his most likely rival. But, says Peacock today, 'I would still be in favour of it, even though it might make the economic rationalists shudder. It bears out what I say about Kennett being an interesting mixture of a guy. He practises conservative economics yet he has a liberal social conscience. As you know, I have a liberal social conscience and I used to get belted for it. He had the same instincts and, through our conversations, we had a mutual understanding. But I don't think people appreciated hisprofile on these issues back in the days when he was hardly known.'

Peacock's outspoken support of the young Kennett cemented one of the longest-standing alliances in Australian politics. The two became a formidable tag team, forming the core of the most influential constellation of power in the Victorian party. Their battles with the Right of the party – the forces of Kroger and Costello, and, by extension, John Howard and his small but devoted coterie of Liberal supporters in Melbourne – were to become legendary. In 1986 Kennett, as Opposition leader, renewed hostilities with John Howard, who had toppled Peacock as leader of the federal Coalition a year earlier. This time, the Victorian accused his federal counterpart of not taking the fight to the Hawke government over its introduction of a fringe benefits tax. 'A lot more pressure should have been applied,' was Kennett's unhelpful advice. Jeff promptly admitted that his pot shot at Howard was purely a way of gaining publicity for his own opposition to the tax. 'I've always been able to attract media attention when I have either abused the media or accosted my federal colleagues,' he told a press conference in Melbourne candidly. 'Now if that will help in getting my message into your columns or cameras today, then consider yourselves accosted, abused and also my federal colleagues abused.'

Jeff Kennett's most vitriolic flare-up with Howard, however, came the following year – the result of a taped phone conversation between the Victorian Opposition leader and Peacock.

The conversation followed a landmark victory by the Victorian Liberal Party in the Central Highlands by-election of March 1987. The by-election had represented a perilous political assignment for Kennett. The federal Coalition was in the throes of the 'Joh-for-PM' campaign, an ill-conceived and highly destructive crusade by the Queensland National Party premier, Joh Bjelke-Petersen, to launch a populist drive to claim power in Canberra. In a brazen challenge to the Liberal Party in both Melbourne and Canberra, Bjelke-Petersen had endorsed the National Party candidate for Central Highlands. The Liberal candidate was a novice, Marie Tehan. If she lost, Kennett knew he would be blamed for allowing Joh to establish a foothold in Victoria. In fact, the Liberals achieved a remarkable 7 per cent swing against Labor to win the largest share of the primary vote. The result was proclaimed immediately as a major setback for the Joh push. But that night, Kennett was in the foulest of moods. He believed the state's party performance had been damaged by the infighting and incompetence of the federal Coalition. Scheduled to address a state council meeting the following day, Kennett was unhappy that Howard would be among those in attendance. Jeff blamed Howard for the federal party's disarray, and earlier that evening had spoken to him bluntly, registering his displeasure and frustration.

On the way home from the central highlands, Kennett picked up his car phone and called Andrew Peacock to report back on the day's events. The phone call was intercepted by a group of civil rights activists scanning the radio frequencies as a hobby. It was taped and a transcript delivered to the *Sun* newspaper. The paper led its Monday edition with a private dialogue that 'turned the airwaves blue'. It is hard to imagine a conversation between two politicians capturing more vividly the behind-the-scenes brutality of public life.

KENNETT: 'I had the biggest run-in with your little mate tonight.'

PEACOCK: 'Why?'

KENNETT: 'Oh, he got on the phone and said, "Are you happy about the result?" and I said, "No, I'm not." He said "Why?" and I said, "Because without your front pages and total disunity . . ."'

PEACOCK: 'You'd have a 10 per cent swing.'

KENNETT: '"I would have got myself another four and you've fucked it up for me." And he went off his brain . . .'

PEACOCK: 'Did he?'

KENNETT: 'And he went off his brain for a long time.'

PEACOCK: 'He went off his brain? He went off his brain?'

KENNETT: 'And he said, "I didn't like the way you kept me out of the campaign" and I said, "I wouldn't have you in it." I didn't have any federal people . . .'

PEACOCK: 'You didn't have me. You didn't have anyone.'

KENNETT: 'And I said to him, "Tomorrow, I'm going to bucket the whole lot of you . . ."'

PEACOCK: 'No, don't do that, Jeffrey . . .'

KENNETT: 'I said, "Tomorrow, John." And he said, "I know where your sympathies lie." I said, "I couldn't give a fuck. I have no sympathies any more. You're all a pack of shits, and tomorrow I'm going berserk." Well, he went off his brain and I said to him at the end of it, "Howard – you're a cunt. You haven't got my support, you never will have. I'm not going to rubbish you or the party tomorrow, but I feel a lot better having told you you're a cunt."'

PEACOCK: 'Oh, shit.'

KENNETT: 'And the poor little fella didn't know whether he was Arthur or Martha.'

PEACOCK: 'Oh, shit.'

KENNETT: 'I just thought I should let you know.'

PEACOCK: 'Well, tomorrow you are humble. You do feel better. And I'm getting out of the car, and I've told Margaret this, I'm getting out of that fucking car, and I'm saying, "It's not Howard's day, it's not my day, it's not anyone's day, it's not Ritchie's day, it is a day for Jeffrey Kennett." I was thinking I would go even earlier, and even if only a third of the bastards are there, I was going to go and grab the mike and say, "This is unprecedented that in the midst of the most horrific difficulties– ", I faced that when I was leader in by-elections, we haven't had 'em for some years . . .'

KENNETT: 'Yeah . . .'

PEACOCK: ' " – we had a great win yesterday and the only person who's deserving – not just earned it, but deserving of support – is Jeffrey Kennett. If you don't give him everything, you are letting down the Liberal Party . . ." '

KENNETT: 'All I can say is I thought I should let you know where I ended up with your little mate . . .'

PEACOCK: 'Well, fuck him. I'm not worried. I almost bloody . . . my fuckin' anger yesterday. As Margaret knows, the first thing when I came in last night, I said, "Oh, fuckin' cunts." I said, "The whole fucking thing could upset tomorrow" and she said, "What are you talking about?" and I said, "Oh, Jeffrey" and she said, "What's Jeffrey done?" and I said, "It's not what Jeffrey's done, it's what everyone has fucking done to Jeffrey." '

KENNETT: 'I thought we came out of it all right.'

PEACOCK: 'All right? The news reports. Have you seen them on television?'

KENNETT: 'No.'

PEACOCK: 'They're saying Labor's down 7 per cent. Cain's claiming that on a two-party-preferred vote – and don't you let that cunt get away with it – it's only 2 per cent. They're saying the Joh campaign has stopped in its tracks. In one of the state electorates, it is something like 2 or 3 per cent down on the last vote and the Liberal Party will walk it in.'

KENNETT: 'We've won on primaries in every lower-house seat and even in the National Party seat. So it's fantastic . . .'

PEACOCK: 'Well, that's exactly what I interpreted from it, mate.

I didn't have the detail. But I'm just going to talk to you [to the media]: "I don't care what you ask me, you can all go and get stuffed. This is Jeffrey Kennett's day."'

KENNETT: 'It's been a good result. But anyway, Howard won't know whether he's Arthur or Martha tomorrow.'

PEACOCK: 'Well, I know. But you feel better. Be humble. Everyone is going to say you're the greatest thing since sliced bread, right?'

KENNETT: 'Well, it's a good all-rounder.'

PEACOCK: 'Where are you?'

KENNETT: 'I'm on my way home.'

PEACOCK: 'Right.'

KENNETT: 'I'm going home to have a reasonably early night and I will see you tomorrow.'

PEACOCK: 'I have got to sit in a chair about four or five rows back from the front and allow Howard, after he's had his tumultuous reception, to come down and sit next to me and be photographed together, smiling . . .'

KENNETT: 'Oh, how pathetic . . .'

PEACOCK: 'I said I would do that . . .'

KENNETT: 'How pathetic . . .'

PEACOCK: 'Yes, but I'm doing it on the basis that when I get out and when I talk – 'cos they'll be chasing me because of the federal issues – I'm just going to talk Kennett. I knew it was going to happen, it should have been better and it would have been better without those difficulties . . .'

KENNETT: 'There's two points. One is the federal difficulties. The other point is how Cain tried to bloody deceive the electorate on this price control thing. The good thing about it . . .'

PEACOCK: 'Be humble, mate.'

KENNETT: 'Oh, I know.'

PEACOCK: 'They're behind you.'

KENNETT: 'The thing is we did not compromise as Cain and the National Party did to try to win political support. It may have

cost us some votes on the price control thing but we've kept very
firmly to our philosophy and that's the most important part of
the whole win, I think . . .'

PEACOCK: 'Make those points. But just tell 'em there are hun-
            dreds of thousands of people in the state who are going to
            support you. You're right and that's it. Just be humble, mate.'

KENNETT: 'All right. I will see you tomorrow.'

PEACOCK: 'Look forward to it. I am just so thrilled.'

KENNETT: 'All right.'

PEACOCK: 'OK, mate.'

KENNETT: 'Give my regards to your good lady.'

PEACOCK: 'OK. Ta. Bye.'

As the story broke that Monday, Kennett and Peacock would
complain, not unreasonably, that there were major privacy issues
raised by the newspaper's decision to publish material gathered
surreptitiously by possibly illegal means. They could also have
argued that the coarse language was not so very unusual in the
bruising game of politics, although it was reserved usually for back-
room chats that occurred well beyond the earshot of voters. Even
so, the fall-out from the mobile phone conversation was momentous. Apart from the incident entering political folklore – a rap
band included excerpts in a recorded song – there were immediate
ramifications for Peacock's career. Howard banished him to the
back bench for disloyalty. As a despairing Peacock would lament,
'Where would you think you were safest? In your own home, after
midnight on a Saturday, in bed with your wife. Save and except for
bloody Kennett.'

At the time, Peacock was deeply resentful of the summary justice
dispensed by Howard, not least because, as the transcript showed,
Peacock had spent much of the conversation trying to placate
Kennett and prevent a brawl. But the episode served to further
undermine Howard's public profile at a time when he could
least afford it. As the Joh-for-PM crusade caused havoc within the

Coalition, Bob Hawke pounced, calling an election for August 1997. Howard's campaign was lacklustre and erratic, reflecting the pressures crowding in on him, and the Coalition lost seats. In hindsight, Peacock concedes that Howard was entitled to be offended: 'It was pretty spicy language by anyone's measure. We both laugh about it these days.'

Howard and Kennett, too, would eventually mend their fences. But unfortunately for Howard, the incident did not dull Kennett's taste for antagonising his federal colleagues. Once he became premier, there might have been an expectation that he would curtail his career-long habit of offering regular commentary on the shortfalls of national policy-making. No such luck for his colleagues in Canberra. It did not take long into Kennett's first term for his government's policy activism to send ripples beyond the state's borders. Despite his abhorrence of air travel, Kennett flew frequently to the other capitals to give speeches at business lunches and party fundraising functions. The media coverage he received outside the state was typically more generous than his treatment at home. Although flattered by the attention, and prepared to flirt playfully with the notion of entering federal politics in his dealings with the media, Kennett would also routinely profess his contempt for Canberra and all it represented. 'I think the worst thing in life would be to die a slow and lingering death. The second-worst thing is to go to Canberra,' he told reporters.

Of course, this is not to say Kennett did not see himself as a major player nationally. Observed one senior Liberal, 'He would love to go down in history as the best prime minister Australia never had.'

In the previous 20 years, perhaps only Neville Wran in New South Wales, Joh Bjelke-Petersen in Queensland and Don Dunstan in South Australia could compare as state leaders who boasted a reputation for fighting in the same weight division as prime ministers. When Dunstan was asked whether he would step into the federal arena, his reply was dismissive. 'Why? I'm doing important work where I am.' Nevertheless, like Dunstan, Kennett was unable to resist the temptation to engage in the grander themes and broader agenda of the national debate. He did so often, with profound impact as the politician who led the charge for tax reform and as the Liberal leader who tackled head on, and at the earliest opportunity, the damaging politics of the One Nation movement. More often than not, however, many of Kennett's colleagues in Canberra saw his intervention as unwelcome sniping from the sidelines.

No example better illustrated this than in May 1994, when Kennett made his extraordinary contribution to the skirmishing over the federal leadership. His decision to attack publicly Peter Costello and Michael Kroger caused a detonation within the federal Liberal Party that ultimately guaranteed the downfall of John Hewson.

Kennett defends his interference, claiming to have been appalled by what he saw as the deliberate undermining of the Opposition leader by his federal colleagues. Although former prime minister Malcolm Fraser had been one of only two senior Liberals to comment publicly on Hewson's beleaguered leadership – calling for 'new faces' to lead the Liberal Party – Kennett suspected Kroger and Costello were key players in the intrigues. Annoyed by their machinations, he signalled to colleagues that he was about to have his say publicly. Andrew Peacock and Petro Georgiou, who was doubling as Liberal state director and Hewson's chief of staff, caught wind of his plans. They went straight to Kennett and spelt out the consequences of him entering the fray. 'If you do this, it will be the end for Hewie. You cannot do this,' they warned him.

Satisfied they had placated Kennett, the two went off to dinner believing the crisis averted. They were wrong. The next morning, in his weekly radio interview with 3AW's Neil Mitchell, Kennett went ballistic. 'This debacle at the moment, and that's what it is, is being generated from Melbourne by the Costello camp. I make no bones about that whatsoever. This has been a very deliberate destabilising effort . . . It is clearly being led by what I would call the Costello interests and camp, and I have very real reasons to be concerned about the integrity of that camp.'

It was a bombshell, and sent convulsions through the Liberal Party across the nation, nowhere more so than in Melbourne. Georgiou, listening to his radio at 104 Exhibition Street, was horrified. So were Kroger and Costello. What issues of integrity? What on earth was he hinting at? It sounded sinister. At noon, Costello emerged to give a doorstop press conference, doing his best to remain outwardly calm. 'I repudiate it. I entirely repudiate it. I especially repudiate any aspersions on my character. Those comments were without foundation. Attacks like that only play into the hands of the Labor Party and destabilise the situation at the federal level. Supporters of the Liberal Party around the country will be appalled when they see Liberal colleagues attacking each other.' Meanwhile, Kroger had marched into Kennett's office at Parliament House in Spring Street to demand an explanation. It was a heated exchange.

KROGER: 'Let's get to the bottom of this. What's this all about? What's the problem?'

KENNETT: 'Your mate's undermining John Hewson.'

KROGER: 'Listen. Your interview alone could bring down John Hewson. Nobody has shafted John Hewson more than you have. What are you on about?'

KENNETT: 'Your mate's trying to bring down John Hewson.'

KROGER: 'Well, what's your problem with me then?'

KENNETT: 'I will tell you what my problem is with you . . . Alan Brown. When I was under attack in '89, Vin Heffernan came to you and said, "We're going to get rid of Kennett," and you said to him, "Well, mate, if that's what you want to do, it's up to you." You should have stopped him and you didn't. I was rolled. Then, in '91, when I came back to the leadership, you were telling the members that if they challenged for the leadership, you would

take away their preselections. So it's all very well for you to back
Alan Brown, and it's fine to get rid of Kennett . . . Double standards, that's your problem.'

KROGER: 'That's complete bullshit. I understand why you are
saying it, but remember that Alan Brown gave an interview where
he said, "If anyone challenges me, the administrative committee
will remove their preselections." Then Alan Brown called me and
said, "I just gave this interview." When I was asked, and everybody was asking, I said, "Yep, Alan Brown's right. We are not
going to muck around with the leadership." You know my rule.
I don't muck around in the parliamentary business.'

KENNETT: 'I don't accept that. I never got any help from you.'

KROGER: 'What's this about integrity? What are you talking about?
Are you talking about any of this stuff with Tricon and Ian Johns?'

KENNETT: 'No.'

KROGER: 'Well, what are you on about?'

KENNETT: 'Just things I hear. I'm not going into it.'

KROGER: 'I work for the Packers at the moment. Is that it?'

KENNETT: 'No.'

KROGER: 'Well really. You are brain-dead. You are a moron.'

Kroger stormed out of the office. In Queensland, the hapless
John Hewson appeared to struggle in his search for a meaningful
response. 'I find what Mr Kennett has to say interesting. Absolutely very interesting.'

As events unfolded, it became clear that Kennett, in effect, had
read the death rites over Hewson's leadership. By the time Hewson
had called a party-room vote the following Monday, the party had
swung in behind a youth ticket of Alexander Downer and Peter
Costello. If Kennett's strategy had been to block Costello's progress
in federal politics, it backfired dramatically. Within a year, Downer,
too, would be finished as leader. Although Costello would continue
to bide his time as deputy, standing back to watch the veteran John
Howard return to the Liberal leadership, the quick demise of

Hewson then Downer had the effect of hand-delivering to Costello a significant core of support within the federal parliamentary party. It also left Kennett, as the senior Liberal premier, with a difficult task in diplomacy on his hands. The history of enmity meant his relations with the two most senior Liberals in the nation – John Howard and Peter Costello – would be testy, if not tempestuous.

Ironically, Kennett at times appeared to have a much better rapport with Paul Keating than with his Liberal colleagues in Canberra. Both were change merchants. Both were stubborn and strong-willed. Both thrived in the rough-house of politics. Despite their famous flare-up over Keating's claims of corruption in Melbourne's casino bidding process, the two were companionable at a personal level. They had the mutual respect you might expect to find between top-of-the-bill prize-fighters, even though in public life they scored points at each other's expense wherever possible. Stockdale, who witnessed their relationship at close quarters, found it a fascinating dynamic. 'They have a number of things in common. They are both a lot brighter than people give them credit for, and they are naturally strong leaders. I don't know what sort of electricity it was, but they liked each other as individuals.'

At the Council of Australian Governments (the annual gathering of federal and state leaders), Kennett and Stockdale would watch Keating's guile as he sought to cajole the states to accept his way of thinking. 'Keating is one of the best chairmen of meetings I have ever seen. He has a gift for it,' comments Stockdale. 'Howard's very good, too, but Keating had one advantage in a philosophical sense. Howard, I think, is a genuine federalist. He actually thinks it is important to have a workable federation. He is looking to find win-win outcomes. Keating was an instinctive and avowed centralist. He understood the power of playing one state off another to get what he wanted. There was always a second agenda. I don't think Keating ever did anything at a COAG meeting that he had not anticipated well in advance. Howard looks for another step. They are different styles. I am not contrasting

Keating favourably against Howard. Their styles and the circumstances in which they operated were quite different.'

There is little doubt Jeff Kennett admired Keating's statecraft. Both were instinctive politicians; they were autodidacts, unimpressed by pomp and pretence. Both were surly, with a brooding propensity to nurse hatreds and crush opponents, yet both were equally capable of thigh-slapping humour and disarming charm. 'They had the capacity to compartmentalise their political activities, their government activities. Their relationship could be quarantined. They knew that on certain occasions they were going to beat the crap out of each other, but on other occasions they knew they had a great deal of empathy,' observes Ken Baxter.

Alister Drysdale, as Kennett's senior adviser, once asked Keating's senior adviser, Don Russell, why he thought the relationship had clicked. Russell said, 'My bloke thinks your bloke is an outcomes bloke, not a process bloke. They do things. They don't care about all the crap.'

Nor was Jeff Kennett, as a Liberal premier, embarrassed to display his friendship. He made a point of this in 1997 when he invited the defeated prime minister to join him for one of the Melbourne Major Events Company showcase occasions, the Three Tenors Concert. Some of his Victorian Liberal colleagues were mortified by the symbolism. Kennett seemed not to care less. It may have been a trifling episode, a sideshow, but there is no doubt it was seen as a transgression in the upper reaches of the Howard government in Canberra.

At the time, the federal government's relative policy inertia was being compared unfavourably to Kennett's foot-to-the-floor approach, especially within Melbourne's business elite. Sensitivity in Canberra over this criticism was compounded by Kennett's constant goading on policy issues, notably over the need for tax reform. In early 1997, when Kennett was complaining regularly of a 'lack of national leadership', Costello, as Liberal deputy, went to Howard to urge the prime minister to retaliate more forcefully.

'When he says there is a lack of leadership, John, he is talking about you. What are you going to do about it?' Howard, after almost 25 years in politics and virtually impervious to insult, especially from Kennett, counselled a more pragmatic response. 'There is no point fighting Kennett. Forget about all that. If I hit back, it will run for three days. If I say nothing, it will only be one day's headlines.'

This marked the beginnings of a thaw in relations between Howard and Kennett. As the ranking Liberal leaders in the country, the two began to establish a more constructive working relationship. Their final rapprochement came during the course of the 1998 federal election. Howard's decision to run his campaign on the platform of tax reform – and the imposition of a goods-and-services tax – won the wholehearted approval of the Victorian premier. In turn, Kennett campaigned strongly in support of the federal Coalition. The Coalition's election win brought a sea change in the two men's turbulent relations. 'Jeffrey may never be invited to Melanie Howard's wedding. There will probably always be personal issues between them. They are very different characters. But in that campaign, Jeffrey was more mature, and genuinely helpful to John,' observes a senior Victorian Liberal. 'From that point on, there was something more solid to the relationship.'

In fact, Howard's performance in the 1998 federal election campaign would see him rated, in Kennett's eyes, as one of the very few postwar politicians worthy of the mantle of leadership. 'Ours is a very interesting relationship,' Kennett would reflect later. 'John's a conservative sort of guy, and I think in the short term he may not get the recognition he deserves. But while he might not like to hear it, I think there is a similarity between Howard, Keating and Kennett. Given the opportunity to govern, we all used the authority to do things better by doing things differently. Keating deregulated the banking sector. Howard challenged the political lexicon in terms of the taxation system.'

In the lead-up to the election, however, many of the premier's federal colleagues were annoyed by the media's unflattering comparisons between Howard and Kennett. Here was a provincial politician who had developed an enviable national profile as a strong leader. Able to rule with the luxury of a two-to-one majority in both houses, Kennett had accumulated the mounting respect of political and business elites outside his home state for his government's swift and sure-footed assault on Victoria's financial distress. Attending a high-powered business lunch for Kennett in Sydney, John Lyons, the former editor of the *Sydney Morning Herald,* remembers being surprised by the level of adulation among the premier's hard-nosed audience. 'The reception was extraordinary. He was seen as this great premier who had revived his state and breathed life into the economy. This guy was the way of the future; the sort of premier all states should have. There was a general view that he was an exemplar of modern leadership. They were asking him about Canberra: why wouldn't he stand? I noticed that a couple of John Howard's staff had come along to watch and listen,' says Lyons, who as a reporter for the Melbourne *Herald* had covered Kennett's troubled years as Opposition leader.

A Morgan poll taken soon after the Liberals' federal victory in October 1998 confirmed Kennett's status nationally. Among Coalition voters, he ranked second only to Howard as the preferred prime minister, 36 to 17. His support was double that for Costello, and he was streets ahead of other federal frontbenchers John Fahey, Peter Reith and Alexander Downer. Kennett's mantle as the oracle from the south meant he could not be ignored; he would go on speaking his mind on issues of national significance no matter how often this irritated his party colleagues in Canberra.

It would be churlish to suggest Kennett engaged in national debates exclusively to gainsay his federal rivals. His campaign to pressure the Howard government to forge ahead with a radical program of tax reform, for example, was driven by his determination not only to secure a more stable income stream for the states, but also to support business demands for a more efficient system of taxing goods and services. The Business Council of Australia's tax reform taskforce was headed by prominent Melbourne accountant Fergus Ryan, and much of the policy formulation was being done at its Melbourne headquarters. Kennett, through his fortnightly round-table breakfasts with the city's leading executives, was close to the action throughout as business leaders lobbied Coalition ministers in Canberra to accept the political risks of taking a radical tax reform agenda to the people. The Victorian premier also had ambitions for a more vigorous and competitive export sector. Although this was not confined to his home state, it is true that Victoria's economic and employment base stood to gain more than most from a broadening of the tax base. A disproportionate burden of wholesale sales taxes fell, in particular, on manufacturing exporters. As early as 1995, Kennett had listed 'generational tax reform' as one of the policy pillars he believed was necessary to reinvigorate the economy and create jobs.

There is no doubt, though, that Kennett's most forceful and far-reaching contribution to national debate was his stout defence of Australia's open-door immigration policies. As early as 1981, as Victoria's minister for ethnic affairs, Kennett had attacked the Returned Services League in Victoria over their attitude towards new migrants from Asia. Kennett decried the RSL's stance as 'anything but Christian' and contrary to the ideals of tolerance for which Australians had fought and died. He would return to this theme dramatically in 1997, when he led the charge against the xenophobic stirrings of Pauline Hanson's One Nation movement.

Kennett, like Keating, was a passionate advocate of greater economic and political integration with Asia. The region was the main stop on the premier's road map into the future. Part of his vision for Victoria was that of an advanced technological society selling know-how, high-value-added food and textiles, and educational and other professional services into Asian markets. Much like former deputy prime minister Tim Fischer, Kennett's formative years serving in the military in Malaysia and Singapore had given him a sense of the possibilities in the fast-developing region.

Through his years in Opposition and government he had made a point of developing an extensive network of high-level contacts in the Asian capitals, from Jakarta to Tokyo. When Cambodia held its first elections after Pol Pot's reign of terror and the Vietnamese occupation, the new minister for education in Phnom Penh, an acquaintance for 17 years, called Kennett for advice on how to rebuild the nation's education system. Kennett flew a team from Victoria's ministry of education to Cambodia to assess their needs.

But not everybody shared Kennett's enthusiasm on the importance of links with Asia – certainly not Pauline Hanson and her supporters on the right-wing fringe of Australian politics. Disendorsed as a Liberal candidate after publicly attacking the level of welfare spending on Aboriginal and migrant communities, the fish and chip shop owner from Ipswich in provincial Queensland had won a federal seat in parliament at the 1996 election running as an independent. In her maiden speech in the House of Representatives, she had claimed Australia was being 'swamped' by Asian migrants. Hanson blamed the 'open-door' policies of successive federal governments for what she characterised as the soul-destroying struggle of the working poor in Australia. According to Hanson, competition from migrants was denying young Australians access to jobs, and imports were threatening the viability of homegrown companies. Her crude and simplistic refrain was targeted, in particular, at deprived communities in rural towns and the urban fringes, where scepticism, if not outright belligerence, about enmeshing Australia's economic interests with those of Asia was highest. In a populist rampage that for a time shook the confidence and internal stability of the mainstream parties, her One Nation movement demanded an end to Australia's postwar consensus on open immigration and its 20-year process of economic deregulation.

The racist undertones of One Nation's pitch to voters were anathema to Kennett, as indeed they were to the vast majority of elected politicians across the nation. Kennett, whose German forebears only two generations earlier had suffered the scars of being scapegoated as migrants, was appalled by the potential for social division within Australia, and for the message this could send to the world. 'We cannot live on our own,' he asserted. 'Let's stop this stupidity before it takes root. It's fine for the public to experiment and it's fine for the public to protest but, at the end of the day, you have to ask yourself if you really want this group of individuals running the country.'

The peak of Kennett's activism in campaigning against One Nation came on 14 June 1998, the day after the nascent political movement gained almost a quarter of the vote in the Queensland election, sending 11 of its endorsed candidates to the state parliament. Watching from Melbourne, Kennett was horrified. He immediately launched a media blitz, pledging to 'chase One Nation down every burrow'. As TV, talkback and newspapers clamoured for a voice of authority to make some sense of the astonishing rise of Hansonism in the northern state, Kennett set out on a personal mission to deflate the One Nation hysteria. Over the next week, he would do five live-to-air interviews on national television, including an appearance on Channel Ten's *The Panel*, one of the highest-rating programs in the youth market. Overcoming his antipathy towards the national broadcaster, he also gave a series of extended interviews to ABC radio. He wrote articles for the *Australian Financial Review*, the *Geelong Advertiser*, the *Ballarat Courier* and the *Bendigo Advertiser*. He gave no less than three formal and informal press conferences, and delivered a major speech to the Australia Summit, a conference of business and community leaders, in Melbourne. Broadly, his message was to warn rural communities of devastation for export markets if Australia reconstructed its tariff walls and gained a reputation for racial intolerance. He spoke of the dangers of 'global bypass' if Australia reverted from its outward-looking and forward-looking policy approach.

One Nation, Kennett said, was a challenge to be met head on. 'I am not one of those that are despairing. I see it as a great opportunity for Australians generally to use the democratic process to articulate the case that has seen Australia develop as one of the most envied, genuinely democratic, multicultural countries in the world and, through ballot boxes in the future, to refute the so-called philosophy of One Nation.'

Kennett was not afraid to offend the sensibilities of those who voted for One Nation. Unlike Prime Minister John Howard, he went public from the outset on his insistence that Labor should be given Liberal preferences ahead of One Nation candidates in order to prevent the new movement gaining a foothold in Canberra. Nor did he pull his punches when queried over why One Nation had proved so successful in provincial Queensland. Asked why Hansonism had not flourished similarly in Victoria, he told a national audience, 'We have a much more mature and intelligent society, if I can put it that way.'

In the October 1998 federal election, Kennett's view was vindicated. One Nation polled less than 2 per cent of the vote in Victoria as a whole. Even in rural seats where it was thought most likely to find support, it struggled to attain more than 5 per cent of the vote. Although One Nation recorded significant support in rural seats elsewhere in the nation, it returned only one senator, from Queensland, to the federal parliament. Pauline Hanson lost her campaign to win the seat of Blair. The One Nation phenomenon had fizzled.

Kennett's role in campaigning against Hanson and her supporters was the high point of his contribution to the national political debate. He had demonstrated courage in taking a higher profile against One Nation than any other conservative politician in the nation. Again, it prompted speculation over whether he might yet make a move to Canberra. But Kennett's full-frontal assault on One Nation was not without hidden costs. At one doorstop press conference, Kennett committed the indiscretion of referring to One Nation supporters as 'hicks'. In an interview on the ABC's *Lateline*, Kennett also issued an explicit warning to voters in the bush that exports in agriculture, dairy produce and coal were at risk if Australia's reputation as a sophisticated and open-minded society was undermined. 'I suspect the public will start to wake up,' he said. 'But if the country says, "We don't care about trade", so be it. There is nothing John Howard or [federal Opposition leader] Kim Beazley are going to be able to do about that. You can blame politicians till the cows come home. But you and I as citizens elect the politicians.'

This performance was a tour de force of the Kennett style: blunt, straight-talking, hard-nosed, unsentimental. Far from pandering to the wounded feelings of aggrieved voters, Kennett gave them a clip over the ears – especially those in rural and regional seats – for flirting with the populist prescriptions of One Nation. In effect, Kennett was like a parent telling a rebellious child to stop grizzling and grow up. For all the kudos he gained in the national arena, however, it was always problematical as to how this message would play in country Victoria, where his government already had a reputation as aloof and uncaring. Out in the hinterland, where funding cuts to state-run services had left deep scars, the electorate was brooding and vengeful. Kennett's imperious lectures on the need for the bush to move with the times can't have helped. Despite the rural rejection of Hansonism, Jeff was soon to feel the brunt of a withering backlash.

CHAPTER SIXTEEN

THE GREAT DIVIDE

'We have had enough. Progress does not have to be like this.'
SUSAN DAVIES, INDEPENDENT MP

Jeff Kennett's first electoral setback of the 1990s blew in like a dust storm from over the horizon. The by-election for the rural seat of Gippsland West in February 1997 was won by Susan Davies. A former Labor candidate, she had resigned from the party to run as an independent on a charter of restoring services to small country towns. The previously safe Liberal seat, embracing the seaside resorts and farmlands of Westernport Bay, succumbed to a swing of 13 per cent. This dramatic shift in electoral sentiment was engineered with the help of a local network of rural activists, many of whom were aggrieved members of the National Party. Together, they crafted a shrewd strategy of preference swapping among a range of single-issue candidates, including two from the gun lobby, to isolate the Liberal frontrunner. Less than a year after its historic second landslide win, this was a moment of foreboding for the Kennett government.

The ironies in the Gippsland West result were many. The by-election had been brought on by the retirement from politics of

Alan Brown, the man who as Liberal leader had negotiated the Coalition deal with the Nationals. Kennett had decided to appoint his former leadership rival to the sinecure of Victorian Agent-General in London. But the story had a twist. Kennett first offered the job to his deputy, Phil Gude, who had been contemplating an exit from politics at the 1996 election. Gude was the member for the super-safe Liberal seat of Hawthorn. A by-election in that seat at the end of 1996 would barely have raised a murmur. But Gude turned down the London offer, and Kennett turned next to Brown. It was a pay-off to an old enemy that was subsequently to haunt the Coalition. It exposed the government's flank to the rural rebellion in Gippsland West. Had Gude taken the London posting, state parliament may never have seen or heard of Susan Davies.

At the time, Kennett sought to downplay the by-election defeat as a one-off result, fought largely on 'local' issues. He insisted that it would not sway the government from pursuing its agenda for reform. In an editorial, the *Age* scolded him for his insouciance. 'The political landscape is littered with examples of governments and leaders who failed to heed the warnings of voters at by-elections . . . The Gippsland West by-election will ultimately come to be seen as either the point at which the government renewed itself, modified its course and started listening, or when it sealed its fate by ignoring the warning signs brandished by some of its erstwhile supporters.'

This prophecy was to prove well founded. The defeat of the Liberals in Gippsland West marked the onset of a fragmentation of voter support for the Coalition in provincial communities. John Brumby, still struggling as Opposition leader to make any headway with middle Melbourne – where elections, traditionally, had been won or lost – pounced on the possibilities raised by the upset result in Gippsland West. Here was an unforeseen window of opportunity for the ALP.

Susan Davies' lament about the impact of government policies on small communities became a highly effective mantra. Hers was a brand of 'retro' politics, resentful of the impact of the global economy and of the processes of deregulation and downsizing by Australian governments and industry to adapt to the new world order. It was a message that often ignored the parallel impact on the lives of city dwellers, especially in the old industrial heartlands where, in the 1970s and 1980s, industry restructuring had brought job losses measured in the hundreds of thousands. Australians living in the big cities had been forced to adjust their thinking and become more outward-looking and more attuned to the rigorous demands of the international marketplace. But as the effects of cutbacks in government spending and industry rationalisations began to ripple across the countryside, small communities felt highly vulnerable. How could they ever summon the critical mass and horsepower to survive in this unforgiving environment? Combined with the impact on farming industries of a slump in commodity prices, many towns and villages began to wither visibly. The mood of protest embodied by Susan Davies and others of her ilk began finding echoes in every corner of non-metropolitan Victoria – indeed, across rural Australia. A backlash in the bush had begun.

Susan Davies arrived in state parliament as a pint-sized, one-woman protest movement. Davies had raised her sons as a working mother, in a small community doing it hard, and brought with her to Melbourne a spirit of struggle against adversity. She could be prickly and querulous, and was fervent in her opinion that Jeff Kennett personified the worst excesses of what she denounced as 'economic rationalism'. He had become too big for his boots, and insensitive to the needs and interests of communities like that from which she came. Davies' forebears had settled and cleared land in the great forests of south Gippsland in the 1880s, near the coalmining town of Outtrim. At the turn of the century, Outtrim had been a bustling community, with 1700 residents and 300 children enrolled in the local school. By the 1990s, however, the township was in decline, a condition reflected across many small towns in country Victoria. Local businesses had shut down, industry had departed, and the schools struggled to survive the financial pressures of servicing too small a population. As job prospects receded, young people would leave for the city, searching for opportunity. This saga of migration to the city and coastal fringe was far from unique to Victoria, but the Kennett government would be held to account for the sense of despondency among those left behind.

In 1903, 40 per cent of Victorians lived in Melbourne and 60 per cent in the countryside. It took another 40 years, nearing the end of World War Two, for the balance to tip slightly in the city's favour. In the postwar era, the trend accelerated dramatically. By the 1990s, Melbourne and its outskirts spoke for three-quarters of the population. The rural and regional communities were losing people, and losing their voice. In her first speech in parliament, Davies took up this theme. 'The depopulation of rural communities is a longstanding problem in the bush. We must put a stop to it. I would like to see the re-emergence of these rural villages so they are like what Outtrim used to be.' Davies left no doubt that she blamed the Kennett government in large part for 'radically dismantling' the way of life of country people, through its policies of privatisation, competitive tendering and budget sector cuts. The Kennett approach, she insisted, served only to destroy the 'small village model' of social organisation. 'We cannot look at this future if we lose so many services that people continue to turn away. We will not find this future when power, telecommunications, gas and water cost more in the bush than the city.'

There was an element of scapegoating in her message. A five-year state government could not be held solely accountable for economic and demographic trends extending over half a century, trends that were just as much an affliction in far west New South Wales and central Queensland as in the hinterland of Victoria. As the emergence of the One Nation movement demonstrated, rural grievances were a challenge for the entire nation. But Davies and her allies in rural politics in Victoria were intent on making Kennett pay dearly for what they saw as his share of the neglect.

The divide between the political values and preoccupations of city dwellers and rural communities is not a new phenomenon. Rural communities have long resented the dominance of Australia's urban culture over political decision-making. In Victoria, the rural constituency has a proud history of organising to protect its interests, often brazenly. It is a tradition built on an electoral gerrymander, and the disproportionate representation of rural communities in the state parliament until well into the 1950s. Via its weighted vote, country Victoria was able to position itself as a formidable third force and counterbalance to the competing claims of the Labor Party and its rivals from the urban middle class, the Liberals and their predecessors. Through an often ruthless guile and a readiness to trade in favours, the old Country Party in fact achieved primacy in the parliamentary politics of Spring Street in the early decades of the 20th century, although frequently at a cost to the concept of stable government.

The party declined in the late 1950s with the emergence of the Victorian Liberal Party's powerful grip on Spring Street and the dilution of the rural gerrymander. The Liberals would win every state election for the next 27 years. Country Party members sat on the cross-benches, marginalised but for their capacity to combine with Labor in the upper house to frustrate government. After 50 years in the thick of the deal-making, the Country Party had become a bit player.

In 1989, Liberal leader Alan Brown set out to end the ancient feuds. His Coalition agreement with the renamed National Party was aimed at ridding the non-Labor forces of their destructive rivalry in nonmetropolitan electorates. Liberals would not run against sitting National MPs; Nats would not run against sitting Liberals. The end to three-cornered contests curtailed Labor's hopes of making any serious inroads into rural and provincial Victoria. However, the deal was not without its risks for the National Party. Although sharing many of the philosophical standpoints of the Liberals, it had survived through the century by setting itself apart

from the preoccupations of its city cousins. Its success had been
in providing a distinctive voice for rural communities. Indeed, its
great expertise was pork-barrelling, using its political leverage to
ensure the country was 'looked after' through a range of subsidies
and concessions. Now its fortunes would be tied to those of the
Liberals. Its policies would necessarily be developed and negotiated
in the framework of a coalition, and it would no longer have the
luxury of going its own way. It meant more discipline, less populism. Inherent in this repositioning was the risk that the Nationals
would come to be seen as part of the political establishment. It
would leave an opening for others to emerge, ideological outriders
who would proclaim themselves as the authentic voice of the bush.

The political dangers in the rise of rural independents had been
apparent even before the Kennett government came to power.
When former National Party leader Peter Ross-Edwards retired
in 1991, it was expected his nominated successor, Don Kilgour,
would have an easy ride into parliament. In fact, an independent,
Valerie McDougall, came within a few hundred votes of forcing
the seat to preferences. That same year, 50 000 country Victorians
marched on the city in what became known as the 'Save Australia'
rally. The march was led by Danny Johnson, a demolition con-
tractor from Warracknabeal in the state's west, who had mobilised
this impressive show of force after writing a protest letter about the
state's financial woes to his local newspaper. The protestors' target
was the Kirner Labor government, and Jeff Kennett had stood on
the steps of parliament to greet them as they swarmed into Bourke
Street from every corner of the state.

Five years later, the Kennett government would become the
target of these same sentiments. Despite a landslide victory in
the March 1996 election, the Liberals lost the northern riverland
electorate of Mildura to an independent, former National Party
member Russell Savage. He was the first independent to be elected
to the Victorian parliament in 40 years. The result was a personal
blow to Kennett, cutting short the political career of one of his

close supporters, Craig Bildstien. Fearing the consequences of the
rise of rural independents and angered by the defeat of a prominent Liberal, Kennett made it known that Savage should not be
made welcome by Coalition MPs. Savage had come into parliament on the rhetoric of standing aloof from the major parties, and
would be held to that principle and given no succour.

Ostracised by most Liberals and Nationals, Savage found his
first months at Spring Street 'an isolating experience'. Having
retired from the police force to make his run for parliament, he
was deeply affected by the hostility he confronted. 'What am
I doing here?' he asked himself. Although a conservative on both
social and economic policy, he drifted into the orbit of Labor MPs,
who at least seemed happy enough to join him in the parliamentary dining room. Savage would never forgive Jeff Kennett. The
old calculus of 'Your enemy's enemy is my friend' would come to
rebound on the premier. The arrival of Savage was merely a taste
of things to come.

In January 1997, only weeks before the Gippsland West by-
election, Danny Johnson emerged again from obscurity to sound
a warning. 'Jeff Kennett has done a wonderful job reducing debt,
but we have all had to pay for it. And his council amalgamations
and privatisation policies are not working. Before the privatisation
of the SEC, I can't remember a power blackout. [Now], blackouts
and surges and damaged equipment are part and parcel of everyday life. They promised we would get a better service and that is
a bloody lie.'

The Liberals knew there was trouble looming. At an administrative committee meeting at the end of 1996, Joy Howley, a
farmer from a soldier-settler property in western Victoria and soon
to become Liberal state president, had warned her organisational
colleagues of a rising tide of antagonism in rural communities.
'People aren't happy out there.' She urged the party to redouble
its research and polling efforts outside Melbourne to pinpoint
the reasons for the growing disaffection. 'Joy had a nose for the

country, so we responded in a variety of ways to try and get to the bottom of it,' recalls a senior Liberal. 'We increased ministerial visits. We tried to get local candidates to go into community forums and defend their decisions. We set up a taskforce, and went to community and business leaders and asked them directly, "What do we need to do for your region?" In many cases, we found they were pretty well looked after. Places like Narracan [in Gippsland] were in fact overrepresented in funding decisions. But we found it incredibly difficult to shift opinions. Part of it was this argument that Melbourne was getting all the attention.'

Government ministers voiced increasing exasperation at being unable to persuade provincial and country communities that they were, in fact, well cared for. Hospitals were rebuilt and refurbished in Bendigo, Geelong and Ballarat. The government set up Partnerships for Growth to encourage business to go back into the regions, and a $50-million-a-year program to advise small business in provincial towns. But still the lament continued. One Liberal strategist reasoned, 'When the banks close, the children leave, small local schools close, and when you have the slump in commodity prices, it's a conjunction of trends that makes it a very difficult context in which to work. People were happily heading off from small towns and driving to the nearest regional centre to shop at the supermarket, because it offered a bigger variety, or to buy their petrol because it was a few cents a litre cheaper, and this became part of the regular Friday routine. Then they discover the local greengrocer goes out of business or the local petrol station shuts down. They tend to look to blame governments. More broadly, there was a feeling of frustration that if you work as hard as they do – and they work damn hard – they were not getting the rewards. The harder they worked, the more they felt they were going backwards.'

Kennett's Minister for Finance, Roger Hallam, concedes that people in small towns felt devastated by the loss of their local schools in the merger and amalgamation process of the early 1990s. 'We did close a lot of schools. And we copped the criticism that we were turning our backs on small communities. But I was a wholehearted supporter in centralising the resources in schools. I want our country children so well educated that they have a choice. I don't want people to stay in the country because they're so poorly educated they have no alternative. I want them to come back by choice. In that circumstance, they would be much better citizens for it. The basis on which we closed small schools was to provide better use of resources, access to the entire curriculum, and, through the latest in technology, giving the students access to the exact equipment and knowledge base available to their city counterparts. It was about getting our children the best education possible.'

In Gippsland West, however, Susan Davies was putting a different view: 'This government has gone too far in reducing our social supports, our local government services, our hospitals, our schools and our towns. We have had enough. Progress does not have to be like this . . . government has a duty to provide basic services. We can change and we will develop, but we cannot move ahead if you keep stripping away our basic support services.'

One of the factors behind Susan Davies' victory was the resentment throughout Gippsland over the federal government's refusal to approve emergency relief funding for the farmers of the region in the midst of a debilitating drought. A crisis committee had been formed to lobby the state and federal governments to answer the cry for help, but conditions in the region did not match the technical requirements of drought assistance legislation. The local farmers felt they were being cheated; state MPs were under fire for not being seen to push harder for the cause. An offer of $1 million in aid from the state was widely seen as an insult to Gippsland farmers, who claimed that, across the region, they were spending that much each day buying in feed for their animals. In April 1997, Swan Hill MP Barry Steggall warned the National Party's state conference in Echuca that there were dangerous cross-currents at play in rural politics, and that the party would lose its power base if it was unable to adapt. The Nationals needed to distinguish their identity more clearly from their Coalition partners. 'The time has come to seriously ask ourselves what philosophical and policy differences we have on the conservative side of politics. We need to determine our goals and objectives for country Victoria and if there are fundamental differences between the parties, we need to identify and highlight them to the voting public. If our nerve fails and we continue on our present ill-defined and confused course, we risk dwindling to a minor fringe party with no power base and poor parliamentary representation.' At the same conference, another National Party MP, Ken Jasper, urged the party to seek more freedom to manoeuvre, supporting a resolution that National Party MPs take 'a stronger public stand within the Coalition government to demonstrate that they are strongly representing country interests.'

By May, the mood in Gippsland had reached boiling point. The Coalition parties were to make a fatal miscalculation. It may have been complacency, it may have been arrogance. But when 700 dairy farmers arrived at a rally at the Korumburra recreational reserve on 28 May 1997, not one Liberal or National MP was there to greet them. Susan Davies was there. So was John Brumby. They shared the stage with dairy farmer Jack Vanderland, a former Leongatha branch president of the National Party. What they heard from the assembled farmers was an outpouring of hostility towards governments in Canberra and Spring Street. Brumby and Vanderland watched and listened as an elderly woman rose to her feet to denounce the deputy premier and National Party leader, Pat McNamara. 'The way the National Party has deserted country Victorians is a disgrace. I move a motion of no confidence in Mr McNamara, and call on him to resign.' The crowd, many of them lifelong Coalition supporters, cheered in acclamation. It was tantamount to a declaration of war on the Kennett government. 'John couldn't believe his luck,' Vanderland recalls.

Brumby reported to shadow cabinet colleagues in Melbourne

that negativity towards the government in rural and regional Victoria was deeply entrenched. 'They will never recover from this,' he predicted. Although Kennett sought to laugh off the no-confidence motion at the Korumburra rally as 'part of the richness of rural life', the event provided the ALP with tangible evidence of the potent mix of anger and alienation in rural communities – a combination of despair over cuts to services, ill will generated by the gun debate, and the squeeze on farm incomes through fickle seasonal conditions and a worldwide slump in commodity prices. In what Brumby would later describe as 'a little revolution', he began formulating a strategy to cripple the Kennett government by siphoning off the Coalition's support in its rural heartlands. He found a willing, if unlikely, ally in Jack Vanderland.

The Korumburra rally marked the beginnings of a schism in rural politics. Vanderland had been a member of the National Party for 15 years, and had been phoned on the morning of the rally by senior party officials. Fearful of what might happen and urging him to keep the crowd under tight rein, they told him, 'Jack, you're one of ours. Don't get stuck into us.' The next day, Vanderland found himself on the wrong end of a series of irate and abusive phone calls from party figures incensed by what they saw as a mutinous uprising. Within days, Vanderland had resigned from the party in disgust. With the remnants of the Gippsland Crisis Committee, a rural network that had been set up in 1987 to raise public awareness of the crippling drought in the region, he began assembling a breakaway group of rebel farmers. They believed the voice of rural Victoria was not being represented strenuously enough and began looking for politicians who would lend a sympathetic ear. With other self-exiles they formed the Victorian Country Lobby Group, a network that spread into east Gippsland and elsewhere in the state. A grapevine of dissent, it began positioning itself as a rival to the Victorian Farmers' Federation as the voice of rural industry and constituted a head-on challenge to the establishment networks of the National Party. Brumby shrewdly kept in close touch. Regularly, and not always with the media in tow, he would assist the drought relief effort, helping to distribute fodder to struggling farmers and donating a personal cheque for $200 to get a fundraising appeal up and running. Labor's shadow cabinet began making appearances in the regions, and the Victorian ALP staged a series of rural summits. As Brumby told colleagues, 'People are hurting. They don't want to be patronised but they want somebody to stand up for them.'

In June 1997, the then state editor of the *Age*, Shane Green, was briefed on Labor's strategy in rural and regional Victoria. In an article of remarkable prescience, two years out from the state election, he wrote of the possibility of Labor being able to win as many as eight rural and regional seats at the next state election and, with a few gains in Melbourne, of perhaps being able to form a minority government. Clearly, Brumby was eager to get the message out that this could be an unexpected lifeline for his struggling party. But not everyone in the ALP was convinced of the efficacy of the plan. Brumby's long absences in country Victoria were causing consternation back in Melbourne, where he seemed to be totally eclipsed by the media presence of the premier. Why, colleagues asked, wasn't Brumby making himself more available for Nine and Seven, Melbourne's prime commercial TV news networks? Despite being told privately by a prominent country newspaper editor that 'people out here think he's on the right track', the ALP hierarchy worried he was overinvesting his time and energy in chasing regional votes. Explains a senior Labor source, 'He'd say, "I'm off to another meeting in Horsham", and we would get frustrated with him. What did he think he was doing? People began talking behind his back, complaining that he was out in the bush too often and not attending to traditional concerns. He started to come under extreme pressure. Of course, the polling wasn't picking up the extent of discontent in the bush.'

But if Brumby was under pressure, so was the National Party. The mood in Gippsland went from bad to worse when floods hit the eastern coastline in 1998, turning farming properties from dustbowls into muddy wastelands. At a time of crisis, the MLA for Gippsland East, David Treasure, was in Europe on a parliamentary trip. As Kennett and McNamara flew by helicopter to the flooded communities, David Treasure continued on his journey, apparently not thinking to fly home. This earned him the name 'Hidden Treasure' and some in his electorate warned they would never forget. It was another setback in his party's attempts to reverse the sullen resentment in the hearts and minds of country voters.

Says Roger Hallam, 'We knew it was a serious problem, but it's very hard to fight the smoke. It became a mantra that we were closing down the schools and hospitals. Then Labor came along and tapped into the potential of envy. Very powerful stuff, in the short term, but entirely unproductive and absolutely destructive in the long term. It made me cross because I saw our people being influenced by superficiality.'

Senior Liberals sensed the pressures building. Within government, also, the cabinet and senior bureaucrats were struggling to find solutions. Kennett was perplexed. He knew the dangers of a backlash, but all governments across Australia were struggling to produce practical answers. Health minister Rob Knowles explains, 'In the 1996 election Jeff had talked about the social agenda. But social policy is much harder in terms of getting a return. There are long lags between designing programs, spending the money and then seeing the returns. In economic management decisions, you often know in a very short space of time whether it's working or not. Social policy is much slower.' Nevertheless, in its April 1999 budget the government looked for ways to address some of the grievances in the community, especially outside Melbourne. It introduced cuts in excise on diesel fuel and petrol, and provided an extra $70 million in spending on country hospitals, schools and roads.

Whatever its success in restoring public finances – and the achievements were dramatic, by any standard – the reality was that voters were beginning to demand reinvestment in social infrastructure. The premier and his senior colleagues were confronting a major challenge in repositioning the government politically. They knew they would need to put greater emphasis on the social agenda, crucial to the government's profile in the beleaguered towns of rural and provincial Victoria. In all the outward signs, the premier appeared to be riding high: the opening of the permanent casino had brought a burst of excitement to Melbourne and the state's economic growth, if not yet effervescent, was steadily gathering momentum. Within government, Kennett remained forceful and methodical in steering policy development through cabinet and the bureaucracy. Through all this, however, there remained an unnerving undercurrent for senior Liberals. For all the good vibes about the state recovering its self-esteem, posting runs on the board in economic and financial reconstruction was no longer winning kudos for Kennett in parts of the electorate. As one astute ministerial adviser remarked, 'People may be taking for granted what's happening in the economy. It could be they have already banked that cheque and are now looking around to see what else is in it for them.'

Ken Baxter comments, 'Policy-makers, and I readily include myself in this, had not come to grips with how to marry the complexity of the requirements of the big cities like Melbourne and Sydney with the distinctive needs of small regional communities. I was buggered if I knew what the solutions were. In fact, one of the criticisms I would make of the government, and some of the fault rests with me, was that we didn't realise we needed to spend a lot more time explaining why some of these fundamental changes were taking place and what were the implications, especially for rural services. It was a huge void, into which Pauline Hanson and others had walked. Kennett was worried, and there were a couple of times in the Council meetings when, in his more reflective moments, he would muse on the dangers. But he didn't see it creeping up behind him in the magnitude that it ultimately did. Nobody saw it coming.'

Almost powerless in the face of the unrelieved gloom in rural and regional communities, one Liberal strategist noted bleakly, 'Brumby was out there bagging us all the time, and people are more likely to listen to a negative message than a positive message. Another beautiful day in Victoria is not much of a news story.' Jeff Kennett found himself trapped in a classic squeezeplay. The ALP had rediscovered the long-forgotten axiom of Victorian politics from the 1940s: divide and rule.

CHAPTER SEVENTEEN

CRACKS IN THE EDIFICE

*'I believe in strong government, but I also believe
a strong party is one which allows strong debate.'*
ROGER PESCOTT

In October 1997, in a speech to mark the anniversary of his fifth year in power, Kennett outlined the government's second-term challenges as he saw them. He turned his sights not to the nostalgia of rural Australia but to the global challenges of the future. 'We are advancing into an era in which the world is being swept up by a king tide of change that no one and no country can hold back. Nor should they try. The forces of change – globalisation, communications and information technology, biotechnology, and a more open international society – will have a dramatic impact on our lifestyles and require new approaches. But they also offer enormous opportunities, and the prospect of individual and community determination and freedom on a scale the world has never before experienced. We need to position ourselves to take advantage of change, to prosper and enrich our social capital.'

The need for Victoria to ready itself to compete more assertively in the global marketplace, and for its people to equip themselves to become highly skilled players in the new industries that would arise from the convergence of technologies, would remain Jeff Kennett's constant theme through the late 1990s. In particular, he took a deep personal interest in the possibilities created by the Internet. He established the first multimedia ministry in the country, attaching it to the state Treasury. This was driven in part by his curiosity over how state governments in the future – with their huge dependence on transaction taxes – would be able to collect revenues in a paper-less society. He phoned prominent stockbroker Laurie Cox and asked for a personal briefing on how the Australian Stock Exchange had made the transition to computer trading. He also sought detailed reports from the lands department on how they handled the transfer of title deeds. In the USA, Kennett made a point of meeting Microsoft's Bill Gates.

In this field, among others, Jeff Kennett showed himself to be a premier capable of looking to distant horizons. He spoke fre-quently of a longer-term policy agenda that cast forward a decade and beyond. Nobody could accuse him of being short-sighted, but wasn't he getting one, two or even three elections ahead of himself? Moreover, did his fascination with the big picture reveal a rising sense of boredom and frustration with the mundane and routine aspects of state administration – the 'municipal drainpipes' syn-drome, as his mate Andrew Peacock once put it?

Sensing a window of vulnerability, Labor began running hard on basic grassroots politics, eagerly exploiting any shortcomings in education and health and seeking to entrench the perception that community services had never recovered from the slashing of budgets in the early Kennett years. The Opposition also looked to generate fresh controversy over issues of accountability and demo-cratic process. Although the ALP had not fielded a candidate in the Gippsland West by-election, the pronounced anti-Coalition swing had demonstrated a gap between public expectations and govern-ment policy that could be exploited. As a result, Kennett would have to contain his passion for the broad horizons of policy reform to deal with a series of demanding tests of his political crisis-management.

Labor's ability to exploit weaknesses in the Kennett government had been sharpened by John Brumby's purge of the party at the end of 1996. Dumping his Socialist Left deputy, Demetri Dollis, along with several other long-serving MPs, Brumby had forged a new-look leadership team. Promising youngster Steve Bracks was made shadow Treasury spokesman and the former chief of staff, Rob Hulls, was elevated to shadow attorney-general. Labor's high-profile health spokesman, John Thwaites, became Brumby's second-in-command. With Brumby at the helm, these three were to represent the nucleus of Labor's attempts to build a more compelling public profile. Thwaites, in particular, worked the media prodigiously. An eloquent lawyer and a former mayor of South Melbourne, he became known to colleagues and to some in the media as 'The Sundance Kid'. Meanwhile, Hulls wasted no time in taking over David White's mantle as chief head-kicker, mounting a relentless campaign to expose what he claimed was corruption and cronyism in government.

As Labor began rebuilding itself as a more credible fighting force, Kennett went out early in an attempt to deflate the sense of revivalism in Opposition ranks. All four of the leadership team came from privileged middle-class backgrounds, an indication of the changing demographics within the ALP's branch membership. All were the products of elite private schools. They had gone on to university and into careers in the professions: Brumby and Bracks as teachers, Thwaites and Hulls in the law. For Kennett, always with an eye to siphoning off the support of Labor's traditional blue-collar working class, the opportunities were too good to pass up. He quickly set about targeting their 'pretty boy' image. In a heated parliamentary exchange, Jeff taunted Brumby and Thwaites, both Melbourne Grammar old boys, by reminding parliament of a saying from his schooldays. 'If you can't get a girl, get a Grammar boy,' he chortled. It was a cheap shot. Thwaites, in particular, was soon to have his revenge.

As Labor's health spokesman, Thwaites had been pursuing the

government's privatisation of ambulance service contracts between 1993 and 1995. Most notably, he had been critical of the success of the US-based company Intergraph in securing the right to operate a state-of-the-art computer-based dispatch system for the Victorian police, fire brigade and ambulance service. On the eve of the 1996 election, Thwaites had been denied freedom-of-information access to key documents which he claimed would reveal serious irregularities in the tendering process run by the Metropolitan Ambulance Service. According to Thwaites, the letting of contracts for the operation of a range of non-emergency ambulance services was also questionable. The controversy would lead to allegations of a high-level government cover-up to protect former health minister Marie Tehan.

Thwaites' suspicions were given a boost in late March 1997, when the government took delivery of the preliminary report from the auditor-general, Ches Baragwanath, on the awarding of ambulance contracts. It was a damning document, finding 'serious deficiencies' in the Metropolitan Ambulance Service's management of $32 million worth of contracts, and identifying a flawed process in which hired consultants had been overpaid hundreds of thousands of dollars. One company in particular, Griffiths Consulting, had received total payments of more than $1.5 million. The auditor provided illustrations of entangled relationships between senior ambulance service managers and private companies bidding for business. Government guidelines had been disregarded, and consultancy firms had reaped significant financial rewards without challenge. In a scathing conclusion, the report said the ambulance contracts saga represented 'at best mismanagement, at worst corruption'.

Rob Knowles, Tehan's successor as health minister, went to see Kennett immediately. Any claims of corruption in the awarding of government contracts, proven or unproven, had to be dealt with firmly. The auditor-general's report should be referred to the police. Kennett agreed, but had a query: 'Does Ches know this is your intention? He should be told.' Knowles said he had not yet notified the auditor-general. Kennett phoned Baragwanath to alert him that his report would become the basis of a fraud squad investigation. Baragwanath, however, believed that the scandal demanded a more high-powered investigation, at the level of a judicial inquiry. As his report lodged in parliament on 23 April would stress, the lack of a paper trail surrounding the contract process would make it difficult for the police to gather evidence. Key documentation about crucial management decisions was not available. A judicial inquiry would have the capacity to call witnesses under oath.

Apart from the suggestions of managerial incompetence or worse, the burning issue politically for the government was how much Marie Tehan had known of the scandal in the lead-up to the 1996 election. Briefing notes had been prepared for her by the chief executive officer of the ambulance service, Peter Olzak, and had pointed to the likely political embarrassment once full details emerged. If these notes had been withheld deliberately from the ALP, in defiance of the freedom-of-information laws, they would constitute evidence of a political cover-up. Tehan claimed she had never seen them. Thwaites ridiculed her claims of innocence: 'We've got the smoking gun. We've got the gunpowder all over Mrs Tehan's fingers.'

Kennett called Tehan into his office. In the presence of Knowles, he asked her to consider her position carefully. 'Did you see these notes?' he queried. 'No,' Tehan replied. 'Are you sure?' the premier quizzed again. Tehan insisted she had behaved with integrity. Kennett ended the conversation bluntly. 'If you have not seen them, I will stick with you. But if it emerges that you have seen them, you will have no choice but to resign.' It was the first time in five years that the premier had been given cause to issue a formal warning to one of his cabinet team.

By April 1999, the Director of Public Prosecutions was to announce that no prosecutions would be laid. Although a report from the fraud squad had outlined possible charges against key figures involved in the tendering process of collusive tendering,

conspiracy to defraud and obtaining financial advantage by decep-
tion, the proposed charges had not offered reasonable prospects of
conviction. Nevertheless, the odour of scandal had persisted. With
the public prosecutor's decision, Rob Knowles announced the
matter closed. But the Opposition accused Kennett and his government of a whitewash. John Thwaites said, 'There's a lesson there
for the future: if you rip off the government, they're going to be too
embarrassed to recover the money from you.' It was left to Knowles
to explain why the government saw no need to take action to
recover $500 000 of undocumented expenditure.

Dangerously for Kennett, the government's handling of the
Intergraph issue was soon caught up in a broader Labor Party campaign to establish an image of his administration as secretive and
resentful of scrutiny. This image was reinforced by one of the
government's most perplexing tactical and political mistakes. On
24 April 1997, the day after Ches Baragwanath's report on the
ambulance services was tabled in parliament, the government produced a bill to implement a major shake-up of the auditor-general's
office. It was an appalling choice of timing that seemed too much
of a coincidence.

Under proposals drawn up by finance minister Roger Hallam,
many of the auditor's duties would be contracted out to private
accountancy firms. Baragwanath and his successors would maintain operational control of a smaller office, although they would
retain autonomy to decide who and what was audited within
government. The legislation set ablaze a controversy that persisted
through the Kennett government's second term in office. A broad
coalition of community groups rose up in anger at what was seen
as a crude and ham-fisted attempt to nobble the state's independent watchdog. Even within the Liberal Party the mood was
restive. The move to restructure the auditor's office proved to be a
public relations nightmare. In the media, broadly speaking, the
issues were black and white. Kennett was out to crush critics and
avoid scrutiny.

The truth, of course, was more complex. The saga was as much a story of bureaucratic infighting as it was about the integrity of the auditor's office. It involved a clash of egos between Baragwanath on the one hand, and Kennett and his senior officials on the other. The government had been involved in a behind-the-scenes test of strength with Baragwanath dating as far back as 1993, when Ken Baxter had made a public speech on the role of the auditor-general, signalling the government's intention to change its operations. Despite the climate of budget restraint, Baragwanath had been insisting that the auditor-general's office could not perform its role effectively without additional resources. With most departments taking 10 per cent cuts to their operating costs, this was a big ask. The only sensible solution, Baxter argued, was for the auditor-general's office to be reconfigured. In order to have the capacity to conduct meaningful performance audits of government departments, Baragwanath should be entitled to recruit some of the top professional accountants in the country – a beefed-up hit squad of auditors, being paid salaries reflective of market rates – to guarantee the public the best possible scrutiny of how its money was being spent. The quid pro quo, however, would be that some of the more routine day-to-day operations – the so-called compliance functions – would be tendered out to private accountancy firms. Baragwanath's reply was blunt. If the government sought to foist these changes on him, he would resign immediately. It became a poisonous feud within government.

At times, the bureaucratic head-butting became farcical. Baragwanath was known as a trenchant critic of Kennett's Black Cabinet, arguing that its very existence flouted Westminster traditions of accountability. Yet Baxter tells of how he took a telephone call from Baragwanath's office after the auditor-general heard that the premier had organised a weekend retreat for Black Cabinet members at an old monastery in the Dandenongs. Baxter recalls that Baragwanath was very displeased that he hadn't been invited.

Baragwanath, a big and burly brahmin of the public service, was viewed within government as an old-style imperialist. Having come through the ranks of the bureaucratic high priesthood at the State Electricity Commission, he was imbued with a keen sense of his authority and strength and a readiness to protect his turf. He knew the enormous power of his office, especially in its symbolism, and proved assiduous in his use of it. Appointed by the Cain government in 1988, Baragwanath promoted himself as apolitical, although he had come from strong working-class traditions in West Brunswick. His father had been known to enjoy a drink at the local pub with former Labor prime minister John Curtin. That said, Baragwanath had shown no mercy to the Cain and Kirner governments, hectoring and harassing Labor administrations over a series of financial bungles. Yet his relations with some Liberals had always been uneasy, and they would point to the failure of the early-warning radar of the auditor-general's office to intercept the single biggest financial disaster in the state's history, the billion-dollar losses of the State Bank's Tricontinental offshoot.

For his part, Kennett as Opposition leader had enjoyed a cordial relationship with the auditor-general. Indeed, Baragwanath kept framed in his office a note from Jeff, sent in 1992, praising him and his officers 'for having the courage to carry out their jobs without bending to pressures'. Thus equipped with a moral justification, written in the hand of the premier himself, the wily auditor-general would hurl this rhetoric back in Kennett's face. 'One of the things that's made me extremely cynical about the political process is the fact that when political parties are in opposition they are strong supporters of the concept of having an independent auditor-general with the capacity to roam right across government affairs. But when they're elected to government, some kind of mystical metamorphosis takes place and, if anything, all they want to do is kind of curb or muzzle or restrict the auditor-general,' he would tell reporters.

Far from a defenceless babe in the woods, Baragwanath proved to be skilful in cultivating strategic media contacts, and understood more than most bureaucrats how to make politicians squirm. Many Liberals would rue the day that they dared antagonise him. 'The debate over the fate of the auditor led to the disaffection of many middle-ground voters, and the intelligentsia,' reflects one back-bencher. 'It became an argument we were never able to win in the public arena.'

Indeed, towards the end of 1997 the public row over the amend-ments to the *Audit Act 1994* was to prove the catalyst for the most open display of division and acrimony within Liberal ranks in the Kennett years. At the party's State Council meeting in Shepparton in October, delegates condemned Kennett for what they claimed was an assault on the abuse of executive power. After the meeting, there was talk of mutiny in the back rooms of the parliamentary Liberal Party, with suggestions that as many as 10 MPs might be prepared to cross the floor in an attempt to vote down the bill. The threatened insurrection never materialised. In the last week of October, Kennett met with 30 MPs led by Victor Perton and Tony Plowman, and listened to their grievances. Consequently, he made some concessions. The auditor-general would retain control over contracting-out of audits, rather than this responsibility being placed in the hands of a tender panel, and he would also maintain a core of his own staff. These changes appeared to satisfy the most strenuous internal critics. The legislation was approved the next day at a full meeting of Coalition MPs.

But not everyone was persuaded. The following Thursday Baragwanath hit out publicly, insisting the changes, even in their amended form, would have a devastating impact on the effective functioning of his office. An auditor-general without auditors, said Baragwanath, was like an admiral without a navy. His stance attracted the support of the Victorian Bar Council, which ridiculed the government's claims that it was in fact intent on enhancing the independence of the auditor. The stand-off continued to simmer.

'An acceptable compromise is so close,' wrote Shane Green in the *Age*. 'The auditor-general wants to keep the power to directly carry out some audits; to maintain an investigatory arm. If the government gave ground on this, the rest of the package would be acceptable.'

Senior ministers and officials had their doubts. 'Ches didn't know how to take yes for an answer,' says one.

Ken Baxter accuses Baragwanath of posturing. 'He was always complaining about the resources available to him and the so-called intervention of the executive. But to my certain knowledge, Kennett offered him a line-item budget, and accountability to the Public Accounts Committee of Parliament instead of the executive. He turned it down flat. Kennett said we were happy to give him a performance contract. He didn't want that either. He didn't want to be judged on performance. Ches was great at producing headlines, but that really adds very little value to the accountability of government. We took the view that the strength of an auditor-general is to ensure effective accountability. That could only happen if the office was properly staffed, and operated with a high degree of intellectual rigour. It's a pity there wasn't a deeper analysis of this as a policy issue, as distinct from a political issue.'

Whatever the rights or wrongs, the controversy soon escalated into Kennett's greatest political challenge. Roger Pescott had nursed a grudge against Kennett ever since his support of Jeff's leadership comeback had translated only to the junior portfolio of industrial services. Now he would use the Audit Act amendments as a platform for his final tempestuous attack on the premier.

Pescott chose the symbolism of Armistice Day on 11 November to announce his resignation from state parliament. In an open letter to the premier, beginning 'Dear Jeff', he denounced Kennett and his leadership style. Citing the contentious changes to the auditor-general's office in particular, Pescott said his decision to retire from public life was in protest against 'examples of bad government in this state'. This was to be Pescott's last stand, and he would sink the knife deep into the rib cage of his old foe.

Your style of government has its advantages sometimes because it summarily dismisses obstacles in the way of commonsense. Yet overall it has many dangers. Liberal Party debate has been constricted to a faint trickle, which has meant many Liberals fear speaking up for the principles which prompted Menzies to form the party many years ago. Members have two options. Speak up and be branded as disloyal to the cause. Say nothing and be part of it. Most follow the latter course because they do not want to be accused of being disloyal. They have been prepared often to give you the benefit of the doubt in the hope that your proposals succeed.

For my part, like most politicians, I entered parliament keen to make a contribution towards winning government, and formulating sound policy. In Opposition, I was very active when given the chance. Increasingly, these chances were restricted and, for nearly a decade, I, like others, have found it difficult to engage you in meaningful policy debate. Yet the party structure, which has only ever relied upon a convention of consultation by the political leadership, seems powerless to enforce a democratic process.

In reality, you have hijacked the Coalition from many of the enduring principles on which it was founded – and because you do not encourage discussion you are not always getting sound advice. How amazed would the community be to learn that the large majority of members in the Liberal party room had not seen the text of the draft legislation on the auditor-general when they approved it. I was unable to get a copy of it myself until three days later . . . as you know, I have put trust in your word in the past. That is why I find resignation from parliament the only effective protest I can make. Like many other Liberals, I wish there were another way.

Even in the brutal and often treacherous world of politics, there had seldom been a more dramatic public outburst aimed at disembowelling a serving leader. Some of Pescott's senior colleagues spoke darkly of this being a final display of petulance and pomposity. The manner of his departure sent shock waves through the party, and indeed through the wider electorate. Most significantly of all, Pescott's mid-term resignation foisted an untimely and unwelcome by-election on the Kennett government. The safe Liberal seat of Mitcham was up for grabs. Pescott issued an explicit plea to the voters of middle Melbourne to send the government a message of protest. The by-election, he insisted, should be viewed as a plebiscite on the controversial changes to the auditor-general's office and, by extension, on the leadership approach of the premier. Kennett refused to engage in a slanging match with his old adversary. 'He won't be missed,' was the premier's blunt retort.

Government MPs closed ranks, knowing that with a by-election ahead this was no time for an outbreak of recriminations. Pescott, for his part, argued that the lack of open support for his stance from fellow Liberals simply reflected a climate in which MPs were afraid to speak out. Even those who privately agreed with him would maintain their silence rather than face accusations of disloyalty. Pescott asserted, 'For many years, I have known that to speak out would mean I was immediately branded a troublemaker. I can't be surprised if others are bulldozed into not saying what they think. I believe in strong government, but I also believe a strong party is one which allows strong debate. The whittling-down of the tradition of debate over time has meant some of the decisions like the auditor-general are not in the best interests of the community.'

The Saturday after Pescott's resignation, an opinion poll published in the *Age* revealed an unprecedented slump in support for the Coalition. Labor had swept past the government to hold an eight-point lead, 54–46, in the two-party preferred vote. It was the first time in five years the ALP had headed the government. A poll published the following Monday suggested the same sentiment at work in the Mitcham electorate, an impregnable Liberal Party stronghold through the 1990s. The Kennett government was confronting a by-election debacle.

According to the poll, voters were registering high levels of disapproval for the changes to the auditor's office. Moreover, another divisive policy debate was causing unrest and anxiety. The decision to reform the state's WorkCover system by removing the right of injured workers to sue for common law damages was also biting deep in the electorate. Here, the government was up against the combined might of the trade union movement and the legal profession, both of which attacked the reform as trampling on workers' rights.

Under WorkCover, the state had been able to reduce insurance premiums for Victorian industry to below the national average, but a surge in litigation through the mid-1990s was causing a blow-out in the scheme's budget. Legal costs had spiralled to more than $110 million annually. The aim of the amendments was to follow the practice of the USA, Canada and two other Australian states in taking the issues of compensation and care for people suffering serious and debilitating workplace injuries out of the hands of litigation lawyers. Instead, a statutory table of benefits would be made available to injured workers so that they would not have to press their claims through prolonged and expensive court action.

Part of the government's irritation was that law firms that had affiliations to the ALP, notably Slater & Gordon and Maurice Blackburn & Co., were market leaders in the industry. Together with the Trades Hall Council, prominent lawyers from these firms – including John Cain junior, son of the former premier – mounted a public campaign insisting that the changes proposed by the government would in fact mean lower payouts to some badly injured workers. With the Mitcham by-election looming, the legal profession and the union leadership had the government on the back foot. Promising a series of protest rallies, Trades Hall Council secretary Leigh Hubbard said, 'If Mr Kennett thought this issue was going to go away, he had better think again. We will not let the people of Victoria forget that he doesn't care about the plight of injured workers.'

There were other factors at work in Mitcham, none of which were positive for the government. A postal survey of Mitcham voters had revealed that the introduction of poker machines into local hotels and clubs was causing community concern. Almost four in every five voters polled had registered their strong disapproval of 'the extent to which gambling has been encouraged in Victoria'. As well, across Melbourne's comfortable middle suburbs there had been a community backlash against the government's decision to allow medium-density developments in leafy residential streets. A protest group, Save Our Suburbs, was gathering support. In electorates such as Mitcham, some of its activists were disaffected Liberal Party supporters.

Given the multiplicity of issues running against the government, overlaid by the spectacle of a premier coming under direct attack from his own back bench, the Liberals knew they were facing humiliation. Kennett's judgement was that the government had no prospect of retaining a seat held by a margin of 5.4 per cent. Mid-term by-elections had a consistent history of voters giving the incumbent government a kick in the shin. Kennett went into the 12 December poll expecting the worst. Feigning nonchalance, he joked that one of his dogs, Elle, might just as well run. It was an idiosyncratic attempt to downplay expectations in anticipation of defeat, but it can hardly have helped Liberal candidate Andrew Munroe in his efforts to defend the seat.

As the votes came in, it was obvious the swing to Labor reflected more than the conventional anti-government protest vote. Although senior Liberals knew defeat in the Mitcham by-election was a foregone conclusion, the swing achieved by the ALP's candidate, Tony Robinson, was in excess of 15 per cent. A triumphant Brumby declared Labor 'back in town'. His party, he said, had scored the biggest by-election swing against a state government in Australia's history. In fact, it ranked second. (Six years earlier, a Labor government in Western Australia had suffered a 30 per cent swing.) But stripping his jubilant statement of its hyperbole, the Opposition leader had a point. This was the first serious repudiation of Kennett's government by the voters of middle Melbourne. Moreover, it was a dramatic affirmation of Brumby's renewal strategy, a result that would surely silence many of his own internal critics. At a subdued Liberal campaign office, Jeff Kennett was forced to eat crow. 'It is a shot across our bow, and it is character-building. We are not ignoring the result. We take it on board.'

In a lengthy interview in the heady mood of resurgence after Labor's victory in Mitcham, Brumby made the claim that Labor was fifty-fifty to win the next state election. 'Four years ago, when I took over, we were at one or two out of 10, pretty close to rock bottom in the big scheme of things. After this by-election, we are probably up around the six or seven out of 10 mark. There's still plenty to do but I think we have got above the Plimsoll line.' Apart from the by-election proving Labor's capacity to dictate the agenda, Brumby insisted that the broader significance lay in what the result said about the premier's campaigning, and the myth of Kennett's invincibility. 'Lots of leaders get the big-head disease. It's not an uncommon problem in politics. Occasionally, they have to be cut down to size and they start again, and so on. But it is usually terminal, and Jeffrey seems to have it. He's gone right off the Geiger counter. People will now see Jeff Kennett as a liability to the Liberal Party. They will see him as a liability in the bush and they will see him as a liability in the Liberal heartland. The pressure is now on him.'

Sniffing the undercurrents of dissent within the Liberal Party about Kennett's role in the Mitcham debacle, Brumby sought to twist the knife, with a cheeky offering of some free advice. 'What Kennett should have done is batted on his strengths, which is getting debt down, finishing the [Eastern] freeway extensions, the [below national average] jobless figures that came out in the last week, the dough he poured into level crossings. If you had a government on its game, a premier in touch and listening, Mitcham should not have been a 16 per cent swing. In terms of the big issues, they had just as much wind blowing their way as ours. Yet they lost it. Why? You've got to conclude one, that we controlled the agenda; secondly, it's Kennett's arrogance, misreading the electorate, misreading the mood. My own view is that it's extremely unlikely Jeff will be around for the next election.'

CHAPTER EIGHTEEN

THE PRICE OF POWER

*'You've got to ask yourself: why would you
want to be in public life?'*
JEFF KENNETT

Amid all the drama at Spring Street, the pressures on Kennett's family life were becoming intolerable. In addition to the ambulance scandal and auditor-general debate, Labor MPs were questioning the government's use of corporate credit cards issued by the state to senior ministers and public servants. Shadow attorney-general Rob Hulls turned his sights to the purchase of a pair of sunglasses for Felicity Kennett on one such card during an official trip by the Kennetts to Athens. It was a $200 controversy concerning a pair of glasses bought at the taxpayer's expense, but, again, it meant the premier's wife was in the headlines. As Kennett was to say later, 'She'd had a gutful.'

The continuing public scrutiny, compounded by a persistent undercurrent of salacious gossip, had pushed the Kennetts' 25-year marriage to the verge of breakdown. The premier had long been assuring his wife that politics would not forever dominate their lives. As early as 1984, he complained to a reporter of always getting home late at night when his small children were already well asleep.

'Why do we do this to ourselves?' he had said to Felicity. Through-out his career, Kennett had promised that he would return to a less harrowing existence in the private sector when he believed his job was done. But as the pressures crowded in on him during those last weeks of 1997, his marriage began to crack under the strain.

In the heady days after his re-election in 1996, Kennett had flirted publicly with the idea of taking a three-month sabbatical overseas, with his wife, to recharge his batteries. This was a truly bizarre proposition, but it provided a glimpse into the nature of the pressures imposed by the media focus on the premier's family during the government's first term. If Jeff was thriving in the excitement of running the state, it was known to his inner circle that Felicity was wearying of the demands it placed on her and the Kennett children. The loss of the family business had been the signal reminder of the price of public office. According to one friend of the Kennetts, the loss of the KNF agency robbed Felicity of any sense of indepen-dence, and left deep scars. As she would reveal in an extended *Good Weekend* interview in 1996, 'I really lost it . . . It's been pretty black. I was feeling sorry for myself. I was depressed.'

In that interview, the premier's wife spoke frankly about the impact of living with the nation's most high-profile politician. Felicity had tried to combine her family responsibilities, her own career and her duties as the consort of a political leader, and had found the task emotionally taxing and, at times, destructive. She was wrestling with the constraints of being seen as bound to the demands and expectations of her husband's job. 'It implies I'm totally beholden to Jeffrey, his life and his way of thinking. That I'm not free to be an individual. And I refuse to take that one. I take it every now and then and I think, bugger that for a laugh – I'm out of here. I'm off.'

On 28 January 1998 came confirmation of the personal crisis that had been the subject of whispers for well over a year. The premier's office issued a brief statement announcing the trial sepa-ration of the Kennetts. 'The premier and Mrs Kennett have decided to issue this formal statement to prevent unnecessary comment and further pursuit of Mrs Kennett and the children that could be hurtful to them at this time. The premier and Mrs Kennett trust that the media will respect their right and that of their family to privacy in regards to this matter. Mr and Mrs Kennett will not be making any public comment.' The marriage breakdown was shattering for Jeff. 'It was devastating,' confirms one close friend. 'Obviously, he was very much devoted to his family. It led to a lot of self-analysis.'

Kennett's home environment had provided balance in the premier's life: a reality check against the delusions and double-speak of the political game. According to friends of the family, the children were encouraged not to take their father and his role in life too seriously. Felicity and the children constantly poked fun at him. When he walked through the door of their Surrey Hills home, he was no longer the premier; he was ridiculed by his family as the household 'dork'. At home, Jeff called the children's mother Flicka; she nicknamed him Basil. Friends described the domestic atmosphere as relaxed and informal, if noisy. 'There was a sense of irreverence. They would all take the piss out of him, and he loved having them take the piss out of him. Felicity has a great sense of humour. She's very quick, very witty, and she just didn't take polit-ical games all that seriously. She had been watching it at close quarters for a long time, watching him through all those ups and downs. As a result, he found it very hard to trust people. That's why she was so important to him. She could make him relax and calm down. She would just laugh at him. He needed people to bring him down to earth a bit.'

From the time Jeff chose to enter politics – he broke the news to Felicity of his plans to run for parliament on the day they brought their second-born child, Amy, home from hospital – the Kennetts had set themselves the task of creating as 'normal' a home environ-ment as was possible for children who have a parent involved in public life. By the time their father became Opposition leader in 1982, there were four children under the age of eight in the Kennett household. They were sent to private schools – the three boys went to Scotch College, like their father and grandfather before them – and grew up in affluent middle Melbourne.

Although they cannot have helped but become aware of the pit-falls of their father's career (Amy, at the age of 13, had sent her dad a private note of condolence after his defeat in the 1988 election), the children were pretty much shielded from the public gaze in their formative years. In 1997 eldest son Ed, an accountancy graduate, was dragged briefly into the furore over family share dealings. But in 1998 middle son Angus, tall and lean like his mother, began attracting constant media attention, through his job as a part-time model at Melbourne's Spring Fashion Week. Soon after, he was named one of five 'millennium models' at Australian Fashion Week in Sydney, and like Patrick Keating, son of the former Labor prime minister, Angus became a hot item in the teen press.

Through this exposure, Angus became the first of the Kennett children to give an extended media interview, thereby providing some insight into the extent of the impact on their lives of their father's career. 'A lot of people refer to me as the premier's son, and I'm always going to be judged by this no matter what I'm successful in,' he said. 'But a name can only get you so far and if I wasn't half decent at what I did I suppose I wouldn't still be doing it.' In fact, the name could also act as a lightning rod for criticism, fair or otherwise. Angus felt the brunt of this when John Wood, a promi-nent television actor, attacked the young man's rising celebrity and denounced him as 'moronic'. Wood's wife, Leslie, was a Labor candidate at the time. Angus spoke in his own defence. 'I think he'll come off worse for saying it. I've always tried to distance myself from politics. Yes, I'm Jeff Kennett's son. But I'm not the premier's son . . . Mum and Dad have always kept us away from the whole media thing. Now I'm a part of it, they still stay away to make the point that if I'm doing it, it's me and not them.'

In fact, as the Kennett children emerged more into the public spotlight as young adults, they came across as confident, relaxed and remarkably unaffected individuals. In 1997 the youngest, Ross, spoke to the media soon after his return from an end-of-school jaunt to Byron Bay, revealing proudly that he had paid $50 to have a black leopard tattooed on a buttock. When he told his parents, his mother had insisted he 'drop his daks' to show them what he had done, while his father, according to Ross, 'just gave me a little smile'.

'We're a very normal family,' Felicity Kennett said in an interview that same year. 'We have disagreements with our kids. If they upset me, I mightn't speak to them for days and we live in the same house. Jeff thinks that's ridiculous [but] we confront the same issues all families do. There are certain moral standards you think your family should uphold and then you find out they don't and you wonder how you're going to tell him.' Felicity cited the example of Amy giving her father a refresher course on the facts of life. 'His daughter . . . sat him down and said, "Well, you know Dad, I am 20. This is how it is for 20-year-old girls." The poor guy, it was hard for him because Dad's daughters aren't supposed to be anything other than perfect little angels.'

The premier's wife had a straightforward 'What you see is what you get' demeanour not unlike Jeff's own, and shared his sense of mischief and his iconoclastic streak. She was capable of making piercing assessments of the duplicity and artifice of political life. Attending one function hosted by the premier for the arts community, she watched the assembled guests gushing over their champagne and canapés and noted acerbically, 'Most of these people wouldn't spit on Jeffrey if they saw him in the street.' Jeff Kennett valued her instincts and judgements. But an influential back-seat role was not much by way of compensation for the intrusions into Felicity's family life. Jeff's commitment to long hours had left her to raise four young children virtually single-handedly, while being subjected to what she saw as a systematic campaign by the premier's enemies in the ALP and the media to chase headlines at her family's expense.

Reflecting on this later, Kennett was to recognise the high price

paid by the family of a senior politician. 'I was working from 5 a.m.
till midnight, six days a week, and usually Sundays as well. Inevitably, over many years, it put an enormous amount of pressure on
Felicity, not only in terms of the household and the children, but
also in terms of her relationship with me. I can see it better now: the
nights, the weeks, the months, the years, of being left alone because
I was never home and there were young children to care for. For an
adult to be at home on her own, night after night, is a terribly lonely
experience. Combined with that was the fact that my relationship
with the media was always full-bore, and she had to read at times
some of the most scurrilous rubbish about me. And about her.
I think this welled up over the years and she decided she wanted to
make a break. She was tired, exhausted, lonely, and there was this
swirling sea in which we were living.'

A fresh wave of media attention would break over the Kennetts
on 29 January, the day after the premier's office had announced
their trial separation. Opening the *Australian* that morning, the
premier was confronted with a feature article which referred to
'rumours, however unfactual' linking him to art gallery director
Maudie Palmer and Grand Prix chief executive Judith Griggs.

As he would later tell the jury during the ensuing defamation
trial, Kennett was angry and disgusted. 'I should not have been
put in that position. No one should be put in that position. Part
of the hurt was not only because it was so absolutely inaccurate,
unfair and unjust, but it was something that I was going to have
to explain to my wife and children.'

Felicity, who also gave evidence at the trial, said the premier
had telephoned her on the day the article appeared. 'He was not
pleased. In fact, he was extremely displeased. He was revolted and
disgusted and I think his language reflected that.' She had gone to
the family home at Surrey Hills that night. Two of their four
children were sitting in the kitchen. Jeff, angry and distressed, was
sitting alongside them. The newspapers were spread on the table.
'This particular article, he was basically hammering it with his

forefinger . . . when he spoke to my children about it, I think that is the only time I've ever seen him really distressed. He wept, he was very emotional . . . already we are talking about a very hard time for us personally, and he couldn't explain to them in simple enough language to say, "This hasn't happened in my life. This is not what has been happening."'

Judith Griggs would appear as a witness for the Kennetts. She denied ever having an improper or intimate relationship of any kind with the premier. She told of being at the office of Grand Prix chief Bernie Ecclestone at his headquarters in London and seeing a small yellow-and-pink baby's bib that arrived in the mail. Attached was a note, with words to the effect, 'Bernie. Please pass on very best wishes to Judith.' Recalled Griggs, 'It talked about Judith and Jeff and then it was signed "Ron". So it was bizarre. To say the least.'

In its defence at the trial, News Ltd did not call witnesses. Instead, counsel for the media organisation, Jeffrey Sher, QC, insisted the article was not defamatory because it did not say the rumours were true; indeed, it had conveyed the very opposite. He urged the jury to read the article rationally, sensibly and calmly. After deliberating for 50 minutes, they found in favour of the newspaper, awarding costs of more than $250 000 against the premier. News Ltd proclaimed it an important victory for freedom of the press. As a crestfallen Jeff Kennett would explain to the media the following day, not only had the jury rejected his complaint of unfair intrusion, but he was also having to ponder how to meet the onerous costs accompanying the litigation. 'I don't have a pot full of money. I don't have a beach house to sell, I don't have a lot of shares – thanks to some issues that ran some years ago – and in the meantime I've tried to educate four children as best I can. I don't have an answer to that. I mean, it's a bit like a Houdini trick. I'm going to have to address that in the next few weeks as the bills start coming in.'

Containing his frustration, Kennett was careful not to criticise the judge or jury. But he took to task defence counsel Sher over his remark, 'If you go into public life, you have to pay a price, and the price is that you get subjected to unfounded and unsubstantiated rumours'. Kennett said this was a view he rejected fundamentally. 'It is going to make it increasingly difficult to get men and women to enter the parliamentary arena. The *Australian* did not care about Jeff Kennett as a private citizen, they did not care about the Kennett family. They only too happily, without making any contact with me or the two women involved, repeated unfounded and unsubstantiated rumours to cause us great harm. You've got to ask yourself: why would you want to be in public life? If that is the norm, and if that is allowed to continue, where is the decency?'

So strongly did Kennett feel about this that he had rejected the offer of an out-of-court settlement from News Ltd and pursued his defamation action all the way to a jury hearing, claiming there was an important principle at stake: the right of politicians to protect their reputations, and their families, against the circulation of unfounded rumours.

Interestingly, though, for a family that shunned media scrutiny, Felicity Kennett would share her husband's interest in a media career. Her decision to leave the family home and build her own career in television as a reporter on the lifestyle program *Healthy, Wealthy & Wise* prompted a fresh bout of speculation within the Liberal Party about how Kennett would react. Inspecting the Domain tunnel project on the day the separation was announced, the premier was asked by reporters if he might soon retire. 'What an appalling question' was his curt response.

Divorce and family break-up were common enough phenomena in Australia in the 1990s, but this was the first time a serving government leader had been forced to deal with these issues in full public view. Inevitably, there would be questions about the impact on his political career. Inevitably, the debate would not always be sensitive to the personal dimensions of private grief. What were the ground rules?

Officially, the Labor Party's response was circumspect. In a brief statement, John Brumby said these were personal matters for the Kennetts to resolve. The following day, after a distressed premier said the ALP should look at whether its tactics had played a part, Brumby's office issued a further clarifying statement rejecting suggestions that Labor could be held responsible for the pressures that led to the marriage breakdown. Hours later, in a moment of clumsiness he would soon regret, Brumby went to a 'Labor Listens' meeting in Prahran and introduced one of his front-bench team to the audience with the preamble, 'This is Rob Hulls. Shadow Attorney-General, ALP bomb-thrower, and marriage-wrecker.' It may well have been intended to be light-hearted, an ironic reference to the premier's criticism of the Opposition; it certainly wasn't intended for wider public consumption. But it was indiscreet in the extreme and appalled some of the guests gathered at the function, including at least one prominent Labor supporter. There were angry calls to talk-back radio, and Brumby's office went into damage-control mode. 'It was not a comment about the Kennetts' marriage. It was a comment about how once again the premier blames the ALP for everything that happens in his life,' declared a party spokesman. The Kennetts' personal crisis was new territory for everyone. Nobody in the media or the political arena seemed quite sure how to handle it, least of all, perhaps, the premier. 'The major anchor in his life had been removed,' said a friend.

'I think that was probably the saddest period in his life,' says Ron Walker. 'I don't think I have ever seen him so disconsolate. He poured his heart out a couple of times in public, and people saw in him things that had happened in their own lives. A lot of people out there don't believe bad things ever happen to people like the Kennetts. It's amazing the perception out there in the marketplace. Nobody could ever believe those two would split up. But public life is a very hazardous affair, very telling, very destructive. A lot of women married to successful husbands don't like the constant attention. I recall Phil Lynch [former federal Liberal deputy] got to the stage where his children wouldn't even have dinner with him in a restaurant because people would be staring all night.'

Public life is littered with shipwrecks, many of them the sons and daughters of prominent politicians who, beyond having to learn to deal with the usual playground taunts, have struggled as they neared adulthood to cope with the pressures of expectations. The Kennetts had gone to great lengths to shield their children from the impact of their father's celebrity. Early in his career as Opposition leader, Jeff had privately approached newspaper editors asking that the children not be photographed or interviewed. Likewise, as they advanced through their school years, he chose deliberately not to impose huge expectations of academic success. The Kennetts were not pushy parents; the children should not feel burdened by a demand to perform beyond their capacity.

In the end, though, and after more than 20 years of building a balanced and well-adjusted home environment, it was Felicity who reached a point where she could no longer deal with prying eyes.

In her only interview during the time of the separation, and angered by a steady stream of rumour and innuendo, she told the *Sunday Herald-Sun* that the separation was entirely amicable. 'People assume there is anger, acrimony – even violence. There has been none of that. I still visit the house. They all visit me. We are still a family. It's just that now I live alone.'

As the premier sought to adjust, he threw himself into his work. He also played more golf. He pedalled furiously on an exercise bike as he watched cable news in the pre-dawn hours at home. He took to the regimen of daily 'power walks' around the parklands of the MCG. At nights, he would cook at home and do the shopping and washing. 'He was lonely more than anything else,' says Walker. 'I think he had to try and fill his weekends. If he kept busy, he wasn't thinking about Felicity as much. But he still maintained a vigil of speaking to her every day hoping it would come back together again. It was the ultimate hurt for him when she left. Be it a prime minister or premier, when your wife leaves you it is a public affair and you can't do anything about that.' Kennett would often invite old allies around for dinner: Alister Drysdale, his former chief of staff John Griffin, and Rob Knowles. The price they paid in joining Kennett on this personal odyssey was to endure a hearty serving of tripe, one of Kennett's favourite dishes.

Meanwhile, the guessing games continued inside the Liberal Party about the effect of the separation on the premier's political life. Would he stay, or would he go? 'There was a lot of discussion, not so much about the marriage separation as his response to it,' confessed a senior backbencher. 'People were not necessarily talking about a challenge, but focusing on whether he was going. People were talking quite openly, is he going to pull the plug or isn't he? If he was out, who would we vote in?'

According to close friends, Felicity's departure made his work an even more important factor in Kennett's life. Says one, 'He loved being busy, he loved having a sense of purpose. He loved putting his fingers into every little pie. If Felicity had been at home . . . she might have been saying, "Let's go overseas for a few months, and put all this behind us." But without her there, the only other constant in his life was the job. If he had given up on that, he could have found himself absolutely rudderless.'

In fact, the family knew by February that Kennett would continue as premier. In the privacy of home, he had discussed the issues at length with his four children. Should he quit? Would this help? The children had counselled him to continue. He had also discussed it with Felicity, believing she would accept his decision with forbearance. 'She understood very well that I enjoyed the job too much, and that if I was going to stay, nothing would really change. It was obviously difficult for her.'

In an interview to mark his 50th birthday, Kennett would tell *Age* readers that he had chosen to stay in office and would look at retiring beyond the next election. In the lonely moments before and after the announcement of the marriage split, he had flirted with giving it away. But he could no longer allow himself the luxury of self-pity and had to separate his public duties from his private anguish. 'The thought has obviously gone through my mind on a couple of occasions. You just have to try to put what's happened personally in one compartment, and your job in another. I am the first to admit it was very, very difficult when it happened. The very fact we are public figures, and we had to make a public statement, and it got the incredible coverage it did, makes it that much harder. But I think it was done with the greatest dignity possible. Flicka and I are still good friends. I talk to her every day, and see her a couple of times a week. But, still, something has happened in my life that I never predicted and never wanted, and that is emotionally very difficult. With the passage of time, you adjust. The difficulty is there is no place to hide. You have your internal emotions, but you still have to be premier of the state. It's been a different month from any month I have ever had in my life. Having said that, I remain politically very motivated.'

Nor did Kennett ever give up on his marriage. A Labor MP remembers seeing a disconsolate premier late at night in a corridor at Parliament House, and expressing sympathy over the impact of the break-up. Kennett insisted he had not given up hope. 'She will come back, you know. She will come back.'

Looking back on this time of upheaval, Kennett believes he was never really close to a decision to leave. Politics had been his abiding interest for most of his adult life, intellectually and emotionally. 'I never actually got to the stage of saying I was going to leave. But the 50th birthday was an option. That obviously gave rise to some of my colleagues anticipating my exit – or, in some cases, trying to manipulate it. That's politics, I guess.'

CHAPTER NINETEEN

———

THE THREAT FROM WITHIN

'Anybody can be loyal to me when I'm right. What I want are people
who are loyal to me when I'm wrong.'
HUGH GAITSKELL, 1950s BRITISH LABOUR LEADER

Jeff Kennett did serve notice of his possible retirement to his close
colleagues as his 50th birthday approached on 2 March 1998.
Despite the recent political and personal upheavals, they were
stunned. Health minister Rob Knowles was one of those called into
Kennett's office at Treasury Place to be forewarned. 'It certainly
came as a bit of a jolt to me,' he recalls. 'As far as I knew he had
not mentioned this before, although he may well have done with
Felicity, but I certainly had no sense of it. I thought that decision
would have come well into the future. We hadn't really contemplated this.' Yet not everybody in the party shared Knowles'
sense of foreboding. One of the senior colleagues to whom Kennett
turned for advice was his deputy and long-standing rival Phil Gude.
Gude responded bluntly. If the premier was so much as flirting with
thoughts of retirement, it was an indication his mind was not fixed
on the demands of office. He should act on his instincts and get out
while he was on top.

Certainly for Kennett's enemies within the party, the Mitcham by-election had created an unforeseen opportunity. Coming on top of the Gippsland West defeat earlier in the year, no leader, surely, could expect to endure electoral setbacks of this magnitude. With the heartland seemingly in rebellion, a group of Liberal MPs began to agitate for change at the top. Kennett had always known the Liberal party room could be fickle. Two landslide election victories would not necessarily protect him against the manoeuvring. Having endured four leadership challenges in the 1980s, he had learned to be distrustful, and had developed strong and secure networks through the party able to detect the first hint of trouble on the back bench.

There had always been cabals within the party hostile to his leadership. Sometimes the names and faces changed, but it was seldom long before Kennett knew who they were, where they met, where they dined and drank – and, usually, what they were up to. In the aftermath of Mitcham, and through the tense months towards the end of 1997, Kennett and his allies were acutely aware of the talk around the corridors. But they also knew that nobody had anything approaching the numbers to challenge him.

The most crucial dynamic throughout this period, therefore, was the calculations going on in Kennett's own mind. His ambivalence about whether he wished to continue in office became widely known in Liberal circles in the weeks leading into the new year. Together with rumours of his marriage breakdown, MPs knew there had been overtures to Kennett to retire from politics and take up a senior role in the private sector. Although Kennett denies there was ever a specific job offer, it is understood he was sounded out informally in 1997 by senior News Ltd heads on whether he was interested in a career as a media executive at the Herald & Weekly Times. Behind the scenes, he was also approached at least once by one of Australia's foremost corporate headhunters. Jeff, however, insists there was never a proposition put to him that was likely to induce him to 'walk the plank'.

Throughout the time the premier was wrestling with his priori-

ties, Phil Gude was emerging as the clear frontrunner to succeed
him. In the absence of Kennett, Gude would be virtually assured of
a majority of the party-room vote. One senior Liberal, a known supporter of Kennett, says, 'Gude's relationship with the back bench
was very, very good indeed, and he was a good minister. Having got
there, you could not fault him, in my view. So what you were seeing
were people looking for a mid-term succession. First question, when
is Jeff going to retire? Second question, who would take his place?
Gude would have got it. He was quite popular. But there were
always those who were asking whether he had the edge in leadership
that a premier requires.'

For all Kennett's personal woes and the policy difficulties confronting the government, Gude did not force the issue publicly.
Although some of his back-bench supporters became highly anima-
ted in the early months of 1998, and senior Liberals were briefing
journalists that Gude was ready and willing to pounce, there was
never a spill motion. In fact, Gude had told one of his supporters
that he would vote personally to uphold Kennett's leadership. That
said, the premier watched warily. 'Although Phil gave the impression of being a benign elderly labrador, Kennett never underestimated him,' a Kennett supporter says. The premier's supporters
also kept a close eye on Gude's adviser John Fetter. Kennett didn't
trust Fetter, and had tried three times to have him removed. Says
another supporter, 'Fetter was a bit of a player. He talked to the
backbenchers a fair bit. Jeffrey would get feedback on the things
Fetter was saying.'

Labor MPs were also keeping a close eye on developments.
Frequently, they would see Liberals gathering in or around Phil
Gude's parliamentary office for a chat. Sometimes there would be
10 or so; sometimes a few more. John Fetter was a ubiquitous presence on these occasions. On the surface, this was no big deal. Part
of Gude's role as deputy leader was to act as a conduit between the
back bench and the cabinet, and to be a sounding-board for their
grievances. Affable and a patient listener, it was his role in political

management to stay plugged into the mood and attitudes of the party room. But, at 57, he had served in two of the most weighty portfolios in government: industrial relations and education. He was a seasoned performer in cabinet and in the parliament. It was not unnatural for him to consider himself a candidate to lead the government if an opportunity arose. Although it proved to be wishful thinking, senior Labor figures suspected this time that Kennett might just be in some danger of being undermined from within.

The relationship between the premier and his deputy remained one of the most intriguing double acts within the Kennett government. In Opposition, they had been rivals. Yet as part of the matrix of deals that brought Kennett back to the party leadership in 1991, Gude had been the only member of Alan Brown's shadow cabinet to vote in favour of the leadership spill. His prize, of course, was the guaranteed backing of Kennett's supporters to take over as deputy. Kennett, for his part, had wanted Stockdale as his deputy. Indeed, for a time he had sought to persuade Gude to consider moving instead to the Treasury role. But Gude, who always had his own agenda, insisted on staying put in industrial relations. The two had to learn to live and let live, in peaceful coexistence.

The common depiction in the Australian media of Gude and Kennett as bitter enemies is a gross oversimplification. In fact, at a personal level they enjoyed a close rapport. In many ways they were confidants, with a sophisticated understanding of each other's interests and egos. Behind the scenes they worked in close partnership, sitting alongside each other in cabinet discussions and regularly conferring privately. There is no doubt, however, that their relationship soured in 1998. This was driven in part by the active role of Gude's supporters in briefing the media against the premier. It was also driven by Gude's resentment that Kennett seldom gave due recognition to his contribution as a stabilising influence. This climaxed when it became evident that Jeff, for whatever reason, did not consider Gude a worthy successor.

Instead, the premier made it known that he believed his treasurer, Alan Stockdale, was the only suitable successor in the short
term. Not even close cabinet colleagues found it easy to accept this
rigid stance. For while there was little doubt that, other than Jeff
Kennett, Stockdale was the biggest brand name in the government,
senior colleagues questioned the treasurer's political instincts. Many
of those who admired his tenacity in chasing through financial
management reforms, and his intellectual depth in engineering big
structural reforms such as privatisation, also held the view that
Stockdale could never be a voter-friendly package. As one Liberal
said famously, 'Stockdale doesn't have a political bone in his body.'
With the government attempting to reposition itself on the social
agenda, the treasurer had the baggage of being seen as too much of
an ideologue. Another factor driving party-room negativity towards
Stockdale had been his role as 'The Minister for Saying No'. In
seeking to restore Victoria's public finances, Stockdale had hectored
and harassed fellow ministers to push harder for budget savings in
the early years of government. He had been a formidable taskmaster
as Kennett's right-hand man in driving the processes of cabinet's
Budget and Expenditure Review Committee, and the success of his
budget reforms had earned him massive kudos in financial markets
and business circles. But his tough-minded approach didn't necessarily earn as much admiration from his ministerial colleagues.
With or without Kennett's imprimatur, Stockdale would simply not
get the numbers.

Party resistance to the prospect of Stockdale as leader was Kennett's great setback as he considered his exit strategy. As he would
recall later, 'I had always hoped that Alan might succeed me. Once
it became clear, for a variety of reasons, that wasn't going to happen,
it became very clear to me that, short of a runaway bus taking me
out of the picture, the interests of the party would best be served by
handing over to the next generation.'

According to one of Kennett's senior cabinet colleagues, 'Jeff
went on because he didn't feel he could rely upon those he saw as

going to replace him. He was very keen to step out on top. The bloke's a realist. He had been up and down like a yo-yo and he knew this was the crest of the wave. But he wasn't prepared to leave the future of Victoria at risk; that's what determined whether he would go on. He put all his personal stuff to one side. He didn't want to go on – Felicity didn't want him to go on – but he was terrified all his work would unravel. It wasn't a personal ego thing. It wasn't driven by animosity. He enjoyed Phil's company. But he didn't want to hand over without being sure they were up to it.' In short, according to Kennett and his confidants, he had no choice but to accept the awkward reality that, unlike Bolte, he was in no position at this time to anoint his chosen successor. If Kennett was not happy to hand the reins to Gude, he would have no alternative but to stay and see off any party-room intrigues.

One reason for restlessness on the back bench was the oldest and most powerful instinct in political life: thwarted ambition. After the 1996 election, Kennett had determined he would reduce the size of the cabinet from 22 to 18. Yet his government had been returned with his back bench bulging. Although three ministers had retired at the election and one, Vin Heffernan, had lost his seat, the streamlined ministry left few opportunities for promotion to cabinet rank. In fact, in order to achieve any turnover at all, Kennett had to axe several serving ministers. Roger Pescott, sensing he was one candidate for the chopping block, circumvented Kennett's plans by announcing he would not be offering himself as a minister. The former community services minister, Michael John, and the former roads minister, National Party veteran Bill Baxter, both had to make way. In the end, Kennett promoted three backbenchers: Louise Asher, Geoff Craige and Ann Henderson. However, with too many candidates for too few vacancies, there were notable omissions. Stephen Elder, the great-nephew of Bolte, who had served as parliamentary secretary for education in the first term, was overlooked, as was the voluble barrister, Victor Perton, who had enjoyed front-bench rank in Opposition. Other ambitious MPs, such as Robert Doyle, Robert Clark and Bernie Finn, were left wondering when their chance would ever come. Kennett would offer no guarantees. Embittered, some MPs began to look to alternatives.

Another ministerial aspirant, Tony Hyams, had resigned from parliament ahead of the 1996 election rather than face another four years on the back bench. Kennett's response to his resignation had also fuelled discontent. A merchant banker, Hyams had told colleagues he would prefer to go back to private industry rather than squander his time on the back bench. He went to see Kennett privately towards the end of 1995 to tell him this, assuming the next election would not be until September or October the following year. When Kennett called the snap election for March 1996, Hyams was caught unawares. Nonetheless, he decided to proceed with his stated intention to retire from politics. Kennett attacked him publicly, chiding Hyams for being selfish and impatient. 'He indicated that unless he had a different role after the election, not that he expected one, he felt he would probably be better going back to the private sector. I refused to give any guarantees. He was a man with a great deal of ability, particularly in the financial and banking industry, but politics is a great leveller . . . and you can't expect just to walk into the ministry.'

The premier's response caused consternation among other backbenchers, who regarded Hyams' decision as defensible in the circumstances. It was also a response that prompted bemusement among Liberals who had watched the young Jeff Kennett barnstorm his way to ministerial rank with no apparent concern for the toes on which he was treading. Their underlying concern was the premier's propensity to assume the right to exercise control over the career paths and life choices of his fellow MPs – and to turn on, often savagely, any who defied him. Whatever happened to the notion of first among equals? To his colleagues, this was becoming an unnerving and oppressive aspect of the Kennett management style.

But who were the credible leadership alternatives? Ian Smith was one possibility. He had been forced to step down as finance minister in 1995 after his chief of staff, Cheryl Harris, went public with revelations that the minister was the father of her child. Through her lawyers, Harris went on to claim that Smith had breached her employment contract and pressured her to abort their child. Smith vigorously denied the allegations, and would later win a substantial defamation payout. But he knew as well as anyone that his ministerial career was over. Rather than face a sex scandal of British tabloid proportions, Kennett called Smith into his office. The two men, rivals over two decades, spoke frankly and without rancour. Their long-standing hatred had dissipated in government. Kennett had come to respect Smith's purposeful approach to the winding-back of the massive unfunded liabilities of the state's superannuation schemes. Even so, he made it clear that Smith's chances of a ministerial comeback were zero. One of Kennett's stated ambitions had been to lead a government through its term in office without one change to his front bench, as a demonstration of the government's discipline and internal cohesion. He referred to his disappointment at failing to meet this target in a simple six-line statement issued from his office, confirming Smith's departure from the ministry, though not from parliament. 'Smithy thought he had more than paid the price,' says one senior cabinet colleague. 'But too many people in the party thought he had been stupid, and brought it on himself. He accepted his lot.' Of the remaining senior Liberals, then, Gude alone had the stature and popularity to be seen as a contender.

The truth was, however, that Gude would always have faced significant and potentially insuperable hurdles if he was to consider a tilt at the leadership. One important constraint was the fact that, as deputy leader, he had no choice but to play his politics cautiously. Another was his health. After suffering polio as a child, he had ongoing physical complications as he advanced in years. The third factor was his age. Gude was 57, and although he might have been able to lead the Liberals to the next election, he would find himself up against a Labor front bench a generation younger. In a presentational sense, who was likely to seem the more compelling alternative to voters to take the state into a new millennium: a two-term government led by a man entering his 60s, or Labor's spearhead quartet of Brumby, Bracks, Thwaites and Hulls, all in their early 40s and bristling with energy?

Fourth, and most fundamentally, it came down to numbers. There was never any prospect of Gude actually rolling Kennett. In a head-to-head contest, the deputy would have struggled to get a quarter of the votes. At first try, he would at best have been able to wound Kennett. And it would have meant resigning as deputy, going to the back bench, and either sitting on his hands or launching another challenge in the lead-up to an election. The politics would be highly destructive, and the recriminations severe. Although a small group of backbenchers were mobilising around him, many of Gude's senior colleagues were not convinced he was willing or able to bring on a contest. Although he was keeping his options open, a blood-and-guts leadership brawl was never likely. That said, the mere hint of leadership manoeuvring within the government sent the party and the media into a frenzy. Kennett claimed to be unfazed, confident throughout that there was never the makings of a full-scale revolution. 'In politics, there will always be people biting at the ankles. It didn't distract us. They were in the minority.'

Rather than hit the panic button, Kennett began the painstaking and arduous process of plotting his personal and political revival. His career had provided plenty of experience in how to fight his way back into a contest. The post-Mitcham debacle and his marriage breakdown had wrong-footed the premier for at least two months. Indeed, they went close to derailing his career. Opinion polls through the first half of 1998 recorded support for the Coalition in Victoria slumping to a 10-year low. But when a talkback caller phoned to complain of the retirement perks available to former premiers, Kennett had a succinct reply waiting: 'Well, you have to see me off first, mate.' One of his shrewd moves to regain the initiative was to prorogue parliament over those difficult months, to be reopened officially early in the new year with a Governor's speech that would give Kennett the opportunity, in effect, to make a fresh start and set out anew the government's directions through to the next election.

CHAPTER TWENTY

ON THE REBOUND

'What are we coming to in this whole society
when our underbelly is so soft?'
JEFF KENNETT

In July 1998, Jeff Kennett flew to Washington. He had been invited to the US capital to attend an America–Australia leadership dialogue. By day, he would join in formal sessions on bilateral relations and world economic trends, or test out his own ideas over coffee, tea or Diet Coke with movers and shakers from Congress and the US business community. On the warm, humid nights he would sit on the steps of the stately residence attached to the Australian Embassy, looking out over the gardens and discussing life, politics and the universe with his old mate Andrew Peacock, now Australia's ambassador to Washington.

Already Kennett had found ways to re-establish his government's momentum. He spoke of a reinvestment in health and education, but made it clear he was not prepared to pander excessively to calls to steer a safer, more populist course. Alan Stockdale's sixth budget, handed down on 21 April, had confined itself to some modest and closely defined spending increases. While boasting proudly that $358 million in extra outlays meant the Kennett government was by this time spending more in real terms on health and education than its Labor predecessors, Stockdale insisted there would be no splurge. 'It would be electorally disastrous for this government if we abandoned prudent financial management,' he insisted in a pre-budget interview. The treasurer sniggered at suggestions that there were some in the party who believed the Kennett–Stockdale double-act was wearing thin on voters, that the pair lacked the political 'smarts' to navigate the government through its slump in popularity, and that Kennett's leadership was in peril. 'If there are any backbenchers saying that sort of thing, they're out of their tiny minds. It's their political smarts that ought to be in question.'

Kennett and Stockdale appeared determined to win the political debate on their own terms. On 22 April, the day after the budget, they were given precisely the reinforcement they needed. In a statement issued by its Melbourne office, Standard & Poor's, the international credit rating agency, announced the restoration of Victoria's AAA status as a borrower. The symbolism was profound. The Kennett government had achieved something they had once believed would take a decade or more. In just over five years, they had tamed the state's debt-interest spiral. This, in Kennett's mind, was a powerful circuit-breaker. It gave him a substantial platform from which to counterattack his critics: here was proof positive of the benefits of his game plan through the hard years. He wasted no time in trumpeting the achievement as a 'wonderful tick of approval' for the government's economic rescue strategy. 'No other government has achieved what we have achieved. I challenge you to find a government in Australia that comes close.'

However, senior Labor figures wondered whether the restoration of the AAA rating might prove a mixed blessing for Kennett. Sure, it provided final confirmation of the success of the government's financial reconstruction strategy, but in their view, this was no longer an issue dominating voter preoccupations. They were looking for something more from government than fiscal puritanism. John Brumby confided to colleagues that he believed the premier was leaving himself vulnerable to a judgement by the public that he had served his purpose. Believing the hard work of budget repairs had been done, the electorate might soon be tempted to turn to Kennett and say, 'Thanks for the clean-up job, old son. Now on your way.' This might have seemed just wishful thinking, except for the fact that similar thoughts were exercising the minds of many Liberals, including senior figures within the government.

Nevertheless, Kennett's political revival seemed to be well in train. Although there were still mutterings of discontent in party circles, the threats of an uprising against Kennett in the party room and at State Council had failed to materialise. Kennett supporters remained firmly in the ascendancy in both the parliamentary party and the broader organisation, leaving the dissidents little choice but to temper their ambitions. If anything, it appeared Kennett's Labor opponents were more at risk of self-destruction. A bitter round of preselection battles was under way within the ALP, amid allegations of branch-stacking in which Brumby himself was being vilified. As Labor turned inward to grapple with these domestic disputes, the Coalition steadily regained its momentum in the polls.

The premier returned from the USA reinvigorated. The existential angst appeared to have lifted, and he was showing all the outward signs of having rediscovered his zest and enthusiasm for the political battlefield. He was on the move, again. As he would tell journalist Shaun Carney, he was thriving on the diversity of the challenges he confronted. 'I get up. I might go to a factory. I might get a briefing on health. I might then see something on multimedia. The next moment I am being called in to solve a problem that might be associated with A, B, C or D. So it's a continual moving feast. I don't know what it trains you for. Probably nothing. But there is no such service as public service.' It was almost as if the premier, like an out-of-form sportsman, was trying to talk himself back into the game. Carney, who had reported Kennett's career over a period of almost 20 years, warned that the premier seemed very much back in character. 'He is a politician incarnate, a man who cannot live without a campaign, an issue, an enemy.'

The overwhelming priority for the Liberal Party in 1998 was to ensure the re-election of the Howard government in Canberra. Jeff Kennett would throw himself into this campaign like no other. The centrepiece of the Howard government's re-election strategy was a radical program of tax reform, including the introduction of a 10 per cent goods-and-services tax to broaden the nation's tax base. It was a daring challenge to the electorate, and Kennett was among its most enthusiastic backers. Likewise, as the federal Coalition looked grimly at the prospect of One Nation undermining its support in rural and regional seats, Kennett determined he would have a role to play in confronting and defeating Pauline Hanson and her supporters. But first, there were a few scores to settle in his own backyard.

In July, Kennett offered his public support for the nomination of a Chinese-Australian, Tsebin Tchen, to take the third winnable position on the Liberals' Senate ballot paper for Victoria. It was, in itself, an important symbolic offensive against the anti-Asian posturing of One Nation. In supporting Tchen, however, Jeff guaranteed yet another confrontation with the forces aligned to Michael Kroger and Peter Costello. Tchen would be contesting the preselection against one of Kroger's long-standing allies and fellow activists in Liberal ranks, Senator Karen Synon. When Tchen prevailed after a tense meeting of the party's preselection convention, it created a firestorm within the party. There were clandestine gatherings at Synon's house in Kew, in effect a war council targeting Kennett, state president Joy Howley and state director Peter Poggioli. There were threats by dissident MPs to challenge the constitutionality of Kennett's role in the elevation of Tchen. One of Kennett's back-bench critics, Peter McLellan, the member for the marginal seat of Frankston East, resigned from the Liberal Party in protest, and later sat in parliament as an independent. But this was to become far more than a local squabble over a minor preselection.

In the lead-up to the preselection vote, Kennett and Kroger swapped insults over the airwaves, including a ferocious exchange through the conduit of 3AW's Neil Mitchell. First Kroger struck out, then Kennett retorted, then Kroger telephoned from Perth to launch another assault. Kroger accused Kennett of ham-fisted interference in the affairs of the federal Liberal Party, of gainsaying his federal colleagues, and of undermining the reputation of the prime minister. 'I think over a long period of time, Jeff has not given the support to the Howard government that he should have. And I think many Liberals have been disappointed in that,' he accused. Kennett dismissed this as nonsense. 'He is saying that I have not been supporting John Howard and Peter Costello. Again, Michael is using those names lightly. He wouldn't be doing it with their authority. He knows, as well as I do, that I have a very good relationship with John Howard and Peter Costello.'

Kroger also set ablaze another bout of speculation over Kennett's federal ambitions. He combined an insistence that Kennett refrain from commentary on the federal party's affairs with the observation that the Victorian premier was ill equipped for the subtleties and detail of the national political debate. This clearly rankled with the premier. 'If Mr Kroger thinks I'm best suited to state affairs and not federal, that's just the sort of challenge that gets me going. It may be that Michael is going to make me reconsider.' Kroger was unrepentant, and demanded Kennett confine himself to his own turf. 'There comes a point when you just have to give Jeff a message, which is: we've had enough of this type of sniping and criticism of federal colleagues and other members of the party he doesn't get on with.'

In Washington, Andrew Peacock watched sombrely. He had tried before to hose down the feuding between Kennett and Kroger. Kennett was Peacock's oldest friend in politics; Kroger was soon to marry his daughter Ann. Although Kennett and Peacock had been able to quarantine their personal relationships (Jeff remained fond of 'Annie' and Peacock dealt amicably enough with both Kennett and Kroger), Peacock bemoaned the constant bickering: 'I have never been much in favour of this public slanging match. It doesn't do anybody any good.' Peacock had made it a rule, however, not to attempt to persuade Kennett to adopt a more diplomatic bent. It was pointless to expect him to behave like a conventional politician. 'I understand what he is like. He doesn't like to constrain himself. What you see is what you get. He likes it to be that way. It leads to a greater comfort within himself. He doesn't express a viewpoint one day, slightly fabricated because it might sound good, and then months later, forget he had set out that position or said it in a certain way. He is honest and it's easier for him to say it as he sees it.'

The enmity between the Kennett and Kroger camps had never been more venomous. When John Howard called the federal election for Saturday 3 October, these virulent undercurrents were still coursing through the Liberal Party in Victoria. In this context, Kroger's public attack on Kennett's purported disloyalty to the federal government was widely interpreted by party colleagues as a calculated pre-emptive strike. It appeared Kroger and his supporters were laying the ground for massive recriminations in the event of Howard losing the election. If the Liberals surrendered more than two or three seats in Victoria, senior Liberals were preparing to point the finger at the premier. Not only would this off-load any blame for defeat on Kennett , but it would prompt a declaration of open season on his leadership. A discredited and enfeebled Kennett would, in turn, be a far less significant obstacle to Peter Costello's leadership ambitions in the event Howard was tossed out by the voters. Of course, all such talk was provisional. The 'blame game' could only come into play if Howard lost. Within parts of the Victorian Liberal Party, however, this became very much the subtext to the 1998 federal campaign. As one senior Liberal commented, 'A tsunami could be about to hit the Liberal Party.'

On 7 September, Kennett flew to Brisbane at the invitation of Queensland Liberals to support their campaigns in Dickson and Blair, two of the crucial contests in the Sunshine State. The first was the seat that the former leader of the Australian Democrats, Cheryl Kernot, would contest as a Labor candidate after her much-publicised defection. But it was the seat of Blair which consumed Kennett's interest. This was the seat Pauline Hanson would contest – it represented the the fulcrum of her Australian campaign to change the temper of politics. The twin imperatives of securing tax reform and removing the threat of One Nation 'is more important than anything I've done in Victoria in the last five or six years', he told voters. Hanson's economics were 'the most half-baked thing I've ever seen' and One Nation was 'a black cloud that needs to be wiped from the landscape'.

Kennett's frontal assault contrasted with the less aggressive tactics of the prime minister, whose strategy had been to deny Hanson the oxygen of publicity. But if Kennett hit the headlines with his withering condemnation of One Nation, it was as nothing compared to the next day, when he travelled to a shopping mall in the town of Toowoomba. There to greet him was Pauline Hanson herself, tipped off by the media about the premier's visit, and eager for a picture opportunity. 'Hello, Jeffrey,' she said as she cornered him at the top of an escalator. 'Welcome to Queensland.' Kennett, wary and caught off guard, made an awkward escape, with the TV cameras whirring. The premier knew he had been set up. Hanson would get free air-time for her stunt. Sensing the dangers, he phoned his office in Melbourne and asked them to forewarn the Liberals' federal campaign director, Lynton Crosby.

Kennett knew there were unusual sensitivities about his role in the campaign. Some in the party, seeing the Hanson footage, would doubtless argue that the whole exercise had backfired. Indeed, within hours, Liberals in Victoria were briefing the media that Kennett had flown to Queensland against a specific request from the 'national secretariat' that he abandon his plans. They argued that he had overridden a tightly controlled strategy towards the One Nation leader, part of which involved government MPs not mentioning her by name or making personal attacks on her.

When the premier's office contacted federal campaign head-quarters, however, the response to the Hanson incident seemed relaxed. For their part, the Queensland Liberals thought the episode had worked to their advantage. Kennett had been calm and unflustered in his handling of Pauline Hanson. It confirmed the growing perception in the electorate that One Nation was disorganised, undisciplined and running out of steam. If Hanson had to engage in bizarre publicity-seeking by heckling the Victorian premier in a Toowoomba shopping mall, it was a strong hint that her party knew she was struggling to maintain momentum of her own.

Nonetheless, John Brumby, perhaps with an eye on the sentiments in rural Victoria, attacked Kennett's trip as 'an outrageous misuse' of Victorian taxpayers' money. 'She's plastered on the front pages all around Australia, and the poor old Victorian taxpayers, who are crying out for assistance for schools and hospitals, they're footing the bill for this jaunt that has backfired and simply promoted Pauline Hanson.'

Not surprisingly, there was continuing dissension within the federal Liberal Party over what further role Kennett should play in the campaign. His unpredictability was always a niggling concern. Some key figures at Liberal campaign headquarters at Nauru House in Melbourne were privately relieved when Kennett took 10 days out of the campaign in September for an overseas visit to the Commonwealth Games in Kuala Lumpur, and then Jakarta. Kennett, though, proved irrepressible. Flying back into Melbourne at 6.30 a.m., he showered at his office, changed his suit, and then paid an impromptu visit to Nauru House. He was anxious to be involved.

On 25 September, however, Kennett was stopped dead in his tracks. It was a Friday afternoon, the eve of the AFL Grand Final. As the city prepared to celebrate its most popular sporting festival, news came through of a massive explosion at the Longford gas plant near Sale, in eastern Victoria. Two workers had been killed, eight more were seriously injured and a fire was burning out of control. There was the risk of a major conflagration that could threaten the state's gas supplies. The Kennett government had a disaster on its hands.

There was no choice but to order a total shutdown of Longford, so that the fire could be extinguished, the gas leak sealed and the plant repaired. Many Victorian households, in the run-up to election day, would have to cope with cold showers and no heating. Many businesses, unable to access alternative fuel supplies, would be forced to shut up shop. Some of the state's hospitals would be unable to run their sanitising units. The community would be denied one of its main energy sources for a fortnight, perhaps longer. In the last week of a federal election campaign, Kennett would have to manage a major civil emergency.

On the Saturday morning, as the extent of damage to the Longford plant became clearer, Kennett spoke to the prime minister. Howard said the federal government was prepared to offer whatever help it could. The defence department was enlisted to help set up alternative power arrangements in hospitals. The Department of Social Security was prepared to process emergency welfare for the tens of thousands of workers likely to be stood down as those industries reliant on gas supplies, such as the major car manufacturers, ground to a halt. But with Canberra in caretaker mode for the election campaign, the Howard government could not readily authorise financial assistance. In the first instance, Victoria would have to cope on its own. Kennett phoned the chief executives of the major banks, requesting leniency for account-holders experiencing financial difficulties through loss of business or employment. He also spoke to New South Wales premier Bob Carr, who authorised the pumping of extra emergency supplies of gas across the border. In Melbourne, the premier set up a special subcommittee of cabinet to coordinate the government's response to the crisis and provide him with detailed status reports twice daily. Moreover, each morning executives from Esso, the company responsible for Longford, would file into the premier's office to provide updates on the progress of repairs to the crippled plant.

Meanwhile, Kennett announced the bad news to the public. Use of gas appliances would have to stop immediately, and there would be heavy fines for breaching the ban. There were perhaps only two days of emergency gas supplies remaining in the state, and these would be needed to maintain the running of essential services in hospitals and nursing homes. The restrictions were likely to stay in place for several days at least. Once supplies were restored, it was intended to phase in their reintroduction through a rationing system. Industry would be given first priority so people could get back to work. Households might have to wait a bit longer.

It was an austere message to be delivering in an election climate. The Victorian Trades Hall Council attacked the premier, demanding an immediate $50 million relief package for workers and small business. The federal Opposition leader, Kim Beazley, said that if he were in power, he would declare the Victorian gas crisis a national emergency. Kennett urged the community to stay calm. The damage would be temporary, and emergency relief should not be needed. 'The reality is most of us and most businesses, big and small, are going to manage their way through this.' On the Wednesday, Kennett flew to Perth to honour an election commitment. Under questioning over the public's reaction to the gas crisis, Kennett assumed his trademark tough-guy persona. Complaining of the tendency of some in the community to 'bitch and moan' about cold showers, he stunned his Liberal colleagues with the taunt: 'What are we coming to in this whole society when our underbelly is so soft?'

Kennett's response was entirely in character. He assumed that the broader community well understood the nature of the emergency, and the need for the government to impose harsh conditions while the dangers were dealt with. He assumed they would be prepared to put up with the inconvenience in order to ensure the safe and reliable restoration of gas supplies. But his apparent nonchalance about the effects on people's lives compounded anxiety in the party federally. It was an unexpected turn in the election campaign, and Kennett was taking unusual risks. This feeling fed into the undeclared private war over who would wear the odium in the event of defeat.

Liberal strategists pored over the polling trends in Victoria for signs that Kennett's conduct during the gas crisis was impacting on voter sentiment. Some senior federal Liberals were claiming that Kennett could cost Howard nine seats. In the week before election day, Michael Kroger visited Liberal state director Peter Poggioli at 104 Exhibition Street to ask how he thought the campaign in Victoria was faring, and to check on indications coming through the party's internal polling. Poggioli was reasonably optimistic. 'Best case, down one, Bendigo is gone. Everything else is in play. Worst case, down five.' Kroger seemed impressed: 'Shit, if you can keep it to five you're a hero.'

Poggioli and other party professionals were aware of the under-currents at work, and the likelihood that this election result would inevitably become part of the dynamics between Kennett and the Kroger/Costello forces. But they tried to banish it from their think-ing. As Poggioli says, 'We couldn't be preoccupied by what Cozza may or may not have done, or what may or may not have happened to Jeffrey. That wasn't our game. I had to worry about getting our candidates over the line. I wasn't concerned about keeping Jeffrey as premier, I was concerned about keeping Howard in government. Jeffrey wasn't a factor in the outcome. Nor was gas. People vote on federal issues at federal elections. This is consistently proved. But had we gone down big time, people could have wound it up and said it was Jeffrey's fault. It would have been wrong, but it would have been hard to counter. If we had lost seven, that would have been enough to point the stick at anyone.'

Early on election night, it seemed the Victorian party could be on the verge of a meltdown. When federal Liberals scanned the exit polls, there was panic. At 5 p.m., the Victorian Liberal Party's leg-endary pollster, the late George Camakaris of Quantum, arrived at 104 Exhibition Street. He found an ashen-faced Poggioli sitting in his office. Lynton Crosby had been on the phone with the results of some polling-day surveys by the federal pollster, Mark Textor. There appeared to be a big slump in the party's vote in Victoria. Indeed, by 6 p.m. whispers began to spread through the national tally room that the party was in trouble in eight seats in the state. Crosby had called John Howard at Kirribilli House to give him the early intelligence. It was anything but reassuring, and it is understood that the prime minister apparently even cautioned his family that defeat was a distinct likelihood.

In Melbourne, Poggioli and Camakaris ran their checks. The gloom-and-doom scenario simply didn't gel with what they were seeing from their own polls and hearing from Liberal officials staffing the booths. They were at a loss to explain the federal party's pessimism. Says Poggioli, 'They had done their exit polls, but it didn't look like what I was seeing. It has to be said that these things are always precarious. Exit polls are about reasons, not about results.' Kroger called Poggioli at 8 p.m. 'What's going on?'

Replying cautiously, Poggioli said, 'It looks like a 2 per cent swing here, mate. I think we're going to hold most of them.' The commentary on national television was still suggesting a disaster. 'People kept saying we were in deep shit in Victoria,' recalls Poggioli. As the frantic assessments continued in both Canberra and Melbourne, the veteran Camakaris insisted that Victoria would hold up well: 'We look all right.' A tense Poggioli wanted to be convinced. 'Is it all right, or does it just look all right?' Camakaris told Poggioli later he had never seen him so stressed.

In the event, the gloomsayers were proved wrong. The Liberals were returned to government, albeit with a much-reduced majority and after having being dangled over the precipice for the first three hours of the count. John Howard had tackled the '800-pound gorilla' of tax reform and survived. In Victoria, the Liberals confined their losses to just three seats, on a par with Howard's home state of New South Wales. Across the nation, the Hanson phenomenon had fizzled. Pauline Hanson lost her fight.

In his victory speech at Sydney's Wentworth Hotel, the prime minister thanked his deputy, Peter Costello – and, then, pointedly, praised the contribution of the Victorian premier. Only party insiders knew the true significance of these remarks. John Howard was not the only Liberal leader in the nation that night whose career hinged on the result. For Jeff Kennett, too, there was a sense of vindication. It seemed the premier had come through his darkest hour.

CHAPTER TWENTY-ONE

The Home Stretch

'He is a champion spruiker with nothing left to spruik.'
STEVE BRACKS

Away from politics, Kennett was working to reconstruct his private world. The circumstances of the federal election campaign had led unexpectedly to an attempt by the Kennetts to reconcile their marriage: while the premier was overseas in Asia, Felicity had moved back into the family home. Shortly after the election, in early October, she accompanied him to a $1000-a-head dinner to celebrate the Kennett government's sixth anniversary in power. Until then, the couple had consciously tried to keep themselves out of the spotlight. Kennett's office had even gone to the point of requesting the media not to publicise the fact that Felicity was back at home. On 8 October, however, the *Australian* ran a page-three story on the reconciliation. Kennett was angry, but knew there was no point in attempting to contain speculation any longer. 'I don't deny it obviously, and I don't want to deny it. I thank all the other media for at least giving us a little bit of privacy. I know it was hard.'

As the end of 1998 approached, any talk of the premier succumbing to the stresses of public life had evaporated. Kennett himself confirmed that he wasn't going anywhere. Indeed, there was a sense of triumph that he had proved yet again his daunting capacities as a political survivor. 'Everyone said, "This is the finish of Kennett." They all wrote it with glee but the reality was that it wasn't the case.' The message from the premier to Phil Gude's supporters was unambiguous: 'Unless I was to drop dead tomorrow, given that I will be here for another four, five, six, 10 years, the likelihood is that people of my age and older will not be the future leader . . . The likelihood is the next leader will come from the next generation.'

The dynamic had shifted again. The premier's political stature had been enhanced through his role in the federal campaign and his sturdy management of the gas crisis. This threw the spotlight back on the Labor Party. Defeat federally was bad enough; Jeff Kennett's resurgence was intolerable. How had he managed to haul himself back into the contest? Senior figures on the Left of the ALP would begin complaining openly that John Brumby, for all the opportunities provided by Mitcham and its aftermath, had been unable to drive home the advantage and bury Kennett once and for all. Suddenly, it was the Labor Party, not the Liberals, that found itself consumed by leadership turmoil. Just as the federal result had entrenched Jeff Kennett in the Liberal Party leadership, so it would prove the catalyst for John Brumby's undoing.

Demetri Dollis, Brumby's erstwhile deputy, had not forgiven his humiliation at the hands of the Opposition leader two years earlier. Through the latter half of 1998, he and other influential figures on the Left had begun mobilising against Brumby's leadership. Their main hurdle was finding a credible alternative. Given the numbers in the parliamentary caucus, any prospective leader would ultimately need the imprimatur of the right-wing power-brokers. This virtually discounted Brumby's unaligned deputy, John Thwaites, notwithstanding his strong profile across the party. Rob Hulls, the shadow attorney-general, was of the appropriate factional stripe but had discredited himself publicly after an un-seemly row in a city bar with a young woman who was a Liberal supporter. The best-credentialled Labor frontbencher to line up against Brumby would, therefore, be shadow treasurer Steve Bracks. He was not a fire-breathing factional warrior. Moreover, he offered the added advantage of having already established a rapport across all factions of the party through his patient and resolute role in driving the party's policy review. Dollis and another left-wing front-bench colleague, Lynne Kosky, began making gentle overtures.

'Demetri has rat cunning,' says a seasoned observer of power plays within the ALP. 'They set out on this strategy over six months or more. It was a slow drip, drip, drip – building support for Bracks and tearing down Brumby – and working through Andre [Haer-meyer, shadow police minister and a leading member of the Labor Unity faction] to ensure they could get the majority of the Labor Unity people in behind them.'

With his party demoralised by the federal election result, and the polls suggesting Kennett was on track for a third consecutive election victory, Brumby went public with a plea that Labor desist from what he called 'the culture of cannibalism'. The Opposition leader acknowledged it would be 'unbelievably difficult' for Labor to win the next state election. 'You'll never defeat the Kennett gov-ernment if the party is obsessed with the spoils of Opposition and squabbles amongst itself. While we are getting better, there is still a tendency for some people in the party to indulge themselves that way.' He went on to credit Kennett for running 'a formidable poli-tical machine' and then predicted that only 12 of the 15 seats Labor needed to win power were 'realistically within our sight'. This was a frank admission from a leader bleeding to death. Brumby's assess-ment was open to the interpretation that he was conceding defeat months before the contest even began. Although what he'd said was true, to say so at a time when his own leadership was under the closest scrutiny served only to empower his enemies. It was a fatal blow, and largely self-inflicted at that.

In December 1998, the *Herald Sun* published a research report from the parliamentary library that revealed 10 501 press mentions for Kennett over the previous two years against 2234 for Brumby. Although the research did not distinguish between positive and negative mentions, the comparative volume of media interest could not be ignored. Kennett was drowning out his opponents. The pop-star premier, after the shakiest period in his years in office, was surging back to the top of the charts.

Entering 1999, Brumby's last chance at survival was a successful launch of Labor's revised policy platform under the rubric of 'New Labor: New Solutions'. But the launch was drowned out by ongoing party squabbles and resignations. At the ALP state conference in February, amid threats that building unions would lead a walkout during Brumby's keynote speech, Steve Bracks was questioned by journalists over his intentions. He ruled out a leadership challenge, but went on to observe that Labor's position politically was not as good as it should be. 'I bloody share the frustration. I do. I know John Brumby does. We all share the frustration. We want to go better.' In the coded language of politics, this was interpreted to mean that Bracks was acknowledging that change was necessary. Within the ranks of the parliamentary party, the demolition of the leader continued unremittingly.

The walkout by 12 left-wing building union delegates at the state conference went ahead as promised. But it was overkill, and many in the Left knew it. Dean Mighell, as head of the powerful Electrical Trades Union, kept his troops on the conference floor. He was persuaded by Lynne Kossky that, at this point, humiliating Brumby served no purpose – it was tantamount to kicking a corpse – and the only effect would be to encourage the ALP national executive to take a much closer interest in the deplorable state of the Victorian branch. The truth is that, by the time of the state conference, Brumby's leadership was terminal. The only question remaining was whether and when he would agree to hand over the reins. From his Treasury Place office, Kennett watched all this with wry amusement. Privately, there may have been some empathy for Brumby's fate. The premier had been on the wrong end of this sort of campaign of destabilisation himself many times before. But he boasted to colleagues that he could see it coming. The signs were unmistakable. Within weeks, there would be a new Labor leader.

With the Labor Party on the brink of upheaval, Kennett was eager to make whatever capital he could. During his Thursday radio interview on 18 March, in a blatant mischief-making exercise, he predicted there would be a leadership spill within the ALP caucus within a week. In fact, this proved to be wrong; events moved far more quickly, and John Brumby would fall on his sword rather than subject himself to the humiliation of being voted down by the caucus. It was the next day, at 3 p.m., when Brumby announced to a press conference he would be standing aside as Labor leader after more than five years in the job. The numbers in the caucus had swung decisively against him. He was sick of the infighting, and the constant corrosive speculation about his leadership. There was no point going on.

At 2 p.m. the following Monday, 22 March, Steve Bracks, a 44-year-old former commerce teacher raised in the provincial city of Ballarat, was elected to the Victorian ALP leadership unopposed. He would be the fifth Labor leader to confront the Kennett colossus. 'Improving our position is a big challenge,' Bracks said, somewhat nervously, at his first press conference. 'But that will be done coherently and patiently between now and the next election. If we do everything right – and that's my intention and plan – I believe we can win.'

In political circles, this was a prediction that brought a few smirks, if not outright guffaws. Bracks had inherited the leadership of a party trailing by 11 percentage points in opinion polls. Labor had been going backwards, not forwards. In March 1999, it looked as far from victory as ever. The premier could barely hide his delight during radio interviews that day. 'It's a new day, I've got a new Labor leader. This'll be the fifth one that I've confronted at some stage or another of my leadership career. There was Joan, sorry, John Cain, and Joan Kirner, Jim Kennan, John Brumby and now Bracks. You like to have change in your life. It's challenging.'

Kennett reminded listeners that he had predicted Brumby's demise as leader and described Bracks as his own choice for Labor leader. He hinted strongly that the ALP's leadership switch was somehow part of his own grand plan. Somewhat smugly, he said he had spent the previous Saturday jotting down his thoughts on what had transpired. 'It's an essay that – how can I put it nicely? – firmly tries to explain what we've been doing in terms of the positioning that goes on in the Labor Party. I've locked that away. I'll make it available after the next election. I can only say that this weekend to me has been a wonderful coming together of a strategy that's been in place for over 18 months.'

It was a foolish boast, arrogant and self-indulgent. Although Kennett was entitled to crow over the demise of another Labor opponent – and to attempt to intimidate the newcomer to the leadership – it was absurd to proclaim the emergence of Bracks as part of his own crafty strategy. For Kennett, this was one ego trip that would haunt him on the return journey.

For the time being, however, the premier had come through the most turbulent episode in the life of his government. Not only had he survived as leader, he appeared also to have rediscovered his sense of purpose and restored equilibrium to his government. What was more uncanny still was that he had appeared to emerge stronger than ever, if anything more assured in his self-belief. Given the pressures at a political and personal level, his resurgence was a performance of unusual durability. His Labor opponents must have begun to wonder how they could ever undo him. He was tungsten tough, no doubt about it. The trouble for the ALP was that he began to look unstoppable. For the government, the trouble was Kennett sounded like he might be starting to believe this himself.

On Sunday 28 March, when he stepped up to the podium to

address the Liberal Party state council, Jeff Kennett had his blueprint for the next election campaign tucked away in his back pocket. There was a sense of expectation among Liberal delegates as they gathered in Hawthorn. Bracks, as the new Labor leader, was struggling to get air-time. The state economy was at the height of a three-year growth spurt, driven by consumer confidence. Unemployment was down to 7.5 per cent. The conditions seemed ripe for a rush to the polls. Was Kennett contemplating an election in June, or perhaps even May? The premier kept his supporters guessing. He was operating to his own timetable. 'I know some of you would be hoping that I'd announce the date today but I've got to say to you, there's a lot of work yet to be done.'

Although the government was clearly on the cusp of an election, Kennett signalled that the party had two basic strategic issues to tackle before the election writs could be issued. First, having largely completed its task of financial reconstruction, the Liberals would need to articulate a new set of policy goals to take them into a different era. Kennett spoke of renewed emphasis on developing the state's intellectual capital to prepare society and industry for competition in the emerging information economy. Second, in a difficult and unprecedented manoeuvre, Kennett was seeking to engineer within government a major turnover of senior ministers ahead of the election campaign. As many as six cabinet ministers were rumoured to be retiring. Back in his chief executive guise, the premier spoke of this matter-of-factly as just another management challenge. 'Very rarely in politics do you see political parties renew themselves from within. You tend to try and hang on to those you started with, until eventually they either drop off the twig, or the party gets sawn down by the electorate. We are going to have the opportunity to renew from within . . . and we have a range of people with experience and backgrounds that are easily going to fill the shoes of those who have gone before them.'

This exodus of personnel would bring with it unavoidable complications. The departure of senior ministers would bring several plum Liberal seats into play, creating the risk of a destabilising round of preselections. Inevitably, with safe seats up for grabs in the affluent eastern suburbs, the tensions between the Kennett and Kroger camps were bound to resurface. Despite a strong lead in the opinion polls, the preliminaries to the 1999 state election would not be easy for Kennett and his party.

On that day at the state council, however, Jeff Kennett was brimful of confidence, so much so that he felt entitled to scold his Liberal colleagues to the north for their failure to topple the Carr government in the New South Wales state election. His call for the sacking of their state director, Remo Nogaretto, was astonishing enough, but there were sharp intakes of breath among his audience when he went on to argue that Liberal leader Kerry Chikarovski was not up to the task. Whatever the validity of his arguments, this was brazen intervention by one state leader in the affairs of another division. Kennett could not be constrained. 'Yesterday's result in New South Wales need not have happened,' he said. 'There is no way we would have ended up with that result. In my opinion, the election was eminently, eminently winnable. There will be those who were instrumental in the outcome yesterday who will now be trying to justify their own position and their own roles. I only mention this to you, absolutely and quite frankly, because it is, I guess, my style. But never forget: the Coalition threw away government. It handed it to Carr because of their own incompetence, because they put personality and disloyalty ahead of the party. And I think that contrasts absolutely with what we have here in Victoria.' His outburst brought applause from the floor.

This propensity of Kennett's to range far and wide in his commentary – extending, occasionally, into subjects that were notionally none of his business – was nothing new. While it reflected in part his hyperactive nature, it also betrayed an element of hubris. This time, as the ALP prepared its own election strategy, it was looking for any opportunity to play up Kennett's tendency for arrogance and bombast. 'The premier has become someone

with an opinion on everything and a solution to nothing,' Steve
Bracks would say in his first major speech as Labor leader. In an
address to the Melbourne Media Club, Bracks began to work
Kennett's obsession with long-distance politics into a potentially
powerful refrain. Rather than a premier preoccupied with issues
beyond the state's borders, or policies throwing forward a generation or more into the future, Victorians wanted a government
that would restore the focus on 'bread-and-butter' issues of immediate concern to its own community – or, as Labor's slogan would
have it, a 'back to basics' philosophy. In developing this theme,
Labor set out to turn one of the Liberals' most successful campaign
strategies back on one of their own. The Victorian ALP would
borrow blatantly from the methods used to great effect by John
Howard in his defeat of Paul Keating at the 1996 federal election.
Labor would go after Jeff Kennett at ground level.

The premier appeared undaunted. He was not afraid to stray
into some of the more esoteric debates on the national agenda if
he felt he had a contribution to make. He penned his own preamble for the federal Constitution; he spoke of the challenges of
population policy, superannuation, corporate tax reform. Kennett
enjoyed the latitude of the 'big picture' debates. However, Labor
would work to portray him as a leader who had lost touch with
the everyday preoccupations of his own community, and seek to
heighten the focus on those issues where it regarded the government as most vulnerable: hospitals, schools, community safety.
The aim would be to generate a perception of Kennett as aloof
and disinterested. Bracks' speech to the Melbourne Media Club
on 30 April 1999 carried eerie echoes of Howard's demolition of
Keating. According to the new Labor leader, Jeff Kennett was
exhibiting all the signs of someone bored and distracted. Unful-
filled by the humdrum tasks of administering a state, he was
forever on the lookout for more stimulating diversions. As a result,
Bracks claimed, the Kennett government lacked focus, energy
and direction.

'He has a swag of ministers whose main concern now is dreaming of life after politics,' said Bracks. 'His front bench looks like a retirement village. They haven't completed their preselections. Their candidates aren't out in the electorate . . . and their only spokesperson will speak on any subject except Victoria.' Road-testing his rhetoric for the forthcoming campaign, Bracks continued, 'There is no new agenda. There are no new solutions. Their leader stands exposed: a champion spruiker with nothing left to spruik.'

By this time, Kennett was in fact well advanced in laying down his re-election strategy. Privately, he was in dialogue with half of his ministry about their future plans. Six, maybe seven, ministers from the class of 1992 were looking to retire or establish careers outside politics. These moves would change irrevocably the face of Kennett's government: more than 100 years of combined parliamentary experience was about to walk out the door. The biggest names among the potential retirees were Alan Stockdale, Phil Gude and Mark Birrell. Stockdale knew by this time he was never likely to lead the party, and his work in privatisation and budget repairs was all but done. He wanted to establish a career in business while still young enough to make a fresh start. For Gude, too, there was little more he could achieve after 20 years in public life. His health problems were a concern, as was the fact that some of his family were living in Queensland, where his first grandchild had been born. With the leadership no longer in prospect, and having served seven years in government in two of the more arduous ministries, it was time to make the break. Birrell was pondering how long he should continue. Although still in his early forties, he had been in the fast lane of politics for longer than his years would suggest. Despite being routinely touted as a future leader, he was not enamoured of the prospect of crossing to the lower house and had turned down several opportunities to make the transition to federal politics. He had a young family; he wanted time and space at weekends. Although one of the most influential forces in the government, Birrell had always preferred policy work to cut-throat politics. After the big public policy shifts engineered through the decade, it was a question for him of whether and for how much longer he could maintain his enthusiasm for the game. He was, however, still undecided.

Kennett spoke to all seven potential retirees privately and at length. As he would explain later, 'Some had told me many months before. Some a couple of years before. Some changed their minds – some to stay, some to go.' Throughout, the premier was insistent on an orderly approach. He was determined that news of the impending departures would not dribble out one by one. 'I didn't want to have a succession of announcements. To be quite honest, I didn't want every retiring minister out there trying to present their own case. It was important to minimise the fallout. What I needed was to get the announcements done as one, and then the party could get on with its preselections.'

No minister was permitted to speak of their plans until the premier was good and ready. Given that the corridors of Spring Street thrived on rumour and gossip, this was a bold attempt at an information blackout. Kennett's reasoning was defensible. In many respects, those who were leaving constituted the shock-troopers of the Kennett revolution, the veterans of the tough early years when the government was at its most vigorous and ambitious. All had come into office steeled by the gruelling and often unrewarding years in Opposition. All had been at the cabinet table in those first torrid months. A mass exodus, unless handled deftly, could give the appearance of a government whose best days were behind it. Gude and Birrell were the last to make up their minds. Gude would go, Birrell would stay, but until they had made their decisions, not a word was to be spoken. For there was a second layer to Kennett's strategem: this time, unlike after the 1996 election, he would strive to ensure he had in place a credible and coherent plan for succession.

Kennett had identified three possible successors among the next generation. In his view the man most likely was community

*'I don't think I've ever seen him so disconsolate,' says Ron Walker of
Kennett after his marriage break-up in early 1998.*

*The loneliness of the long-distance politician. On his 50th birthday, and
on his own, Jeff Kennett takes time out for a walk through the gardens
of the Melbourne Cricket Ground.*

Reunited, the Kennetts dance at the Grand Prix ball.

*Rumblings within. Deputy Liberal leader Phil Gude (left) becomes
the lightning rod for back-bench dissent, and Michael Kroger (right)
is the premier's foremost internal Liberal critic.*

Looming large. New ALP leader Steve Bracks has the premier in his sights.

Kennett announces the retirement in June 1999 of his most faithful lieutenant, Alan Stockdale, marking the end of an era.

State Liberal director Peter Poggioli briefs the media on the launch of the Liberals' 1999 campaign.

Knee-deep in the hinterland: Kennett goes bush. Too late, perhaps.

Travelling north to the rural township of Ouyen, the premier judges the Great Vanilla Slice Competition, with no hint at this time that country electorates would later swallow him whole.

Two Taps: Labor's secret weapon across the rural networks.

Cliffhanger: Kennett salutes party supporters despite the shock result in the 1999 election.

The morning after the night before. The Kennetts stroll through a tulip farm in the Dandenong Ranges as the reality of the outcome sets in.

His fate in their hands. The three rural independents, Craig Ingram, Susan Davies and Russell Savage (from left), weigh their decision on who will form the next government.

Exit strategy. Kennett ponders his parting words as he prepares to resign as premier.

services minister Denis Napthine, a vet from Portland and holder of a Masters degree in Business Administration. Earnest and diligent, Napthine had demonstrated a strong grasp of policy and a sharp intellect. That he hailed from regional Victoria was an added bonus. But he had very little media profile, and would need time to establish himself in the public mind as a putative premier. Kennett saw tourism and small business minister Louise Asher as another potential leader. But she would have to cross from the upper house to a front-bench role in the Legislative Assembly. It was here that governments were formed, that the decisive political battles were usually fought, and that potential leaders strutted their stuff. Stockdale would be vacating the prized lower-house seat of Brighton and Kennett urged her to run, but with a sobering proviso: it had to be all or nothing. As he remembered from his own preselection campaign two decades earlier, it was far too easy for rivals to undermine attempts by upper-house ministers to make the shift downstairs. Preselectors had to know that if they voted against a talented minister, that minister would be lost to the party. Asher agreed. Events later proved that hers was one of the most gruelling preselection contests in the party's history.

Behind the scenes, Kennett was also encouraging former state president Ted Baillieu to make his run for parliament. As president of the Victorian party through its most successful phase in the modern era, Baillieu had the unusual attribute of being admired and respected across the full spectrum of party opinion. From the early 1990s, he had been earmarked as a politician with the skills to compete in the heavyweight division. Phil Gude's seat of Hawthorn was identified as an ideal avenue for Baillieu to make his move. His imminent arrival generated almost immediate speculation about Baillieu being groomed as a leader-in-waiting, but the truth is that this was long-range thinking on Kennett's part. Although he was destined to be fast-tracked into the senior ranks, Ted Baillieu would need time to find his feet in the parliamentary sphere.

As he went about these preparations, though, Kennett remained concerned that the departure of such prime movers as Gude, Stockdale and attorney-general Jan Wade would sap the government of significant horsepower in the lower house. With Gude departing, Kennett wanted a ready-made deputy who could be trusted to step into his shoes if he was hit by the proverbial runaway bus. He approached his closest friend in politics, Rob Knowles, with a proposition both would come to regret. Kennett wanted Knowles in the lower house. To achieve this, Knowles would need to shift from the safe Legislative Council seat of Ballarat Province and contest the neighbouring Assembly seat of Gisborne. At the time, it seemed relatively risk-free. The retiring Tom Reynolds held Gisborne, in central Victoria, with a comfortable buffer of 7.9 per cent. But Knowles was health minister, a tough and thankless portfolio, and it had fallen to him to manage the government's response to the explosive Intergraph affair.

With Knowles primed to make the crossing to the lower house, Kennett had most of his chess pieces in place. He needed the final word from Gude, but it all seemed to be coming together. Self-evidently, he was masterminding an incredibly complex matrix of moves, any of which could potentially backfire. The mere fact that he managed to keep the nature of these discussions pretty much under wraps for the entire first half of 1999 was a tribute to the government's internal discipline. All that remained was to manage public perceptions of the changes. Kennett had to succeed in crafting an image of a government able to renew itself, both in policy and personnel.

On 4 May 1999, Alan Stockdale delivered the Kennett government's pre-election budget, its last set-piece opportunity to articulate its agenda and spread some largesse, ahead of the campaign proper. For the first time, this was a genuinely upbeat budget. 'It is a budget which marks the end of Victoria's Labor-induced austerity, and focuses squarely on the opportunities of the future,' declared Stockdale. The budget provided for $383 million in new spending, and $1.36 billion was pledged for additional capital works outlays. There was an important totemic pledge of $310 million to boost science and technology training, aimed at providing incubation and sustenance for high-tech industries. Payroll tax was cut to 5.75 per cent, and regional Victoria was to receive more than $100 million in new capital works on hospitals, schools and police stations over the financial year, more than a third of the capital-works budget for 25 per cent of the population. So as not to be accused of pork-barrelling country electorates, Stockdale argued that sensible investment in rural and regional areas was vital to future economic prosperity, and said the government's spending initiatives constituted 'a sound platform for self-reliance'. This served as further confirmation, however, that the government was nervous about its standing in the bush.

Likewise, the government sought to outflank Labor on another populist issue – community safety – by promising to recruit an extra 400 police over two years. Bracks accused the government of blatant vote-buying – and then added that 400 more police were nowhere near enough. Symbolically, the key element of the budget was the formal admission by the Kennett government that the hangover from the Cain and Kirner years was no longer driving policy. The end of the hard grind of financial repairs meant that the Coalition could look forward to moulding a vision of its own – but it also meant it had to be ready and willing to stand or fall on its merits. As the budget speech conceded, the political contest had changed in nature.

With this in mind, the budget was designed to cast Kennett and his team as forward-looking and optimistic, offering tangible proof to voters that here was a government – and a leader – with the ideas and energy to govern for the good times, as well as the bad. The creed of austerity had gone. Now was the time to broaden the government's repertoire. With the budget well received in the next day's media, the premier set off to sell the message hard. But in a radio interview on the 3AW breakfast program, he allowed himself

to be side-tracked, bizarrely, into more ruminations over his retirement plans. The day after a 'feel-good' budget, and with an election
imminent, his candour got the better of him. 'I think I should have
got out last year for a whole range of reasons,' he confessed.

The implication that Kennett had still to convince himself that
it was worthwhile continuing in office lay begging. Bracks was quick
to pounce, suggesting Kennett would disappear quickly after the
election. 'I don't think he'll see out the full term.' This, of course,
was an admission in itself: the Labor leader hinting he believed
Kennett was likely to win. But predictably, the comments of Kennett, not Bracks, were the ones to attract headlines. By Thursday, the
premier was having to run a damage-control exercise. Whatever the
plans afoot in his private discussions with retiring ministers, the fin-
de-siècle scenario was never intended to include him. During his
weekly radio session with Neil Mitchell, he denied he was bored
with the job. Belatedly, he produced his standard 'dead bat' response
to Mitchell's questions. He should have done so 24 hours earlier. His
lapse served only to heighten election speculation, and intensify the
focus on whether this was a government at the fag-end of its best
years, running out of ideas and energy.

In the fortnight following the budget, Kennett was pursued
constantly on the timing of the election. June 12 was the first date
available to him, under a constitutional requirement that all governments must serve at least three of the maximum four years in
office before returning to the polls. Labor was certainly readying
itself for a June election, and there were commentaries in the media
pointing to the propitious circumstances in which the government
found itself. Kennett himself admitted in a radio interview that 'if
you were going to maximise your opportunity, we should be going
to an election now'. But privately and publicly, he ruled this out.
No matter what the polls – or the so-called media 'experts' – said,
he was working to his game plan, and would not be diverted.

Then and since, Kennett has scoffed at suggestions that a June
election was a golden opportunity gone begging. His defensive

reflex on this is understandable. Ultimately, it was a decision for which he alone carried the responsibility. Inside his department, advisers had been urging him to keep the June option open. Government MPs were canvassing the benefits of a lightning strike. One clear advantage was that the issue of the writs would mean the proroguing of parliament: without that forum, where and how could Bracks, as Opposition leader, possibly generate momentum? Even in hindsight, however, Kennett is not ready to admit his decision to hold off was a miscalculation. 'June was never an option,' he insists. 'I had in fact hoped to go for a full four years. Then people started talking about June, lazy journalists with nothing better to write about. I think people [in the electorate] would have reacted against that. We have a four-year term. To go for three and a half years is fine. But to go on the knock of three years is, I think, obscene. We never considered going in June, and nor was there any approach from within the party to go in June. None at all.'

The truth is that Kennett's protracted negotiations with his fellow ministers precluded him considering the early option. As the end of May approached, Kennett had still to finalise the arrangements with Phil Gude, among others, about whether he was staying or going. 'Phil was up to his old tricks,' says one insider. 'He'd say to Jeff, "Look, I think I'll go. Can I have the weekend to think about it?" Then he would change his mind. Phil always ran his own agenda.' This procrastination was, in turn, delaying the party's preselections. Here, too, there were logistical difficulties. The preselections could not be done in a rush. Some of the seats likely to become vacant were situated deep in the Liberal heartland. As blue-ribbon electorates, the candidates chosen could expect to sit in parliament for many years hence. They could expect to be ministers, and potential leaders. For the Liberal organisation, these were prizes not to be awarded lightly. The influential party branches likely to be involved in preselections would rise up in anger if they felt they were being railroaded into having candidates imposed on them in the haste of preparing for an election campaign. Given the acrimony that had followed Karen Synon's demotion on the Senate ticket, Kennett had no choice but to hasten slowly.

On 26 May, some Liberals breathed a sigh of relief that Kennett had held his nerve. Signalling his intention to retire in July, Ches Baragwanath delivered his last report to parliament. Clearly, the auditor-general intended to leave an indelible mark. The report accused the Kennett government of excessive secrecy, and warned that traditional notions of accountability to the public were under threat through the increasing resort of government to confidential contracts. 'There appears to be a widely held belief, particularly prevalent among senior bureaucrats, that financial arrangements should be shielded from the public gaze. Unless parliament is provided with appropriate information, its capacity to exercise its constitutional right to monitor the operations of the executive will be restricted, and accountability and good governance in Victoria may be irreparably harmed.' The report took the government to task on hospital funding, the tendering process within the education system, the quality of water in country Victoria, cost blowouts at the new museum, and the failure to tighten the rules governing credit cards. His job done, Baragwanath posed for pictures in his office. Kennett rose in parliament to thank him for his work on behalf of all Victorians. One of the government's most unrelenting critics had finally departed the scene – or so the Liberals thought.

On 1 June, the premier finally made the announcement that had been so long anticipated. It wasn't an election date, but a precursor that signalled the election countdown was on in earnest. At a Treasury Place press conference, the premier calmly told the media that six ministers would be leaving at the election, along with the speaker, Jim Plowman, former minister Ian Smith, and five other MPs. A third of the cabinet would be turned over. Kennett was about to kick his renewal strategy into top gear. Stockdale would go, so would Gude. Marie Tehan and Jan Wade would retire. Most were household names in Victoria, spear-carriers for Kennett's reform agenda through the 1990s. But they did not announce their own decisions. It was done by the premier, much in the style of a chief executive announcing a corporate shake-up. It was a duty he performed with military efficiency; almost as if throwing out an old pair of shoes. None of the ministers were to give interviews ahead of the election. Kennett insisted on this. He wanted the appearance of discipline, not disarray. 'None of us are irreplaceable, individually. All will be missed, but all will be replaced,' he said bluntly. 'I'm sorry that some of them are going, obviously. Sorry that all of them are going, in one sense. Regardless of that, I haven't asked any of them to reconsider their position.' Kennett went on to signal that the party would open preselections for several prime Liberal seats the following weekend. Out with the old, in with the new. Somehow, it seemed too well stage-managed. No valedictory speeches in parliament; not even an opportunity for these senior ministers to reflect on their achievements.

His task complete, the premier took Phil Gude to lunch. As they strolled to the République restaurant, it is hard to imagine that Gude would not have cast a quick glance at the facade of the parliament at the top of Bourke Street. After spending 20 years of his life in this place, rising to the role of Leader of the House, he must have sensed he had seen the last of his days of jousting and jollity in the Legislative Assembly. In fact, as events transpired, parliament would not sit before the state election. Gude would never set foot in the chamber again. But as he and Kennett chatted over a bottle of wine, who would have guessed that Gude was not the only one to have made his final appearance at Spring Street?

For Jeff Kennett, however, there was no sense of nostalgia. The premier had only one hurdle to clear before calling the election: the preselection battle for the seat of Brighton. It was a contest that brought his tourism minister, Louise Asher, into direct conflict with the Kroger–Costello forces. Mitch Fifield, a senior adviser to the federal treasurer, had been cultivating support in the Brighton branches for months in a bid to succeed Alan Stockdale. On a margin of 18.2 per cent, it was the safest Liberal seat in the state, embracing Melbourne's most affluent bayside suburbs. Asher, of course, had been unable to declare formally her intention to stand until Stockdale's retirement was announced. Behind the scenes, however, the battle had been simmering for weeks. On 17 June it erupted into a clash of the titans, with Kennett and Costello, Victoria's two most senior Liberals, engaging in a ferocious public display of head-butting. Angered by press reports of negative briefings against Asher by the Kroger forces, the premier opened hostilities in his Thursday morning radio session. 'What I'm trying to do is get the people that are available to me in the best positions to do the best job by the people of Victoria. And I've made a decision that I need Louise in the lower house . . . She's not doing it because she wanted to do it, she's doing it because the leader of the party – and, in this case, also the premier – has asked her to put at risk her whole parliamentary career by moving out of a safe seat to come down to a place where she has to compete for preselection. Once you're asked to come down, I don't think you've got much option.' Although Kennett was not demanding that Fifield withdraw, he argued he was within his rights to lobby on Asher's behalf. 'She's what the government wants; she's what I've requested.'

The premier could not have made his endorsement more explicit. In the eyes of the Kroger–Costello camp, however, he had gone further. He had virtually put the preselection delegates under instructions. Asher was his choice, the government's choice; she should also be their choice. The federal treasurer, who was in Melbourne and had heard Kennett's comments on the radio, wasted no time in delivering a withering response. 'This is a party of Menzies, not of Marx. Decision-making flows upwards from the grassroots, and the branch members will make their own decisions. The Liberal Party is a party where people join to have a say. I don't think members of the Liberal Party take directions,' Costello snapped.

Over the succeeding weeks, the confrontation became one of the most gruelling power plays in the Liberal Party for a decade. It featured all the base instincts of politics: revenge, paybacks, the dissemination of rumour and scuttlebutt. Although much of the poison was being generated at the local level, powerful egos were on the line, and somebody – either Kennett or Costello – was going to suffer a considerable loss of face. One drawback for Fifield's campaign was the anger in the Victorian party over the role of federal ministers in a state preselection. Fifield clearly had Costello's imprimatur to run. Moreover, he had the strong support of David Kemp, the member for Goldstein, the federal electorate which embraces Brighton. Just as premiers could not anoint in preselections, nor could federal ministers, even federal treasurers. Shrewdly, Prime Minister John Howard kept a respectful distance, noting pointedly, 'This is a state preselection. It's got nothing to do with me.'

When the preselection panel gathered at Liberal headquarters at 104 Exhibition Street on 11 July, the battle for Brighton proved to be a non-event. Asher won convincingly in the first round by a margin of more than three to one. Given the limited support for Fifield, Costello came in for criticism for not persuading his candidate to pull out. It was an unnecessary public scrap, and a rare rebuff for the federal treasurer. Kennett, for his part, was on a winning streak, and the final chess piece of his re-election strategy appeared to be in place. Now, there were only the opinion polls to consult. Here, too, Kennett was gaining in confidence. An AC Nielsen poll published in the *Age* on 21 July suggested the Coalition could increase its landslide majority. It appeared that Steve Bracks had made little impact on the electorate. Primary vote support for the Kennett government was at 51 per cent, with Labor at 39 per cent. In the two-party preferred vote, the Coalition led Labor 55 to 45. The approval rating for Kennett was at 60 per cent, compared to 35 per cent for Bracks. Kennett led by 29 per cent as preferred premier. John Stirton, AC Nielsen's associate research director, said, 'This underlines the fact that the problem for Labor is not the leader, the problem is the premier. He is dominating and there is nothing much they can do.'

The AC Nielsen poll reaffirmed what the Liberals were picking up in their private research. Their own surveys in June had indicated that while there were still issues of concern for the government in the bush, attitudes were improving outside Melbourne. 'All the research and information we had in the months leading up to the election indicated we had very strong standing throughout the community, rural and metropolitan,' Kennett would later claim. 'It was getting stronger and stronger. We had begun preparing at the start of '99, with our strategy groups, doing different sorts of research. All of that was very solid. Bear in mind, we had been using these frameworks and techniques for 10 to 15 years, and they had been proved up. The only thing that worried me was this incredible expectation factor. Eighty-nine per cent of people in our surveys were saying they expected the government to win. Labor never got higher than 8 per cent.'

On any conventional reading, this was not the worst problem ever to face a political leader contemplating an election date. Unbeknown to Liberal strategists, however, significant events were taking place 200 kilometres north-east of Melbourne. Unlike Kennett, Pat McNamara was not enjoying the same success in imposing his will on crucial preselection contests. In April, the National Party had revolutionised its membership rules in order to attract fresh blood into the party in time for the election. The one candidate that senior National Party figures hoped to secure through these changes was the popular mayor of Bairnsdale, Shaun Beasley. Beasley was mounting the second-only challenge to a sitting National MP in the party's history. He was out to depose the member for Gippsland East, the man known derisively by locals as David 'Hidden' Treasure. When the preselection vote was taken, however, Treasure survived on the strength of the branch vote. Beasley's failure to win the nomination was a bitter disappointment to senior Nationals. Worse, it fuelled disillusionment among the party's erstwhile supporters across a vast electorate.

Others would stand against Treasure come election day, one of them a Bairnsdale abalone diver, Craig Ingram, who would run as an independent. Ingram had confided to friends that if Beasley had been preselected, he would have abandoned his plans to run for parliament. At the time, of course, nobody could have begun to imagine the potential ramifications of the National Party's decision to spurn Shaun Beasley.

CHAPTER TWENTY-TWO

MELTDOWN

'It's an unbroken summer, and all the weather forecasts say tomorrow's going to be beautiful. Why shouldn't you have a barbecue? Show me anybody in the party who was saying, "Don't do it, Jeff."'
A LIBERAL MP, SEPTEMBER 1999

Jeff Kennett went into the 1999 election with one eye on the scoreboard. In election campaigns as leader of his party, he had won two and lost two. As he admitted himself: 'This election will decide which side of the ledger we'll end up. I have a vested interest in doing well.'

There was considerable insight behind Kennett's observation. In the televisual age, three-term governments were becoming a rarity, as the 'chew 'em up, spit 'em out' pressures of constant media exposure – or what former British prime minister Harold Macmillan called the 'hot eye' of public scrutiny – took their toll. Even the master politician, former Labor prime minister Bob Hawke, a four-time winner of election campaigns and something of a folk hero, had served only eight years in power. In plotting to secure a third term, the Victorian premier was looking to the prospect of more than 10 years in office. If he triumphed in the campaign, he would rise to a new level as the most successful Liberal leader of his generation and a man who had endured far beyond the expected shelf life of contemporary political leaders. This would be Jeff Kennett's big chance at immortality.

On 24 August, the premier went to Government House to recommend a general election be held on 18 September. It would be an election, he said, about 'maintaining the momentum'. It would also be a 25-day campaign – calculated to provide the ALP with precious little time to close the gap. The September date carried with it some risks, not least because it challenged conventional wisdom about the dangers of forcing Victorians to the polling booths on any Saturday in September. The election would clash with one of the state's great religious festivals, the Australian Football League finals series. As his pretext for going early, however, Kennett, like many leaders, would claim that business and the wider community were demanding an end to the uncertainty of incessant election speculation. Despite the likelihood that the football would take at least some of the focus off the state election campaign – again making it hard for Labor to establish traction in the electorate – and notwithstanding the sense of assurance inherent in the party's internal polling, Kennett was careful at the outset of the campaign to guard against complacency. Of course Labor could win, he told the media. 'We are the incumbent and often people want to hit the incumbent. Also, I think, after a period in office, the opportunity for an alternative team to simply promise the world in order to gain what I would call sectional interest support is very high. This is a two-horse race.' Then, with a mischievous smile, he added, 'It's Coalition or bust – the ALP.'

Steve Bracks had known an election was fast approaching. At the ALP's new headquarters in Melbourne's west, the campaign team was determined not to repeat the mistakes of 1996. This time, they would aim to adhere to a strict and well-planned strategy, not relying as often on responding to the day's headlines. To the outside observer, however, the Labor campaign didn't seem as sure-footed as insiders wanted the media to believe. Labor had a bad first few days, and it showed up in the party's internal polling, where even heartland seats looked in extreme danger. 'Our support dipped,' one senior official would admit later. 'The impetus was all with Kennett. But we hadn't started our advertising.'

In contrast, the Liberal strategy was running like clockwork. Kennett leapt from the blocks on Tuesday, smothering the airwaves. Outflanking Labor, the Coalition's first policy launch on Wednesday outlined its proposals for the education system. This was territory the ALP was desperate to make its own. But the Coalition made the running, and put the spotlight immediately on one of Labor's least experienced frontbenchers, Mary Delahunty. The Liberals had gone out after the early psychological ascendancy, dictating the agenda and forcing the ALP to respond. Certainly, in Melbourne, Labor appeared to be caught off balance, and had to play catch-up. The word from the Kennett bunker was upbeat. 'I don't think many of the guys expected the premier to be as happy as he is in the first week,' said one of his senior advisers.

The following night, though, Labor got the kick-start it desperately needed. Ches Baragwanath intervened. The retired auditor-general delivered a barnstorming speech at Melbourne University, attacking the government over secrecy and lack of accountability. Citing the increasing power of the executive, the reduced capacity of parliament and the electorate to hold ministers to account, and the implications for the public's right to know of the increasing use of confidential contracts, Baragwanath said these issues went to the heart of democracy. Victorians, he said, should be marching in the streets. The protocol of a senior bureaucrat saying such things during an election campaign – especially given his long-proclaimed status as an independent voice – would have been problematic. But Baragwanath was by now a private citizen who could do and say as he wished. Labor strategists were mightily pleased. 'I think it's going to hurt them,' one confided cheerily. 'I am not that surprised. Once the campaign began, I thought he would enter it somehow. We were hopeful.' By Thursday morning, his speech had all but eclipsed coverage of the government's education policy. Kennett was forced to defend his integrity. It shook up the dynamics of the campaign, gave Labor an issue to chew on, and cut across the Coalition's momentum.

Another ploy enabling the ALP to generate helpful publicity was the announcement that Justin Madden, a popular ex-footballer, would be standing for Labor in the upper house seat of Doutta Galla. Born and raised in Melbourne's north-western suburbs, 'Harry' was a genial giant, standing 210 centimetres tall and enjoying almost iconic status as a 'local hero'. Madden was to prove a valuable asset for Labor as it sought to consolidate its standing in its own heartlands, especially regarding the bid to recapture the seat of Tullamarine.

At the same time, the party appointed former lord mayor of Melbourne Dick Wynne to take over the seat of Richmond from Demetri Dollis, the former party deputy who had been so instrumental in engineering Brumby's downfall and Bracks' ascendancy. In the first week of an election campaign this was a daring gambit, especially given Dollis' history as a mover and shaker in the Left. It could easily have escalated into a major brawl. However, Dollis' interests were focused elsewhere – namely on the Greek foreign ministry, which was offering him a senior international role as the head of an office responsible for liaising with Greek communities around the world. Indeed, Dollis had been spending so much time on his extracurricular activities in Athens that for the Labor Party's supporters in Richmond, it was almost as if he were an absentee landlord.

The ALP's most important work at this time, though, had nothing to do with what was happening in its inner-city fiefdoms. This would not to be a campaign won or lost by what was said or done in the metropolitan media. Instead, Labor frontbenchers were spanning out far and wide across the state. Even in that first week, high-profile MPs such as John Thwaites and Mary Delahunty were pushing hard to ensure that the ALP got exposure on the crucial issues of health and education across a string of regional TV and radio news networks, notably WIN television. It was an unprecedented tactic for Labor, and it also made the party's campaign hard to track. But the ALP constantly monitored the impact its presence in the bush was having. The strategy worked. The availability of high-profile frontbenchers for interviews and picture opportunities meant Labor's message was featuring strongly in news bulletins across country Victoria. Yet, as ever, wider perceptions of how the major parties were performing were governed by what appeared in the Melbourne media. In the first week, there seemed little doubt that Kennett had outclassed and outmanoeuvred his opponents.

Moreover, although Labor had steadied itself, it appeared to be making no inroads into Kennett's massive lead in most of the polls. Only one pollster, Gary Morgan of the Roy Morgan Research Centre, had been arguing since June that the election was far from a foregone conclusion. Morgan also argued that Kennett had made a strategic error by refusing to agree to a televised head-to-head debate with Bracks. 'That's what George Bush did and he lost, and that's what the Nationals did in Queensland in ignoring One Nation and they lost. When you ignore the Opposition, they have a field day.' In this assessment Morgan had isolated an issue that was to blow up into perhaps the single most damaging campaign miscalculation by Kennett and the Liberals. In accordance with the same strategy they ran in 1996, the aim was to deny 'air' to the ALP. Kennett had what seemed a decisive ascendancy over his opponent in public perceptions: why, then, allow Bracks to share a platform with him? Most of the downside risks in such an exchange would be carried by the frontrunner. The Liberals had no intention of allowing Bracks to piggyback his way to prominence by bouncing off the pop-star premier.

But the party took this control mechanism further. Liberal members of parliament and candidates were instructed not to engage in debates with their Labor opponents in the major metropolitan media. Local newspapers were fine, but the party did not want confusing or contradictory messages to emerge on the main election showcase – the major daily newspapers, the ABC and commercial radio stations and, most of all, Melbourne's prime-time TV news bulletins. State director Peter Poggioli issued instructions that MPs and candidates were not to talk across each other: all communications with the big news outlets would be channelled through the premier and senior ministers. In many respects, this was a standard campaigning technique employed by most political parties. Kennett and the campaign strategists were fearful of the dangers of allowing inexperienced backbenchers to be mauled by the media, in a campaign environment where news organisations might be on the lookout for any hint of conflict or incompetence in Liberal ranks. Tedious and one-sided contests, after all, do not make for good copy.

The backlash was ferocious. It climaxed with the *Herald Sun*, on Tuesday 31 August, devoting its entire front page to the so-called 'gagging' of Liberal MPs. Under the headline 'Kennett's campaign order: silence', it carried photos of 10 members of parliament who had refused to discuss campaign issues when approached by the newspaper's reporters. 'Liberal MPs and candidates have been gagged for the election campaign on the orders of Jeff Kennett,' the story began. Poggioli went on radio the next day to defend the strategy, but in doing so, confirmed that the discipline imposed by Liberal headquarters would stay in force. The issue began to dominate talkback radio and fed exquisitely into Labor's campaign theme that here was a government fearful of scrutiny, close questioning and open debate. As Liberal insiders would later admit, the issue got away from them. Internal discipline, something on which the party organisation prided itself, had suddenly became a glaring political liability. 'It became a crunch point,' says one of the party's advisers. 'The radio jocks were making a meal of it. It was running away from us.'

Backbenchers began phoning the premier's office, saying they were under constant demand to do media interviews. They were told to do the locals, but no more. Although the 'gag' had never been official policy, the Liberal campaign team decided to tough it out and ride over the controversy. Although senior Liberals knew it was an unnecessary diversion, and that the party had handled it badly, the damage had already been done. The saga would confirm at least in some people's minds that Kennett was antidemocratic. 'It was pretty awful,' admits one senior strategist. 'Here we were, saying "Vote for these people", but we won't let them loose on radio or TV.'

While the Liberals' problem related to overexposure, the ALP's problem was quite the reverse. After only 150 days in the leadership, Bracks was struggling to build a positive profile in the electorate. His recognition factor was extraordinarily low for the leader of a major party going into a campaign. With Kennett refusing to share a platform, how was the ALP to get its man into the public eye, and to stamp him as a genuine leadership alternative? Running on the 'big L' leadership theme was always fraught: after all, this was Kennett's strong suit. As one former Labor minister concedes bluntly, 'Kennett had ownership of that issue.' How could the premier's all-pervasive profile be countered by a Labor leader who was still widely regarded as a political novice? Flicking through the newspapers months earlier, at the time of the May budget, long-time Labor Party advertising and marketing consultant Bill Shannon had come across a comment piece in the *Age* which discussed the issue of how long a leader of Kennett's ilk could expect to survive in government. 'The biggest threat to the Coalition's chances of winning a third term – perhaps the only real threat – is a shift in the electorate's sentiment triggered by a belief that the hard times are over, and that a new era calls for a new style of leadership,' the article said. Shannon began to ponder the possibilities. Was this an opening for Bracks?

Over subsequent weeks the ALP's image-makers agreed on a risky strategy. Using the 'New Style of Leadership' banner, they would run Bracks head to head against Kennett through juxtaposition. The premier would be conveyed as arrogant, surly and

uncaring; Bracks as fresh-faced, sincere and accessible. It was a
'Here is the problem and now here is the solution' theme. Labor's
advertisements would feature the premier, distorting his image
slightly to distend his jaw. The aim was to portray him as too much
of a 'strongman'. Bracks would be filmed in slick studio shots, chatting earnestly with voters at hospitals, at schools or on farming
properties, oozing compassion. Across the range of issues Labor
believed were its most potent – health, education and rural
grievance – Bracks would be promoted as offering a new and more
inclusive approach, under the catchcry, 'Who Cares? Labor Cares!'
Says Shannon, 'Our advertising had to provide an opportunity to
use Bracks. It was very important to give him visibility.'

The advertising strategies of political parties during election
campaigns is forever the stuff of intrigue and mystery. The common
assumption in Victoria during the 1990s was that the Liberals had
the capacity to outspend Labor by several multiples. Indeed, in
1996 the Liberals were believed to have spent 10 times more than
Labor. In 1999, however, it was a very different story. The ALP
had far more in its war chest than $800 000. This time the Liberals
were thought to be spending $2.8 million on their showpiece adver-
tising campaign, a glossy production casting Labor as the voice of
the past and the Liberals as the party of the future. The production
qualities were exquisite, but the campaign fell into the genre of
goodwill advertising for major companies rather than the hard-
hitting, often downright nasty propaganda voters had come to
expect at election time. 'What we tried to do,' explains a senior
Liberal, 'was to compare the Victoria we had now to what they had
in 1992. What we tried to do in these vignettes was to show how
we had achieved all this growth, and as a consequence, business had
gained in confidence and people were finding jobs.'

Oddly, Jeff Kennett did not feature at all in the advertisements.
Over at the ALP, Bill Shannon, for one, was mystified. 'I had always
admired his strength, as do most people. The style of photography was very upmarket, but the campaign was wishy-washy.

Our commercials were cobbled together but they delivered a very strong message.'

The contrasts between the advertising approaches adopted by the two parties provides an illustration of why public perceptions that Jeff Kennett dictated every twist and turn of Liberal strategy are often overstated. When Kennett suggested to a strategy meeting that the Liberals should sharpen the focus of their advertising campaign – he suggested it would be worthwhile splicing parts of his official campaign launch into the ads – Poggioli had the idea tested with focus groups. He told the premier bluntly that it did not appear to go over too well in research. 'OK,' said Kennett, with a shrug of the shoulders. What bemused some senior Liberals was the failure of the party's advertising to focus on the negatives of Steve Bracks' leadership. Bracks had been in charge of the Opposition for less than six months, had never served in ministerial office, and here he was seeking the confidence of the electorate to lead Australia's second most populous state – or, as Kennett would put it, a $19 billion business. In crude political terms, Bracks was only just out of short pants. Surely there had to be some mileage in raising doubts about whether he was up to the task? After all, in recent Victorian experience, the only previous premier who had gone into the job 'cold' was John Cain. When the Liberals tested some negatives on Bracks with its focus groups, though, the feedback suggested the approach might well be counterproductive. Scowls one Liberal veteran, 'All that tells you is that they tested the wrong negative ads.'

Questions were also asked over why the Liberals weren't saturating the market with their message. The disparity in the number of screenings of Labor ads, compared to Liberal ads, had narrowed dramatically when compared to 1996. Although Bill Shannon, for one, denies it, some Labor people were almost ready to concede that the ALP was very close to matching if not exceeding the Liberals' spend. In fact, party strategists counted seven days during the campaign where the Liberals didn't appear to advertise at all in metropolitan Melbourne. The ALP sat back nervously, awaiting a last-minute blitz. It didn't come.

On Sunday 5 September, the Liberals staged their official campaign launch at the Dallas Brooks Hall in Melbourne. It began as a techno presentation, with expensive, high-quality video productions featuring bright and shiny images of a state in renewal. Then Jeff Kennett emerged on the stage, in the company of his wife. After the ritual standing ovation, Felicity took her seat off-stage, in the front row alongside her children and Kennett's parents. For the next 25 minutes, the premier set out his vision for the next 10 years. Education would be the first priority. A $600 million backlog in the maintenance of schools, inherited in 1992, would be eliminated by 2002. Another 600 welfare counsellors would be employed through the state education system to provide support for children suffering as a result of family breakdown, drugs and other emotional distress. The government would provide incentives to attract students into science, maths and information technology courses, to equip them for the industries of the future. And, in a cradle-to-grave education initiative, the government would set up a new headquarters for the University of the Third Age in Victoria.

In health, with an anticipated increase of 500 000 patients per year by 2004, 10 new hospitals would be built to help the system. On the environment, the government would create a new marine park in Melbourne's Port Phillip Bay. On rural and regional policy, Kennett acknowledged the government had much work to do. 'You must appreciate, given the appalling condition of Victoria in 1992, our starting point had to be to revive the heart of the state – Melbourne – in order that the body could be restored as well. The heart is now beating strongly again, and we are extending out into the regions and rural areas.' In an effort to silence the claims that his government had neglected nonmetropolitan Victorians, Kennett announced a proposal to create a ministry specifically dedicated to policies of decentralisation. Finally, he confirmed plans to proceed with his pet project, a major research program to investigate the causes of dementia and depression. 'Governments have often tended to respond to issues rather than reading the trends and working in advance of them becoming major problems. With the homeless, drugs and suicide, policy has generally been reactive . . . by tackling depression now, I believe there is a very real chance of achieving significant results and making a substantial long-term contribution to the wellbeing of our society.' In conclusion, Kennett observed, 'Victoria has come a long way in seven years, but in real terms, we have only rebalanced the scales. We now arrive at the starting point of a new decade, a new century, a new millennium . . . a new and heroic era awaits us.'

Behind the rhetoric, the stark political message remained that Kennett would not be indulging those, even within his own government, who were demanding a loosening of the purse strings to salve community concerns over funding for schools, hospitals, police and rural infrastructure. Prudent financial management would continue to be the crucial underpinning of his policy framework, election or no election. As he told his audience of supporters, 'It has taken us seven years to overcome the gross mismanagement of the Labor decade. We have added new infrastructure, new facilities and new programs without adding one dollar of debt to the people of Victoria. Our recurrent budget, which pays our operating costs – the salaries for teachers, nurses, police and so on – is back in the black.' That, insisted Kennett, was where it would stay. 'My government will never again accept or allow deficit budgeting.' This defiant declaration represented Kennett's belief that he could repeat the miracle of 1996 – that is, to put policy integrity ahead of political imperatives and still survive.

What was not known to most people outside the inner sanctum of government, however, was that Kennett in fact had much more latitude for new spending than the May budget forecasts had implied. Just before the campaign, both Kennett and Stockdale were advised that revenue growth had far exceeded expectations. The state's coffers were bulging. The sustainable surplus had soared well beyond the $66 million forecast at budget time. In fact, it was running closer to $600 million. The premier, the treasurer, the two other most senior Liberals, Phil Gude and Mark Birrell, and their advisers knew there would be a revenue windfall available to the next government – certainly more than enough to match any spending initiatives Labor put forward, including the ALP's $170 million regional development fund. Yet Kennett, in those crucial final days before launching the campaign, was insistent that the government would not review its spending proposals. Despite the heaven-sent opportunity to appease voters, especially in country electorates, he could not be shifted. Additional spending promised by the Coalition would not exceed $70 million. During the campaign, the premier spoke of the government having only a 'thin sliver' of extra resources at its disposal. In hindsight, this may have been his greatest miscalculation.

For his part, Kennett claims that the electorate would have been suspicious if a government that had based its reputation on sound financial management suddenly began lavishing funds on its most vulnerable electorates. 'I insisted on there being a surplus on both recurrent and capital expenditure. This was unprecedented. We were putting stuff aside for a rainy day.' A more cynical interpretation is that Kennett was being too clever by half, and that his commitment to fiscal sobriety in fact revealed he was excessively confident of victory. Why commit to extra spending if the election result was already in the bag? To admit publicly to a far higher budget surplus would only create an opening for Labor to feel less constrained about keeping its campaign initiatives modest. Kennett sought instead to perpetuate the myth that the government accounts were running close to balance, and that the state simply did not have the capacity to increase its outlays significantly. This strategy denied Labor any prospect of engaging in a vigorous bidding war, but it also bound the Coalition to fiscal puritanism beyond the call of duty. Even in defeat, Kennett defends his judgement. 'You can't just buy

votes. You can't do these things unless you can justify them internally.' Nobody can accuse Kennett of not being consistent – but
in this instance, and with the benefit of hindsight, some senior
colleagues believe he was under the delusion of thinking the election
was as good as won. He was already planning strategies for his next
term.

Kennett's signal that he intended to tough out the demands for
more resources, especially in the regions, came through loud and
clear in his public pronouncements. On the Monday prior to his
campaign launch, he had given an interview to Ballarat radio
station 3BA. A recent poll had shown Labor leading convincingly
in Ballarat East, the most marginal seat in the state. Was Labor
outmanoeuvring the Liberals with its intense focus on regional
electorates? Kennett defended his government's performance in
Ballarat, citing in particular the establishment of a leading-edge
information technology park. Then he issued a stern warning: 'If
the people, as is their right, decide that they want a change, then
what they are putting at risk is whether Ballarat maintains the
momentum into the 21st century, or whether it is going to stop in
its tracks and see Bendigo and Geelong go ahead in leaps and
bounds because the people of Ballarat want to see a return to the
party of the past that left Ballarat for dead and got the state into
so much trouble.' Far from being reassuring, the tone of Kennett's
'with us or against us' message came across as almost punitive. The
premier complicated matters further in a subsequent radio interview when he referred to Melbourne as the vital heart of the state,
and to rural towns as the 'toenails'. One Liberal official winced
visibly: 'He has a way with words, doesn't he?'

On Wednesday 8 September, Bracks officially launched Labor's
campaign. The location was strategic: the Ballarat Town Hall. He
was introduced by federal Opposition leader Kim Beazley to wild
cheers from his hometown audience, with the pacy Hunters and
Collectors anthem 'Do You See What I See?' thumping away in
the background. In his speech, Bracks went straight for Kennett's

Achilles heel. 'In his narrow focus on a few square miles of the Melbourne CBD, this premier has become blind to the outer suburbs and oblivious to our regions and towns. He's forgotten who he's meant to be governing for.'

Bracks pledged to cut class sizes, employ an extra 650 teachers, end the privatisation of hospitals and reopen 290 public hospital beds. Eight hundred more police would be recruited. Then, in a precise, surgical strike at the government's most marginal provincial electorates, he promised $120 million to fix road-accident black spots across country Victoria and $20 million a year for 'community infrastructure projects' in areas of high unemployment. There would also be an $80 million investment in fast rail links from Melbourne to Geelong, Ballarat and Bendigo, and an upgrading of the rail link to Traralgon. He also promised $40 million to standardise the rural rail freight network. 'These services will be the new lifelines of our state. They will put regional Victoria on the map.' Bracks had declared open a bidding war for the hearts and minds – and votes – of the one million Victorians living outside Melbourne. It was a contest Kennett refused to be drawn into on anyone's terms but his own.

Soon after the campaign launch, Labor unleashed its advertising masterstroke: the 'Two Taps' television campaign. This was an advertisement that was never seen in Melbourne, but which ran prominently in the final weeks of the campaign across regional Victoria. Dreamed up by party strategists at Bill Shannon's office, it relied on a simple, stark image. The tap on the left gushed pristine water and carried the caption: 'Melbourne $2 billion'. The right-hand tap was rusted and decrepit. When turned on, it squeaked and spluttered, releasing only a feeble trickle. This was captioned 'Country $Zero.' Says one Labor strategist, 'It was brutal. It was simple. And it cost absolutely nothing to make. This was to the point: the city getting everything, the country nothing.'

Labor was playing on the politics of envy – shamelessly, and with ruthless efficiency. As the strategist says, 'How scandalous, that we should resort to the same tactics as John Howard in 1996. He wiped us out in the regions with a very similar message.'

The campaign proved highly effective. 'The tap ads didn't create the perception, but they confirmed what people thought,' admits a Liberal official. 'The broad sweep was that people in the country thought they had done the hard yards. They went along with us in 1992 so that we could clean up the mess. After 1996, however, they said, "Right, where are the rewards?" What we delivered as benefits were not perceived by them as benefits, and they stopped listening. Everything looked a bit rosier in the city. Why were things not so great in the bush? I am not sure they ever understood that Melbourne, too, had unemployment and that some people were doing it tough.'

By mid-campaign, it was evident that this was an election being fought in two parts. Labor was making little, if any, impact in Melbourne itself. The Liberals were staggered by Labor's inertia east of the city. Apart from the seats of Oakleigh, where the ALP's Ann Barker had been active for years, and Mitcham, where Tony Robinson had been working diligently to defend the seat he had won at the December 1997 by-election, the ALP, according to the Liberal organisation, seemed to have no energy or impetus. But beyond the city's borders, it was almost another world. Here, Labor found it hard to believe the charmed run it was enjoying in provincial seats.

In fact, senior Liberals were having serious misgivings about the party's fortunes in country Victoria. Three weeks out from election day, health minister Rob Knowles, running for the rural seat of Gisborne, was picking up on the sullen mood in his electorate. He notified party headquarters. Some polling was done. The report transmitted back to him was that although the Liberal vote had slipped, it was not a life-threatening scenario. Working with a buffer zone of 7.9 per cent from 1996, there was no cause for alarm. Kennett, too, was getting what he called 'uncomfortable vibes', but nothing he could get a fix on. 'It wasn't that we were not being well received around the traps. We were. But I was still concerned about the expectation levels. That measure didn't fall below 82 per cent of the electorate who thought we would win. Our research suggested that the vast majority of people were supporting what we had done, and if there was this huge differential between city and country, our polling wasn't showing it.' In the middle of the campaign, though, Liberal Party polling had indeed picked up a downturn, just as Labor officials were coming to believe they had a chance to go close. Poggioli had discussed the softening of the provincial vote with Kennett's staff, but if the alarm bells were sounding, it seems Jeff Kennett, for one, was either not aware of the threat, or not convinced of its magnitude.

The third week of the election campaign was overwhelmed by news from East Timor of the appalling violence inflicted by pro-Indonesia militia following the province's independence vote, and the angry international reaction. It was clear Australia would take a leading role in any military intervention. For the first time since Vietnam, Australian ground troops would be deployed on foreign soil. The nation was immersed in a major regional security crisis that drowned out the state election coverage.

On the surface, this would have seemed to favour the Liberals: if the task facing Bracks to establish his profile in the electorate was not difficult enough already, the preoccupation of the community with the events in East Timor would make it almost impossible. No political message could rise above the humanitarian disaster taking place across the Timor Sea. The Liberals knew it; so did Labor. But the ALP needed desperately to make up ground. Denied 'free time' on air through the relegation of the state election to the inside pages of the daily newspapers and beyond the second or third ad breaks on TV news bulletins, Labor redoubled its advertising efforts. Says an ALP insider, 'The Libs made a conscious decision to stay below the media level of East Timor. We tried to punch through. We had no choice. It was the only way we were going to make any impact. So the only media

message that was getting out there at all was ours.' Labor was still
despairing of its struggle to keep itself in the headlines, but there
was a perverse benefit for the ALP in the diminished focus on the
state campaign. The East Timor drama served as camouflage for
the fact that Labor was beginning to creep up from behind on
Kennett and make serious inroads into the Liberals' lead. In the
final week of the election campaign, as the crisis in East Timor
eased, the ALP expected the Liberals to strike back and strike back
hard. 'We got to the last seven days, wondering when is this going
to hit, and nothing happened. We actually ran the same number
of ads as they did,' says a senior ALP source.

Labor strategists were also expecting a final furious assault from
the premier. To Labor's dismay, their polling had reached a plateau
on the weekend prior to election, and then had begun to slip backwards. The only glimmer of hope in these figures was the unusually high number of undecided voters. But Labor also received
some heartening intelligence from within the Liberal Party. A journalist confided to an ALP official that senior Liberals were growing
increasingly concerned about their vote in the bush. Reflects one
Labor MP, 'This was 23 days into the campaign. Where had they
been? The only place they ever had a problem was in the bush.'

Labor expected Kennett to go through the entire last week of the
campaign focusing on one undiluted message – the strength
of the economy, and the dangers of handing control back to Labor.
'Any time he said the word "economy" our polls would drop,' says
one campaign insider. 'What we had tried to do was to distract him
and keep him on the back foot so that we could keep the focus on
our issues, not his issues. We went out of our way to create any
diversions, to keep Kennett and Stockdale off-message. We had
something every day to ensure that Jeff was answering questions
about anything other than the economy. This was our big vulnerability. We were way ahead in health and education, but any
time it came to issues of economic management, our approvals
would fall down into the low 20s.' According to the ALP, this was

Kennett's biggest failure in the campaign: his inability to shape the agenda in the crucial last days by steering the public debate back onto core issues of financial management and the levels of confidence in the local economy.

Instead, his most notable performance in the final week was an acrimonious exchange with ABC morning announcer Jon Faine. On Wednesday 15 September, Faine grilled the premier over the earnings of Rebecca Cooper, a cabinet minister's daughter who had left her job as a senior government adviser to work as a private sector consultant for the gas industry. Kennett became so irritated by the line of questioning that he refused point-blank to answer.

KENNETT: 'You go on, I'll just sit here and drink my tea.'

FAINE: 'And that's the only response.'

KENNETT: 'Well, you're pathetic. Absolutely pathetic.'

The ALP could scarcely believe its luck. Kennett sounded harried and uncomfortable. Instead of scoring big hits on economic management, he was coming across as a politician on the defensive. 'They ran a shocker in that last week,' says one senior ALP source. 'They needed him talking the economy, and instead he got tangled up in all these other issues. Kennett had got away for so long without doing interviews. He really had distanced himself from any degree of pressure. In campaigns you can't do that. He was totally unprepared for the fact that he had to answer questions every single day. He had become so used to keeping the media at bay, and simply refusing to answer when anyone asked a hard question. He would drift off onto other issues or he would simply go into hiding for a couple of days. In the campaign, he got himself into a situation where he demonstrated he was unaccustomed to having to deal with these pressures. The interview he did with Jon Faine was a disaster. It showed he had forgotten how to handle himself under pressure. Whenever anyone put difficult questions, he was totally unprepared for the fact that he was expected to answer them.'

As surprised as Labor officials were by the premier's volatile performance, they were equally nonplussed – and relieved – that nobody in the media was bothering to ask detailed questions about Labor's financial management strategy. Despite attempts by Stockdale and Kennett's office to ignite interest in their 'black hole' argument, which said that Labor's spending promises would take the budget back into deficit, the financial management issue virtually disappeared from the campaign debate in the first week, after Bracks issued a letter from private consultancy Access Economics affirming that Labor's costings had been authenticated.

In fact, nobody in the media saw the costings until three days out from election day, when Bracks released them at a briefing of journalists at Parliament House. It was 3.30 in the afternoon, and no TV cameras were present. The strategy, simply, was to chloroform any intensive analysis of Labor's alternative budget. For a leader running on issues of openness and accountability, this was curious footwork, yet it succeeded. Apart from a comment piece in the *Age* on election day suggesting one or two elements of jiggery-pokery in Labor's calculations, the package slipped through virtually unnoticed. The ALP was chuffed. Says one source, '[The media] should have been screaming at us, "Give us the costings, and if you don't we will write the fact that you are refusing to provide us with the documents."' Down at Liberal headquarters, media attitudes towards the Labor leader were also noted, one official complaining wearily, 'Bracks got this treatment from the media as if to say, "Well, he's doing all right for somebody who's going to lose." Nobody said, "This man could be premier next week." Nobody put him under the microscope.'

In the aftermath of the election, the Liberal campaign was roundly criticised. However, one official argues that much of this was wisdom in hindsight. 'The inescapable fact is that nobody expected Jeff to lose. Nobody. That goes all the way up and down the scale. The voters didn't expect him to lose. In lots of ways, they disarmed us. If we attacked Labor, they said, "They're not going to win anyway. What are you talking about?" If we said, "If Labor gets back they will run up deficits," they said, "They've got no hope of winning. Who cares about their budget strategy?" Eighty-five per cent of the electorate expected Jeff to win. Less than 10 per cent, and sometimes 5 per cent, expected Labor to win. Those people who were persuadable, or undecided, were all saying they expected Jeff to win. What happened in the last 24 to 36 hours was that there were lots of people who hadn't made up their minds and they all went one way. They were people who were Liberal voters in 1996. They voted Labor in 1999.'

The media, of course, were operating on much the same assumptions as the political parties. Labor would be unlikely to get itself into a position where it could form government. Doubtless, this sentiment intruded on coverage and story selection. The 'Guilty Party' days were long gone. It was Kennett's style of leadership that became the issue, not the fine print of the Opposition's policy documentation. This was a mindset that gave the ALP convenient shelter, especially in the economic management debate. Within Labor, the use of Access Economics as a third-party endorsement of the ALP's financial management policies was seen as a serious coup.

By election eve, Peter Poggioli was increasingly apprehensive. He was up until 3 a.m. poring over the opinion polls published in the election-day newspapers. AgePoll suggested another landslide victory for the government, while the *Herald Sun*'s Quadrant poll showed Labor gaining between three and seven seats – nowhere near enough to claim government. Newspoll in the *Australian*, however, showed the two parties running neck and neck. Moreover, it reported plunging support for Kennett in rural Victoria. But even Newspoll's Sol Lebovic, appearing on the ABC's *7.30 Report*, was cautious not to make too much of this. He concluded, 'It's going to be a very close election. But the very fact I say that may mean it's not going to be close.' Poggioli was taken aback, but his concern was more with the tone of the coverage in the major

Melbourne dailies. In their election editorials, both newspapers had supported the return of the Kennett government, albeit in both cases with a plea for wider community consultation and enhanced democratic safeguards. Moreover, their lead news stories were suggesting the election was pretty much one-way traffic, as if the result were already guaranteed for Kennett. The expectation factor was becoming a monster. Petro Georgiou had been warning in his regular election commentary in the *Age* of the dangers of universal expectations of a Liberal win. At a meeting of party supporters one week out from polling day, he had grown alarmed at the sense of complacency, even among hard-nosed Liberals, about the certainty of victory.

For its part, though, Labor could find no joy in the polls. Underdog status had had its advantages in structuring a campaign, but here, on the verge of election day, everything was pointing to the state ALP facing a third successive debacle. Although Bracks was saying publicly – and privately – that Labor was a chance to win, this was interpreted, even among his own party colleagues, as the bravado of a man who had no option but to hope for the best. He perhaps betrayed his true feelings on election day when he cornered a reporter from the *Australian* for a word about that morning's headline, 'Shock surge against Kennett'. Grinning, he told the reporter, 'I know Newspoll is always right, and I hope it's right, but I think the *Australian*'s on drugs.'

Labor's predicament was that it had made almost no impact in the outer-eastern suburbs – the 'claybelt' seats that followed the course of Whitehorse Road from the city and onward to the Yarra Valley and Dandenong Ranges. It was accepted wisdom that these were the seats that determined who governed in Victoria. On election eve, it seemed beyond doubt that, with the possible exception of Mitcham, which was too close to call, most if not all of these seats would remain safely in the keeping of the Liberal Party. How, then, could Labor possibly win?

The only possible chink of light for the ALP in its own polling came through the detailed seat-by-seat breakdown of samples. These indicated a blow-out in the number of undecided voters in country electorates, described by one ALP source as 'a massive variable of indecision'. As Newspoll was indicating, a rural backlash was still a possibility.

As both parties in Melbourne were intensely studying the last-minute polls, news was coming through from the Canadian province of Saskatchewan of an election upset. Despite leading impressively in all the pre-poll forecasting, popular two-time premier Roy Romanow had suffered a massive swing against his government and would have to negotiate with minor parties to form government. His support had evaporated in the conservative prairie districts of rural Saskatchewan. It was a result that shocked almost everyone, reported the correspondent for the Canadian Broadcasting Corporation. But even if anyone in the ALP had heard of this boilover, a quirky election outcome in a faraway place could hardly be seen as an omen. Almost all of the objective evidence suggested Labor would not even go close. On election eve, some Labor frontbenchers had been telling journalists bleakly that the party would do well to gain two or three seats. The prepositioning to protect Bracks' leadership in the event of a disaster was already under way. Right-wing powerbroker Steven Conroy was telling colleagues that if Labor picked up more than five seats he would sprint naked down Bourke Street.

On a cold and blustery Saturday 18 September, Jeff Kennett left his Surrey Hills home at about 8 a.m. to vote early at the Ashburton Primary School. Together with Felicity, he toured some of the local booths in his four-wheel drive, chatting amiably with voters. Then he went back to the family home. Apart from an election verdict to await, there were also preparations to make for the 21st birthday of his son Angus. Kennett's parents, Ken and Wendy, had also arrived to lend moral support. Election days were never easy. The premier, having been through four previous campaigns as the leader of his party, had learned to be fatalistic. Yet this time there seemed little cause for concern. Although he had expressed his apprehension publicly over the expectation factor emerging through the polls, and had warned his colleagues to guard against complacency, this was a contest he never dreamed he would lose.

For Kennett, this was to be a day of endless shocks. The first blow for the premier was when word came through from Frankston East that the former Liberal MP, Peter McLellan, who had resigned from the party in protest over Kennett's autocratic leadership and was defending his seat as an independent candidate, had died unexpectedly. The Frankston East campaign had been stressful and debilitating. The Liberal candidate, Cherie McLean, who had once worked in McLellan's office and was one of his close friends, had been the victim of a violent attack at her campaign office near the Pines estate, and this incident was known to have deeply affected McLellan. On election eve, he was found dead at his home. Kennett was distraught when he heard. McLellan may have been one of his most strenuous internal critics, and a rebel MP in his last months, but the two had shared a common background in the military and a blunt, upfront approach to politics. In Kennett's eyes, McLellan was always part of his team – the class of '92. The reports of his death cast a shadow over the premier's day.

More bad news was soon to come. At 5.50 p.m., Peter Poggioli got the first results of his exit polling. He looked twice, disbelieving. The figures indicated that Labor would make significant gains, and that the result could be on a knife edge. Poggioli wondered for a moment why he ever bothered with exit polling. It had a history as an inexact science. But the omens could not be ignored.

By this time, Jeff Kennett was among friends and family in a suite on the 50th floor of the Hotel Sofitel in Collins Street. Poggioli didn't call. Before imparting this sort of news, he wanted firm confirmation from his polling booth officials and scrutineers. However, one of Kennett's staffers phoned soon after and asked, 'What's going on?' Poggioli replied soberly, 'There's a swing on.'

The state director was clearly agitated and unhappy, and the conversation was brief. As the election telecasts began to beam through the first results of the formal count, Kennett stayed with his family. In an adjacent room, his chief advisers, Anna Cronin and Steve Murphy, gathered in a huddle with Kennett speechwriter Kevin 'The Quill' Balshaw, Mark Birrell and Petro Georgiou. Felicity Kennett wandered out occasionally to join them for a cigarette. She rarely smoked, but it soon became evident this was going to be an arduous night.

By 7.30 p.m., Kennett staffers knew the unthinkable was happening. Labor had won the seat of Oakleigh – easily. It had also surged to the front in Tullamarine. But the true shock waves were rolling in from the countryside. Labor was winning Ballarat East, Ballarat West and Narracan. All had been marginal, and therefore vulnerable.

Over the next hour came the rumble of thunder. Labor was achieving swings of up to 10 per cent in rural and provincial Victoria. Bendigo East was the first domino to fall, then previously safe Liberal seats such as Ripon and Seymour. Unbelievably, the Liberal vote had also collapsed in the seat of Gisborne. The 23-year political career of Rob Knowles, Kennett's closest friend through all their years in parliament, was over.

The news for the National Party was worse still. In Gippsland East, the swing against David Treasure was 12 per cent. He would be forced to a count of preferences. The Nationals had gone into the election campaign with eight of the safest seats in the state. But now, the smallest swing against a sitting National Party MP was 6 per cent. Even in Benalla, held by Pat McNamara, the party's vote had plummeted by almost 8 per cent.

At ALP headquarters in West Melbourne, the mood was euphoric. Labor was a chance to win nine seats outside the city, its best showing in country Victoria since 1952. In Melbourne, it had managed to win only three, maybe four, seats. Although this meant that they could not hope to achieve an outright victory, the party's performance had surpassed all expectations – even those of its leader. Astonishingly, the election was a cliffhanger: too close to call. For Labor, this was as good as a victory. Shortly before 9 p.m., Steve Bracks and his wife, Terry, left excited party officials to make their way across the West Gate Bridge to the Williamstown Swimming and Surf Life Saving Club, where, after a decade of rejection and dejection, frenzied celebrations of Labor supporters were erupting.

At about 9.15 p.m., Kennett came out to join his staff and colleagues. He was weary and gaunt, and could not disguise the worry on his face. The premier had been briefed by Poggioli: the Liberals had lost at least seven seats. The government's majority had been emasculated; it was guaranteed to hold only 43 seats, two short of a majority. However, Gippsland East, Geelong and Carrum still looked promising, and there remained some hope of regaining Mitcham once postal votes were counted. Frankston East would go to a supplementary election. All was not lost, and Poggioli was forecasting that the government would squeak over the line with a narrow majority. Kennett did his best to sound optimistic, although he was clearly startled – and stung – by the extent of the swing against the government outside Melbourne. Nothing in the polling had hinted at a backlash on this scale. For his colleagues, Kennett put on a stoic front. 'He was a rock,' says one.

Reflecting on this later, Kennett believes he had been toughened by his experience in previous campaigns. 'I had been through a lot of elections. There is no point in histrionics and tears. I saw the result coming in, I saw the huge differential between city and country. When something like this happens, you've just got to wear it. There's nothing you can do to change it. I thought we had run a good campaign. I knew we had been an honest government. I was satisfied we had achieved a great deal for the state. We were very disappointed with the loss of seats, but at this stage, of course, the election result was still in the mail. We still thought we would be able to form a government.'

For all his attempts to maintain a steely exterior, Kennett was deeply distressed, in particular, by the plight of two of his cabinet colleagues, Rob Knowles and Ann Henderson. Kennett held himself personally responsible for Knowles' loss. 'I had asked him to come down to the lower house. He would not have done it if I hadn't asked him. It was all part of the succession strategy. He was my closest friend in the political sphere and that was a big blow.' If anything, though, Kennett was even more perturbed by the fate of housing minister Henderson, the member for Geelong, who would have to wait another week before knowing the final outcome of the ballot. 'To me, she was in one sense the spirit of Geelong. She had been through awful trauma in her own health and that of her husband. She had contracted cancer back in 1996, and she had fought through that campaign while receiving treatment. Tragically, she had a relapse, and had to fight the thing again during this campaign. We worked very hard to make sure it didn't get out. She didn't really want anyone to know. In the end, it came down to the fact that if eight people had voted differently, she would have held the seat. I felt great sorrow for her on election night.'

At 9.30 p.m., as Kennett consulted staff on the speech he was preparing to deliver to shell-shocked party supporters gathered in a downstairs ballroom, Steve Bracks emerged on the stage at the official ALP function in his electorate of Williamstown. 'This is the end of the one-man band and the start of democracy in Victoria,' he told a delirious crowd. 'I can tell you that Labor has gained more than 50 per cent of the vote in Victoria. We have won more seats in country and regional Victoria than the Liberal and National parties combined. This is a victory for decency. I am so proud, so, so proud that Victorians stood up and said there is a better way for Victoria. Good on you.'

At 10.05 p.m., Kennett took the lift downstairs. He hummed a tune as he walked alongside Felicity. He knew by now that he faced the prospect of a hung parliament. Whoever formed the next government would do so with the barest of margins. Policy would be conditional – the stuff of negotiations, deal-making, horse-trading – in order to secure a workable parliamentary majority. As he began his speech, which was televised live nationally, Kennett said he took responsibility for the backlash against his government. This prompted whoops of delight from the Labor supporters in Williamstown. Kennett then went on to attribute the swing to the 'unprecedented expectation' that his government would be returned in a landslide. This was a protest vote, he argued, cast by an electorate believing it had the luxury of voting against a government that was certain to be returned. Certainly, Kennett's argument had some merit, but it sounded suspiciously like he was blaming voters for making a stupid and reckless mistake. Continuing on this theme, Kennett said the state faced up to two months of uncertainty, and there might yet be a need for fresh elections. No matter who ultimately won, Victoria would be a very different place. 'There is no other conclusion that you can draw. A lot of the excitement, a lot of the consistency, a lot of the achievements we have gained, a lot of the respect we have earned will quite quickly dissipate.' In this new and uncertain climate, the days of bold and brash decision-making were over. Whatever the final outcome, the Kennett era, as Victorians had come to know it, was over.

Around the nation, Labor leaders rejoiced. Secretly, so did some of Kennett's federal Liberal colleagues. Even if Jeff held on to office, he would surely be enfeebled by this experience. The New South Wales premier, Bob Carr, chided by his Victorian counterpart only six months earlier for being a weak leader who didn't deserve to be re-elected, could not resist the opportunity to offer a piercing observation. 'If you spend most of your time boasting about how good you are, you're really inviting the gods to strike you down. In a democracy, the gods are the voters.'

Kennett had not been repudiated by the voters en masse. But for Oakleigh and Mitcham, which remained too close to call on that night, none of the Liberals' vast string of marginal seats in the city's east had fallen. The knockout punch, the one that Kennett had not seen coming, was the utter collapse of the Coalition vote among its traditional supporters in country and provincial Victoria. Given the patterns of voting, this result had to be due to something beyond conventional politics. It had about it the old and familiar refrain of 'Them and Us'. The voters of regional Victoria, brooding over their sense of neglect, had combined to give those uppity city slickers the lesson of their lives.

CHAPTER TWENTY-THREE

ENDGAME

'Most nights are slow in the political business, but every once in a while
you get a fast one, a blast of wild treachery and weirdness
that not even the hard boys can handle.'
HUNTER S. THOMPSON

Back in his suite at the Hotel Sofitel that election night, Jeff Kennett interrupted the bleak postmortems to lead a rousing chorus of 'Happy Birthday' for his son Angus. As the youngsters then went off to party, Kennett stayed to mingle with his staff and study yet again the seat-by-seat breakdowns provided by Poggioli. The final result would not be known for days, perhaps weeks. The death of Peter McLellan meant that the poll in Frankston East had been declared void. A supplementary election could not be held for least 25 days. Unless the counting of postal votes delivered the seats of Geelong, Mitcham, Carrum and Gippsland East to the government, neither Labor nor the Coalition would be able to form government until Frankston East was decided, and only then on the say-so of independents. It shaped as a never-ending nightmare. The premier reflected on this over a few drinks. He waited until just after the stroke of midnight, then turned to his guests. 'Ah,' he said with a sigh of relief. 'A new day dawns.'

The next morning, he had scheduled a Sunday lunch in the

Dandenongs with his old friends the Tesselaar family. On a sunny afternoon, in the idyllic surrounds of their tulip farm, the premier would normally have been chirpy and amiable, at one with the world. But the impact of the election result was beginning to sink in, and there was no escaping the media interest in how a once-dominant premier was coping with the dramatic diminution of his power. Kennett was jaded and disconsolate. When interviewed, he conceded for the first time that he might have to quit.

The following morning, when he arrived in his office, the mood was funereal. Kennett spoke to the staff, saying he feared the government was in danger of defeat, and they might all lose their jobs. He apologised. When cabinet met for lunch, Kennett delivered the same sombre message to his ministers. Rob Knowles was visibly distraught. Susan Davies, the independent from Gippsland West, was telling the media that Kennett was a 'dead duck'.

By Monday afternoon, however, there appeared to be a Liberal resurgence as the count progressed. Ann Henderson was making up ground on her Labor opponent, Ian Trezise, in Geelong. Likewise, David Lean was making a comeback in Carrum. Mitcham, according to Poggioli, would come down to a few hundred votes, and the National Party seemed more confident about holding Gippsland East. Kennett's spirits began to lift. If favoured by fortune in the postal votes, and if the Coalition held its nerve, his government might yet survive in its own right.

Within the National Party, however, the mood was inconsolable. Mortified by the collapse of its vote, the junior Coalition partner was looking to its own survival as a party and there was talk of abandoning the Coalition immediately in order to set the party apart and give it more freedom to manoeuvre in this new and chaotic environment. Even before it was certain of defeat, the government was fragmenting. Kennett was furious about what he saw as National Party brinkmanship at this time of crisis. Publicly, he tempered his criticism of McNamara, 'I think it's regrettable that Pat is out there now trying to position himself in this way.'

The panic in the National Party was compounded on Tuesday night, when it became apparent that Labor preferences were likely to give the independent, Craig Ingram, victory in Gippsland East.

The pressures were crowding in on Kennett. The Nationals were threatening to scrap the Coalition agreement, his own Liberal colleagues and the business community were urging him to do whatever necessary to survive in office, and the independents were lurking. Under the greatest political strain he had faced in seven years, Jeff was having to swallow his pride and rediscover the pragmatism he had brought to the job of Opposition leader. On Wednesday morning he strolled out into the Treasury Gardens and gave an expansive press conference. He was about to present a different face to the public. First, he conceded there could be no protest vote without grievance. 'We've been given a real kick in the provincial cities, and I don't see it as a protest vote so much as I see people deliberately deciding how they were going to vote.' Second, he issued a form of an apology for his brusque leadership style. 'If, along the way, I have trodden on some toes, if I have offended some, I am sorry. I didn't set out to offend or hurt.' Thirdly, he signalled he was ready to change his approach if that meant retaining power. 'The human being can be a pretty flexible animal.' The media were sceptical. Here was the 'Can-Do' leader sounding gentle, contrite, almost vulnerable. It didn't look or sound convincing.

The following day, Kennett made his usual appearance on 3AW. 'I'm not a quitter,' he said. 'I never have been. I've been written off more times than the Bible has been printed. I'll be hanging in there. I never left town, I ain't gonna leave town.' The premier remained steadfast in his refusal to acknowledge that he was facing political oblivion, characterising the election result as a 'huge wake-up call' rather than a repudiation. Then, mysteriously, he read over the air a poem sent to him by a woman in Geelong. It revealed Kennett's bitterness at what he saw as the fickleness of human nature. It was also interpreted as the premier scolding the electorate for their ingratitude and shortsightedness.

People are unreasonable, illogical and self-centred. Love them
anyway.

If you do good, people will accuse you of selfish ulterior
motives. Do good anyway.

If you are successful, you will win false friends and true enemies.
Succeed anyway.

The good you do today will be forgotten tomorrow. Do good
anyway.

Honesty and frankness makes you vulnerable. Be honest and
frank anyway.

The biggest person with the biggest ideas can be shot down by
the smallest people with the smallest minds. Think big
anyway.

People favour underdogs, but follow only top dogs. Fight for
some underdogs anyway.

What you spend years building may be destroyed overnight.
Build anyway.

People really need help but may attack you if you help them.
Help people anyway.

Give the world the best you have and you will get kicked in the
teeth. Give the world the best you've got anyway.

Leaving the media pack dumbfounded, the premier then headed
to a special party-room meeting to confront for the first time his
own MPs. The Liberals had counted their dead, and remained in a
state of shock. Recriminations were beginning. A handful of MPs
were saying Jeff was finished. 'The public is fed up,' said one.
'Kennett has lost the element of awe. Nobody is afraid of him. The
emperor has lost his clothes. He can't come to grips with what has
happened. In the past, he has somehow managed to find a way to
come back. He's clutching at straws: how can he can get out of this
to prove what he has proved before, that he can pull success out of
failure? This is what's driving him. That's what he's about. But,
frankly, he's history.'

In the party room, however, these voices fell silent. When Liberal MPs wandered in, they found Kennett sitting in a chair off to the side of the head table. He had presumed they would want to vote on who should lead them. He waited for others to nominate. Nobody did. The premier was re-elected as Liberal leader, unopposed. Despite what some of his internal critics were saying privately to journalists, none summoned the nerve to speak up in his presence. Later, one or two were to complain of the lack of rigorous analysis of the election result at the meeting. 'The party is in denial,' they told journalists. But for the vast majority of Liberals there that day, there was obviously no sentiment whatsoever for a change in the leader – or at least, nobody with the courage to say so. Rationalising this later, one critic snarled, 'Let him stew in his own juice.'

By lunchtime on Thursday, Jeff Kennett knew that his world had changed forever. The premier's office took a call from Susan Davies. She and one of her fellow independents, Russell Savage from Mildura, were coming to see Mr Kennett at Treasury Place. They would be there at 1.30 p.m; could his staff make sure he was there to meet them? A receptionist called Kennett's senior adviser, Anna Cronin. 'I see. You had better call the premier back from parliament.' Thus began the power play that would ultimately determine the future of Jeff Kennett and his government.

Measured on the basis of their combined first-preference votes, the three independents spoke for only slightly more than 30 000 people in a statewide electorate of three million. Crucially, though, they would have three votes in a Legislative Assembly of 88, with the Liberals and Nationals likely to have 43 seats, Labor 41 and Frankston East still to be decided. Unless everything ran the Coalition's way in the final counting of postal votes, there was every likelihood that the independents could dictate who would form government. They had come to see Kennett to outline the conditions on which their support would depend – a shopping list of demands for a series of policy changes that would later be formalised as their 'Charter of Good Government'.

This was unfamiliar and uncomfortable territory for Kennett. Through his second term in office, the premier had treated Savage and Davies with near-contempt. The feelings were mutual. Now, he had to bite his tongue and listen to their lectures on how and why he should overturn or amend some of the most contentious decisions of his second term. Kennett's advisers were suspicious from the start about the intentions of the independents. Susan Davies had been a Labor candidate back in 1996, and under both Brumby and Bracks had been a regular visitor to the Opposition rooms. Kennett had come to regard her as an unreconstructed socialist, and had told her so to her face. Savage was more conservative in his leanings, but he too had clashed heatedly with the premier. Although the incident was never recorded in Hansard, the former police sergeant was known to be deeply offended by one exchange in parliament during which he insists he distinctly heard the premier call him a vulgar name. The two independents had been assigned a shared office in the so-called 'Chook Shed' – the annexe to the parliament building. The Labor Party had given up some of its space to accommodate them. Liberal MPs had laughed at the time.

On election night, Davies and Savage had watched the count from their rural electorates. Both were returned comfortably and they spoke by phone late in the night to discuss the implications. Davies also spoke to a reporter from the *Age* but was quoted as being somewhat hesitant and coy about her potential role in the new parliament. 'Oh God, I don't want the balance of power,' she said. 'That would be too much altogether.' Kennett did not believe this for a minute. 'Susan absolutely loved having us on toast,' agrees one of his advisers.

During their opening round of discussions, Kennett invited Mark Birrell to join him in his office with Savage and Davies. The two independents told them they would be speaking to Craig Ingram that night, and that they would be putting together a charter. While there was no detailed discussions of its likely contents,

Savage and Davies had sought an immediate commitment from Kennett that he would overturn the changes to the office of the auditor-general. The premier said he would take advice and urged that they meet again soon. They told him they would be drawing up a list of issues on which they would seek his formal response. Kennett and Birrell finished the meeting still sceptical about the process, but heartened that the conversation had been calm, relatively cordial and constructive.

'There was always a huge risk this was a charade,' recalls one senior government insider. 'In our heart of hearts, we thought it probably was. But there was a feeling we had to give it absolutely our best shot. Maybe they had already made their decision, and we were going through the motions. Maybe what we said or did was not going to make one whit of difference. Susan was relishing just sitting there in Jeff's office, laying down demands. But Russell was totally professional. Very hard to read. He seemed to take it very seriously. There was no posturing or square-ups. He asked reasonable questions, substantial questions. He listened carefully, almost deferentially, to the responses. At a personal level, he didn't seem to have any problems with Jeff at all.' Kennett, for his part, could not afford to be other than polite and businesslike. If his government was to survive beyond a few weeks, he had no choice but to hear the independents out. As he would say later, 'We had to fight the good fight.'

On Friday 24 September at the final count of postal votes, however, there was heartbreak for the Liberals in both Geelong and Carrum. David Lean lost his seat by 116 votes, and Ann Henderson fell short in the battle for Geelong by a mere 16 votes. The government's last hopes of holding office in its own right evaporated. Henderson's near-miss in Geelong was excruciating for the Liberals, especially when they learned that 40 or more players from the Geelong Football Club had been on their end-of-season trip to Bali on election day. Would they have made the difference? The point remained that Henderson had needed only nine people in an electorate of 32 000 to vote differently in order for the Coalition to creep up to 44 seats. With precisely half the Legislative Assembly, the government would have been in a far stronger position to defend its right to continue in office.

As an intellectual exercise, Liberal officials could argue – and did, despairingly – that Kennett, in effect, had been stranded short of a governing majority by a mere 69 votes. All it would have taken was for 69 people entering the polling booths of Geelong and Carrum on 18 September to have changed their minds and voted Liberal, not Labor. But as they knew only too well, these calculations were academic and futile. The party flirted with the notion of mounting a challenge over the result in Geelong through the Court of Disputed Returns, but the reality was that the votes were in and Labor was guaranteed at least 41 seats in the lower house against the Coalition's 43, with three independents. Now all eyes would be on Frankston East, and all ears tuned to every utterance by the independents. The negotiations over the coming fortnight would be life or death for Kennett and his government.

By now, Labor knew it was in the driver's seat. Its polling had been strong in Frankston East. ALP officials believed that their candidate, Matt Viney, would have won the seat on 18 September had the count gone ahead. After the election, the wind was blowing even more strongly Labor's way. Confident of the outcome, Bracks sought to cast the supplementary election as a referendum on who should form government. Ominously for the Coalition, the independents appeared to accept this. Kennett became progressively more disheartened. 'That seat was never going to be a win for us. Before 1992, it was fundamentally a Labor seat. And of course, there was this mood swing happening, particularly in the media. Obviously, a tall poppy had been pulled down to size, and they were having a field day. I've never seen anything like it.'

On Monday 27 September, the independents provided Kennett's office with their charter of demands. A copy was sent to Bracks, although this seemed pretty much a formality. Almost every item specified in the charter featured in Labor's election platform. Susan

Davies had been the key figure in preparing the document – and some Liberals suspected that Labor's chief parliamentary strategist, Peter Batchelor, had also had a role in its drafting. This Batchelor denied, although not before stressing that he enjoyed very amicable relations with Savage and Davies. The independents' headline demand was for the powers of the auditor-general to be enshrined in the Constitution, a protection they deemed 'non-negotiable'. They also sought a move to a system of proportional representation to elect the Legislative Council. The charter stipulated an increase in the number of parliamentary sitting days, more staff and resources for independent MPs, the strengthening of freedom-of-information laws and a firm commitment to greater infrastructure investment in the regions. Davies told Kennett's office that the charter would not be released publicly. Government ministers awoke the next day to find it leading all media, print and electronic. One National Party minister noted tersely, 'Their concerns didn't seem to have much to do with the interests of people in rural and regional seats.'

The independents gave both the Coalition and the ALP until 12 October to provide formal responses. Despite the gloom descending over the government, Mark Birrell and Anna Cronin began the task of drafting the government's stance. Cronin sat down with the premier and went through each item in the package to ascertain his level of flexibility. Birrell worked through the issues relating to parliamentary procedures; Cronin focused on the policy ramifications. Kennett held further meetings with Savage, Davies and Ingram, in which Savage would lead the questioning for the three independent MPs. Davies would sit to his left, Ingram to his right. Other members of the Coalition leadership group also joined in. 'We did fight it out very hard,' says Kennett. 'We argued our case very strongly. Anna Cronin deserves the greatest credit there. Her work in that three- or four-week period was nothing short of extraordinary.'

As they watched the dynamics, it appeared to the Coalition ministers that Russell Savage was the pivot. One of those involved says, 'It seemed to us that where Russell went, Craig would follow. He had a lot of respect for him. He regarded Russell as the elder statesman. Even Susan seemed to defer to him to a degree.' As they parried with the Mildura MP, though, the National Party leaders were finding it hard to contain their frustration. Here were three rural-based politicians, representing seats that had never once been in the hands of the Labor Party, arguing that the fate of government was to be decided by a charter that seemed built to serve the ALP's purposes. At the first meeting in which he was involved, Roger Hallam found it impossible to bite his tongue. 'Russell Savage was going on about sustainable farming, and I said, "Let's just remember that the folk you're supposed to represent are going to survive depending on their ability to thrive in the international market. They are going to have to be efficient before they are sustainable."' Kennett wasn't pleased by Hallam's outburst and called him aside for a quiet word. 'You can't do that. You're not going to solve the world's problems. We just have to find our way through this, so let's get on with the job,' he scolded. Hallam took it as it was intended: a clear rebuke from the premier for his minister's lack of diplomacy.

Hallam remained perturbed throughout the process. He feared that the government, anxious to placate the independents, was stepping back from too many hard-fought principles, especially over the reforms to the Audit Act. He watched, bemused, as Kennett engineered the shift.

'He just said, "Fine, get rid of it." After all we had invested in it, having held the line for so long, I didn't think we could go back on it. It's not possible for a human being to do it. He said, "You watch me." He gave the impression it was almost a test of his pragmatism: we would do what we could to survive. "The vision we have for the state is much more important. Let's not bleed over something that's not worthwhile." Jesus, I remembered when it was worthwhile. That was a side of him I hadn't seen before. It was not that he was being mercenary. But I was in awe that someone who had fought so long and so hard over a particular issue was prepared to jettison the whole thing.'

'This was a whole new ball game for Kennett,' says another close colleague. 'But we could not deliberately give up government. If there was a small chance – maybe it was totally unrealistic – to stay in office, the pollies wanted him to follow it through. Some were going to become ministers if the government held on. And they were desperate to be ministers.'

By Friday 8 October, Birrell and Cronin had completed the Coalition's 42-page response to the independents' charter. Given its history, the concessions made so readily by the Kennett government were breathtaking. They amounted to an acceptance of all the terms laid down bar one: the proposal to introduce proportional representation voting for upper-house elections. The cover note to Savage, Davies and Ingram was deferential in the extreme. Here were the Coalition leaders down on bended knee, seeking mercy and forgiveness.

> We acknowledge the independents' wish not to control any government's program or policies and the independents' desire not to be a formal part of government – and your determination to maintain your independent status. Further, we acknowledge the need for substantial reform in particular areas of government practice and the need to provide you with clear evidence that we are both willing and able to address these reforms. We recognise the particular needs of rural Victoria and are committed to ensuring that all Victorians can benefit from government services and that the benefits of economic growth are distributed equitably across the state.

The document promised reforms to the parliamentary committee system, heightened powers for the police commissioner and the director of public prosecutions, fewer exemptions on freedom-of-information requests, fixed four-year terms for parliament, and a $65 million program to educate farmers in new technologies aimed at achieving higher productivity without damaging the natural resource base. It also promised to 'step back from the purist deregulation model' imposed by the national competition policy. There was an additional undertaking to review all contracting-out procedures, and a pledge to give local councils greater influence over planning decisions. The auditor-general would be commissioned to conduct an independent review of privatisation, and the Coalition would order a judicial inquiry into the ambulance contracts scandal. On page 17, on a personal note, the document stressed, 'The Coalition Members of Parliament undertake to treat all Members of Parliament, including Independent Members, with courtesy and respect.'

On Tuesday 12 October, Kennett took the government's response to a full meeting of Coalition MPs. A copy was faxed to the office of Susan Davies at 4.45 p.m., as Liberal and National MPs studied the contents. Some saw it as capitulation, pure and simple. The offer gave the independents almost all they had asked for, at the cost of a significant loss of face to Kennett and the government. Indeed, as their subsequent behaviour would suggest, the independents were offered far more than they had bargained for. The government, against all expectations, had been neither stubborn nor arrogant. It appeared the independents had expected a straightforward and uncomplicated choice. They had not expected Kennett to go even halfway to matching what Labor had put on the table. Suddenly, the veil lifted. The independents had to show their hand. It was apparent to many Liberals, within hours of the document being sent, that there had never been any intention by the three MPs to do other than support the ALP.

Before Coalition MPs had emerged from their discussions, Susan Davies had put the offer document in the public arena via her web site. In another unsettling development for the government, the *Sunraysia Daily* in Mildura ran a poll suggesting that 54 per cent of Russell Savage's supporters wanted him to vote Labor into power.

Savage was later forced to deny rumours that he had phoned a local ALP official to say, 'Make sure you win the poll.' More evidence emerged when he began telling the media that the obstacle all along had been the premier himself. Savage didn't trust him, and never would. If only Kennett had resigned the leadership, the independents would almost certainly have voted the Coalition back into power.

This was not a condition Savage had advanced during the formal negotiations, although he claims he sent these signals privately to Coalition MPs. In fact, Savage has since argued that the Liberals should have sensed it intuitively. 'I always avoided putting it specifically. I didn't have that right. It was a matter for the Liberals to decide. But they were obviously a bit thick if they thought we could deal with Jeff Kennett. The relationship I had with Kennett was very bad. I didn't respect him as premier or as a person. He had sacked me as a councillor in Mildura, and now I was to have a hand in removing him. Look, he had taken away our *Vinelander* train, he had damaged the office of the auditor-general, and these were things I reflected on. If Kennett wasn't there, we would have been hard pressed to justify our decision to support the ALP.' Savage's admission that his decision was driven in part by personal animus was reinforced by another frank concession about the negotiations over the charter. 'I am not interested in what a leader is in terms of political reference. We were looking for honesty, accountability. Bracks was way ahead in these attributes.'

In hindsight, it can be said that the Coalition's response to the independents' charter was dead on arrival. The process was proving to be fiction. Which way the independents would vote had never been in serious doubt. This was finally confirmed on Thursday 14 October – the day the Coalition was due to hold its final round of talks with the independents before the Frankston East supplementary election. Susan Davies appeared on the ABC's *AM* program and launched a personal attack on the premier, describing him as a bully. 'I don't like bullies. It makes me feel like vomiting actually, if you want to know the truth. Because I'm afraid of bullies, that makes me realise that you can't – you don't – give in to bullies.' In response, Kennett said this left no doubt – if ever there had been any doubt – that Davies would support the ALP. 'I don't think anyone genuinely believes that she is genuinely independent.' The premier still held out hope of securing the support of Savage and Ingram. Their two votes would be enough to secure a majority for his government. The discussions were protracted, and continued through until 7 p.m.; Kennett asked that they resume the following day.

On the Friday morning, however, Craig Ingram bumped into a group of Labor frontbenchers. During some good-humoured banter, Ingram mentioned he was none too popular at home. When they asked why, he dropped the much-anticipated revelation, 'My missus is not too happy about me going with you blokes.' Jaws apparently dropped. Twenty-four hours in advance of the Frankston East poll, the decision had already been made. When Bracks was told, he instructed Tim Pallas, his chief of staff, to draw up the paperwork immediately. They needed Ingram to sign up in writing that very day. Nothing was to be left to chance. At 8 a.m. the talks between the independents and the Coalition leadership resumed in Kennett's office. The premier was downbeat. He sensed his chances might be slipping away. 'He was distracted. He was on tenterhooks. I think he had a strong feeling it was all a bit of a charade. He was finding it hard to put his all into it,' says a colleague. But Ingram gave no indication at this stage that the talks were futile. He kept his cards close to his chest.

When the talks broke up that afternoon, the newcomer from Gippsland East promptly went across to the Opposition rooms at Spring Street. A fortnight before he was officially sworn into parliament as an MP, Craig Ingram signed the Kennett government's death warrant.

By this time, the Frankston East poll was all that stood between the premier and defeat. If Labor failed to win the seat, the independents, despite their preference for Bracks, would have faced

a hung-parliament scenario – and a choice of either supporting
Kennett to remain in power, or voting down the government by
a single vote. It could have meant fresh elections, and this was the
last thing the independents wanted. They believed Kennett would
look to the first opportunity to take the parliament back to the
people, confident that neither Labor nor the independents were
likely to run him as close a second time around. The voters of
Frankston East were crucial to the arithmetic. If Labor failed, the
independents could not take the risk of voting Kennett out.

As expected, however, Labor romped home with a swing of
8.3 per cent, more than twice what it required to take the seat.
Savage spoke that night to the *Sunday Herald Sun*. He told the
newspaper that the independents would announce their support for
Steve Bracks to be appointed premier and for Labor to form the
next government. Davies had already signed up on the Saturday to
support the ALP. Savage gave the deal his imprimatur on the Sunday. They would seek to justify their decision on the grounds that
Jeff Kennett was unfit for office. Savage attacked Kennett as a 'disgraceful fellow' prepared to stoop to dirty tricks to intimidate the
independents. The Mildura MP said he had been disturbed by
rumours that Kennett intended to force a showdown in the parliament so the independents could be filmed voting the government
down.

Certainly the premier had taken constitutional advice on
whether he should force the issue to a vote in the parliament. But
when he arrived in his office at Treasury Place on Monday, Kennett
ordered his staff to begin packing up. He would go to see the governor, Sir James Gobbo, the next day to advise of his intention
to resign. 'It's curtains,' Kennett said in a 10-minute speech to the
staff. He made no attempt to disguise his fury at the role of the
independents. 'I bear no animosity whatsoever towards Bracks.
This is not his doing. Good luck to him. But that incredible process
with the independents . . . the only thing that will ever be remembered of them is that they combined to defeat the government of

the day. The public didn't change the government; they did. They will bear responsibility for having thrown out what was often described as one of the best governments of its time.'

When the independents formally announced the reasons for their decision, they said that although there were doubts about Labor's readiness to govern, they believed Bracks would deliver 'honest, ethical and transparent government'. Davies prompted sniggers from close political observers when she claimed it was a decision she had never savoured. 'My guts have been rolling over and over for several weeks.' Ingram, claiming he was basically a conservative, confessed to being slightly uncomfortable about supporting Labor. He went on to offer the explanation that his decision had been influenced in part by the Coalition's response to the independents' charter – the fact that they had agreed to so many of its demands and ditched their own policies to do so, was, he thought, 'a bit cynical'. As for Savage, he said he could not trust Kennett, whom he had come to regard as 'a rat and a charlatan'. But with an eye on the potential backlash in his own electorate, Savage went on to lament the fact that he was in the invidious position of having to make the choice. 'This was the hardest decision of my life.' Again, he specified that the premier was the stumbling block: 'Had Kennett fallen on his sword with an element of humility and some statesman-like qualities, the outcome would have been different.' Vexed senior Coalition ministers were never convinced. 'That was his rationalisation for his own constituency,' says one. 'He had to blame Kennett. Without that, it all looked pretty cheap and nasty.'

At lunchtime on Monday, Jeff Kennett called a final meeting of his cabinet. Although some senior colleagues were still urging him to force the issue to a vote in the parliament on 3 November, Kennett knew that the governor would favour a quick resolution of the five-week stalemate. He was also conscious that many of his cabinet colleagues feared the consequences of an ongoing parliamentary stoush. Philosophically, this was a position he himself had already reached. The fact that he had made up his own mind contributed to his anger when he heard that some backbenchers had been plotting a party-room uprising to bring about his downfall if he refused to step aside. He phoned several of the agitators from his office, reminding them and himself of the homily, 'Part of the quality of your service is the quality of your departure.' He would go gracefully. For his part, he did not see himself as a loser.

The premier next spoke to his deputy, Denis Napthine, telling him he would have his support for the leadership. Napthine, perhaps startled, made the curious offer to serve as a caretaker if, at some point in the future, Kennett thought the time was ripe for his return. Politically, of course, this was a nonsense. Jeff Kennett was not only resigning as leader of the party. His announcement would be merely the precursor to his retirement, very soon afterwards, from public life.

At 1 p.m. the next day, Kennett rose to his feet in the Liberal party room and announced he would be resigning both as premier and as leader of the Liberal Party. There was a standing ovation. Many MPs wept openly. Two hours later Kennett spoke to Bracks, alerting the Opposition leader to his plans to visit the governor that afternoon. 'Once the independents had made their decision, and we had another government, they were entitled, and I thought they should be encouraged, to get on with it and do the best job possible. The last thing I wanted was for all we had achieved to be put at risk. Once I had made that decision, albeit with tinges of regret, it was fairly easy to activate.'

At 4 p.m., Kennett contacted the governor to formally resign his commission and advise that Bracks should be invited to form government. At 4.47 p.m. on Tuesday 19 October, he walked into the press room at Treasury Place to announce his plans to the public:

I genuinely believe that the government that I have had the honour of leading for the last two terms – seven years – will be the benchmark . . . against which many governments in Australia will now be judged.

Some Victorians have not appreciated the style and some will not have appreciated the outcome [but] it has been a period of extraordinary discipline from which we, as Victorians, are all going to benefit. Obviously, I am disappointed that tomorrow, at 11.30, I leave government to our political opponents. But that is life . . . Can I also indicate that I informed the Liberal Party today that at Tuesday's meeting next week, I will resign the leadership of the Liberal Party. I have done this with a heavier heart than most of you can imagine, given that most of you don't think that I have any heart at all . . .

Victoria is without doubt my life. I have given everything I have to doing the job that I thought the public expected of us in 1992. Again, some might not have liked the style, but importantly, Victoria has never been in a stronger position than it is today and, for our political opponents who will assume office shortly, they are inheriting a state in which confidence levels are high, the financial position is extraordinarily strong, and they are being served by what I consider to be the most professional public service in Australia . . .

In making my decision, it is my view that one era has ended and another is about to start, and if part of that healing process for the community is my withdrawal from a position of author- ity, then that is a small part to play . . . Tomorrow, Mr Bracks is given the opportunity of forming government. I rang him this afternoon after I had left our Coalition meeting to indicate that . . . I wish them well, I wish the people of Victoria well.

Kennett's struggle was over. Although some colleagues urged him to stay on in politics, his only agenda from that point onwards was how to execute his final exit from a 23-year parliamentary career. 'I could have hung on as Opposition leader or I could have sat on the middle benches, but in the end I decided I was better out of the place. It was better for my family. We could have a quieter life. It was better for the party, because if I had been there, whoever took over the leadership would always be subject to comparisons, or my presence would be used for mischief-making.'

As Kennett would later admit, he also had cause to ponder, and not for the first time, whether and for how long he could have continued even if circumstances had allowed him to serve on as premier. He had been through harrowing times, and he had been on the wrong end of an election result he regarded as a quirk of fate. Even if the Liberals had held the seat of Geelong, allowing the Coalition to cling to power, would he have wanted to lead a government in such an environment? He was not a man suited to the demands of governing with an eye over his shoulder. The great days were over; his best work was done; he was proud of his record of achievement. 'You often can't see it clearly at the time – maybe I don't even see it clearly now – but if I had stayed on, it might have affected my relationship with my wife; it might have been that the pace of life I was leading just could not be sustained. Regardless of anything I said, I would probably have kept working at the same pace. It might have been that we would start to do some things badly. I don't know, but there is a rhyme and reason for everything. Convinced of that, I had no qualms about going.'

On 3 November, Alex Andrianopoulos, the Labor-appointed speaker of the new parliament, stood to his feet to read a letter of resignation from the member for Burwood. Kennett was calling it quits.

> It has been a great honour to have served as a Victorian parliamentarian. I leave having served in many positions ... the last seven years as premier of this great state. I remain very proud of the new Victoria we have created ... To my Liberal colleagues, former and present, I thank them for the faith they have placed in me to lead the party for the best part of 16 years. To all parlia-

mentarians, I wish you the very best in your deliberations on behalf of the people of Victoria. I leave you enormously proud of our achievements over the years, but prouder still of the state of Victoria and its people. I remain convinced there is no greater service than public service.

Then came the sign-off familiar to all Victorians: 'Have a good day.' Even Jeff Kennett's most bitter enemies, sitting in a chamber that had been his domain for so many years, found it hard not to grin.

POSTSCRIPT

'I hate mediocrity – it's such a waste of time and space.'
JEFF KENNETT

In December 1999, a new security attendant at the government offices at Treasury Place was doing the rounds of the basement car park. He noticed a Mercedes occupying a premium reserved space but carrying private number plates. Suspicious, he went upstairs and queried his fellow officers: 'I have an unidentified Merc downstairs. Does anyone know who owns it?'

Concealing their smirks, they shook their heads and suggested that perhaps he should follow the procedures and report it to police. Dutifully, the attendant phoned police and gave the car's registration number. They checked their computer files as the attendant waited. There was an awkward silence from the desk officer when the registration data was located. After a pause, he said, 'Yes, that car is registered. In the name of Jeffrey Gibb Kennett. Need we say any more?'

Democracy can be a dangerous business, especially for those like Jeff Kennett, who burst free of the carefully constructed corsetry of modern political dialogue. The voters put you up, and they can just as readily knock you down. They don't have to state their reasons. Those are the rules of the game.

And yet the downfall of Jeff Kennett somehow transcends the routine ebb and flow of political fortune. This was no ordinary political leader slipping from office, sapped of ideas and energy and resigned to fate. A high roller, Kennett didn't hedge his bets. He thought he had one more election win in him and went for the all-or-nothing result. The drama of his departure was lost on nobody. Even to Russell Savage, who was so central to the machinations that produced Kennett's defeat, this was an awesome spectacle. 'It's like when the *Hindenburg* went down. One minute he is so vast, so overpowering. Then there's a little pinprick in the fabric, and the whole thing just falls to earth.'

The Kennett government held office for two weeks short of seven years – not a long time, even in the small pond of Victorian public life. There have been four premiers who have served longer in office. Among Kennett's Liberal predecessors, both Bolte and Hamer enjoyed greater electoral success. Even John Cain – the man ridiculed by Kennett as 'an abject failure' – succeeded at three elections and led a government for eight years. But is this form of calculation appropriate in assessing the Kennett phenomenon? To adopt a cricketing metaphor, it is the equivalent of measuring the contribution of a batsman by the length of time he occupies the crease. Jeff Kennett was a strokeplayer, a swashbuckler. He ran his government outside the natural rhythms of political behaviour, cramming more far-reaching change into his first two years in office than many other governments have attempted over two terms. He left big footprints.

In the 1990s, Australia produced two political leaders of this ilk: Paul Keating and Jeff Kennett. The differences between Keating and Kennett were many: opposite sides of the fence, different political bloodlines, different styles and sensibilities. Yet they shared common strengths – and weaknesses. It is not surprising that they found an empathy at the personal level which transcended their politics. Both were ardent reformers, change merchants. Both had big visions, and the capacity and force of personality to drag people with them. Inevitably, though, not everybody wanted to embark on the great journey.

The advent of the Coalition government in Victoria in 1992 unleashed a starburst of dynamism and aggression, which expired just as abruptly as it started. There have been few more eventful periods in the life of the state, and no political leader has generated more headlines, good and bad. It was one of Jeff Kennett's precepts that politics need not be dull and boring. This was a promise on which he duly delivered. But beyond the theatre and the pyrotechnics, the more telling judgements of his era will hinge on whether his government achieved permanent shifts in the public policy framework and the political culture. The overarching question is whether Kennett's unexpected fall from power will come to be seen as the end of an era of reformist government in Australia.

Certainly there were many cautionary lessons to learn from the defeat of a government that had been universally expected to retain power. One is that success in financial management and economic strategy is no guarantee of electoral reward. By 1999, growth in Victoria's economic output had been outpacing the rest of the nation for two years, debt was at its lowest in 30 years, unemployment had fallen from almost 12 per cent to 7 per cent, inflation was below the national average, and the productivity of the Victorian workforce had grown faster than any other state. Not all of this can be credited to the Kennett government – Victoria shared in the national recovery – but without the rigorous financial management disciplines set in place by the Kennett regime in its early years, the state's resurgence would have been slower and less certain. Moreover, such was the pick-up in confidence in the mid-1990s that a state that had once retarded national growth emerged as a powerful engine in the low-inflation, high-growth climate enjoyed by Australia in the latter half of the decade. Victoria lifted its

performance as an exporter of services and high value-added manu-
factures, and by 1999 was surpassing New South Wales, the most
populous and wealthy state, in jobs and output growth. As Kennett's treasurer, Alan Stockdale, observed wryly, 'If this is a rustbucket, let's all live in a rustbucket.'

At least part of this outcome was due to Jeff Kennett's success in
achieving a turnaround in the intangibles of community confidence
and self-esteem. Maybe it was clever marketing. Maybe it was pop
psychology. Maybe it extended at times into crass parochalism. But
Kennett's activism created a mood of reinvigoration. Gone was
the 'Bleak City' epithet. 'Renaissance' may be too strong a word to
describe the phenomenon, but there was, at the very least, a spirit of
revival. Of course, economic growth can only ever be part of the
story of measuring a society's progress, but it happens to be the part
that puts bread on the table. The mystery of the Kennett government's unexpected demise is how it lost the faith and confidence of
a decisive slice of the electorate at the very time when the economic
fundamentals were in peak condition.

'Back to basics' is a good political slogan. It worked powerfully
for the Victorian ALP in 1999. Its message lands slap bang in the
middle of the comfort zone. It is about political leaders not getting
too uppity, not getting ahead of themselves or the community
they serve. It is cosy and cuddly and reassuring. It implies a return
to the certainties of the past.

Kennett, though, believed there was no choice but to confront
the daunting challenges of the future and embrace the dynamics of
globalisation and the knowledge economy. He wanted the state to
enhance its standing in the new growth industries of multimedia
and biotechnology. An indomitable internationalist, he was also
committed to building networks of mutual interest with Australia's
near neighbours in Asia, notably in establishing new markets for
high value-added exports in food and advanced manufacturing.
Here, again, there are parallels with Keating. Hubris and impatience
for change combined to play a part in both leaders' downfall. But

they fell out of favour, also, because of the ideas and images they came to represent: aggressive, outward-looking and eager for Australia to ready itself for a different world. In the major policy shifts of the last 15 years, both leaders were ready to be first over the barbed-wire fence, goading others to follow. It is not surprising that the strategies used to bring them undone were uncannily similar. Adventurism has its price.

Witnessing their fate, will others dare to step into the breach? Roger Hallam says of Jeff's seven years in power, 'I don't walk away from anything we have done. We were thrown out. We were dumped. We lost ground in the country. I understand all that. But our strategy was the one that would bring the best long-term outcome and I am actually proud of the fact that we were prepared to put the short-term stuff to one side. Some people would like to think it's a matter of going out there and cuddling people. The truth is, the people we need in positions of influence are those who take the big-picture view and who know there is no long-term choice. They are now carrying a very big monkey on their back.' In the days after Kennett's defeat, the former Queensland Labor premier, Wayne Goss, voiced similar fears. 'The danger is that this will give a lot of encouragement to those who want the world to slow down.'

Jeff Kennett had a habit of downplaying any sense of curiosity on his own part about how history would judge him. In 1988, he told a reporter: 'Walk around Parliament House and you walk over tiles that have been down there for 156 years. I can't remember anyone who was in the first parliament. I can't remember anyone who was serving in 1930, and in 30 years' time, no one's going to remember Jeff Kennett.' In January 2000, in a reflective discussion for this book after his defeat as premier, he said much the same thing: 'In one sense, what does history matter?' Kennett knew the state he had governed was but a small corner of an underpopulated island nation: prosperous and favoured by fortune, but threatened by the condition of irrelevance he called 'global bypass'. Its people and political leaders would need to beat the drum loudly to make themselves heard. Politicians would come and go. Some would make more noise than others; few would leave enduring legacies.

Yet this feigned indifference to history's verdict is not borne out by Kennett's actions. The mere fact that he saw it as necessary for his government to commission, at the taxpayer's expense, an official history by Monash University academic Dr Malcolm Kennedy suggests a profound sensitivity about how his years in office would be seen. If Kennett was uncomfortable with the conventional analysis of the way he exercised power, it is likely he was more wary still of explanations of how and why he lost power.

Jeff Kennett must wear much of the odium for his government's surprise election defeat. Self-evidently, his policy rigour and unyielding style were key factors in the alienation of a significant segment of voters in rural and regional Victoria. But in the official Victorian Liberal Party postmortem on the 1999 election, former federal president Tony Staley cautioned his party colleagues against cannibalising the Kennett legacy out of frustration at having lost power: 'It is difficult to envisage a campaign in which Jeff Kennett would not have dominated. The media's fascination, and that indefinable quality known as "presence" were always going to place Jeff Kennett at centre stage. Jeff Kennett's success as Victorian premier – a success that can be measured in terms of higher employment, surging investment and dramatic debt reduction – will forever be associated with his style of leadership. But to criticise this style, to remember it exclusively as a factor in one disappointing campaign, is to ignore its central role in the extraordinary recovery of our state.'

However historians in the future may choose to characterise his years in power, whatever spin they put on his achievements and failings, it is unlikely Jeff Kennett will be quickly forgotten. This will be as true for his enemies as for his admirers. All governments have their virtues and failings, and Kennett was a politician always destined to polarise opinion. People will remember what they want to remember, according to their own prejudices – but remember him they will. The face of Victoria changed under Kennett's leadership.

His reform effort after coming to government in 1992 remains a tour de force in Australia's postwar political history. In the climate of the times it became a groundbreaking agenda, pursued assuredly, often courageously, and against the tide of expectations.

For a politician who lived dangerously, we should not be surprised he departed so unpredictably. In a sense, it would have been odd and almost out of character if it had happened any other way. Jeff Kennett, from start to finish, was a freak phenomenon. A one-off. This alone is likely to keep his name in our collective memory.

NOTES

The sources on the following pages have been quoted or otherwise referred to in this book. I am grateful to those publishers, authors or other copyright holders who, where appropriate, granted me permission to do so. Private interviews were conducted with the following individuals and are quoted in various chapters.

Jeff Kennett (chapters 1–8, 15, 18, 19, 21–3, Postscript)
Ken Kennett (Chapter 2)
Graham Cornes (Chapter 2)
Tim Fischer (Chapter 2)
Ron Walker (chapters 3, 6, 7, 10, 12, 13, 15, 18)
Andrew Peacock (chapters 4–7, 15)
David White (chapters 5–7, 13)
Tom Austin (chapters 5–7)
Ted Baillieu (chapters 5–8)
Ian Baker (chapters 5, 7, 10)
Geoff Connard (chapters 6, 7)
Alan Stockdale (chapters 6–10, 15)
Reg Macey (chapters 6, 8)
Peter Poggioli (chapters 6, 7, 10, 13, 20)
Bruce Guthrie (chapters 6, 13)
Victor Perton (chapters 6, 7)

Tania Price (Chapter 7)
Alister Drysdale (chapters 8, 15)
Rob Knowles (chapters 8, 16, 19)
Ken Baxter (chapters 8, 9, 13, 15–17)
Roger Hallam (chapters 9, 16, 23, Postscript)
John Lyons (Chapter 15)
Russell Savage (chapters 16, 23, Postscript)
Jack Vanderland (Chapter 16)
Bill Shannon (Chapter 22)

CHAPTER ONE: BEGINNINGS
Advertisement, *Australia Today*, 8 December 1906.
Richard Yallop, *Royal South Yarra Lawn Tennis Club: 100 Years in Australian Tennis*, Currey O'Neil, South Yarra, Vic., 1984.
Peter Blazey, *The Secret Diary of Jeffrey Kennett, Aged 45¼*, Pan Australia, Chippendale, NSW, 1993.
Peter Blazey, correspondence with Sandra McKay, November 1995.
Bill Birnbauer & Sandra McKay, 'Kennett: unauthorised', *Age*, 9, 11–12 December 1995.

CHAPTER THREE: YOUNG MAN IN A HURRY
Victoria, Legislative Assembly 1976, *Debates*, vol. 326, p. 39.

CHAPTER FOUR: INTO THE FRAY
Bill Birnbauer & Sandra McKay, 'Kennett: unauthorised', *Age*, 9, 11–12 December 1995.
'Yes, but why Mr Kennett?', editorial, *Age*, 18 December 1980.
Michael Yates, 'Kennett sticks to his guns', *Herald*, 2 September 1981.
Shaun Carney, 'Speaking Kennett's mind', *Age*, 22 September 1988.

CHAPTER FIVE: THE WAITING GAME
John Hurst, 'Boy babbler's race against the Liberals' knives', *National Times*, 3 November 1983.
Tim Duncan, 'Leading the Liberals out of the wilderness', *Bulletin*, 29 November 1983.
David Broadbent, 'Big talk blunders in big government', *Age*, 29 March 1984.
'The nun's story', *National Times*, 12 August 1986.
'Not a time to gamble', editorial, *Age*, 1 March 1985.
Michael Gawenda, 'A hard day's night', *Age*, 4 March 1985.

CHAPTER SIX: WILDERNESS YEARS
Tim Colebatch, 'Four good reasons why Kennett should stay', *Age*, 31 December 1985.
Lim Say Boon, 'Kennett called colleagues wimpish bastards', *Australian Financial Review*, 20 October 1986.
Paul Chadwick, 'Kennett looks at brighter side', *Sun News-Pictorial*, 6 December 1986.

'The case for maintaining the momentum', editorial, *Age*, 30 September 1988.

CHAPTER SEVEN: THE PATH TO POWER
Victoria, Legislative Assembly 1991, *Debates*, vol. 403, p. 499.
Geoffrey Barker, 'How Alan Brown sealed his own fate', *Age*, 27 April 1991.
Neil Mitchell, 3AW, 23 May 1991.
'Mr Kennett: the blackmail option', editorial, *Age*, 24 May 1991.
'Kennett's reckless road', editorial, *Australian Financial Review*, 29 May 1991.
Jeff Kennett, campaign speech, September 1992.

CHAPTER EIGHT: SHOCK OF THE NEW
Tony Parkinson & Ewin Hannan, 'High speed reformer', *Australian*, 2 October 1993.
Jeff Kennett, 'Victoria's commonsense revolution', Alfred Deakin Lecture, 29 August 1995.
Geoffrey Barker, 'Crisis? What crisis?', *Age*, 10 April 1996.

CHAPTER NINE: REINVENTING GOVERNMENT
John Cain, *John Cain's Years: Power, Parties and Politics*, Melbourne University Press, Carlton, Vic., 1995.
Colin Clark & David Corbett, eds, *Reforming the Public Sector: Problems and Solutions*, Allen & Unwin, St Leonards, NSW, 1999.
Brian Costar & Nic Economou, eds, *The Kennett Revolution: Victorian Politics in the 1990s*, University of New South Wales Press, Sydney, 1999.
Evatt Research Centre, *State of Siege: Renewal or Privatisation for Australia's State Public Services*, Pluto Press, Sydney, 1989.
Office of the Victorian Auditor-General, *Privatisation: An Auditing Framework for the Future*, special report no. 38, 1995.
Mark Skulley, 'Private man, private power', *Australian Financial Review*, 3 May 1999.

CHAPTER TEN: THE CAN-DO CULTURE
Les Carlyon, 'His other side', *Sunday Age*, 24 March 1996.

CHAPTER ELEVEN: OPEN FOR BUSINESS
Jean Holmes, *The Government of Victoria*, University of Queensland Press, St Lucia, Qld, 1976.
Tony Parkinson, 'Kennett's biggest test', *Australian*, 1 April 1995.
'Jeff, Felicity and that share deal', editorial, *Sunday Age*, 19 May 1996.
Stephen Mayne, jeffed.com web site, September 1999.
Michelle Grattan, 'Doing business with Jeff Kennett', *Australian Financial Review Magazine*, 28 February 1997.
Victoria, Legislative Council 1993, *Debates*, vol. 414, p. 539.

CHAPTER TWELVE: HIGH ROLLER
Sue Neales, 'Casino losing bidder licks its wounds', *Age*, 7 September 1993.
Rowena Stretton, 'It's Jeff's business', *Australian Financial Review*, 29 March 1996.

CHAPTER THIRTEEN: RAISING THE STAKES

Jeff Kennett, 'Letter to the editor', *Age*, 2 June 1996.

Karl Quinn & Misha Ketchell, 'From the (former) editor's desk', *Melbourne Weekly*, 5–11 May 1998.

Shelley Gare, 'Who's editor now?', *Australian*, 5 August 1999.

Robert Haupt, 'Campaign notebook', *Age*, 23 September 1988.

Russell Skelton, 'Revealed at last: what Mary really asked', *Age*, 7 September 1998.

Mary Delahunty, 'Why Kennett savaged me over that interview', *Age*, 29 September 1998.

CHAPTER FOURTEEN: CROSS-CURRENTS

Hamish Fitzsimmons, 'Victoria: Jeff-tastic', *Beat Magazine*, 27 March 1996.

Paul Conroy, 'The night they busted Tasty', *Age*, 18 November 1995.

Department of Premier & Cabinet, Drug Advisory Council, *Report*, 10 April 1996.

Neil Mitchell, 3AW, 23 May 1996.

James Button, 'It's Kennett v. The Church', *Sydney Morning Herald*, 30 December 1995.

Gareth Boreham & Meaghan Shaw, 'Stay out of politics, Kennett tells G-G', *Age*, 19 November 1997.

Sushila Das, 'Premier to meet expert on gambling', *Age*, 28 May 1998.

Productivity Commission, Inquiry into Australia's Gambling Industries, *Draft Report*, 19 July 1999.

Amanda Hodge, 'Victorian politics enters the kingdom of God', *Australian*, 3 January 2000.

CHAPTER FIFTEEN: A LARGER STAGE

Pamela Williams, *The Victory: The Inside Story of the Takeover of Australia*, Allen & Unwin, St Leonards, NSW, 1997.

Michelle Grattan, 'Doing business with Jeff Kennett', *Australian Financial Review Magazine*, 28 February 1997.

Tape of mobile phone conversation between Jeff Kennett and Andrew Peacock, 22 March 1987.

Neil Mitchell, 3AW, 19 May 1994.

Tracey Aubin, *Peter Costello: A Biography*, HarperCollins, Pymble, NSW, 1999.

Roy Morgan Research Centre poll, *Bulletin*, 3 November 1998.

Jeff Kennett, speech to the Australia Summit, 16 June 1998.

A Current Affair, Nine Network, 16 June 1998.

Lateline, ABC TV, 18 June 1998.

CHAPTER SIXTEEN: THE GREAT DIVIDE

'A cry from the heartland', editorial, *Age*, 3 February 1997.

Victoria, Legislative Assembly 1997, *Debates*, vol. 434, p. 298.

Shane Green, *Age*, 'A minority view of the next election', 27 June 1997.

CHAPTER SEVENTEEN: CRACKS IN THE EDIFICE

Jeff Kennett, *Delivering a Modern Social Agenda*, Melbourne, 6 October 1997.

Office of the Victorian Auditor-General, *Annual Report*, 1996–97.

Peter Barber, 'Lights go out for Victoria's official watchdog', Australian Associated Press, 27 July 1999.

Shane Green, 'How Kennett stilled cries of dissent on A-G', *Age*, 1 November 1997.

Roger Pescott, 'Open letter to the premier, Jeffrey Kennett', *Age*, 12 November 1997.

AC Nielsen poll, *Age*, 15 November 1997.

Brian Costar & Nic Economou, 'The Monash Mitcham survey', *Age*, 4 February 1998.

Tony Parkinson, 'The man who would be premier', *Age*, 19 December 1997.

CHAPTER EIGHTEEN: THE PRICE OF POWER

Bruce Guthrie, 'Kennett tills the marginal country', *Herald*, 23 October 1984.

Sue Neales, 'Felicity Kennett on personal pain', *Age*, 2 November 1996.

Damon Johnston, 'We're just an ordinary family', *Herald Sun*, 16 September 1997.

Cheryl Critchley, 'The premier's youngest son has bared all about that tattoo', *Herald Sun*, 6 December 1997.

Amanda Ruben, 'The model son', *Herald Sun*, 11 May 1999.

Amanda Ruben, 'Angus casts protest vote', *Herald Sun*, 14 September 1999.

Stuart Rintoul, 'A house divided', *Australian*, 29 January 1998.

Rachel Hawes, 'Kennett sues preferred paper over rumours', *Australian*, 5 March 1999.

Peter Gregory, 'Court told of Kennett's tears', *Age*, 6 March 1999.

Tony Parkinson, 'At 50, Kennett seeks time out', *Age*, 27 February 1998.

Graham Pearce, 'Life on my own', *Sunday Herald Sun*, 1 March 1998.

Jeff Kennett, press conference, 12 March 1999.

CHAPTER NINETEEN: THE THREAT FROM WITHIN

Newspoll, *Australian*, 27 April 1998.

Neil Mitchell, 3AW, 12 February 1997.

CHAPTER TWENTY: ON THE REBOUND

Tony Parkinson, 'The tale of brave Ulysses', *Age*, 17 April 1998.

Shaun Carney, 'Solitary man', *Sunday Age*, 28 June 1998.

Neil Mitchell, 3AW, 10 July 1998.

Gay Alcorn, 'Kennett: I'll work to defeat Hanson', *Age*, 8 September 1998.

CHAPTER TWENTY-ONE: THE HOME STRETCH

Kimina Lyall & Michael Magazanik, 'Jeff and Felicity trying again', *Australian*, 8 October 1998.

John Brumby, 'Why *The Age* is wrong on my leadership', *Age*, 10 November 1998.

Ewin Hannan, 'Kennett: I'm here to stay', *Age*, 28 November 1998.

Damon Johnston, 'Brumby out of the public eye', *Herald Sun*, 25 December 1998.

Australian Labor Party, *New Labor, New Solutions*, platform document, 18 February 1999.

Ewin Hannan, 'Brumby's big day spoilt by continued brawling', *Age*, 19 February 1999.

Ewin Hannan, 'Plan to dump Brumby: claim', *Age*, 26 February 1999.
Neil Mitchell, 3AW, 18 March 1999.
Steve Bracks, press conference, 22 March 1999.
Breakfast Crew, 3MMM, 22 March 1999.
Jeff Kennett, speech to Liberal State Council, Melbourne, 28 March 1999.
Steve Bracks, speech to Melbourne Media Club, 30 April 1999.
Neil Mitchell, 3AW, 5 May 1999.
AC Nielsen poll, *Age*, 21 July 1999.

CHAPTER TWENTY-TWO: MELTDOWN
Jeff Kennett, press conference, 24 August 1999.
Ches Baragwanath, speech at the University of Melbourne, 25 August 1999.
Roy Morgan Research Centre poll, *Bulletin*, 1 September 1999.
Jeff Kennett, Liberal Party campaign launch, Melbourne, 5 September 1999.
Steve Bracks, ALP campaign launch, Ballarat, 8 September 1999.
Jon Faine, 3LO, 15 September 1999.
Jeff Kennett, Liberal Party keynote address, Melbourne, 16 September 1999.

CHAPTER TWENTY-THREE: ENDGAME
Farah Farouque, 'The independents who hold the key', *Age*, 20 September 1999.
AM, ABC radio, 14 October 1999.
Felicity Dargan & David Wilson, 'Trio's pact for Labor', *Sunday Herald Sun*, 19 October 1999.
Victoria, Legislative Assembly 1999, *Debates*, vol. 444, p. 4.

Photographic Credits

The photographs in this book, identified below by abbreviated caption, are from the following sources, whose assistance is appreciated. (Jeff Kennett is referred to as 'JGK'; Felicity Kennett as 'FK'.)

Age: JGK with fellow army officers (2 photos); KNF Advertising office; JGK newly elected to Liberal leadership; JGK and FK celebrate his election as Liberal leader; JGK and Henry Bolte; JGK and Andrew Peacock; Michael Kroger and Peter Costello; young JGK portrait shot; JGK and Felicity claim victory at 1992 election; Ken Baxter; anti-Kennett demonstration; JGK and John Brumby in parliament; JGK in motorcycle gear; anti-Grand Prix rally; JGK, Judith Griggs and Ron Walker.

John Lamb/*Age*: JGK with his parents and FK; JGK and Roger Pescott.

Scotch College: JGK as a cadet.

Michael Rayner/*Age*: Fred Nelson.

Bruce Postle/*Age*: JGK uses car phone; JGK congratulates Labor on election win 1985; JGK and FK greet each other.

Craig Abraham/*Age*: Former Victorian premiers.

Jerry Galea/*Age*: Alan Stockdale and JGK in parliament; John Brumby and Tony Robinson.

Vince Caligiuri/*Age*: JGK and Ron Walker at motorcycle grand prix.

Sebastian Costanzo/*Age*: JGK 'On the Move'.

Ray Kennedy/*Age*: JGK and Ron Walker at Port Phillip Bay.

Jason South/*Age*: JGK and Lloyd Williams; David Penington addresses parliament.

INDEX